MW00619311

THE OTHER
IN THE LIGHT OF THE ONE

The Universality of the Qur'ān
and Interfaith Dialogue

FROM THE LIBRARY OF
Seher Siddiqee

THE OTHER IN THE LIGHT OF THE ONE

The Universality of the Qur'ān and Interfaith Dialogue

Reza Shah-Kazemi

THE ISLAMIC TEXTS SOCIETY

Copyright © Reza Shah-Kazemi 2006

This first edition published 2006 by
The Islamic Texts Society
22A Brooklands Avenue,
Cambridge, CB2 2DQ, UK

All rights reserved. No part of this publication may be reproduced, stored in a retrieval system, or transmitted in any form or by any means, electronic, mechanical, photocopying, recording, or otherwise, without the prior written permission of the Publisher.

British Library Cataloguing-in-Publication Data.
A catalogue record for this book is
available from the British Library.

ISBN–13: 978 1 903682 46 3 *hardback*
ISBN–10: 1 903682 46 0 *hardback*

ISBN–13: 978 1 903682 47 0 *paper*
ISBN–10: 1 903682 47 9 *paper*

Cover design copyright © The Islamic Texts Society

Contents

Dedicated to the Memory of
MARTIN LINGS
(1909-2005)

Introduction
Interfaith Dialogue: The Contemporary Context

IN THE SUMMER OF 2001, when the idea of writing this book was first conceived, the principal aim was to present, on the basis of traditional Sufi exegesis, an exposition of the universality of the Qur'ānic message of *tawḥīd*,[1] and the implications of this universality for dialogue. This exposition was intended for a readership comprising scholars and students in religious studies generally, together with all those interested in Islamic esoterism and spirituality. Now, however, in the post-September 11 era, it seems more appropriate to address a somewhat wider audience. For it would not be exaggerating to say that the events of September 11 have catapulted Islam to the epicentre of international relations; and as a result, the Qur'ān as the guiding text for over one billion Muslims, its essential nature and message, the ways in which it is interpreted and applied—all of these issues have suddenly assumed new global dimensions and are unavoidably replete with political implications.

[1] The word *tawḥīd*, often wrongly translated as 'oneness', is a verbal noun, stemming from the verb form *waḥḥada*, which means 'to make one'; in theological terms it means declaring or affirming that God is one; in mystical terms, as will be stressed in this book, it comes to acquire in addition the connotations of realizing, actualizing and finally, being extinguished within, that oneness.

Given this new role of the Qur'ānic discourse in the transformed international environment, the present work will doubtless be perceived by many in a different light, and in relation to a particular set of questions: does the Qur'ān promote peace and harmony or discord and conflict, does it contribute to pluralism or exclusivism, is its message spiritual or fanatical? Without pretending to go into all of these questions in depth, the content and also the tone of this work have been somewhat modified in order to try and demonstrate, among other things, the way in which the Qur'ānic discourse, appreciated in its most profound and spiritually transforming aspect, can and does function as an antidote to fanaticism parading as Muslim piety.

This is not to say that an apologia is being made for the Qur'ān. Nor is it being claimed that a formal commentary in the tradition of classical *tafsīr* is being presented, an exercise for which this writer is not qualified. Rather, the intention is to bring to light the profound, and urgently required, message that the Qur'ān conveys, not just to Muslims but to all those concerned with the deeper wellsprings of meaningful dialogue and peaceful coexistence between the adherents of the different religious traditions. Particular attention will be brought to bear on those verses in the Qur'ān which most clearly contribute to a positive evaluation of the other faith-communities, and thus to the basis for meaningful and fruitful dialogue between the upholders of different beliefs; and this presentation will be firmly grounded in the commentaries and insights of some of the most renowned spiritual authorities of the Islamic tradition. While it is always of intrinsic value simply to give voice to this aspect of the tradition, doing so in the current climate has the additional merit of ensuring that contemporary discourses on the Qur'ān are not drowned out by those with an ideological agenda.

It is spirituality, we believe, that reveals, more effectively than any other aspect of the Islamic tradition, the reductionism inherent in the attempt to ideologize and politicize the message of the Qur'ān. For it is precisely when the spiritual appreciation of Revelation is weak, that its message becomes susceptible to ideological distortion. There is a clear relationship between the decline of spirituality and the rise of ideology, in Islam as in other religions; and it would not be going too far to say that, deprived of a living spirituality at its core, Islam will inevitably be reduced to an empty shell, the vacuum within soon becoming filled with worldliness in all its guises: its revealed text becomes an ideological pretext; morally reforming oneself gives way to violently rectifying the other; spiritual contemplation is scorned in favour of political machination; the subtleties of revelation become submerged by the exigencies of revolution.

The new environment has merely sharpened, and not produced, the need to take cognizance of the universal message of the Qur'ān; and to say 'universal' is to say spiritual and ethical, not ideological or political. That the Qur'ān contains the principles for guidance in respect of politics, economics or any other aspect of human society is not being denied, of course; but what must be forcefully refuted is the idea that the Qur'ān is *in essence* about politics or economics. The fact that the Qur'ān is applicable to the realm of politics does not mean that it is reducible to this realm. The Qur'ān transcends such relativities by its universal spiritual and ethical content; and it is this essential content that, properly assimilated, will ensure that in the domain of applications, intelligence and moral sensibility will be brought to bear. It is to this universal content of the Qur'ānic discourse that the Sufis have traditionally addressed themselves, and this is the reason why we have chosen to focus here on their interpretations rather than those of other schools of thought in Islam. Sufi commentaries on the Qur'ān are thus particularly relevant to the contemporary intellectual and 'dialogical' situation, offering precious keys to those who are seeking to unlock the depths and the mysteries of the revealed text, and to do so in a way that includes all that is sacred, in whatever religious tradition it is to be found.

As we have mentioned above, events over the past few years have caused Islam to enter the consciousness of everyone in unprecedented ways. From this has emerged an astonishing and, in the view of some, a paradoxical thirst for literature on Islam. In the words of Jeremy Rifkin, President of the Foundation on Economic Trends, Washington: 'Like so many others, I have been reading up on Islam... I'm not alone. Seven of the fifteen lead books on the New York Times paperback bestseller list are devoted to Islam. The Koran has become a bestseller. The whole world, it seems, has been converted into a classroom as we try to make sense out of the tragic events of September 11 and its aftermath.'[2]

Such a situation offers both challenges and opportunities. It behoves all those Muslims concerned with the deeper aspects of their faith to ensure that discourse on Islam is not monopolized by what was aptly referred to as the 'rhetoric of rage' by Shaykh Hamza Yusuf—one of a new breed of charismatic, intelligent and 'home-grown' Imams in the West.[3] The different dimensions of traditional, normative Islam must be expressed, and be given the importance they deserve both in the configuration of the Islamic faith and amongst the overwhelming majority of its practitioners; and so too must the dimension of depth, or of spirituality, be brought to the fore. Without an appreciation of these spiritual, ethical and intellectual dimensions the religion of Islam will appear as a series of external forms—legal, ritual, dogmatic—deprived of that inner power which undergirds and sustains the normative traditions of Islamic culture, and provides formal Islam with its spiritual 'infrastructure', its life-giving sap. It is this normative, traditional Islam, buttressed by spiritual values, that

---

[2] Jeremy Rifkin, 'Dialogue is a Necessity', *The Guardian*, November 13, 2001.

[3] He was described by journalist Jack O'Sullivan as 'arguably the West's most influential Islamic scholar'. See the two-page profile of this figure, in *The Guardian*, October 8, 2001. The term 'rhetoric of rage', which has been quoted frequently since Shaykh Hamza coined it, was contained in the following remark in the course of the interview. 'Islam has been hijacked by a discourse of anger and the rhetoric of rage. We have lost our bearings because we have lost our theology.' See also the more detailed profile of him in *Q-News—The Muslim Magazine*, no. 337, November 2001.

constitutes the most important and effective bulwark against all forms of extremism masquerading as Islam.

Throughout its history, the spiritual values of Islam have ensured that outward forms of the faith are respected but not 'idolised'. This, indeed, is the best way of conserving those forms; for it is precisely when forms are absolutised or idolised that they are subverted. As Rida al-Sadiq puts it: 'Deprived of the vivifying sap of their spiritual roots, forms wither away—or else collapse in on themselves in violent self-destruction... It is a paradox that those who are most fanatical about the forms of the religion end up violating those forms themselves: suicide and mass murder are alike illegal in any school of Islamic Law. A slippery slope thus leads from religious formalism to sacrilegious fanaticism.'[4]

What also needs to be stressed, now more than ever, as a counterpoint to the tendency to reduce Islam to the dimensions of a monolithic, political ideology,[5] is the rich diversity within the Islamic faith communities, both past and present. Within 'Islam' there is a wide range of cultures, traditions, opinions, and attitudes such as belies any reductive, homogenizing effort to reify the religion; the view of 'Islam' as a single, undifferentiated entity is the first step to identifying it with extremist policies, *tout court*, in order the easier to reject, oppose and vilify it. Such an attitude has aptly been referred to as 'Islamophobia'.

In an important address, 'The First Annual World Humanities Lecture', at the University of Leicester, April 2000, T. J. Winter of Cambridge University, defined Islamophobia as 'the emotive

---

[4] Sayyid Rida al-Sadiq, 'At War with the Spirit of Islam', in *Dialogue*, December 2002, p. 6.

[5] See S. H. Nasr's decisive rebuttal of this tendency in his *Traditional Islam in the Modern World* (London & New York: Kegan Paul, 1987); Gai Eaton's eloquent critique of political reductionism in Islam in his latest work, *Remembering God—Reflections on Islam* (Cambridge: Islamic Texts Society, 2000) (especially pp. 101-135); and, from a different perspective, the essays by Ibrahim M. Abu Rabi', *Intellectual Origins of Islamic Resurgence in the Modern Arab World* (Albany: State University of New York Press, 1996).

dislike of the Islamic religion as a whole, rather than of its extreme manifestations; or rather... the assumption that the extremes of the religion have normative status.'[6] This lecture was also important in that Winter not only criticised western prejudices of Islam; he also called upon Muslims not to regard Christianity as a monolithic force, inherently hostile to Islam. He concluded the lecture with an appeal to Muslims to take seriously the fact that if one part of Christianity—the polemical, dogmatic and aggressively anti-Muslim part—is part of the 'problem' in terms of Muslim-Christian relations, there is another part 'which is emphatically part of the solution, advocating hospitality in a world which has never been more in need of a transcendently-ordained tolerance.'[7]

A tolerance that is 'transcendently-ordained' is one which carries with it some divinely revealed sanction; tolerance of a non-transcendent order ultimately derives only from a kind of social or humanistic utilitarianism, and is thus at the mercy of the contingencies of pragmatism. The first kind of tolerance is of a much more absolute nature, being sealed, as it were, by Heaven; the second, though laudable in its positive effects, is more fragile, and depends more on the evaluation of what is opportune in any given situation. It is our contention here that the Qur'ānic discourse, read in depth and not just on the surface, contains the principles for elaborating just such a 'transcendently-ordained tolerance', a tolerance that is not simply the outcome of a sentimental desire for peaceful relations between adherents of different religions, but one which is deeply rooted in a recognition of, and respect for, the holiness that lies at the core of all revealed religious traditions. Jeremy Rifkin asks, in the above-mentioned article, whether 'most Muslims can accept living in a pluralistic world, with respect for different faiths, creeds and ways of life.' Our answer would be yes, in harmony with the answer given overwhelmingly by Muslims through the

[6] T. J. Winter, 'Islam and the Threat of Europe' in *World Faiths Encounter*, no. 29, 2001, p. 7.

[7] *Ibid.*, p. 11.

centuries. This positive attitude to the beliefs of the 'other' is deepened in the measure that the spiritual aspects of the Qur'ānic discourse determine one's approach to other faiths. One should add that these spiritual aspects, rather than contradicting the legal principles enshrined in the text, on the contrary contribute to the cultivation of that inner substance which enlivens the Shariʿa, and which ensures that in its application, the widest possible latitude be given, the most sensitive and tolerant interpretations be forthcoming,[8] and, most important of all in the contemporary Muslim world, the most creative adaptations of legal principles to current circumstances be made, in accordance with the crucial juridical principle of *ijtihād*, literally, the creative 'exertion' on the part of the jurists to apply themselves to the sources of the law.[9]

Rifkin, to his credit, ends the above mentioned article with an appeal for a global dialogue between Islam and the West. The opposite point of view was acerbically expressed by Jonathan Meades, a *Times* columnist. He objected to the fact that al-Qāʿida prisoners at Guantanamo Bay were given copies of the Qur'ān to read, likening this act to the presenting of Hitler's *Mein Kampf* to Nazis awaiting trial at Nuremberg.[10] For, he writes, 'the Koran, like any other *vade mecum* of the mind, is hardly shy of exclusivity, is not loath to calumnise the Christians and Jews, and, if read with sufficient partiality, is an inviting incitement to abominations.'

---

[8] We are thinking here of the efforts of such scholars as M. H. Kamali, *Freedom of Expression in Islam* (Cambridge: Islamic Texts Society, 1997) and Khaled Abou El-Fadl, *Speaking in God's Name—Islamic Law, Authority and Women* (Oxford: Oneworld Publications, 2001).

[9] See M. H. Kamali, *Principles of Islamic Jurisprudence* (Cambridge: Islamic Texts Society, 1991) pp. 366-394, for a concise explanation of the principle of *ijtihād*.

[10] *The Times*, January 26, 2002. He also seems to object to their being allowed to pray: 'It is some measure of how far we've come, or how fully emollient we are, that we allow the shaven, shackled former warriors of al-Qaeda at Guantanamo Bay to pray and assist them by giving each one a copy of the Koran.'

We hope to show in this book how far this statement is from the truth. No one can deny that, in the hands of violent fanatics, even the most innocuous of texts will be interpreted in a fanatically violent way. But to limit the scope of the Qur'ān to these erroneous interpretations is to do it a gross injustice. We shall illustrate how the discourse of the Qur'ān points to coexistence and not conflict, promotes dialogue and respect rather than diatribe and vilification. This is not to deny the existence of exclusivist verses in the Qur'ān; as we hope to show in Chapter IV, what one needs to do is to situate such verses correctly, and to view them in the light of the spirituality of the Qur'ān—rather than allowing the converse to happen: that is, allowing one's perception of this spirituality to be clouded by giving precedence to the exclusivist verses. One needs to put first things first, to attribute primary, determinative significance to those verses which express the spirituality of the revelation, and which contain principles of universal import; then one can appropriately contextualise, and give due weight to, those verses which are of a particularist or exclusivist character. The particular can best be appreciated in the light of the universal; to reverse this principial priority is to put the cart before the horse.

Those readers of the Qur'ān who are incited to 'abomination' by it are those whose perception of the text is already predetermined by political extremism; those who read it with an open mind and for whom principles—spiritual, intellectual, moral—take precedence over politics should be able to see clearly that these principles are of universal import, and, as such, not only surpass the realm of politics, but also transcend, ultimately, the entire plane on which the differences between religions have any significance: for intrinsic morality, faith, spirituality are always recognisable as such, whatever be the formal religious environment in which they are located.

The Qur'ān is indeed unique among the revealed scriptures of the world not only in the way it promotes dialogue between adherents of different faith-communities, but also in the way it explicitly refers to the divine ordainment of religious diversity.

In consequence, it upholds the spiritual value of these diverse religious paths, which are presented in the Qur'ānic discourse as so many outwardly divergent facets of a single, universal revelation by the unique and indivisible Absolute. If we let the Qur'ān speak for itself in this regard, we will find in it such verses as the following:

> *He hath ordained for you of the religion* (min al-dīn) *that which He commended unto Noah, and that which We reveal to thee* [Muḥammad], *and that which We commended unto Abraham and Moses and Jesus, saying: Establish the religion, and be not divided therein. . .* (XLII: 13)
>
> *Say: We believe in God and that which is revealed unto us, and that which is revealed unto Abraham and Ishmael and Isaac and Jacob and the tribes, and that which was given unto Moses and Jesus and the prophets from their Lord. We make no distinction between any of them, and unto Him we have submitted* (III: 84)
>
> *For every community* (umma) *there is a Messenger* (X: 47)
>
> *Naught is said unto thee* [Muḥammad] *but what was said unto the Messengers before thee* (XLI: 43)
>
> *For each We have appointed from you a Law and a Way. Had God willed, He could have made you one community. But in order that He might try you by that which He hath given you* [He hath made you as you are]. *So vie with one another in good works. Unto God ye will all return, and He will inform you of that wherein ye differed* (V: 48)
>
> *Truly those who believe, and the Jews, and the Christians, and the Sabeans—whoever believeth in God and the Last Day and performeth virtuous deeds—surely their reward is with their Lord, and no fear shall come upon them, neither shall they grieve* (II: 62).

All the above verses are compelling arguments in favour of religious dialogue, based on the metaphysical premise that the different revealed religions are truly and effectively paths to salvation precisely on account of having been revealed by God. However, among the obstacles in the way of meaningful and constructive interfaith dialogue few are more insuperable than the entrenched belief that one's own religion alone holds out the prospect of salvation and that all others are irremediably false. In key verses of the Qur'ān this exclusivist chauvinism is explicitly criticised, and in many others like the ones cited above, an inclusivist vision is evoked. But citing such verses is not enough, however immediately intelligible such a presentation might be to some; for it would beg the question as to the diverse ways in which the verses in question have been interpreted, and how they ought to be interpreted and applied in today's context.

What follows, therefore, is a presentation of these key verses from a particular point of view, that adopted by those most steeped in the spiritual and mystical tradition of Islam, Sufism.[11] This is not to deny the importance of the other exegetical genres—linguistic, legal, philosophical or theological; each has its place in the overall matrix of interpretation and application. But what should be stressed is that we are today more urgently in need of a return to the spiritual source of Islam than ever before; thus, special attention should be paid to the mystical, spiritual and metaphysical dimensions of the revelation, and to those authorities within the tradition who probe and disclose the depths of meaning within the Scripture. In sayings attributed to the Prophet, each verse of the Qur'ān is said to have seven (or seventy) levels of meaning; and in one saying, cited by several Sufi commentators at the beginning of their commentaries, the Prophet is reported as saying: 'There is no verse of the Qur'ān which does not have an outward sense (*ẓahr*), an inward sense (*baṭn*), a limit (*ḥadd*) and a place to which one ascends (*muṭṭalaʿ*).'[12]

It is the Sufis who have brought to light these inner aspects of the revelation, as well as the ramifications in 'height' resulting from the spiritual 'ascent' occasioned by the verses of the revealed text. It is because the Sufis are so concerned with moving from

[11] See Chapter I for a brief overview of the Sufi phenomenon within the Islamic tradition.

[12] See note 124 of Chapter I.

the form to the essence, from appearances to realities, that they are able to perceive the religious phenomenon in a completely different light: religion for them is divine dis-closure, not human 'closure', openings to higher truths and deeper realities, not just exclusive affirmations of simple dogmas combined with perceptions limited to surface phenomena. It is for this reason that Sufi expositions of the mystical, metaphysical and spiritual dimensions of the Qur'ānic revelation can be of inestimable value to all those who are engaged in religious dialogue, and to those, in particular, who see the different religions not so much as mutually exclusive and inevitably antagonistic systems of dogmatic belief, but rather as so many 'paths to the heart'.[13]

The essay by Seyyed Hossein Nasr, 'Islam and the Encounter of Religions' is one of the most important contemporary expressions of this vision of the inner unity of religions[14] from an Islamic perspective.[15] It is a wide-ranging application of the principle of the 'transcendent unity of religions' from the point of view of the Islamic tradition as a whole. After describing the encounter between Islam and other religions on different planes—historical, legal, theological, philosophical, and

---

[13] This is part of the title of an interfaith conference that was convened at the University of South Carolina, October 5-7, 2001: 'Paths to the Heart: Sufism and the Christian East'. The present book is an expanded version of a paper delivered at the conference. See our 'The Metaphysics of Interfaith Dialogue: Sufi Perspectives on the Universality of the Quranic Message', in *Paths to the Heart: Sufism and the Christian East*, ed., James S. Cutsinger (Bloomington: World Wisdom, 2002), pp. 140-189.

[14] Or what Frithjof Schuon referred to as the 'transcendent unity' of religions. The unity in question pertains exclusively to the deepest dimensions of spiritual realization, and the highest aspects of the truth; on the non-transcendent level, the religions are distinct and irreducible. See F. Schuon, *The Transcendent Unity of Religions* (Wheaton: Theosophical Publishing House, 1993). T. S. Eliot wrote of this book that 'I have met with no more impressive work on the comparative study of Oriental and Occidental religion.' Quoted by Huston Smith in his introduction to the revised edition of the book.

[15] Published in his work, *Sufi Essays* (London: George Allen & Unwin, 1972) pp. 123-151.

scientific—Nasr writes that it is on the level of Sufi esoterism that,

> '. . . the most profound encounter with other traditions has been made, and where one can find the indispensable ground for the understanding in depth of other religions today. The Sufi is one who seeks to transcend the world of forms, to journey from multiplicity to Unity, and from the particular to the Universal. He leaves the many for the One, and through this very process is granted the vision of the One in the many. For him all forms become transparent, including religious forms, thus revealing to him their unique origin.'[16]

This unique origin is described as the 'Centre where all the radii meet, the summit which all roads reach. Only such a vision of the Centre,' he continues, 'can provide a meaningful dialogue between religions, showing both their inner unity and formal diversity. . . '[17]

The present work takes this affirmation as one of its main points of departure. In Chapter I, our hermeneutical approach to the Qur'ān will be outlined, together with the reasons for adopting a traditional Sufi rather than modern or postmodern perspective on the text of the Qur'ān. In Chapter II, the focus is on the Qur'ānic message of unity, as understood by the Sufis. Here the relationship between the One and the many will be examined in order to undergird the notion of religious dialogue with a metaphysical foundation, and to demonstrate that the principle of oneness, far from implying the negation of multiplicity, embraces and infuses it. The one and only Reality, being infinite, cannot but manifest itself infinitely in diverse ways—without detriment to the distinctiveness of each and every particularity thus manifested, and without the One sacrificing anything of its oneness. Thus human diversity—and the religious

---

[16] *Ibid.*, p. 146.

[17] *Ibid.*, p. 150.

diversity it calls forth—is one reflection and expression of divine infinity. The self-manifestation of the One to Itself through the mirror of creation is proposed in this chapter as the ultimate prototype of all dialogue.

Another major point in this chapter concerns the dialectic between selfhood and its correlate, the 'other'. The discussion here involves a perception of the ego in the light of the spiritual realization—and not simply theological affirmation—of the central, definitive message of the Qur'ān, *tawḥīd*, the affirmation or realization of the oneness of God. On the one hand, the bonds of egocentricity are loosened; and on the other hand, the holiness that is innate to the other is affirmed. One comes to see the 'Face' of God in the other—that divine face that the Qur'ān tells us is there, *wherever ye turn* (II: 115). Humility and generosity are the two key virtues generated in the realm of dialogue by this perception of integral oneness. This 'metaphysics of dialogue', then, will be presented in terms of the principle of divine self-disclosure, and as an integral aspect of Sufi wisdom, or realized knowledge (*maʿrifa*). In addition, the discussion of 'ontological' *tawḥīd* provides us with a more subtle approach to the question of the 'truth' of *tawḥīd*. This truth is situated in relation to spiritual reality, a reality which calls out to be assimilated within one's being, and not simply 'understood' as a notion or a mental construct. Such a conception helps one to grasp more firmly the points made in the following chapters—in particular the argument that dialogue can be spiritually fruitful despite the existence of outwardly incompatible dogmatic beliefs.

In Chapter III, the chief aim is to show how a spiritual appreciation of the meaning of 'Islam', based on Sufi exegesis of certain Qur'ānic verses, opens up a path leading to the heart of religion as such; and how such a conception, in turn, helps to situate the different religious traditions within a spiritual universe defined by quintessential 'Islam'; that is, Islam understood as universal submission to God, rather than as just a particular religious denomination. On the one hand, historical Islam is one expression of this universal principle, and is thus to be both respected and upheld in all its particularity; and, on the other, its relativity *qua* religious form must also be acknowledged, this very acknowledgement opening up a perception of the spiritual, intellectual and moral values present in other revealed religious traditions. These values are rooted in the primordial and inalienable substance of the human soul—the *fiṭra*—and are brought to fruition by the graces inherent in submitting to a revealed religion; the innate perfection, from within, is catalyzed and realized through divine revelation from above. The Qur'ān refers to the 'right religion', which is based on the unalterability of the primordial soul, the summit of creation: *So set thy purpose for religion with unswerving devotion—the nature* [framed] *of God* (fiṭrat Allāh), *according to which He hath created man. There is no altering God's creation. That is the right religion* (al-dīn al-qayyim), *but most men know not* (XXX: 30).

In Chapter III, then, we hope to stress the importance of verses, such as those cited above, which address the universality of the religious phenomenon; to show that it is at the hands of the Sufi commentators that the deeper meanings and implications of these important verses are brought to light; and to relate the principles derived from this encounter between Sufi spirituality and Qur'ānic universality to themes germane to dialogue.

Chapter IV addresses itself to the question of competing readings of the Qur'ānic discourse, and the extent to which the spiritual perspectives on universality and dialogue presented here can be accepted by those upholding majoritarian exoteric norms within contemporary Muslim communities. Insofar as the aim of this work is not simply academic but also practical, such a question cannot be ignored. For the intention here is not simply to demonstrate how the Qur'ān can be read in such a way as to highlight its universality, its affirmation of the holiness of religions other than Islam, and thereby its encouragement to Muslims to reach out to the religious other with respect. It is also intended to present these 'openings' to the other in a way which allows Muslims to recognise this position as an authentically Qur'ānic one, and not as compromising the integrity or the normativity of the tradition. In other words, one is hopeful that the spiritual principles expounded here will help in some way to articulate more explicitly that innate sense of the holiness of all religions, that deep-rooted respect for the believers of all faith-communities, which has in fact characterised the overwhelming majority of Muslims, past and present;[18] and in this way to contribute in a small way to the process by which the hostile attitude towards other faiths, animating a small minority of politicized Muslim extremists, will be shown to be unfaithful to the authentic spirit of the Qur'ānic revelation and thus to the spirit of Islam itself.

However, one has to acknowledge the truth in much of what is claimed about Muslims in dialogue today, particularly those in the West. Richard Neuhas has a point when he writes, in connection with those who are deemed to be representatives of Islam in inter-faith dialogue: 'As for conferences, it is not hard to get "Muslim spokespersons". There are teams of them flitting from conference to conference all over the world... I have met them in Davos, Switzerland, where top CEOs and heads of state annually gather with select intellectuals to chatter about the state of the world in the esperanto of an internationalese that is not spoken by real people anywhere. The Muslims in such settings are for the most part westernized, secularized, academic intellectuals who are there to "represent the Muslim viewpoint", but have little more connection with living Islam than many Christians and Jews.'[19]

---

[18] As Nasr notes in his latest work: '... for the vast majority of Muslims, the Quranic doctrine of the universality of revelation and the plurality of prophets under the One God still resonates deeply in their hearts and souls, and they remain ever mindful of the many verses of the Quran concerning the reality of One God *and* the multiplicity of revelations sent by Him.' *The Heart of Islam—Enduring Values for Humanity* (New York: HarperCollins, 2002), pp. 53-54.

[19] From his review of, *The Decline of Eastern Christianity Under Islam: From Jihad to Dhimmitude* by Bat Ye'or, in *First Things*, no. 76, October 1997, p. 93.

It is sadly the case that so many of those engaged in dialogue on behalf of Muslims are not seen as representative of mainstream Muslim opinion. Those who are in dialogue are, in a sense, those who do not need to be, as they already possess a respectful attitude to the religious other; and those who stay away from dialogue, out of suspicion or ignorance, are those who most need to open up to, and respect, the other. The main drawback of the many well-intentioned efforts to present a Qur'ānic 'approach' to, or 'perspective' on, religious dialogue is that they fail to connect sufficiently with those who most need to be convinced of the argument, those for whom the normativity of Islam is threatened or undermined by the kind of pluralism or universalism propounded by modern liberal Muslim thinkers.[20]

The attempt made in this book may be no more successful, but the metaphysical perspective elaborated here on universality enables the universalist to uphold the normativity of Islam without detriment to his or her universalism; indeed, to uphold it precisely as an expression of this universalism. The essence of the argument here, based on the metaphysics of Ibn ʿArabī, is that a universalism that does not include particularism is itself particularist and exclusivist—it excludes exclusivism. The danger of excluding those who can only open up to the religious other on the basis of rigorously adhering to the normativity of their own faith was vividly brought to light by the controversy over the recent book by the Chief Rabbi, Dr Jonathan Sacks. The manner in which Dr Sacks was compelled by senior theologians in his own community to retract certain sentences from his latest book, *The Dignity of Difference*[21], highlights well the intellectual challenge involved in reaching out to the other without alienating one's own community.

---

[20] One is referring here to such authors as Abdulaziz Sachedina, Farid Esack, and Hasan Askari, to whose writings particular references will be made later.

[21] Jonathan Sacks, *The Dignity of Difference—How to Avoid the Clash of Civilizations* (London & New York: Continuum, 2002).

Dialogue normally implies that one has something to learn from the other; does that mean that one's own religion is deficient? Dialogue normally presupposes that no one religion is to be promoted as the only true religion, or even as the 'best'; does that mean then that one's own religion is no longer to be considered normative? These questions must have been in the mind of the Chief Rabbi when he was writing his book, a courageous one, in which he went further than any other major Jewish leader of our times in asserting that he and his religion can indeed learn from the Gentile, the non-Jewish other. But his endeavour went too far for the conservatives within his community. It was reported that he was compelled by senior theologians to 'amend' the following sentences for the next edition of the book: 'God has spoken to mankind in many languages, through Judaism to the Jews, Christianity to Christians, Islam to Muslims... no one creed has a monopoly of spiritual truth... In heaven there is truth, on earth there are truths. God is greater than religion. He is only partially comprehended by any faith.'[22]

We hope that some of the ideas presented here may complement the theological perspective boldly proclaimed by the Chief Rabbi in these sentences, at the same time as minimising the reasons for anathematisation by the exoteric authorities. Likewise, it is hoped that such laudable theological endeavours as those of Mohamed Talbi, one of the most important contemporary Muslim spokespersons in dialogue, and a most effective proponent of tolerance and respect of the other within Islam, will be complemented and supported by some of the principles given expression in this book. For an inclusivist theology can be greatly assisted by, to give just one example, a rigorous metaphysical conception of oneness; on its own level, theological oneness—the oneness of God—is of limited scope, whereas a conception of oneness that embraces all that is—the

[22] See the report in *The Guardian*, September 27, 2002.

oneness of reality—holds out far richer possibilities as regards comprehending and respecting the other.

It should be noted that in this work, the terms 'exclusivism' and 'inclusivism' are being employed in their obvious lexical meaning, and not with the implications the terms have acquired in the context of the on-going debate within Christian philosophical theology. In the latter context, an 'exclusivist' is described as one who believes one of two things: either that his religion is alone true, authentic, and valid, excluding all others, or that it, alone, is *fully* true, authentic and valid; an 'inclusivist' is one who, while believing in the normativity of his own religion, 'includes' the other within that religion, and therefore allows salvation as a possibility for the other; finally, pluralists are those who believe that all religions are equal, none has the right to claim to be unique, for all are human, 'cognitive responses' to the ineffable Real—in the words of its chief proponent, John Hick.[23]

The position argued for in this book cannot be fitted into any of these categories. It can instead be characterised as 'universalist': a position which shares with pluralism the basic premise that the major religious traditions are valid paths to salvation, but parts company with the pluralist in asserting that this salvific efficacy stems from the fact that these religions are divinely revealed, not humanly constructed. While many of the aims and motives of the pluralists are laudable and deserve support, this does not mean that one has to agree with all its premises and concomitants; in particular, one disagrees with the kind of

[23] The first presentation of this threefold typology was given by Alan Race, in his *Christians and Religious Pluralism* (London: SCM, 1983). See Gavin D'Costa's very helpful analysis of these three principal positions in his *Theology and Religious Pluralism* (Oxford: Blackwell, 1986), in which exclusivism is analysed with reference to Hendrik Kraemer, inclusivism, in relation to Karl Rahner, whose 'anonymous Christians' consist in all those who live a life of truth and virtue, without being formally members of the Church, and pluralism in relation to John Hick. I shall discuss the position of Hick briefly in Chapters III and IV.

pluralism which is constrained to deny the uniqueness of each religion in order to subsume them all under some putatively 'global theology'. For it is by the same token constrained to contradict the self-definition of all the religions.

As regards the 'inclusivist' position, while sharing with it the assertion that there is a single religious essence which underlies all outward forms, the universalism expounded here upholds as irreducible the differences of outward religious forms, for these differences are seen as divinely sanctioned:[24] they are diverse forms reflecting the principle of divine infinity, not just accidental expressions of human diversity. Thus the very otherness of the other is rigorously maintained and respected, rather than being domesticated and appropriated as part of oneself or one's formal religion, and thereby in practice denying its otherness. Rather, the other in its very otherness, in all its particularities, in all its irreducible difference, is respected not simply out of a sentiment of religious tolerance, but on the basis of a perception that the other is an expression of the One. The One reveals itself in diversity and infinite differentiation; it does not deny or abolish differences on the plane of its infinite unfolding. The difference between oneself and the other is therefore simultaneously upheld and transcended: upheld on the plane of irreducible form, and transcended only on the supra-phenomenal plane of the divine Principle itself in which all differences are embraced and unified.

[24] Rahner, by contrast, asserts that the Christian mission must persist in its efforts to convert 'anonymous Christians' to Christianity in its institutionalised form, this form alone being given the final divine sanction. The 'anonymous Christian' can be turned by conversion 'into someone who also knows about his Christian belief in the depths of his grace-endowed being by objective reflection and in the *profession of faith which is given social form in the Church*.' (emphasis added) K. Rahner, *Theological Investigations*, vol. 5, p. 32; cited in D'Costa, *op. cit.*, p. 88. One of the positions argued for later in this book may appear to be identical with this inclusivism of Rahner—for the Muslim universalist also calls for the 'conversion' of the other to Islam—but the basis on which this call is made differs in a significant respect, as will be made clear in Chapter IV.

Finally, as regards the 'exclusivist' position, even though universalism clearly transcends one type or aspect of exclusivism—the absolute denial of the validity of other faiths—it evinces a certain solidarity with another type or aspect of exclusivism—the notion that one's religion is normative and binding. The way in which these two apparently contradictory positions can be reconciled will be one of the key leitmotifs of this book.

CHAPTER I

The Hermeneutics of Suspicion or of Sufism?

THE APPROACH TO the Qur'ān adopted in this book is based in its essentials upon the rich tradition of Sufi exegesis in general, and on one hermeneutical principle expounded by *al-Shaykh al-Akbar*—the 'Greatest Shaykh', Muḥyī al-Dīn Ibn ʿArabī (d. 638/1240), in particular.[1] Moreover, it is not only formal works of exegesis in this tradition that will be looked at, but also 'informal' commentaries, that is, fragments of commentary on Qur'ānic verses that are to be found in works which are not designated as formal commentaries—such as the *Mathnawī*[2] and the *Discourses* of Jalāl al-Dīn Rūmī (d. 672/1273), the *Futūḥāt al-makkiyya*[3] of Ibn ʿArabī and the *Mishkāt al-anwār*

[1] Ibn ʿArabī is given this honorific in the Sufi tradition on account of his authoritative and encyclopedic exposition of metaphysics, spirituality, cosmology, theology, law, exegesis, and many other branches of Islamic thought and practice. For the most comprehensive biography of this seminal figure of Islamic spirituality, see Claude Addas, *Quest for the Red Sulphur—The Life of Ibn ʿArabī* (tr. P. Kingsley), (Cambridge: Islamic Texts Society, 1993).

[2] The *Mathnawī* is often referred to in Persia as a poetic commentary on the Qur'ān. Indeed, as Corbin notes, it is 'meditated and practised as the "Persian Qur'ān" (*Qur'ān-i Fārsī*)'. *En Islam iranien* (Paris: Gallimard, 1971), vol. III, pp. 216-217.

[3] In the words of Michel Chodkiewicz, the foremost expositor of Ibn ʿArabī's hermeneutics in the West, 'It is not incorrect to consider that the

of Abū Ḥāmid Ghazālī (d. 505/1111). This is done out of a recognition that esoteric commentary on the Qur'ān is by no means restricted to that corpus of works designated as *tafsīr*. As Abdurrahman Habil writes:

> '. . . we tend to ignore the fact that almost every work that deals with the religion of Islam involves, directly or indirectly, a certain understanding of the Quran and certain interpretations of particular Quranic verses. This is simply due to the obvious fact that the whole Islamic religion revolves around this Book. Sometimes even an incidental reference to a verse indicates an implicit, particular interpretation of it. This applies especially to Islamic esoterism. After all is said and done, one comes to the conclusion that the whole Islamic esoteric tradition is essentially an esoteric commentary on the Quran.'[4]

Needless to say, Sufi exegesis is by no means monolithic. The genre is complex and multifaceted, but there are certain features that define its essential character, as will be discussed below. For the most part, the commentaries to be examined here fall under the 'Akbarī' category, that is, they are written by members of the school inaugurated by the Shaykh al-Akbar.

---

work of the Shaykh al-Akbar. . . is in its entirety a Qur'ānic commentary.' M. Chodkiewicz, *An Ocean Without Shore—Ibn Arabi, the Book and the Law* (tr. David Streight), (Albany: State University of New York Press, 1993), p. 24. In this masterly exposition, to which we shall return below, Chodkiewicz demonstrates how not only the content of the *Futūḥāt*, but also the very structure of this apparently randomly assembled work, derive from the Qur'ān, in a clearly discernible numerical pattern. In the words of Ibn ʿArabī himself: 'All that of which we speak in our sessions and in our writings proceeds from the Qur'ān and from its treasures.' (*Ibid.*, p. 64)

See Chapter III of this work for the presentation of the structural and thematic correspondences between the chapters of the Qur'ān and those of the *Futūḥāt*.

[4] Abdurrahman Habil, 'Traditional Esoteric Commentaries on the Quran', in S. H. Nasr (ed.) *Islamic Spirituality*, vol. 1 Foundations (London: Routledge & Kegan Paul, 1987), p. 24.

The principal source of formal exegesis will be the esoteric commentary on the Qur'ān written by ʿAbd al-Razzāq al-Kāshānī (d.730/1329), a distinguished representative of the school of Ibn ʿArabī. This work has played a role of considerable importance in the tradition of esoteric commentary in Islam, its renown having been amplified in recent times as a result of its erroneous attribution to Ibn ʿArabī.[5] Its value lies principally in the fact that it presents a complete exegesis, chapter by chapter, of the Qur'ān, and it does so from an uncompromisingly esoteric perspective. It thus leads us, in the words of Pierre Lory, 'to the very root of the Sufi endeavour: the encounter with the holy word, and the spiritual force proper to it, not only on the level of meaning, but in the most intimate dimension of the meditating soul.'[6] A careful reading of this commentary, Lory insists, helps one to appreciate the way in which the Qur'ān—'a "closed" book for many western readers'—has sown the seeds of a deep spirituality, seeds 'which have enriched and enlivened the religious life of the Islamic community for the past fourteen centuries.'[7]

The aim in this book is not to be comprehensive but illustrative. That is, the fragments of the commentaries examined here are intended to illustrate and illuminate the relevance of fun-

---

[5] The commentary was published under the name of Ibn ʿArabī, with the title *Tafsīr al-Shaykh al-Akbar*, in Cairo (1283/1866), and in Cawnpore (1883); and under his name, with the title *Tafsīr al-Qur'ān al-Karīm* in Beirut (1968), and in several other editions since then. We have used a recent reprint (Cairo: al-Maktaba al-Tawfīqiyya, n.d.) of the Cairo 1283/1866 edition.

[6] P. Lory, *Les Commentaires ésotériques du Coran d'après 'Abd ar-Razzāq al-Qāshānī* (Paris: Les Deux Océans, 1980), p. 7. It is also noteworthy that Kāshānī was, in a certain respect, a 'Shiʿi Sufi', and that his work thus constitutes, as Abdurrahman Habil writes, 'one of the several points where the Shiʿite and Sufi commentary traditions meet each other.' (*Op. cit.*, p. 34) See also the excellent work by Abū Bakr Sirāj ad-Dīn, *The Book of Certainty* (Cambridge: Islamic Texts Society, 1992) which offers a concise and profound exposition of Sufi gnosis based principally on Kāshānī's commentary on certain Qur'ānic verses.

[7] Lory, *Les Commentaires*, p. 8.

damental Qur'ānic themes and principles to the contemporary context of religious diversity and dialogue. But before outlining the exegetical approach that underlies this book, it is necessary to do two things: first, we need to situate, in broad terms, the phenomenon of Sufism itself in the context of the Islamic tradition; and secondly, in anticipation of certain objections to the approach here, we must state briefly why it is that we are, as it were, 'looking back' to the Sufi tradition, rather than adopting a modern, or postmodern, hermeneutical approach to the sacred text. This will help to clear the ground for a deeper appreciation of the Sufi approach to exegesis, and also show how radically this differs from postmodern hermeneutics.

Sufism in Context

When considering Sufism as a historical phenomenon, it is important not to confuse its outward manifestations in time with its inner spiritual principles. One should not, in other words, regard Sufism as a later addition to the Islamic tradition, and portray it as something new or original; for this would lead directly to the idea that Sufism is a kind of *bidʿa* or innovation. It also credits the Sufis with much more than they claim for themselves. For they see themselves simply as the inheritors of the spiritual legacy of the Islamic Revelation, nothing more. Moreover, this spiritual legacy is not to be confined within the boundaries of the Sufi tradition alone. For, despite the fact that the spiritual values of the Islamic revelation are expressed with particular vigour, subtlety and depth by the Sufis, these values are also present and active, in differing degrees, within all the major expressions of Islamic intellectuality and piety. Sufis do not claim a monopoly on these values; they simply endeavour to raise these values to their highest pitch, on the level of metaphysics; to realize their deeper ramifications, on the level of mystical *praxis*; and to implement with utmost sincerity their ethical implications, on the plane of morality. One should also note that what is referred to as *taṣawwuf* in the Sunni world often finds expression as *ʿirfān* (spiritual knowledge or gnosis) in Shiʿism.[8]

One can, however, agree completely with S. H. Nasr when he writes: 'Islamic esotericism or gnosis crystallized into the form of Sufism in the Sunni world, while it poured into the whole structure of Shiʿism, especially during its early period.'[9] Thus, the esoteric essence of Islam expresses itself in Sunni Sufism and in Shiʿi *ʿIrfān* with different 'accents', its fundamental message remaining the same. Indeed, according to one of the commentators dealt with in this study, Sayyid Ḥaydar Āmulī, the true Shiʿi is a Sufi without realising it; and the true Sufi is a Shiʿi who has forgotten his origins. For Āmulī, it is *walāya*,

[8] That is to say, when contemporary Shiʿi scholars discuss the origins and doctrines of *ʿirfān* they in fact describe the origins and doctrines of Sufism. See for example, the overview by the late ʿAllāma Muṭahharī, "ʿIrfān: Islamic Mysticism", in his *Understanding Islamic Sciences* (London: Islamic College for Advanced Studies, 2002), pp. 89-141. This not to say that Shiʿi *ʿirfān* is simply Sunni Sufism by another name. While there is much in common between the two traditions on the plane of essential spiritual principles, aims and intentions, the relationship between them is rather more complex, as they differ in ways that are not negligible. Among these, the following distinctive features of Shiʿi *ʿirfān* should be noted: the preponderant spiritual functions attributed to the twelve Imams—with a particular eschatological function attributed to the twelfth—together with the intellectual, spiritual, and moral role occupied by their sayings; the existence, independent of the more formal Sufi orders in the Shiʿi world, of informal, highly secretive initiatic relationships between master and disciple, shorn of the public organisational features (titles, hierarchies, distinctive dress, regular public sessions of incantatory rites (*majlis al-dhikr*)), etc., which characterise most Sufi orders; and finally, one must take into account the practical consequences of adherence to the Shiʿi school of Law by all those affiliated in one way or another to the tradition of *ʿirfān*.

Also, Sufi orders are of course to be found within the Shiʿi world. See Kamil Mustafa al-Shaibi, *Sufism and Shi'ism* (Surbiton: LAAM, 1991), for a good overview of the relationship, doctrinally and historically, between the two traditions.

[9] This statement comes in his important essay, 'Shiʿism and Sufism: their Relationship in Essence and in History', in *Sufi Essays* (London, George Allen & Unwin, 1972), p. 105.

sanctity, that constitutes at once the true substance and the goal of Sufism and Shiʿism alike.[10]

We can begin this brief discussion of Sufism with a famous definition of *taṣawwuf* quoted by ʿAlī al-Hujwīrī (d. 456/1063) in his *Kashf al-maḥjūb* ('Disclosure of the Veiled'), one of the most important early manuals of classical Sufism: 'Today, Sufism is a name without a reality; formerly it was a reality without a name.'[11] In other words the Sufis regard their spiritual way to have been present, in all its pristine plenitude, at the time of the Prophet and his Companions, as an inner, unnamed reality, a profound attunement to the overwhelming reality of the Qur'ānic Revelation, a way of life and thought that was consonant with the values and principles enshrined therein. After giving us this definition, Hujwīrī writes that those who deny the intrinsic principles of Sufism are in fact denying the 'whole sacred Law of the Apostle and his praised qualities'.[12]

Now it might seem surprising to assert that a denial of Sufism is tantamount to a denial of the whole Sacred Law; but the stress here should be on the word 'whole'. For if Islam is reduced to just a mechanical observation of outward rules, then it is not a religion in the full sense. Or, it is a religion without inner life: hence we find the great Ghazālī naming his *magnum opus* the *Iḥyā' ʿulūm al-dīn*, literally, 'enlivening the sciences of religion'; and it is clear from his writings that the spiritual values proper to Sufism provide this inner life of religion.[13]

For a true religion must comprise not just a formal Law but also a spiritual Way; a law that requires obedience, and a way that teaches sincerity of heart, that is, *ikhlāṣ*, or *ṣidq*, terms by which

[10] See Corbin's *En Islam iranien*, vol. II, pp. 154–155, 178–190, for this aspect of Āmulī's thought.

[11] *The Kashf al-Maḥjūb—The Oldest Persian Treatise on Sufiism*, ʿAlī al-Hujwīrī (tr. R. A. Nicholson), (Lahore: Islamic Book Service, 1992), p. 44.

[12] *Ibid.*, p. 44.

[13] *Iḥyā' ʿulūm al-dīn* (Beirut: Dār al-Jīl, 1992), vols. 1-6.

Sufism is often defined.[14] All of the great masters of what one might call 'normative' Sufism have stressed the interdependence of the Law and the Way, the *Sharīʿa* and the *Ṭarīqa*. For them, any spiritual way which disdains the Law is like a disembodied spirit—a 'ghost' as it were; but the Law, deprived of the spirit, is a lifeless form—a kind of 'corpse'. The Law, in other words, should be conceived as a framework, a structure, within which the life of the spirit can be cultivated; it is this spirit that leads one to God, and not the Law *per se.* Ghazālī makes this point very clearly: after mentioning different forms of divorce, contracts, hire rental and lease and money-changing—all oft-discussed subjects in Islamic Law—he declares: 'Anyone who acquires knowledge of these things, hoping thereby to draw nearer to God would certainly be mad. Indeed, nothing but engaging body and soul in the service of God and His worship would draw people nearer to God.'[15]

One could also refer in this context to the Prophet's own definition of the three aspects of religion in a famous exchange, known as the 'Ḥadīth of Gabriel', for the questioner of the Prophet in this exchange, unbeknown to the Companions who were present, was the angel Gabriel, in human guise. The narration is from ʿUmar ibn al-Khaṭṭāb:

> 'O Muḥammad, tell me about Submission (*islām*)', the stranger asked. The Prophet replied: '*Islām* is to testify that there is no god but God and Muḥammad is the Messenger of God, to perform the prayers, to pay the poor-due (*zakāt*), to fast in Ramaḍān, and to make the pilgrimage to the House if you are able to do so.' The narration continues: 'He [Gabriel] said: You have spoken truly, and we [the Companions, according to ʿUmar]

---

[14] See for example *The Book of Truthfulness* (*Kitāb al-ṣidq*), Abū Saʿīd al-Kharrāz (ed. and tr. by A. J. Arberry), (London & New York: Oxford University Press, 1937).

[15] *The Book of Knowledge* (tr. N. A. Faris), (Lahore: Sh. Muhammad Ashraf, 1966), p. 45.

> were amazed at him asking him and saying that he had spoken truly. He said: 'Then tell me about faith (*īmān*).' He said: 'It is to believe in God, His angels, His books, His messengers, and the Last Day, and to believe in divine destiny, both the good and the evil thereof.' He said: 'You have spoken truly.' He said: 'Then tell me about virtue (*iḥsān*).'[16] He said: 'It is to worship God as though you are seeing Him, and if you see Him not, yet truly He sees you.'[17]

It has been remarked by many in the Islamic tradition—and not just by the Sufis—that the *fuqahā'*, the jurists, are the specialists in the first domain, that of how to enact the rules of the religion; the *mutakallimūn*, the theologians, are the specialists in the second, that of formal beliefs; while to the Sufis pertains the third domain, that of spiritual virtue, of 'doing what is beautiful'.[18] There is an interpenetration between the three spheres, but their distinctiveness can be easily discerned in the unfolding of the overall tradition. While it is fair to refer to Sufism as the 'mystical' dimension of Islam, as does Schimmel in the title of her work, *Mystical Dimensions of Islam*, one of the

[16] This can also be translated as 'excellence' as 'goodness' or, more literally, as 'doing what is beautiful', the root of the word being related primarily to beauty, *ḥusn*, as is stressed by Sachiko Murata and William Chittick in their excellent introduction to Islam, *The Vision of Islam* (New York: Paragon House, 1994), pp. xxxii, 267-273. In drawing attention to the aesthetic connotation of this key term, the authors cast into a different light the many verses in the Qur'ān that mention *iḥsān* and its derivatives. For example, LXXX: 31:... [*that He may*] *recompense those who do what is beautiful with the most beautiful.*

[17] This is the first part of a tradition related by Bukhārī and Muslim; see for the full text in English and Arabic, *ḥadīth* no. 2 of *An-Nawawī's Forty Hadith* (tr. E. Ibrahim, D. Johnson-Davies), (Cambridge: Islamic Texts Society, 1997), pp. 28-33 (translation slightly modified).

[18] It is no coincidence that the overwhelming majority of artists—calligraphers, painters, poets, musicians, etc.—were practising Sufis. See S. H. Nasr, *Islamic Art and Spirituality* (Ipswich: Golgonooza Press, 1987).

most comprehensive accounts of Sufism in western scholarship,[19] it would be incorrect to disassociate this dimension from the overall matrix that it presupposes, and to the spiritual and ethical integrity of which it makes such a vital contribution.[20]

Another tripartite distinction of the different aspects of the Islamic tradition, one that is frequently cited in Sufi texts, is the following: *Sharīʿa, Ṭarīqa, Ḥaqīqa*—Law, Path and Truth. Rūmī refers to these three elements, and gives an analogy with the science of alchemy. In his introduction to the fifth book of his poetic masterpiece, the *Mathnawī*, he says his poem shows that the Law 'is like a candle showing the way. Unless you gain possession of the candle, there is no wayfaring; and when you have come on to the way, your wayfaring is the Path; and when you have reached the journey's end, that is the Truth. Hence it has been said, "'If the truths (realities) were manifest, the religious laws would be naught"... the Law is like learning the theory of alchemy from a teacher or a book, and the Path is (like) making use of chemicals and rubbing the copper upon the philosophers' stone, and the Truth is (like) the transmutation of the copper into gold. Those who know alchemy rejoice in their knowledge of it, saying, "We know the theory of this (science)"; and those who practise it rejoice in their practice of it, saying, "We perform such works"; and those who have experienced the reality rejoice in the reality, saying, "We have become gold and

---

[19] A. Schimmel, *Mystical Dimensions of Islam* (Chapel Hill: University of North Carolina Press, 1975). See also the three volumes of *The Heritage of Sufism*, ed. L. Lewisohn (Oxford: Oneworld, 1999); and the two volumes of *Islamic Spirituality*, ed. S. H. Nasr, cited above. For a succinct and profound account of Sufism from within the tradition, see Martin Lings, *What is Sufism?* (Cambridge: Islamic Texts Society, 1993). See also M. Lings, *A Sufi Saint of the Twentieth Century—Shaikh Aḥmad al-ʿAlawī, His Spiritual Heritage and Legacy* (Cambridge: Islamic Texts Society, 1993), for a vivid account of the concrete, lived aspects of Sufism in relation to one of the great spiritual masters of the last century.

[20] See Victor Danner, *The Islamic Tradition* (New York: Amity House, 1988), for an overview which makes very clear the integral role played by Sufism within Islam.

are delivered from the theory and practice of alchemy: we are God's freedmen." *Each party is rejoicing in what they have.*'[21]

The complementarity between the legal and the spiritual should be noted in this passage, which sums up well the traditional Sufi conception of the relationship between these different aspects of Islam. Although the Truth surpasses the Path and the Law, it is nonetheless only by means of obeying the Law and following the Path that one can attain ultimately to the Truth. The Law thus functions as a framework within which the Path is followed, a Path leading to a summit which transcends that framework, together with the Path. In transcending that framework, certain Sufis were seen as so radical as to be undermining it, but, as Corbin wisely notes, they were in fact strengthening the framework of the religion, precisely by revealing the spiritual potential contained within it. Sufis like Ibn ʿArabī and Ḥallāj may have scandalised many, but they never pretended that they had 'gone beyond' Islam: 'They lived it and actualized all of its latent spiritual power. What they certainly did go beyond was the purely legalistic, social and political conception of Islam, a conception which would have been the death of the religion.'[22]

Turning to a less controversial figure, Ghazālī, Sufism was often referred to by him in terms of the 'science of the hereafter' and the 'science of the heart'. Only those with practical experience in such sciences are competent to teach them. The jurist has no authority in this domain: if the jurist addresses himself to questions of inner sincerity or the heart, that is, to questions which pertain to the science of the hereafter, he 'oversteps his bounds'.[23] This spiritual aspect of Islam is altogether fundamental: it is the substance of inner worship and all that goes to condition this supreme gift of oneself to God. If this dimension of religion be weak or denied, the very integrity

---

[21] *Mathnawī* (tr. R. A. Nicholson), (London: Luzac, 1934), vol. VI, Book V, p. 3. The final sentence is a verse from the Qur'ān, XXX: 32.

[22] Corbin, *En Islam iranien*, vol. I, p. 19.

[23] Ghazālī, *The Book of Knowledge*, p. 43.

of the Sacred Law as a whole will be fatally undermined. For the Law can be obeyed outwardly but at the same time denied inwardly, and this is hypocrisy; and as regards belief, one can assert various beliefs with the mind without their true reality being present in the heart, and this is superficiality. To attain higher degrees of faith and realization, one needs more than just a theoretical description of the theological creed; one needs, as Ghazālī stressed repeatedly, a practical science aimed at purifying the heart. 'To know God, His attributes and His works... does not result from theology—in fact theology is almost a veil and a barrier against it.'[24]

It is difficult to over-emphasise the role of Ghazālī in synthesising the Spirit and the Law, or Sufism and the Sharīʿa, within the framework of Islamic piety. In the words of Victor Danner, '... al-Ghazzālī describes the illuminative knowledge of the path, which confers immediate certitude and graces, as the very summit of the believer's life. In brief, the *Sharīʿah* did not suffice unto itself... After his day, it would not be easy for any religious scholar to reject the *ṭarīqah* without exposing his ignorance about the spiritual contents of the Islamic message. All that the future critics of Sufism, like the Ḥanbalī theologian Ibn al-Jawzī (d. 597/1200), could do was to criticize certain Sufis, or some of their teachings, but not the path itself.'[25]

As regards the origin of the term 'Sufi', various theories have been proposed.[26] Of these the most plausible is the connection with the word for wool, *ṣūf*. We should also remember that the *ahl al-ṣuffa*, a group of poor people who lived in the Prophet's mosque and who were renowned for the intensity of their

---

[24] *Ibid.*, p. 55.

[25] V. Danner, 'The Early Development of Sufism', in *Islamic Spirituality*, vol. 1, p. 262.

[26] See the chapter entitled, 'How the Ṣūfis account for their being called Ṣūfis', by one of the most important early expositors of Sufism, Abū Bakr al-Kalābādhī (d. 380/990) in his *The Doctrine of the Ṣūfis* (*Kitāb al-taʿarruf li-madhhab ahl al-taṣawwuf*), (tr. A. J. Arberry), (Cambridge: Cambridge University Press, 1935), pp. 5–11.

worship, wore woolen garments, and that they, along with the Prophet himself and his closest companions, can legitimately be called the first 'Sufis' even if they were not referred to at the time by this name. In fact, many Sufis refer to themselves as *al-ṭā'ifa*, the 'group' or 'tribe', because of the following verse of the Qur'ān: *Verily thy Lord knoweth that thou keepest vigil almost two-thirds of the night, and half of it and a third of it, as doth a group* (ṭā'ifa) *among those with thee...* (LXXIII: 20)

The pre-eminence of this group is also referred to in the following verse, telling the Prophet to keep close to these people rather than paying attention to the vanity of this world: *Restrain thyself with those who cry unto their Lord at morn and evening, seeking His countenance; and let not thine eyes overlook them, desiring the pomp of the life of this world...* (XVIII: 28)

It is important to cite in this connection other verses with which the Sufis identify in a particularly direct manner, verses which are fundamental to the spirituality of the Islamic tradition, and which demonstrate that one need look no further than the Qur'ān—and the Prophetic norm, or *Sunna*—for identifying the source of Sufism.[27]

> *And unto God belong the East and the West; and wherever ye turn, there is the Face of God.* (II: 115)
> *He is with you wherever ye may be.* (LVII: 4)
> *We are nearer to him* [man] *than the jugular vein.* (L: 16)
> *God cometh in between a man and his own heart.* (VIII: 24)
> *Is He not encompassing all things?* (XLI: 54)
> *He is the First and the Last, and the Outward and the Inward.* (LVII: 3)

[27] The researches of Louis Massignon put paid to the Orientalist thesis that Sufism had its origins in borrowings from other religions. See his *Essay on the Origins of the Technical Language of Islamic Mysticism*, (tr. B. Clark), (Notre Dame, In.: University of Notre Dame, 1997). See also P. Nwyia, *Exégèse coranique et langage mystique* (Beirut: Dār al-Mashreq, 1970), for further substantiation of this position.

Each of these verses contains the seeds of the most profound spiritual doctrines;[28] and each has given rise to the most fecund meditation upon that most mysterious of all realities, the immanence of the Absolute in all that exists. While the thrust of the Qur'ānic discourse is to emphasise the transcendence of God, His remoteness and incomparability (the aspect referred to classically as *tanzīh*), the complementary dimension, that of divine immanence, proximity, and similarity (*tashbīh*) is also expressed, and the Sufis give special attention to this aspect of the divine Reality, cultivating a receptivity to the inalienable presence of the one-and-only Reality within the entire sphere of relativity, of all that which is, from another point of view, 'other than God'.

Sachiko Murata's work, *The Tao of Islam*,[29] demonstrates the way in which the Sufis valorise this *yin* aspect of God—the divine beauty (*jamāl*), proximity, and compassion—whereas the theologians and jurists on the whole stress the *yang* aspect—the divine majesty (*jalāl*), remoteness, and wrath. She makes the important, and often neglected point that 'dogmatic theologians with their almost exclusive emphasis upon God's incomparability, represented only a small number of intellectuals who had relatively little influence on the community at large. Popular Islam, the philosophical tradition, and the spiritual tradition, represented by the great Sufis stressed, or at least found ample

---

[28] See the article 'The Quran as the Foundation of Islamic Spirituality', by S. H. Nasr in *Islamic Spirituality*, vol. I, pp. 3–10. The following point by Frithjof Schuon is relevant here. He cites the following verses: *The Hereafter is better for thee than this lower world* (XCIV: 4); *The life of this world is but sport and play* (XXIX: 64); *In your wives and your children ye have an enemy* (LXIV: 14); *Say: Allāh! Then leave them to their vain talk* (VI: 91); *Whoso feareth the station of his Lord and restraineth his soul from desire* (LXXIX: 40). Then he adds, 'when the Qur'ān speaks thus, there emerges for the Moslem a whole ascetic and mystical doctrine, as penetrating and complete as any other form of spirituality worthy of the name.' *Understanding Islam* (Bloomington: World Wisdom, 1994), p. 60.

[29] S. Murata, *The Tao of Islam—A Sourcebook on Gender Relationships in Islamic Thought* (Albany: State University of New York Press, 1992).

room for, a second point of view that is clearly supported by many Koranic verses.' Instead of perceiving God as 'a distant, dominating, and powerful ruler whose commands must be obeyed,' the Sufis 'maintain that mercy, love, and gentleness are the overriding reality of existence, and that these will win out in the end. God is not primarily a stern and forbidding father, but a warm and loving mother.'[30]

Receptivity to this aspect of divine reality is cultivated not only by reflection and meditation upon such verses as the above, but also by contemplative practices that are themselves clearly indicated in the Qur'ān itself, and embodied in the conduct, or *Sunna*, of the Prophet. In the Qur'ānic chapter cited above, *al-Muzzammil* (LXXIII) 'The Encloaked One', in which mention was made of the *ṭā'ifa*, one finds an explicit reference to the practice that lies at the heart of the Sufi endeavour, the 'remembrance of God' (*dhikr Allāh*), a remembrance or consciousness of the divine reality that is generated by the accomplishment of the invocation of the Name of God, the word *dhikr* comprising both the goal—recollectedness, awareness of God—and the means to attain it:[31] *And invoke the Name of thy Lord, devoting yourself to it with utter devotion* (LXXIII: 8). Here, the pronoun indicated in the word *ilayhi* can refer either to Him as 'your Lord' or to 'it' as the 'Name of your Lord', so that the verse can also mean, for the Sufis: invoke the Name of God and

[30] *Ibid.*, pp. 8-9.

[31] In his lexicon of terms in the Qur'ān, al-Rāghib al-Iṣfahānī gives us the following definition. *Dhikr* is that by means of which 'man preserves that knowledge (*ma*ʿ*rifa*) which he has attained, so it is akin to memory (*ḥifẓ*) except that memory is spoken of in respect of its function of acquisition (*iḥrāzihi*), whereas *dhikr* is spoken of in respect of its function of "rendering present" (*istiḥḍārihi*). *Dhikr* is also used to refer to the presence of a thing in one's consciousness (lit. 'heart') or in one's speech. Thus, it is said that there are two types of *dhikr*: *dhikr* of the heart and *dhikr* of the tongue, and each comprises two further kinds of *dhikr*: a *dhikr* which follows forgetfulness, and a *dhikr* which does not follow forgetfulness but which on the contrary expresses a continuous remembering.' *Mu*ʿ*jam mufradāt alfāẓ al-Qur'ān* (Beirut: Dār al-Fikr, n.d.), p. 181.

devote yourself to this Name with utter devotion. This recalls the explicit injunction contained in such verses as the following:

> *Glorify the Name of thy Lord, the Exalted* (LXXXVII: 1)
> *And invoke the Name of thy Lord morning and evening* (LXXVI: 25)
> *O ye who believe! Invoke God with much invocation* (XXXIII: 41)
> *Call upon thy Lord in humility and in secret* (VII: 55)
> *And invoke thy Lord within thyself, in humility and awe, and beneath thy breath, in the morning and in the night* (VII: 205).

All of these verses appear to point to an actual practice, one which is to be maintained according to different modes ('in yourself' 'with humility', 'with awe', 'in secret', 'under one's breath', etc.)[32] The aim of this practice is to become aware of the divine presence through the opening up of a mode of perception that, following the Qur'ān, the Sufis refer to in terms of the 'heart'.

The relationship between remembrance and the heart is clearly affirmed in this Qur'ānic verse: . . . *Those who believe and whose hearts are at peace in the remembrance of God; is it not in the remembrance of God that hearts are at peace?* (XIII: 28) And also in the following verses: *Truly therein is a reminder* (dhikrā) *for him who hath a heart* (L: 37). *Those are true believers whose hearts quake with awe when God is invoked* (VIII: 2). And in the following verse, negatively: . . . *woe be to those whose hearts are hardened against the remembrance of God, they are in plain error* (XXXIX: 22). By contrast, the verse that follows this one, verse 23, refers to hearts that 'soften' to the *dhikru'Llāh*.

[32] For the most comprehensive exposition of the theory and practice of *dhikr* in the Sufi tradition, see the volume by Ibn ʿAṭā'illāh al-Iskandarī, *The Key to Salvation—A Sufi Manual of Invocation* (*Miftāḥ al-falāḥ wa miṣbāḥ al-arwāḥ*) (tr. Mary A. K. Danner), (Cambridge: Islamic Texts Society, 1996).

While the formal, canonical prayer is binding upon all, and is defined by particular times, places and conditions, the invocation, by contrast, can be practised at all times, in all places and in all conditions. It is thus a universal, unconditional imperative—though it is not incumbent legally.[33] In one verse, the 'people of substance' (*ūlu'l-albāb*) are described as those who *remember/invoke God standing, sitting, and reclining on their sides. . .* (III: 190–191)

Moreover, for the Sufis, a life devoted to contemplation and prayer does not preclude an active life in the world; for their aim is to be like those *whom neither commerce nor trade diverteth from the remembrance of God* (XXIV: 37). This remembrance is intended to be a continuous inner awareness which is not ruptured by outward activity, but rather determines the whole of one's life, infusing all of one's activity, both worldly and spiritual, with the consciousness of God. Since this inner consciousness or remembrance takes precedence over outward actions, the Sufis judge all of their activities according to the criterion of this

[33] The *dhikr* is universal in another sense, for the methodic practice of the invocation of a 'name' or 'word' symbolising the Real is found in the most diverse religious traditions. Although we will not enter into this aspect of universality in the following two chapters, it is important to at least draw attention to this little studied evidence, on the plane of religious practice or experiential realization, of the inner unity of the religious traditions. See the citations on the practice of invocation, drawn from all the major religions of the world, given by Whitall Perry in his *Treasury of Traditional Wisdom* (London: George Allen & Unwin, 1971), the section entitled 'Colophon—Invocation', pp. 1001–1042. For an insightful treatment of the invocation within the context of Islamic contemplative disciplines, See J.-L. Michon, 'The Spiritual Practices of Sufism', in *Islamic Spirituality*, vol. 1 Foundations, pp. 265–293; and M. I. Waley, 'Contemplative Disciplines in Early Persian Sufism' in *The Heritage of Sufism*, vol. 1, pp. 497–548. See also the article '*Dhikr*', by L. Gardet in the *Encyclopedia of Islam* (2nd edition). See also the excellent article by James Cutsinger, '*Hesychia*: An Orthodox Opening to Esoteric Ecumenism' in *Paths to the Heart*, ed. James S. Cutsinger (Bloomington: World Wisdom, 2002), pp. 225–250, in which the Christian Orthodox practice of the 'prayer of the heart' is related to the appreciation of the unity of the world's religions on the level of esoteric realization.

remembrance; and they quote the following verse to justify this attitude: *Truly prayer keepeth* [one] *away from lewdness and iniquity, and the remembrance of God is greater.* (XXIX: 45)

Numerous sayings of the Prophet attest to the primacy of the remembrance. For example, it is related that the Prophet asked his companions: 'Shall I not tell you about the best and purest of your works for your Lord, and the most exalted of them in your ranks, and the work that is better for you than giving silver and gold, and better for you than encountering your enemy, with you striking their necks and they striking your necks?' Thereupon the people addressed by him said: 'What is that, O Emissary of God?' He said, 'The perpetual invocation of God—exalted and glorified be He.'[34]

In the light of such verses and sayings, one can better appreciate the following claim by the Shaykh al-ʿAlawī, which sums up the Sufi approach to the practice of religion:

> 'Remembrance is the mightiest rule of the religion... The law was not enjoined upon us, neither were the rites of worship ordained but for the sake of establishing the remembrance of God... In a word, our performance of the rites of worship is considered strong or weak according to the degree of our remembrance while performing them. Thus when the Prophet was asked what spiritual strivers would receive the greatest reward, he replied: "Those who remembered God most". Then when questioned as to what fasters would be most rewarded he said: "Those who remembered God most", and when the prayer and the almsgiving and the pilgrimage and charitable

[34] Cited in *Al-Ghazālī Invocations and Supplications* (Book IX of *The Revival of the Religious Sciences*), trans. K. Nakamura (Cambridge: Islamic Texts Society, 1990), p. 8 (we have slightly modified the translation of the last sentence of the *ḥadīth*). This *ḥadīth* is found in the collection of Ibn Māja (*Sunan*, Adab, 53) and in that of Ibn Ḥanbal (*Musnad*, VI. 447). See the Arabic text for this and several other *ḥadīth* of similar import in Ghazālī's *Iḥyā' ʿulūm al-dīn*, vol. I, pp. 391–2.

> donations were mentioned, he said of each: "The richest in remembrance of God is the richest in reward".'[35]

✸ ✸ ✸

As regards the first manifestations of Sufism in Islamic history, one has to address the question: How and why did it develop as a distinct system of doctrine and practice in the second/eighth to third/ninth centuries? In brief, and at the risk of simplification, one can answer as follows. It was in this period that many of the dimensions of Islam were crystallizing as distinct branches of the developing civilization; it is at this time that the five great schools of jurisprudence were established, when rules of Arabic grammar according to the schools of Basra and Kufa were codified, hadiths were being written down, as were rules of Qur'ān recitation, poetry, and lexicography.[36] It was, in other words, a time of fixations, of codifications, an institutionalisation of aspects of Islamic culture that were previously transmitted orally. It was therefore altogether natural that the purely spiritual legacy of the Revelation should also be expressed in a distinctive fashion.

This was also a time when the empire of Islam was burgeoning, and great fortunes were amassed; in such a context, the dangers of greed and worldliness loomed large in the eyes of the pious. Now such worldly tendencies would most definitely have been intensified if the exterior aspects of the religion alone were stressed and formalised. There were, then, two main tendencies against the background of which the early development of Sufism can be viewed: worldliness and formalism. In the face of these two dangers, the first Sufis played a fundamental

[35] Cited in M. Lings, *A Sufi Saint*, pp. 96-97.

[36] See Marshall G. H. Hodgson, *The Venture of Islam—Conscience and History in a World Civilization* (Chicago and London: University of Chicago Press, 1977), vol. 1, for a good overview of these processes by a historian who possessed a sensitive and illuminating appreciation of the dynamics of intellectual history.

role: on the one hand they were the living witnesses to the otherworldliness of religion, and on the other hand they were a kind of guarantee against the risks of legal formalism, that is the stifling of the spirit by the letter of the law.

This was also a period in which theological controversies abounded: Murjiʿites, Qadarites, Jahmites, then Muʿtazilites and Ashʿarites[37]—all these schools were asserting the correctness of their views of God and faith. Just as these groups and schools acquired a name, so, gradually those who asserted the primacy of worship over theological controversy, self-purification over legal obedientialism, asceticism over worldliness—such people came to distinguished by the term 'Sufi'. Moreover, these different groups, and those specialising in other religious disciplines, all claimed to be dealing with *ʿilm*—knowledge in the formal, discursive sense. At this early period one notices a certain shift in Sufi discourse, an increasing—but by no means exclusive—employment of the term *maʿrifa* to designate *spiritual* knowledge. As Rosenthal puts it: 'The pre-emption by others of *ʿilm* as a technical term prevented the Sufis permanently from selecting *ʿilm* for employment as one of the numerous technical terms of their own vocabulary and from using it to designate by it one of their specific states and stations. Since *maʿrifa* and *yaqīn* lent themselves without much difficulty to doubling for *ʿilm*, they were indeed widely substituted for it.'[38]

This is how Hujwīrī expresses the difference between the two types of knowledge: '. . . the Sufi Shaykhs give the name of *maʿrifat* (gnosis) to every knowledge that is allied with (religious) practice and spiritual state (*ḥāl*). . . and the knower thereof they call *ʿārif*. On the other hand, they give the name of *ʿilm* to every knowledge that is stripped of spiritual meaning and devoid of

[37] See Wilferd Madelung, *Religious Schools and Sects in Medieval Islam* (London: Variorum Reprints, 1985).

[38] Franz Rosenthal, *Knowledge Triumphant—The Concept of Knowledge in Medieval Islam* (Leiden: E. J. Brill, 1970), p. 165.

religious practice, and one who has such knowledge they call *ʿālim*.'[39]

As we have stated elsewhere,[40] one finds, parallel to this early shift of discourse from *ʿilm* to *maʿrifa*, a corresponding shift of emphasis from the *ʿaql*, intelligence, to the *qalb*, heart, as the seat of spiritual awareness;[41] together with a more frequent use of the Divine Name, *al-Ḥaqq*, the Real or the True, to refer to God. In other words, there is discernible here a three-fold change of doctrinal exposition regarding knowledge: first, in the nature of knowledge itself, from discursive to spiritual; then in the faculty of knowledge, from the mind to the heart; and finally, in the object of knowledge, from discrete, formal data, to the essential principles of Reality as such.

Turning now to the more formal, institutional expression of Sufism, the eleventh/fifth century marks a decisive turning point. It was from this time that the Sufi orders (*ṭuruq*, sing. *ṭarīqa*) began to crystallise, and to assume prominence throughout the length and breadth of the Muslim world.[42] From the medieval

---

[39] *Kashf*, p. 382 (partially modified). Nicholson prefers to translate *ḥāl* as 'feeling', which is too vague and superficial to convey the subtlety, depth and transformative power of a *ḥāl*, a spiritual state.

[40] R. Shah-Kazemi, 'The Notion and Significance of *Maʿrifa* in Sufism', in *Journal of Islamic Studies*, vol. 13, no. 2, 2002, pp. 159-160.

[41] This is not to say that the *ʿaql* is always seen in this limitative sense; it can also designate consciousness as such, thus comprising not only both reason and intuition but also both the created intelligence and the uncreated intellect. See S. H. Nasr, 'Intellect and Intuition: Their Relationship from the Islamic Perspective', esp. pp. 68-74, *Studies in Comparative Religion*, vol. 13, nos. 1, 2, Winter-Spring 1979. Moreover, the harmony between *ʿaql* and *qalb* is affirmed in the following words of the Qur'ān: . . . *have they hearts* (qulūb) *wherewith to understand* (yaʿqilūna bihā)... (XXII: 46). *Yaʿqilūna* shares the same triliteral root as *ʿaql*.

[42] For a comprehensive account of the origin and development of the major orders, see J. Spencer Trimingham, *The Sufi Orders in Islam* (Oxford: Oxford University Press, 1998); for more insight into the spiritual principles and practices of eight of the most important orders, seen from within, see Nasr, *Islamic Spirituality*, vol. II, 'Manifestations', pp. 3-193; and for a concise account of the orders, see John O. Voll's article 'Sufi Orders' in *The Oxford*

period up to modern times, the influence of Sufism has been transmitted primarily through these orders, to which not just mystics, but also rulers and scholars, merchants and craftsmen, soldiers and peasants have all been affiliated. Indeed, as Arnold clearly demonstrates in his classic work, *The Preaching of Islam*, the spread of the religion itself from the eleventh century onwards was largely achieved through the peaceful 'preaching' of the Sufis—the most impressive example of this means of propagation being observable in the Malay world, where Islam was established, and became deeply rooted, without any military conquest by Muslim states or empires.[43]

Marshall Hodgson, in his unsurpassed history of Islamic civilization, makes clear not just the centrality of Sufism to the practice of spirituality in Islam, but also the relationship between the piety fostered by Sufism throughout Muslim society and the maintenance of the normative prescriptions of the Shariʿa:

> 'Sufism... became the framework within which all popular piety flowed together; its saints, dead and living, became the guarantors of the gentle and co-operative sides of social life. Guilds commonly came to have Ṣūfī affiliations. Men's clubs claimed the patronage of Ṣūfī saints. And the tombs of local saints became shrines which almost all factions united in revering. It is probable that without the subtle leaven of the Ṣūfī orders, giving to Islam an inward personal thrust and to the Muslim community a sense of participation in a common spiritual venture quite apart from anyone's outward power, the

---

Encyclopedia of the Modern Islamic World (New York/Oxford: Oxford University Press, 1994), ed. John L. Esposito, vol. 4, pp. 109-117.

[43] Thomas Arnold, *The Preaching of Islam* (London: Luzac, 1935). Arnold's work makes clear that conversion to Islam in large regions of Africa, India and Central Asia was likewise based upon peaceful propagation; and that, even in those places where military conquest by Muslims occurred, conversion to Islam was but rarely the result of coercion by the Muslim rulers.

mechanical arrangements of the Sharīʿah would not have maintained the loyalty essential to their effectiveness.'[44]

It is this traditional role of Sufism in the normative traditions of legality, piety, and intellectuality within Islam that should be borne in mind when we come to deal with the metaphysical intricacies of Sufi interpretations of the Qur'ān. These commentaries must not be seen in a kind of vacuum, as if they emanated solely from subjective, individualistic inspirations, divorced from the living piety of the majority of the faithful. The importance of these commentaries, together with the teachings embodied in the lives of these spiritual authorities and their disciples, lies not just in their timeless philosophical value, but also in the very real impact they had upon the environment in which they lived and operated. The oral tradition of transmission plays a significant role in this connection.

As regards the contemporary exigencies of dialogue and tolerance, the universal values espoused by the Sufis have a particular relevance, on the practical as well as the doctrinal level. In the chapters that follow, these spiritual values will be explored in the context of the Qur'ān, but we shall also try to present these values in a way that minimises the alienation of the less mystically-inclined, more legally-minded representatives of Islam, not to mention the non-mystical majority of Muslims generally. The latter will no doubt be challenged by many ideas expounded here, but this challenge can be a constructive one, if it be couched in terms that, rather than eliciting knee-jerk opposition, might be successful in causing some of the more thoughtful readers to re-evaluate entrenched positions regarding the other, to read once again what the Qur'ān actually says about religious diversity, to consider with greater subtlety the relationship between upholding one's own faith and opening out to that of the other, and to deepen one's assimilation of the content of one's own faith in the process.

---

[44] Marshall G. H. Hodgson, *The Venture of Islam*, vol. 2, 'The Expansion of Islam in the Middle Periods', p. 125.

One key aspect of the success of the Sufis in the Islamic tradition lies, as noted above, in the symbiosis achieved between Sufi spirituality and *Sharʿī* legality. Although our principal aim in what follows is to highlight the universality of the Qur'ānic discourse, and to demonstrate the particular relevance of this aspect of the discourse to philosophical and spiritual questions concerning interfaith dialogue, we shall try to make our arguments reflect and build upon this traditional symbiosis; particularly as regards the relationship between universality and particularity, or between opening up to the other and maintaining fidelity to one's own tradition.

As will be argued in Chapters III and IV, an approach which reconciles Sufi universality with *Sharʿī* particularity has at least some chance of being accepted by those who most need to be won over to the cause of tolerance, dialogue, plurality, cooperation and co-existence; that is, the Muslim universalist needs to make his or her case without provoking defensive reflexes on the part of those—the overwhelming majority of Muslims—who feel duty-bound to maintain and promote the normativity of Islam. One aspect of the hermeneutics of Ibn ʿArabī will be of particular relevance in the formulation of this argument, as will be seen shortly.

Traditional Exegesis versus Postmodern Hermeneutics

Turning now to the question of exegesis, it should be made clear that we refer to such spiritual authorities as Ibn ʿArabī, a Rūmī or a Kāshānī not out of an uncritical prejudice in favour of the category 'traditional hermeneutics', but as a result of intellectual conviction. The perspectives and principles born of the spiritual insight of such sages, we believe, are not only compelling and illuminating; they are also timeless. They are only things of 'the past' if we decide to place them there, confining their relevance to their own time. It is therefore difficult to agree with the following statement by Farid Esack, a contemporary interpreter of the Qur'ān:

> 'Qur'ānic scholarship today does not require appeals to the intellectual genius or the spiritual heights of pious predecessors. What is required of the interpreter today is a clear understanding of where he or she comes from, a statement of his or her baggage as the Word of God is being approached.'[45]

To this one can reply: One certainly can make 'appeals' to the spiritual heights of our great predecessors, without this implying any derogation of intellectual responsibility; indeed, not to benefit from the insights of those predecessors whom we recognize as outstanding authorities is itself both irresponsible and presumptuous. A cavalier attitude towards the tradition to which one belongs deprives one of invaluable intellectual resources, and, in spiritual terms, radically diminishes receptivity to the nourishing sap that flows from the roots of the tradition to all its branches. This is not to say of course that one accepts everything traditional simply because it is traditional: blind imitation of traditional authorities, born of sentimental prejudice, is one thing; creative application of traditional principles, born of intellectual conviction, quite another. As will be apparent in the course of this work, we are not merely reproducing, parrot-fashion, the ideas of the Sufis; rather, the aim is to build upon principles, take advantage of insights, interpret values and to apply them creatively to contemporary conditions, even if this latter task is barely begun in this book—the principal aim of

[45] Farid Esack, *Qur'an, Liberation and Pluralism* (Oxford: Oneworld, 1997), p. 62. While we agree with several of the important points made by Esack in his book, we feel it goes too far in the direction of excluding the exclusivists, thus it is being exclusivist in its turn; a true inclusivism must, however, also find a place for exclusivists. A truly inclusive Sufi approach, rather than mutually exclusive theological perspectives, helps one to arrive at such a position, as will be argued shortly, and elaborated in the following chapters.

which is to make better known, and more assimilable, esoteric perspectives on the Qur'ān.

Prejudice, moreover, is by no means the exclusive preserve of those upholding tradition: if anything, the prejudice of modernism—the knee-jerk cognitive reflex against all things traditional, merely because they are situated in the pre-modern era, together with an eager readiness to accept modern ideas merely because they are 'up-to-date'—such a prejudice might in reality be more insidious than that of 'traditionalism', in that it is so pervasive and subtle, indeed, subliminal, and therefore largely unacknowledged. One who wishes to remain faithful to a tradition, by contrast, is compelled to swim against the intellectual tide,[46] to justify his or her preference for values that are rooted in a revealed tradition, and thus, where necessary, consciously and explicitly reject those paradigms of modern thought which clearly and radically undermine the continuity of the spiritual tradition or the interpretive community to which one belongs. The following words of Alasdair MacIntyre are apposite here: '. . . the story of my life is always embedded in the story of those communities from which I derive my identity. I am born with a past; and to try to cut myself off from that past, in the individualist mode, is to deform my present relationships.'[47] This identification with tradition, for MacIntyre, does not imply accepting the moral or philosophical limitations of 'the particularity of those forms of community'; for a living tradition

[46] See in this connection Martin Lings, *Ancient Beliefs and Modern Superstitions* (London: Archetype, 2001), a work whose title expresses well the intellectual challenge it mounts to the modernist mind-set. It demonstrates well the truth of Jacques Maritain's statement: '. . . a loss or weakening of the metaphysical spirit is an incalculable damage for the general order of intelligence and human affairs.' *The Degrees of Knowledge* (New York: Charles Scribner's Sons, 1959, p. 59).

[47] Alasdair MacIntyre, *After Virtue* (London: Duckworth, 1981), p. 205. This book, together with *Whose Justice? Which Rationality?* (London: Duckworth, 1988), and his *Three Rival Versions of Moral Enquiry* (London: Duckworth, 1990), are excellent antidotes to the pretensions of Enlightenment reason and the rootlessness of modern systems of morality stemming therefrom.

'is an historically extended, socially embodied argument, and an argument precisely in part about the goods which constitute that tradition.'[48] Herein lies the projective aspect of adherence to tradition, for 'an adequate sense of tradition manifests itself in a grasp of those future possibilities which the past has made available to the present.'[49]

With this kind of adherence to tradition in mind, the simultaneous support for fundamental norms of the tradition by no means implies an uncritical acceptance of all attitudes, postures, concepts that are ostensibly rooted in those norms. On the contrary, the likelihood of the success of a critique of particular negative attitudes is all the greater if it is itself clearly rooted in those fundamental norms. As stated above, this is one of the reasons for the continuing positive influence of Sufism: its sometimes radical attitudes and challenges are assimilable at least partly because they are deemed to be still 'within' the tradition, a tradition that is thus continuously re-vitalised by fresh influxes from the Spirit.

The rejection, then, of certain paradigms of modern thought, follows naturally from one's allegiance to the continuous narrative formed by one's own tradition; as in the radical, philosophically articulate approach of MacIntyre, such a rejection need not be dogmatic and uncritical. In the words of Frithjof Schuon:

> 'When the modern world is contrasted with traditional civilizations, it is not simply a question of seeking the good things and the bad things on one side or the other; good and evil are everywhere, so that it is essentially a question of knowing on which side the more important good, and on which side the lesser evil, is to be found... to confine oneself to admiring the traditional worlds is to stop short at a fragmentary point of view, for every civilization is a "two-edged sword"; it is a total good only

[48] *Ibid.*, p. 207.
[49] *Ibid.*, p. 208.

by virtue of those invisible elements that determine it positively.'[50]

The 'more important good' is, clearly, that which orients consciousness to absolute values, to final ends, to 'the one thing needful'. Modern paradigms of thought are to be rejected in direct proportion to the extent to which they negate or detract from this 'more important good', and, in particular, to the extent that they undermine the principle that essentially defines and justifies a spiritual tradition: the principle of transcendence, together with the paths—conceptual and practical, intellective and transformative—that lead thereto.[51]

The challenge, then, for those who adhere to a given tradition is not so much to reproduce an irretrievable past for which one yearns nostalgically, but to realize—first and foremost within oneself—those immutable, essential values of which tradition is the ever-living, formal vehicle. As Corbin eloquently puts it:

> '. . . a Tradition transmits itself as something alive, since it is a ceaselessly renewed inspiration, and not a funeral cortège or a register of conformist opinions. The life and death of spiritual things are our responsibility; they are not placed "in the past" except through our own omissions, our refusal of the metamorphoses that they demand, if these spiritual things are to be maintained "in the present" for us.'[52]

---

[50] Frithjof Schuon, *Light on the Ancient Worlds* (Bloomington: World Wisdom, 1984), pp. 42–43.

[51] See our *Paths to Transcendence—Spiritual Realization According to Shankara, Ibn ʿArabī and Meister Eckhart* (Bloomington: World Wisdom, 2006).

[52] *En Islam iranien* vol. 1, p. 33. Earlier in the same volume, Corbin makes a similar point, but relates this dynamic conception of tradition to gnosis, or *maʿrifa*. Referring to the teachings of Mullā Ṣadrā, he writes that the 'perpetual revival' demanded by authentic tradition is inseparable from true gnosis (p. xvii). In similar vein, T. S. Eliot writes that traditions 'cannot be inherited'; they are acquired only 'by great labour'. (Quoted in Aziz Esmail,

This statement by Corbin is a good contemporary reflection of the principle given poetic expression by Rūmī in his masterpiece, the *Mathnawī*. In the middle of one of his stories concerning Moses and Pharaoh, he suddenly breaks off the narrative and speaks directly to his readers—in what might be interpreted, in modern parlance, as the poet's own 'deconstruction' of 'reifying' processes of thought in his readers' minds:

> 'The mention of Moses has become a chain to the thoughts (of my readers), for (they think) that these are stories which happened long ago.
> The mention of Moses serves for a mask, but the light of Moses is thy actual concern, O good man.
> Moses and Pharaoh are in thy being: thou must seek these two adversaries in thyself.[53]
> The (process) of generation from Moses is (continuing) till the Resurrection: the Light is not different (though) the lamp has become different.'[54]

From this point of view, tradition is that which connects the light of prophetic revelation, symbolised here by Moses, to all the 'lamps' that transmit it. The lamps of tradition are varied and, importantly, man-made, but the light transmitted by them remains one and the same. God is not only the 'light' of the heavens, He is also the 'light' of the earth, according to the famous 'verse of light'.[55] One has to overcome the disbelieving element in the soul, the 'Pharaoh within', if one is to see clearly, with the 'eye' of the Moses of one's being, the Light of God, and not be distracted by the 'lamp' made by man. As will be noted

The Poetics of Religious Experience, London: Institute of Ismaili Studies—Occasional Papers I, 1998, p. 5).

[53] Cf. Kāshānī's comment on *And when We delivered you from the folk of Pharaoh* (II: 49) cited below.

[54] *Mathnawī*, III, verses 1251-1255. (The words in parentheses are by Nicholson.)

[55] See the following chapter for Ghazālī's commentary on this extremely important verse.

below, the tendency of postmodernism and deconstructionism is to focus exclusively on the lamps—to their forms, the way they are made, the materials of which they are made, the places from which these materials came, etc. etc.—to the detriment of the light transmitted by them. Rūmī, on the contrary, asks the following, a question that challenges the very mentality of which pedantic postmodernism appears to be a hypertrophied form: 'How long will you play at loving the shape of the jug? Leave the shape of the jug; go, seek the water.'[56]

A more comprehensive description of the elements that enter into the definition of an integral, still living religious tradition is given by Marco Pallis:

> '...a source of... Revelation; a current of influence or Grace issuing forth from that source and transmitted without interruption through a variety of channels; a way of "verification" which, when faithfully followed, will lead the human subject to successive positions where he is able to "actualize" the truths that Revelation communicates; finally there is the formal embodiment of tradition—the doctrines, arts, sciences and other elements that together go to determine the character of a normal civilization.'[57]

Holding such a position carries a great deal of what Esack called 'baggage'; that is, preconceptions, assumptions, latent philosophical positions, not all of which can be 'unpacked' here and now.[58] But what must be addressed, if briefly, is the key

---

[56] *Mathnawī*, II, verse 1021.

[57] M. Pallis, *The Way and the Mountain* (London: Peter Owen, 1991), p. 9.

[58] See our essay, 'The Spiritual Function of Tradition: A Perennialist Perspective', in *Sacred Web—A Journal of Tradition and Modernity*, no. 7, 2001, pp. 37-58, in which we offer an overview of the most essential spiritual aspects of Tradition from the viewpoint of the school of writers known as the 'Perennialists' or 'Traditionalists'. This school, inaugurated in the late nineteenth century by René Guénon and Ananda Coomaraswamy, flowered in the twentieth century through the works of Frithjof Schuon,

metaphysical assumption implicit in these important statements on tradition: that there is in 'tradition' a spiritual core, a sacred substance that transcends the changing human contexts that enclothe it with extrinsic forms, contexts which both reveal and veil that substance, both elaborate and dissimulate it. One who upholds tradition perceives it as making accessible, to some degree or another, the revelation that inaugurates the tradition in question. A spiritual hermeneutic, such as *ta'wīl*,[59] starts from the premise that the human *context* of revelation is derivative, secondary, and strictly subordinate to the transcendent *content* of revelation. Historicism—the tendency to view all texts as being inevitably and exhaustively determined by the conditions of their particular moment in history—is vigorously resisted; the quest is for universal spiritual principles, which are expressed *through* time, space and all other phenomenological categories but are not reducible *to* them. One moves from a conception of time as historical, quantitative, and phenomenal to one that is trans-historical, qualitative and principial. This is the distinction between *zamān āfāqī* (outward, literally 'horizons' time—thus, horizontal time) and *zamān anfusī* (spiritual, literally 'souls' time—thus the vertical axis that transcends the outward flow of time by integrating it within inward 'space', that of the soul).[60]

The hermeneut's task is, from this point of view, not so much to perceive—still less, deconstruct—the transcendent content through the ever-changing prisms of human context; on the

Titus Burckhardt, Martin Lings, Seyyed Hossein Nasr, Huston Smith, and several other authors. We shall return to the perspectives associated with this school in the final chapter.

[59] This kind of hermeneutic, according to Corbin, is not so much 'a construction as a spontaneous act, an innate aptitude.' *En Islam iranien*, vol. 3, p. 104, n. 137.

[60] This distinction, drawn by 'Alā' al-Dawla Simnānī, is well defined by Corbin: 'The "before" and the "after" presuppose the uniformity of continuous and irreversible time, measurable by the stellar revolutions; but the event which takes place in the soul, and in the time of the soul, cannot be situated—as regards that which constitutes it—before or after a given date in the calendar.' *En Islam iranien*, vol. 3, p. 221.

contrary, it is to make an effort to discern and assimilate at least some aspects of that transcendent content—to glimpse, 'taste' or intuit them—despite the inevitable relativities attendant upon the process by which absolute truths and principles are communicated through relative contexts.[61] From this point of view—as will be elaborated in Chapter II—the archetype of all 'dialogue' is the self-disclosure of the Absolute to the relative, the expression of infinitude in finite form, the revelation of the 'hidden treasure' that 'loved to be known', in the words of the *ḥadīth qudsī* or sacred utterance so central to Sufi metaphysics.[62] It is human consciousness, alone, that can come to 'know' this treasure of divine reality. And the revealed text is one of the central means by which this knowledge of transcendent truth is communicated.

Ta'wīl is described by Corbin as the single hermeneutic task common to all three Abrahamic faiths: it is essentially the returning of a thing to its origin or source—this being the etymology of the term, which is a verbal noun deriving from the word *awwala*, to take back to what was 'first' or at the beginning. This movement from the outward/literal to the inward/spiritual

[61] Frithjof Schuon refers to the 'human margin' as a key to help explain the diversity of theological positions, often engendering mutual anathematisation, that can be found in one and the same religious tradition. In regard to the relationship between human action and divine influence within the unfolding of a religious tradition, he writes that 'the divine influence . . . is total only for Scripture and the essential consequences of the Revelation, and it always allows for a "human margin" where it exerts itself only in an indirect fashion, yielding to ethnic or cultural factors.' *Form and Substance in the Religions* (Bloomington: World Wisdom, 2002), p. 201. This leaves open, of course, the question of where to draw the line between 'essential' and inessential 'consequences' of the revelation. The important point is that such a line exists; for the postmodern mind, not only is the existence of such a line of demarcation denied—all 'consequences' of the founding revelation are inessential because they are all ineluctably 'constructed'—but the very fact of divine revelation itself is denied, implicitly if not explicitly, by being itself regarded as 'constructed' by the supposed recipient thereof.

[62] See the discussion of this theme in the following chapter.

he calls the essence of 'Abrahamic ecumenism'; and rightly asserts that this common hermeneutic task aims at the discovery of the esoteric sense of the revealed text, the 'real' meaning of the Book.[63] In other words, the traditional exegete is one who perceives—or makes an effort to perceive—the relative in the light of the Absolute, or phenomena in relation to principles, or the text in the light of its origin, and not *vice versa*. Modern and postmodern hermeneutics, with their all-consuming interest in human agency, their stress on socio-historical context, their negation of the principle of objectivity, and their explicit or implicit denial of the Absolute, thus have precious little to offer those who wish to engage in a mode of reflection upon scripture that is both intellectually coherent and spiritually meaningful.

Moreover, there is an inherent contradiction in postmodernism, an 'unstable paradox that permeates the postmodern mind', in the words of Richard Tarnas. 'On its own terms', he writes, 'the assertion of the historical relativity and cultural-linguistic bondage of all truth and knowledge must itself be regarded as reflecting but one more local and temporal perspective, having no necessarily universal, extrahistorical value. Everything could change tomorrow. Implicitly, the one postmodern absolute is critical consciousness, which, by deconstructing all, seems compelled by its own logic to do so to itself as well.'[64]

[63] *En Islam iranien*, vol. 1, pp. xx, xxviii. One should note, however, that the term *ta'wīl* does not always connote spiritual exegesis. In Ibn ʿArabī, for example, it almost always refers to a rational process of explaining away such inconvenient references in the text to God's 'hands' or His 'throne' and so on. See William Chittick, *The Sufi Path of Knowledge* (Albany: State University of New York Press, 1989), pp. 199-202. See also C. H. M. Versteegh, *Arabic Grammar and Qur'ānic Exegesis in Early Islam* (Leiden: E. J. Brill, 1993), pp. 63-5, for the variety of meanings associated with *ta'wīl* in the earliest period of exegesis.

[64] R. Tarnas, *The Passion of the Western Mind* (London: Pimlico, 1991), p. 402. Postmodern deconstructionism can thus be seen as an extreme manifestation of the basic theme of epistemological relativism, which refutes its own thesis: 'Relativism sets out to reduce every element of absoluteness to a relativity, while making a quite illogical exception in favour of this

Derrida himself seems fully aware of the inherent contradiction of deconstruction. Proving the futility of his own endeavour, he confesses:

> 'There is no sense in doing without the concepts of metaphysics in order to shake metaphysics. We have no language—no syntax and no lexicon—which is foreign to this history; we can pronounce not a single destructive proposition which has not already had to slip into the form, the logic and the implicit postulations of precisely what it seeks to contest.'[65]

In the search for stable, enduring and meaningful values, it is evident that the postmodernist enterprise cannot be relied upon. It can deconstruct, but not reconstruct, and this flows naturally from its preoccupation, not with ideas as such, still less with the spiritual transformations which those ideas are intended to set in motion, but with the various processes that can be identified as having entered into the formation of ideas; more specifically, it evinces such a degree of interest in language and context that one forgets about meaning—one cannot see the wood for the trees. Such ideas as transcendence, divinity, absoluteness, are no longer treated as philosophical themes but as verbal constructions determined exclusively by historical process; as such they are worth studying only as fossils, for their 'archeological' significance. For what has been 'constructed' in the past must by that very fact be 'deconstructed' in the present. One who argues in favour of transcendence cannot begin talking without being told that this very word already

---

reduction itself. In effect, relativism consists in declaring it to be true that there is no such thing as truth, or in declaring it to be absolutely true that nothing but the relatively true exists... its initial absurdity lies in the implicit claim to be unique in escaping, as if by enchantment, from a relativity that is declared alone to be possible.' F. Schuon, 'The Contradiction of Relativism' in *Logic and Transcendence* (London: Perennial Books, 1984), p. 7.

[65] Quoted by Richard Bernstein in his 'Metaphysics, Critique and Utopia', *The Review of Metaphysics*, no. 42, 1988, pp. 266-267.

bespeaks an outmoded epistemology. As Huston Smith observes ruefully:

> 'If modernism led us to play down religion's transcendent referent where we did not deny it outright, postmodernism is doing something equally disturbing. It is reshaping language in ways that make it difficult to consider the *possibility* of ontological transcendence without being charged with speaking ineptly. If we wish to ask—open-endedly but seriously—whether (another) reality. . . exists, we are blocked from the question by being told that we are off on the wrong foot in framing the issue as we have. Our wording betrays "metaphysical tendencies", metaphysics here being tagged to repression. It is trapped in a this-worldly/other-worldly binary bind. It slopes towards "realism", which "reifies" its referents and turns God into a "being among beings", which would lead us to seek its "essence" through "referential language" that purports to "correspond". As all those words and phrases are dismissive epithets for postmoderns, a language is being woven that places theism in double jeopardy. Theists are made to feel that before they get to the substance of their claim, they violate language in the way they propose to state it.'[66]

Insofar as hermeneutical approaches incorporate this postmodern prejudice against transcendence, their utility for those of us concerned with what gives tradition all its meaning and transformative power will be diminished. Likewise the type of hermeneutic which intends to incorporate—albeit with

[66] From his article, 'Postmodernism's Impact on the Study of Religion', in *Journal of the American Academy of Religion*, LVIII/4; quoted in Lynn C. Bauman, '"Mystery" and Scriptural Text in the Post-Modern Age', *Sacred Web*, no. 3, June, 1999, pp. 71-72. See also the important work by Huston Smith in this regard, *Beyond the Postmodern Mind* (Wheaton, Ill.: Quest Books, 1989); and also the useful article 'Through the Idols of Twilight: Postmodernism and Tradition', by Algis Uždavinys, in *Sophia—A Journal of Traditional Studies*, vol. 5, no. 1, Summer 1999, pp. 147-170.

reservations—ideological viewpoints which explicitly undermine or deny the principle of transcendence, the reality of the Absolute, or, quite simply, all that makes religion 'religious', will be of little relevance to us.

We are thinking here of the well-intentioned effort of Paul Ricoeur to 'recapture' the sacred in what he calls a 'post-critical' stage. He understands well that without a sense of the sacred—what he refers to as a 'naïve' acceptance of the supernal reality—the act of hermeneutics is meaningless. It becomes reduced to a profane, worldly exercise, which usurps the place held by the sacred. On the other hand, he believes that we cannot ignore the 'insights' of Nietzsche, Freud and Marx; that, together, these insights must predispose us to a 'hermeneutics of suspicion'.[67] One must regard, with a 'healthy' suspicion, the way in which human hands may have interfered with texts and their interpretation throughout history. One looks, suspiciously, for signs of interpretive activity motivated by, respectively, a hidden 'will to power', by repressed 'subconscious drives', by disguised 'class interests'. Having passed through this 'moment' of critical hermeneutics, constituting the second stage of the hermeneutic 'arc', one proceeds to the third stage, the return to naïveté,[68] a second 'immediacy', a re-adoption of the sacred, but now in 'post-critical' mode.

But, one might ask, what can possibly be left of the original sacred perspective after the content of these radically anti-transcendent ideologies has had its impact? For it is extremely

---

[67] This advocacy of the hermeneutics of suspicion is made in Paul Ricoeur's *Freud and Philosophy* (tr. D. Savage), (New Haven and London: Yale University Press, 1970). See Dan Stiver, *The Philosophy of Religious Language* (Oxford: Blackwell, 1996), pp. 100-107, for a summary of Ricoeur's position.

[68] What he calls naïveté we would prefer to refer to in terms of a natural, initial, as it were 'virgin' receptivity to a knowledge with which, however, one is already 'pregnant'. Revelation from 'on high' brings to fruition the seed that is already 'within'. This point will be mentioned briefly below, and elaborated more fully in the following chapter, in relation to the Qur'ānic principle of the *fiṭra*, the primordial nature of the human soul.

difficult, if not impossible, to return to the pristine state of receptivity, which, Ricoeur knows, hermeneutics cannot dispense with. The only naïveté at this post-critical stage would appear to reside in the belief that the sacred can survive the onslaught of these ideologies; for if one accepts the violently anti-spiritual content that determines, in a fundamental and not accidental manner, the perspectives of such thinkers, how can the sacred subsist as the determinative element of one's viewpoint?

We are neither claiming that Ricoeur has no longer a sense of the sacred,[69] nor denying the many positive aspects of his own contribution to the interpretation of scripture; but the

[69] One may note here his volume of essays, *Figuring the Sacred* (Minneapolis: Fortress Books, 1995). However, one cannot help seeing the negative consequences of his espousal of the 'hermeneutics of suspicion' in, for example, his essay, 'Religion, Atheism and Faith', where, referring to the use of the atheism of Freud and Nietzsche in destroying 'superstitious' religion, he writes: 'atheism clears the ground for a faith beyond accusation and consolation.' (Quoted by David Detmer, 'Ricoeur on Atheism: A Critique' in *The Philosophy of Paul Ricoeur*, The Library of Living Philosophers, Chicago, ed. Lewis E. Hahn, Open Court, 1995, p. 478). What we have in such 'atheism' is but a parody of a basic esoteric principle: the Essence of God, apophatically conceived, transcends 'God', conceived positively as Creator, Revealer, Judge, and so on. This principle is expressed concisely by Eckhart: '... let us pray to God that we may be free of God, that we may gain the truth and enjoy it eternally' (*Meister Eckhart—Sermons & Treatises* (tr. Maurice O'Connell Walshe), (Dorset: Element Books, 1979), vol. II, p. 271). The simplistic notion of God is transcended by Eckhart, but in a manner that deepens the faith of believers rather than negating it. For his words are meant, he says, only for the 'good and perfected people' in whom dwell 'the worthy life and lofty teachings' of Christ. (*Ibid.*, vol. I, p. 6) The ostensible 'transcendence' of the simplistic notion of God aimed at by thinkers like Freud, on the other hand, does nothing but undermine and subvert faith. The fact that Eckhart was accused by the Church of his day of coming close to heresy does not affect the argument being made; more to the point, his doctrines have been 'officially' reinstated by the Roman Catholic Church of today, in recognition of the positive value they have in deepening, not subverting, the faith of Christians. This also shows the importance, in an age dominated by doubt, rationalism and scepticism, of metaphysical and esoteric doctrines generally.

case for engaging in a 'hermeneutics of suspicion' does not convince us. For there is a total incompatibility between the ontological claims of such thinkers as Marx and Freud, on the one hand, and those of religion on the other. Each side can claim to situate the other in its own light: for Marx, religion is but 'false consciousness', the 'opium of the masses'; just as for Freud, religion is the projection of subconscious neuroses. For both thinkers, religion is reduced to an accidental category within a totalist ideology, that is, an ideology which claims to explain the totality of existence within its own terms, an ideology which is based on a particular ontology, a particular view of what constitutes reality. Religion, likewise, makes this kind of 'totalist' claim and subsumes the categories deemed essential by its rivals. 'Class interest' is not so much denied as a category as given an altogether relative importance; it can be acknowledged as an element in the social domain, which itself is not determinative of religion, it is surpassed by the principles which make religion what it is in essence—a sacred path of salvation. As for the 'subconscious', this is the preserve of those who, through the centuries, have cultivated and refined consciousness such that they are fully aware not only of subconscious drives, but also of transcendent states of consciousness, the attainment of which indeed, presupposes the channelling of the positive energy within those drives towards spiritual goals.[70]

Faced with these incompatible ontic claims, we willingly and unabashedly choose those of religion, a choice which should appear altogether natural when the subject we are investigating is religion, not psychology or sociology. If one allows psychologists and sociologists to formulate theories *about* religion, one should, *a fortiori*, allow theologians, philosophers and scholars of religion also to continue to develop and articulate

[70] See the fine article on Sufi psychology by Mohammad Ajmal, 'Sufi Science of the Soul', in *Islamic Spirituality*, vol. 1, pp. 294–307. See also the excellent critique of modern psychology by Titus Burckhardt in his *Mirror of the Intellect* (tr. & ed. William Stoddart), (Cambridge: Quinta Essentia, 1987), pp. 45–67.

ideas *within* religion. It should be evident that sound scholarship and religious commitment are by no means incompatible; indeed, to discourage intelligent scholarship within religion would be tantamount to encouraging the tendencies and postures of 'dogmatic closure' within religious circles. Religious thought is enriched by the presence within it of serious scholarly work, and impoverished if it is abandoned by scholars and left to the devices of narrow-minded dogmatists, from within, or hyper-critical secularists from without.

If one's aim is to contribute to the quest for meaning within a religious tradition—whilst respecting contemporary norms of scholarly discourse and, at the same time, combating dogmatism within religious discourse—one's basic approach to religious hermeneutics ought to be consonant with the axiomatic premises of the religious tradition in question. If, however, one wishes to analyse aspects of the tradition from without, purely as an academic observer, one should at least intend to bracket out one's own beliefs to the greatest extent possible, in the manner of the phenomenological *epoché*,[71] and not allow these beliefs to intrude upon one's perception of the subject-matter, or to attack

[71] The phenomenological approach to religion, associated with such figures as Mircea Eliade, Jacques Waardenburg and Henri Corbin, begins with a recognition of the irreducibly sacred character of religion, its status *sui generis*, as a category in its own right. The 'bracketing out' of one's own assumptions and prejudices is intended to let the 'phenomenon' of religion speak for itself, in its own terms. It is in this manner that the imperative of scholarly objectivity and respect for the sacred aspects of religion are brought into harmony. For an overview of this approach see the article 'Phenomenology of Religion' by Douglas Allen in the *Encyclopedia of Religion* (New York: Macmillan, 1987), vol. 11, pp. 272–285. The approach is well expressed in Eliade's important and influential work, *The Sacred and the Profane* (Harcourt: Brace & Co., 1959); and, for a fine analysis of Eliade's hermeneutical principles, see Douglas Allen, *Structure and Creativity in Religion* (The Hague: Mouton, 1978). See also Randall Studstill, 'Eliade, Phenomenology and the Sacred' in *Religious Studies*, vol. 36, 2000, pp. 176–194, for a concise presentation of the importance for Eliade of arriving at meaning by focusing on the manifestation of the sacred (hierophany) as opposed to the historical matrix within which such manifestation occurs. The latter aspect is not negated, but is definitely

outright the basic axioms of the tradition being studied—such attacks being all too often mounted, ironically, in the name of a putatively 'scientific' objectivity.

Mohammed Arkoun seems partly to confirm this point of view, calling upon the scholars of 'the peoples of the Book' to 'suspend' rather than 'disqualify' all theological statements of belief about the status of the Qur'ān; but then seems not to abide fully by this injunction himself. Though he rightly criticizes the destructive 'scientistic' tendency that characterises some western scholars in their attitude towards Islam and Muslims, his own deconstructive 'subversion' of the premises of traditional Muslim thought certainly seem to 'disqualify' rather then 'suspend' statements of belief.

On the one hand, he appeals to the scholars to 'suspend any theological statements about Qur'ānic Discourse as the word of God until all of the linguistic, semiotic, historical and anthropological problems raised by the Qur'ān as a text, are clarified. I say "suspend" rather than "disqualify", "ignore" or "eliminate", as modern linguists arrogantly do when they refuse even to listen to the rightful demands of believers who are rejected in an non-scientific category. By doing so, they substitute and oppose a positivist, pseudo-scientific, self-promoting interpretation to the dogmatic, theological one which, over the centuries, has imposed its own form of arrogant self-entitlement to the exclusive Truth.'[72]

This sensitivity to the need to address a living community of practising believers, and to take their faith seriously, is reinforced in another passage, where he writes that the elucidation of basic epistemological principles connected with the Qur'ān must appeal not only to the scholars and thinkers of the

---

subordinated to the principle of the sacred as such. See, finally, Schimmel, *Deciphering the Signs of God—A Phenomenological Approach to Islam* (Albany: State University of New York Press, 1994), for a fine application of this approach to the Islamic tradition.

[72] M. Arkoun, *The Unthought in Islamic Thought* (London: Saqi Books, 2002), p. 73.

academic community, 'but also to those believers who consider themselves practising and orthodox. This is a crucial point if one intends to overcome the arrogance of scientific reasoning which provides believers with no opportunity to speak out, and which interprets, cuts and pastes, categorizes and judges, without actually elucidating the mechanisms, omnipresence, results and significance of belief for every human being.'[73]

However, in his own application of the modern sciences to the study of the Islamic tradition—in his own proposed 'historical or philosophical deconstruction of the system of postulates and premises perpetuated as an intangible dogmatic posture of what I have called Islamic reason'—Arkoun appears to go much further than simply 'suspending' all theological statements about the Qur'ān as the revealed Word, for he maintains that

> 'Methodologically, the theological-exegetic reading should be attempted only on the new critical basis established by the two first approaches [the 'historical-anthropological' and the 'linguistic-semiotic']. This means that all the axiological principles, postulates and themes which have predominated thus far in all systems of thought, should be intellectually and culturally subverted.'[74]

Given that one such 'axiological principle' is belief in the Qur'ān as the Word of God, subverting this principle becomes

---

[73] *Ibid.*, p. 51. Cf. the following prudent note by Khaled Abou El-Fadl: borrowing epistemologies of western provenance, he writes, should be done with 'measured restraint, and a degree of reasonableness so that the receiving body will not violently reject them.' *Speaking in God's Name: Islamic Law, Authority and Women* (Oxford: Oneworld, 2001), pp. 99-100.

[74] *The Unthought in Islamic Thought*, p. 84. He also writes that, while Ibn ʿArabī's 'creative freedom' is a 'potential model' for the kind of liberation from dogmatic enclosures Arkoun espouses, 'in the case we are presenting, the desired freedom is more subversive, since it would include all forms and experiences of subversion ever attempted by mystics, poets, thinkers and artists.' *Ibid.*, p. 65.

an inescapable necessity for the proposed methodology. One cannot, however, in good logic 'suspend' judgment about the status of the Qur'ān and 'subvert' belief in it as a revealed text at one and the same time. One can surely affirm belief in the revealed status of the Qur'ān whilst simultaneously challenging dogmatic 'closures' in regard to its interpretation—the likelihood of the success of this challenge being greatly enhanced by the credibility of one's adherence to the traditional community of interpretation.[75] Suspending belief in the Qur'ān, or worse, subverting it, tends to vitiate in advance whatever positive intellectual values might be contained within one's contribution. Detaching oneself from the axiological principles of one's tradition is not the best way to bring positive influence to bear upon it, nor is it an appropriate way of appealing, as Arkoun insists we must, to 'those believers who consider themselves practising and orthodox'.

A similar kind of problem is observable in Arkoun's approach to transcendence. On the one hand, he claims that his approach does not exclude the transcendent as a meaningful category;[76] on the other hand the traditional notion of transcendence is to be radically deconstructed, for 'The transcendence claimed in the traditional theological interpretation of the Book is the projection of the religious *imaginaire* back to the inaugurating age of revelation. It becomes a psychological, cultural process of transcendentalization, mythologization, sacralization and ideologization in various changing conditions.'[77]

The only kind of 'transcendence' that seems capable of escaping from these historically conditioned processes of 'transcen-

[75] It is precisely the ambiguity of Arkoun's position in regard to Islamic tradition—however defined—that results in the kind of outburst against him by Mohamed Talbi, an intellectual figure noted for his tolerance and open-mindedness. His attack on Arkoun is quoted by Arkoun himself. See *The Unthought in Islamic Thought*, p. 52, n. 1.

[76] See his *The Concept of Revelation: From the People of the Book to the Societies of the Book* (Claremont, Cal.: Claremont Graduate School, 1987), p. 27.

[77] *Ibid.*, p. 27.

dentalization' is one that is erected by what Arkoun calls 'the true rationality'.[78] It is only this kind of rational, neo-Kantian transcendence that is deemed to be untainted by theological dogmatism and historical conditioning. Hence, Arkoun appears simply to be rejecting one notion of transcendence—one ontological principle or axiological premise—in favour of another, which, from our point of view, is actually far less 'transcendent' than that which he is rejecting. For transcendence must transcend reason, if it is to be truly transcendent. Arkoun appears to be simply replacing theological dogmatism with rational dogmatism, or erecting reason to the status of a new dogma. There is here a new 'dogmatic enclosure', defined by reason itself. As James Smith notes, in regard to Kant's attempt to establish religion 'within the limits of reason alone':

> 'The notion of an autonomous or "pure" reason—untainted by either history of faith (or prejudice) is an Enlightenment myth... [reason] always begins from certain cultural assumptions... is always already grounded in a worldview which constitutes a fundamental trust or commitment.'[79]

From the viewpoint of esoteric Islam, it is both dogmatism and rationalism alike that are transcended. As will be clear from what follows, the 'dogmatic, theological' claim to Truth

---

[78] *Ibid.*, p. 27.

[79] James K. A. Smith, 'Re-Kanting Postmodernism? Derrida's Religion Within the Limits of Reason Alone', in *Faith and Philosophy*, vol. 17, no. 4, 2000, p. 568. In another fine article, Smith deconstructs the 'messianicity' claimed by Derrida to be a form of rational religion that transcends the historically constituted 'messianisms' responsible for exclusivist violence. Citing Caputo, Smith asserts that Derrida's ideal content-free, rational structure of messianicity in fact posits 'a pure Greco-modern universal of the most classical species that remains immune to history and space. And that, as far as deconstruction is concerned, is heresy, along with being a little *incroyable*.' James Smith, 'Determined Violence: Derrida's Structural Religion', in *The Journal of Religion*, vol. 78, no. 2, 1998, p. 210.

is indeed transcended, but without subverting the tradition whence this claim emerges; it is transcended, in other words, by the spiritual interiorization of the same revealed data that give rise to dogmatic theology. Thus, formal theology is not subjected to rationalist subversion from without but to spiritual conversion from within: what is *defined* dogmatically is not *confined* existentially, for the essences or principles that are outwardly given dogmatic expression in theology are not the prisoners of that mode of expression; these principles, rooted in revelation, go infinitely beyond the boundaries of rational conception, of dogmatic expression and of socio-historical process.[80] If transcendence has any meaning, it must be located in that which transcends human reason, together with time, space and all other existential categories; otherwise, by the logic of Arkoun's own methodology, it cannot but be the product of the processes of 'transcendentalization, mythologization, sacralization and ideologization in various changing conditions'; and must therefore in its turn be subjected to deconstruction or subversion. No 'reason'—Islamic reason, Enlightenment reason, or post-Enlightenment reason—can escape from the process of 'rationalization' which inexorably accompanies it and which, in the post-metaphysical age, elevates it to the status of a transcendent (or rather, 'transcendental'—in the Kantian sense) category.[81] The transcending of reason itself is what

[80] 'Truth,' writes Frithjof Schuon, 'does not deny forms from the outside, but transcends them from within.' *Spiritual Perspectives and Human Facts* (London: Perennial Books, 1987), p. 118.

[81] Ernest Gellner's *Reason and Culture* (Oxford: Blackwell, 1992) is a good *exposé* of the culturally conditioned premises of the rationalist claims to have transcended culture. On the one hand, the 'essence of the rationalist programme' is defined in terms of its opposition 'to the acceptance of reality of the world on trust. It knows no loyalty to a culture and its custom.' (p. 23) On the other hand, though, 'The rationalists did not, as Descartes thought, transcend culture. They created and codified a distinctive, special, individualist culture... This is not the first time that a society has believed itself to be in possession of a superior, exclusive, and saving truth, and damned all others as benighted heathens.' (pp. 164-165)

transcendence is, at least initially, all about. But, it should be noted, this apparent limitation of the scope of reason does not mean the abdication of reason but rather the expansion of the domain within which it operates: for the data with which it functions are expanded to include all the fruits of revelation and inspiration.[82]

As noted above, Arkoun calls for the 'theological-exegetic reading' of the Qur'ān only to be attempted on a 'new critical basis' which is constituted by the 'historical-anthropological' and the 'linguistic-semiotic' approaches. The present book is based on what can be called a 'theological-exegetic' reading—even though I would prefer to call it an 'esoteric-exegetic' reading—without making any reference to the other approaches. This by no means implies a rejection of such approaches, but it does imply that creative thinking about ideas contained within the tradition of exegesis need not stop—or be 'suspended'—until such time as the other approaches are deemed to have successfully erected the 'new critical basis'.[83] Therefore, one is not objecting, Luddite fashion, to the use of such disciplines as linguistics, philology, sociology, anthropology, historiography and so on; nor to the critical investigation of that whole gamut of phenomenological factors which configure the various matrices within which the revelation is transmitted. One is simply asserting that none of these disciplines can replace the perennial quest for deeper meanings and implications of the revelation. The search for intellectually stimulating, spiritually

[82] See René Guénon, *The Reign of Quantity and the Signs of the Times* (New York: Sophia Perennis, 2004), and Frithjof Schuon, *Logic and Transcendence*, *op. cit.*, chapters 1–3, for a rigorous critique, from a traditional metaphysical perspective, of the rationalistic assumptions underlying modern thought.

[83] This attempt to establish a 'new critical basis' is also referred to by Arkoun as a 'Critique of Islamic Reason'. As regards the stage it has reached, he writes as follows: 'I do not claim to have personally completed all the operations of deconstruction required by the founding texts called Holy Texts; I am merely opening up some perspectives and developing tools and issues, in order to initiate a complex work of research depending upon many teams of excellent scholars. . . ' *The Unthought in Islamic Thought*, p. 132, n. 2.

transforming, and morally uplifting values in the roots of one's tradition ought not to be postponed until some indeterminate time in the future, when the 'historical-anthropological' and the 'linguistic-semiotic' approaches have attained sufficient maturity for the exegetical endeavour to be resumed.

Moreover, many of the concerns of these sciences can, in differing degrees be accommodated within an expanded conception of the traditional Muslim exegetical science of *asbāb al-nuzūl* ('occasional causes of revelation'), and of the study of the *maqām* (context) of the scripture. As Muhammad Abdel Haleem argues, the importance of context 'was recognised and formulated for the study of the text of the Qur'ān by Muslim linguists, whose work in this respect anticipated by many centuries modern linguistic thinking.'[84]

Toby Mayer, in his penetrating critique of Andrew Rippin's approach to the Qur'ān, puts the case well: 'Muslims themselves have always maintained a lively concern with the historicity of the sources of their tradition... it is conceivable that this time-honoured Muslim concern with the historical context of early Islam might in due course take aspects of contemporary historical method in its stride. An implicit assumption that history and religion are at odds is itself, surely, *anti*-religious. What is there to fear in an honestly and sincerely deployed historical or textual criticism, philology, archaeology, etc., etc.? The religious tradition must be strong in a versatile, not brittle way, and it contains ready-made tools for these challenges.'[85]

It can readily be admitted that all such tools and disciplines are useful in situating and defining the *form* assumed by the revelation, together with the community of interpretation that flows therefrom; but they cannot in and of themselves help us to plumb the spiritual depths of the *content* of the revelation. On the contrary, they can all too easily obscure the most

[84] Muhammad Abdel Haleem, *Understanding the Qur'an—Theories and Style* (London: I. B. Tauris, 1999), p. 158.

[85] T. Mayer, 'Review Article: *The Qur'ān and its Interpretive Tradition*, by A. Rippin', in *Journal of Qur'ānic Studies*, vol. IV, no. 2, 2002, p. 104.

revealing aspects of this content, diverting us from in-depth interpretation by an all-consuming interest in peripheral issues. Moreover, in the hands of certain critics, these sciences, instead of explaining revelation, end up explaining it away; instead of acting as auxiliaries to the principal interpretive task, they eclipse or supplant it; rather than enhancing the basis for comprehension, such sciences can end up masquerading as comprehension itself.

Returning to the hermeneutics of suspicion: if one takes seriously the philosophical underpinnings of such an approach, one ends up attempting to locate the religious phenomenon in some putatively universal structure—'class', 'power', etc.—that reveals its 'true' nature. It will then, however, not be recognisable as 'religion'. Our starting-point, on the contrary, is located within a community of interpretation, and is intended to contribute to the search for meaning within that community, taking as authoritative and divinely revealed the scripture that inaugurates and defines the religious tradition of Islam. What matters is not so much how the scripture that we now possess has come to assume its present form; it is, rather, the question of how to assimilate more deeply the content of this dazzling message that has been the spiritual wellspring for countless communities across the globe for the past fourteen centuries, and which continues to galvanize the souls of over a billion people today; and how to relate some of the most profound interpretations and elucidations of this content to the contemporary exigencies of dialogue and religious diversity.

For, as said earlier, it is the content and not the context of the text that counts for us. The content leaps out of its context, proving, for some of us at least, its revealed nature by the transformative impact it makes upon our consciousness: thus our belief in it as divinely revealed is as much the consequence of our reflection upon it as the reason for wishing to study it in the first place. This is not unrelated to the following, more profound observation by Rūmī, which will lead us to a brief consideration of Gadamer's approach to hermeneutics: instead of being the cause of certitude of the Absolute, belief in the

Qur'ān as a revelation of the Absolute can be regarded as the consequence of an already existent certitude of the Absolute. This principle of what one can call 'spiritual epistemology' is expressed by Rūmī as follows:

> 'There are certain servants of God who proceed from the Koran to God. Others more elect come from God, find the Koran here, and know that God has sent it down: *It is We who have sent down the Remembrance, and We watch over it* [Q. XV: 9]. The commentators say that this refers to the Koran. This too is good; but it can also mean, "We have placed in you a substance, a seeking, a yearning. We watch over that, not letting it go to waste, but bringing it to a definite place."'[86]

While the 'more elect' ones are of course fewer in number, in rigorously metaphysical terms, all those who believe in the divine origin of the Qur'ān arrive at this belief on the basis of an already existing knowledge embedded deep within their souls—in the absence of which they could not 're-cognise' the text as true, as divine. This knowledge is pre-personal, it pertains to the 'primordial nature' of the human soul, the *fiṭra* which we shall be examining in greater detail in the following two chapters. From the point of view of this spiritual epistemology, this innate knowledge of God confirms the divinely revealed character of the Qur'ān, rather than being engendered *ex nihilo* by the Qur'ān. Even when faith in God is apparently the result of reflection upon the text, the function of revelation is to 're-mind' the soul of the divine reality, knowledge of which is ingrained in the very substance of the soul. It is for this reason that the Qur'ān refers to itself repeatedly as a 'reminder': *And it is nothing but a reminder to creation* (LXVIII: 52 and LXXXI: 27); *We have not revealed unto thee this Qur'ān that thou shouldst be distressed, but as a*

[86] *The Discourses of Rūmī (Fīhi mā fīhi)* (tr. A. J. Arberry), (London: John Murray, 1961), p. 125.

reminder unto him that feareth (XX: 2–3); *Nay, verily this is a reminder, so whoever will, shall remember it* (LXXIV: 54–55).[87]

One might ask here: is there not a similarity between this conception of innate knowledge, proper to the *fiṭra*, and the 'pre-understandings' posited by Gadamer as determining in advance all possible interpretive activity? Gadamer takes these pre-understandings, defined by Heidegger[88] as the inevitable concomitants of *Dasein*, of 'being-there', and elevates them to the status of principles of interpretation and understanding. Rather than perceiving these individual premises of thought as negative prejudices, he regards them as indispensable foreshadowings of cognition, whose fruitfulness increases in the measure that they are identified as such, and insofar as their ramifications are properly elucidated.

One of Gadamer's aims is to undo the Enlightenment's 'prejudice against prejudice': 'There is one prejudice of the Enlightenment that defines its essence: the fundamental prejudice of the Enlightenment is the prejudice against prejudice itself, which denies tradition its power.'[89] Although he admits that 'authority' may be a source of prejudice in a negative sense, he adds that 'this does not exclude the possibility that it can also be a source of truth, and this is what the Enlightenment failed to see when it denigrated all authority.' This leads directly to one of Gadamer's most controversial points—and, for us, one of his most positive contributions to hermeneutics—namely, the assertion that the authoritativeness of received texts, and of particular persons within a tradition is not necessarily opposed to reason; indeed, critical reason has strong grounds for upholding their authority.

---

[87] We shall return to this theme in Chapter III.

[88] 'Whenever something is interpreted as something, the interpretation will be founded essentially upon fore-having, fore-sight, and fore-conception. An interpretation is never a presuppositionless apprehending of something presented to us.' M. Heidegger, *Being and Time* (trs. J. Macquarrie & E. Robinson), (Oxford: Blackwell, 2000), pp. 191–2.

[89] Hans-Georg Gadamer, *Truth and Method* (New York: London: Continuum Press, 1989), p. 270.

The authority of persons is based 'not on the subjection and abdication of reason, but on an act of acknowledgement and knowledge—the knowledge, namely, that the other is superior to oneself in judgement and insight, and that for this reason his judgement takes precedence, i.e., it has priority over one's own.'[90] It is perfectly reasonable, in other words, to assert that what one perceives as 'authoritative' is to be treated as such, not simply because of one's ignorance before the received text or person, but also, and more fundamentally, because 'what the authority says is not irrational and arbitrary but can, in principle, be discovered to be true.'[91]

It is at this point that both the similarity and the difference between a Gadamerian approach to interpretation and a traditional Sufi one emerge. The similarity lies in the fact that, for both approaches, the text received as authoritative can be 'discovered as true'; an active investigation, and not mere passive reception is what is called for, so that the 'truth' therein be verified for oneself and not merely obeyed 'on authority'.[92] But when we attempt to go further, and ask what is meant by 'the truth' for Gadamer, we encounter the following insuperable difficulty: the criterion by which we can evaluate true prejudices—those which engender understanding—and false prejudices—those which produce misunderstanding—is not provided by Gadamer; indeed, the very search for such a criterion 'that would certify objectivity once and for all' is, according to Gadamer, 'a vestige of historicism'. As Jean Grondin, a faithful student of Gadamer notes, although everything revolves around the question of distinguishing between these two types of prejudice, 'the problem persists unresolved'.[93]

---

[90] *Ibid.*, p. 279.

[91] *Ibid.*, p. 280.

[92] This is the well-known distinction in Sufism between *taḥqīq* (realization) and *taqlīd* (imitation).

[93] Jean Grondin, *Introduction to Philosophical Hermeneutics* (New Haven and London: Yale University Press, 1994), p. 113. Grondin points out that in the

This inability to ascertain the objective veracity of one's understanding of the meaning of a text follows naturally from the limited scope bestowed upon one's 'pre-understandings': for these latter appear to be limited to the purely horizontal transmission provided by the environment and culture into which one is born—in stark contrast to the knowledge of the Absolute which the Islamic tradition sees as being ingrained in the substance of the soul, this being the basis upon which one is able to recognise as true the revealed scripture, and the foundation upon which all other cognitions are predicated.

Gadamer's failure to resolve this fundamental question of veracity in interpretation is the inevitable consequence of a hermeneutical enquiry that feels itself constrained to abandon any claim to objectivity, hence truth, for fear of 'lapsing' into 'metaphysics'. Although Gadamer claims above that what the authority says is not necessarily irrational 'but can, in principle, be discovered to be true', it seems that in practice, such a discovery is all but excluded for want of any criteria for discerning between the truth and falsity of the prejudices upon which understanding is founded. Without recourse to transcendent values, it is evident that no claim to have attained objectivity can be substantiated: there is no 'point of view' that can be said to escape the conditions—of myth, history, culture—which impinge on all rational activity.

It might now be asked: is there not a great deal in common between Sufi hermeneutics—which goes beyond 'the letter'

1960 edition of *Truth and Time* Gadamer asserts confidently that 'It is only temporal distance that can solve the question of critique in hermeneutics, namely how to distinguish the true prejudices, by which we understand, from the false ones, by which we misunderstand'. But in the 1986 edition, he revises this sentence and more modestly proffers the opinion that 'Often temporal distance can solve the question of critique. . . ' Grondin puts a positive gloss on this revised opinion, praising Gadamer for being 'continually ready to alter [his] opinion when better insight comes along, but cannot escape the conclusion: the problem—the most important problem in hermeneutics—'persists unresolved'. *Ibid.*, p. 113.

of the text, and dissolves the reifications and coagulations of rational cognition—and postmodern hermeneutics, *à la Derrida*, in which the confidence of Enlightenment 'reason', Cartesian dualism, and the certitudes of modernist rational thought are all radically deconstructed? Is there not a convergence between the Sufis and the postmodernists in that they both accept the principle that reason and language cannot yield certainty and objectivity?

This is what Ian Almond proposes in an interesting, but flawed, attempt to compare Ibn ʿArabī with Jacques Derrida in regard to the role of 'bewilderment' (*ḥayra*) in their perspectives.[94] Before looking at this article, let us note the following irreducible differences between the hermeneutics of deconstruction and Sufi exegesis. In Derrida's hermeneutics, the 'meaning' of a text—any text—is endlessly deferred; from a Sufi exegetical perspective, the meaning that can be derived from a revealed text is limitlessly plumbed. In the first case, there is an indefinite expansion on the plane of linguistically defined concepts, in the second, an infinite unfolding of divine self-revelation, assimilated in the measure of the intellectual and spiritual receptivity of the interpreter. Derrida's hermeneutics of *différance* proposes the endless deferring of meaning from one word-symbol to another: every word is but a sign, whose meaning is derived exclusively from other signs in the same system of which it is a part; and it rejects totally what he calls 'western logocentrism', that is, the idea that there is something, a real entity which is the 'transcendental signified'.[95] Whereas Sufi exegesis, in total

[94] Ian Almond, 'The Honesty of the Perplexed: Derrida and Ibn ʿArabi on "Bewilderment"', *Journal of the American Academy of Religion*, vol. 70, no. 3, 2002, pp. 517-534. Ian Netton also sees a similarity between the approaches of the two figures: 'In his peculiar and very individual way, Ibn ʿArabī foreshadows the advent of the deconstructionist movement.' *Allah Transcendent—Studies in the Structure and Semiotics of Islamic Philosophy, Theology and Cosmology* (London: Routledge/Curzon, 1994), p. 292. The meaning of transcendence in Islamic metaphysics appears to evade Netton's analysis.

[95] Quoted in Stiver, *The Philosophy of Religious Language*, p. 183.

contrast, begins with the transcendent Real and returns to It, all possible dogmatic reifications in this conception being precluded not by some rationally constructed formula, but by the spiritual transformations wrought by, among other things, contact with Revelation: there is no mental fixation on any concept to the exclusion of others, but rather a metaphysical suppleness that, on the intellectual and intuitive plane, reflects the spiritual capacity proper to that faculty of inner perception referred to as the 'heart'. To quote the famous words of Ibn ʿArabī:

> My heart has become capable of every form: it is a pasture for gazelles and a convent for Christian monks,
> And a temple for idols and the pilgrim's Kaʿba and the tables of the Tora and the book of the Koran.
> I follow the religion of Love: whatever way Love's camels take, that is my religion and my faith.[96]

This universal capacity of the heart reflects the fact that the Real—the 'transcendental signified'—is both beyond and within all conceptions and beliefs (we shall return to this theme in Chapter III). While the simple notion of God is radically transformed through spiritual interiorization, it is by no means subverted: it is a starting point for an infinite unfolding, not a mere reified linguistic form which needs to be deconstructed.[97]

As regards the article by Almond, despite the fact that certain parallels can be found between the two thinkers—for example, in the similarity between Ibn ʿArabī's 'untying the knot of belief'

---

[96] Ibn ʿArabī, *The Tarjumān al-Ashwāq—A Collection of Mystical Odes* (tr. R. A. Nicholson), (London: Theosophical Publishing House, 1978), p. 67.

[97] Carl Raschke lays bare the true nature of deconstruction as regards its impact upon religious thinking: 'Deconstruction must be considered the interior drive of twentieth century theology rather than an alien agenda... [it is] in the final analysis the death of God put into writing.' This is from his article, 'The Deconstruction of God' in T. J. Altizer *et al.*, *Deconstruction and Theology*, as cited by Netton, *Allah Transcendent*, p. 325.

and Derrida's undoing of the 'fabric' of the text[98] —one simply cannot ignore the fundamental difference between the two both in principle and as regards 'bewilderment'. For Ibn ʿArabī, this bewilderment is a state that is ultimately subsumed as part of the knowledge of the Real which produces it in the first place; it characterises the highest 'knowers'. For Derrida, bewilderment is the result only of ignorance, of the realization that all of one's efforts to understand 'rest upon interminably shifting sands', to quote Almond.[99]

While both will agree on the inability of reason alone to attain certainty they differ fundamentally on the way to resolve this difficulty—indeed, Derrida would regard the very search for a solution to be doomed in advance. Ibn ʿArabī, however, on the one hand, indicates that reason and imagination can work together—these being the two 'eyes' of the soul;[100] and on the other, that a methodology of spiritual practice[101] opens the soul up to an altogether superior mode of knowledge, one by which are apprehended the higher realities to which reason has no access; but reason may nonetheless register something of these higher realities, in the very measure that it yields to Revelation from God:[102] its 'reasoning' will then not be based

[98] Almond, 'The Honesty of the Perplexed', *op. cit.*, pp. 516–518.

[99] *Ibid.*, p. 524.

[100] See W. C. Chittick, *The Sufi Path of Knowledge*, pp. 29–30, 70; and chapter 20, entitled 'Seeing with Two Eyes', pp. 356–381.

[101] 'In our view, knowledge requires practice, and necessarily so, or else it is not knowledge, even if it appears in the form of knowledge.' *Ibid.*, p. 151. Elsewhere, he writes, in his reply to the objection that his 'way' is just as much based on reason as is that of the rational philosophers, 'occupy yourself with following that which God has commanded you: practicing obedience to Him, examining (*murāqaba*) the thoughts that occur to your heart, shame (*ḥayā'*) before God, halting before His bounds, being alone (*infirād*) with Him, and preferring His side over yourself, until the Real is all your faculties and you are "upon insight" [XII: 108] in your affair.' *Ibid.*, p. 168.

[102] 'God knew that He had deposited within the rational faculty acceptance towards that which is given both by the Real (*al-ḥaqq*) and by the reflective faculty. . . ' *Ibid.*, p. 74.

on 'interminably shifting sands' but on the firm ground of faith, initially, and indubitable certitude, finally. It can thus at least participate, to some extent, in the kind of knowledge (*maʿrifa*) that is realized in its plenitude by the 'folk of unveiling':

> 'For the Tribe,[103] *maʿrifa* is a path (*maḥajja*). Hence any knowledge which can be actualized only through practice (*ʿamal*), godfearingness (*taqwā*), and wayfaring (*sulūk*), is *maʿrifa*, since it derives from a verified unveiling which is not seized by obfuscation. This contrasts with the knowledge which is actualized through reflective consideration (*al-naẓar al-fikrī*), which is never safe from obfuscation and bewilderment, nor from rejection of that which leads to it.'[104]

This last phrase, 'rejection of that which leads to it', sums up the 'deconstructionist' aspect of Ibn ʿArabī's attitude to reason: knowledge which comes about through the use of reason alone is by that very token liable to be 'deconstructed' by reason as well: it is only that which goes beyond the confines of reason that is not subject to deconstruction by reason or by 'bewilderment' from any other source. The contrast with Derrida could hardly be clearer. What emerges from an Akbarī perspective is not, however, a monotonous stability in contrast to Derrida's endless variegation, but rather 'stability in variegation' (*al-tamkīn fī'l-talwīn*).[105]

In the article above, Almond also compares Derrida's deconstruction with the apophatic or negative theology of Dionysius the Areopagite.[106] However, once again, the two approaches

---

[103] As noted above, in relation to verse LXXIII: 20, this is one of the terms by which the Sufis refer to themselves.

[104] *Ibid.*, p. 149.

[105] *Ibid.*, p. 108.

[106] Almond, 'The Honesty of the Perplexed', pp. 525-526. For an interesting and original analysis of apophatic discourse in comparative context see Michael Sells, *Mystical Languages of Unsaying* (Chicago and London: Chicago University Press, 1994).

to ultimate reality remain fundamentally irreconcilable: in apophatic theology, the kind of 'deconstruction' in question is of an ascendant nature, affirming—albeit in negative terms—the absolute reality of the Divine, whose very absoluteness defies all attempts at positive ('kataphatic') definition.

Dionysius, the founding father, one might say, of the tradition of negative theology in Christianity, makes the following prayer to the Deity 'above all essence, knowledge and goodness' at the very beginning of his treatise *The Mystical Theology*: '... direct our path to the ultimate summit of Thy mystical Lore, most incomprehensible, most luminous and most exalted, where the pure, absolute and immutable mysteries of theology are veiled in the dazzling obscurity of the secret Silence, outshining all brilliance with the intensity of their Darkness...'[107]

It is already clear from this passage that for Dionysius, there really is a 'transcendental signified', even if it is described in a series of paradoxes, such as 'dazzling obscurity'. The purpose of defining the ultimate reality in terms of darkness, and as that which goes beyond being, is not simply to shroud that reality in utter, impenetrable obscurity, but rather to precipitate receptivity to that reality by showing the inability of the human mind in and of itself to attain comprehension of, or union with, that reality. It is the contrast between ultimate reality and mental abstraction that is in question. To take another example, the *koans* of Zen Buddhism are designed to highlight this same chasm between reality in itself and all mental constructions of reality. In the words of D. T. Suzuki: 'The intellect may raise all kinds of questions—and it is perfectly right for it to do so—but to expect any answer from the intellect is asking too much of it... The answer lies deeply buried under the bedrock of our being. To split it open requires the most basic tremor of the will. When this is felt, the doors of perception open and a new vista

[107] Dionysius the Areopagite, *Mystical Theology and the Celestial Hierarchies*, (Fintry: The Shrine of Wisdom Press), 1965, p. 9.

hitherto undreamed of is presented.'[108] It is this 'tremor of the will' that the *koan* is designed to precipitate.

To continue with Dionysius, he addresses the following words to his disciple:

> '... do thou, dear Timothy, in the diligent exercise of mystical contemplation, leave behind the senses and the operations of the intellect, and all things sensible and intellectual, and all things in the world of being and non-being, that thou mayest arise by unknowing towards the union, as far as is attainable, with Him who transcends all being and all knowledge. For by the unceasing and absolute renunciation of thyself and of all things, thou mayest be borne on high, through pure and entire self-abnegation, into the superessential Radiance of the Divine Darkness.'[109]

It is clear that the intent behind this apophatic discourse is to direct the seeker from the interminable play of ratiocination to the interiorizing art of contemplation. As in the Advaitin tradition, every concept is regarded as a 'form' (*rupa*) upon which apophasis (*apavada*—its cognate) is to be performed; this 'false attribution of form followed by apophasis' (*adhyaropana-apavada*) is an inherent part of the meditative and contemplative discipline that leads to realization of the Absolute, of 'That from which words fall back'.[110] Shorn of this positive, spiritual counterpart to apophasis one is left with nothing but negation: the dead-end, precisely, of deconstruction.

The contrast between the traditional mode of 'deconstruction'—predicated entirely on a spiritual 'reconstruction' on the transcendent plane—and the deconstruction of Derrida is thus clear.

[108] D. T. Suzuki, *Studies in Zen* (London: Rider, 1986), p. 48. Suzuki quotes such *koans* as the following: 'Let me hear the sound of one hand clapping'; 'Walk while riding a donkey'; 'Talk without using your tongue'(p. 49).

[109] *Ibid.*

[110] *Samkara on the Absolute* (tr. A. J. Alston), (London: Shanti Sadan, 1987), vol. 1, p. 147.

Derrida deconstructs and relativizes all linguistic expression 'from below', not so as to indicate or affirm a transcendent reality that eludes all linguistic definition, but rather in order to deny that there is anything in thought or being (which are, ineluctably, linguistic 'constructions') that can escape the indefinite play of *différance*, of indefinitely extended significations which only signify further significations, this merry-go-round playing itself out on the same level of linguistically definable cognition. To further underline the chasm that separates this paradigm from traditional mystical approaches to language, or indeed, from any context in which spirituality is the defining element, the following extract from the *Discourses of Rūmī* should be carefully pondered:

> 'Someone asked: Then what is the use of expressions and words?
> The Master [i.e. Rūmī] answered: The use of words is that they set you searching and excite you, not that the object of the quest should be attained through words. If that were the case, there would be no need for so much striving and self-naughting. Words are as when you see afar off something moving; you run in the wake of it in order to see it, it is not the case that you see it through its movement. Human speech too is inwardly the same; it excites you to seek the meaning, even though you do not see it in reality.'

Rūmī then reinforces the point, stressing the incommensurability between the kind of learning that comes through reading and the understanding that arises from the spiritual discipline of self-transcendence:

> 'Someone was saying: I have studied so many sciences and mastered so many ideas, yet it is still not known to me what that essence in man is that will remain forever, and I have not discovered it.
> The Master answered: If that had been knowable by means

> of words only, you would not have needed to pass away from self and to suffer such pains. It is necessary to endure so much for yourself *not* to remain, so that you may know that thing which *will* remain.'[111] (Emphasis added)

As will be seen in the following chapter, the relationship between the 'passing away' of the self, and the emergence of the perception of reality is a key dimension of the spiritual way which the Sufis derive from the Qur'ānic discourse. This apparently negative exigency of self-abnegation is but the prelude to an eminently positive realization; for this self-effacement is the essential 'alchemical' element, as it were, which dissolves all coagulative tendencies—that is, all tendencies to abusively identify oneself in absolute terms with anything of an extraneous, superficial or transient nature. It is when the veil of the ego—and all of its extensions in terms of family, tribe, nation or religion—is rendered transparent that a new mode of perception is born.[112]

Having made clear the contrast between a Sufi epistemological orientation and a postmodern one, we shall complete this chapter with a very brief outline of the specific hermeneutical principle that informs the exposition that will be presented in the following three chapters.

---

[111] *Discourses*, p. 202.

[112] The following assertion by the great metaphysician and art-historian, Ananda Coomaraswamy brings closer to home the ideal of self-effacement: 'A long stride has been taken if at least we have learned to accept the idea of the naughting of self as a good, however contrary it may be to our "natural" desire... For if the spirit be thus willing, the time will come when the flesh... will no longer be weak. The doctrine of self-naughting is therefore addressed to all, in the measure of their capacity, and by no means only to those who have formally abandoned name and lineage [that is, the *sannyasins*].' Roger Lipsey, (ed.), *Coomaraswamy 2: Selected Papers—Metaphysics* (Princeton: Princeton University Press, 1977), p. 237.

Ibn ʿArabī: From Ontology to Hermeneutics

It is difficult to overstate the importance of the Andalusian Sufi, Muḥyī al-Dīn Ibn ʿArabī, in the constellation of the Islamic intellectual universe. Given the extent to which this universe has been moulded by Sufism, and given the dominance of Ibn ʿArabī within Sufi discourse, one can readily agree with William Chittick, one of Ibn ʿArabī's foremost expositors in western academia, when he writes: 'In the Islamic world itself, probably no-one has exercised deeper and more pervasive influence over the intellectual life of the community during the past seven hundred years.'[113] One should note the use of the phrase 'intellectual life' here, for the Shaykh al-Akbar's influence was by no means restricted to the mystical or esoteric domain of Islam and its adherents, the Sufis. Despite the fact that his legacy has been controversial, and subject to attack from exoteric Muslim scholars throughout the centuries, one can only understand the depth and the breadth of his influence in all the domains of thought in Islam with reference to the *support* his ideas have received from members of that same class of exoteric scholars; that is, from orthodox representatives of the normative values of Islam.[114] It was in this way that his influence acted—and continues to act[115]—like a leaven within orthodoxy, stretching

[113] Chittick, *Sufi Path of Knowledge*, p. x.

[114] As is clear from the detailed study by Alexander Knysh, *Ibn ʿArabi in the Later Islamic Tradition* (Albany: State University of New York Press, 1999), there were, throughout the centuries, heated debates over the question of Ibn ʿArabī's orthodoxy—it was by no means a foregone conclusion that he was heterodox. See, for example, the tabulation of *fatwas*, both for and against him, on p. 135; and a more comprehensive list, on the question of the status of the *Fuṣūṣ*, provided by Osman Yahia in his *Histoire et classification de l'œuvre d'Ibn ʿArabī* (Damascus: Institut Français de Damas, 1964), vol. 1, pp. 122-135.

[115] In our own times, despite the recent controversy in Egypt over the re-publication of his *al-Futūḥāt al-makkiyya*—for which refer to Th. Emeril Homerin, 'Ibn ʿArabī in the People's Assembly' in *Middle East Journal*, vol. 40, no. 3, pp. 462-477—one only has to ask the scholars of al-Azhar, the 'citadel' of contemporary Sunni orthodoxy, their opinion of the Shaykh al-Akbar

its boundaries, adding a dimension of mystical depth to its initial dogmas, whilst also challenging and overturning narrow-minded, pharisaical attitudes.

One important reason why his esoteric influence was so pervasive was that, like Ghazālī, his stress on the 'spirit' did not contradict the 'letter', it complemented it; the inward (*al-bāṭin*) and the outward (*al-ẓāhir*) were two sides of the same coin. As much as he railed against the pettiness of the 'folk of the outward' (*ahl al-ẓāhir*), the Shaykh gave short shrift also to those antinomian Sufis who believed that attachment to the inward and the mystical dimensions of Islam implied or required an abandonment of its outward and legal dimensions. James Morris argues convincingly that Ibn ʿArabī's 'esotericism' can only be properly understood against the background of his firm adherence to the defining principles of the Islamic tradition, principles which he applies in depth and with subtlety.[116]

As was noted above in connection with Corbin, mystics such as Ibn ʿArabī and Ḥallāj were not trying to go beyond Islam or to exit from it, they merely brought to fruition the spiritual power that was latent within the religion; what they transcended was a conception of Islam defined exclusively by its legal, social and political aspects. As with Hujwīrī's claim that without Sufism, the 'whole' of the Law would be destroyed, Corbin's point is that, without an opening towards its *ḥaqīqa*, its spiritual truth/reality, religion inevitably degenerates into a parody of its true nature. For it is only the *ḥaqīqa* that can operate

to be made aware of the continuing support his perspective receives even amongst those deemed to be 'exoteric' authorities. Needless to say, a high proportion, if not a majority, of these Azharī shaykhs are themselves practising Sufis at the same time as being experts in Islamic law and theology. While Egypt is somewhat exceptional in this regard, the situation is not so dissimilar in other Muslim countries; the former Grand Mufti of Syria, for example, Shaykh Kiftaru (d. 2004), was one of the most senior Sufi masters of the Naqshbandī Ṭarīqa in Syria.

[116] See his 'Ibn ʿArabi's "Esotericism": The Problem of Spiritual Authority', in *Studia Islamica*, LXXI (1990), pp. 37–64.

the necessary 'metamorphoses' which prevent the Shariʿa from being 'denatured' by 'political socialisation'.[117]

We shall return to the significance of this point in the final chapter, when we come to consider the extent to which the esoteric ideas presented in this book might be acceptable to the contemporary upholders of exoteric norms in the Muslim communities.

Turning now to the hermeneutics that informs this book, the Shaykh al-Akbar sums up the Sufi approach in general in the following statement:

> 'It is known that when the Scriptures speak of the Reality, they speak in a way that yields to the generality of men the immediately apparent meaning. The elite, on the other hand, understand all the meanings inherent in that utterance, in whatever terms it is expressed.'[118]

Sufi commentaries are distinguished from exoteric exegesis by their tendency to relate the verses of the scripture to sacred symbolism, to the inner life of the soul, to the spiritual substance of ethical values, to eschatological themes and to metaphysical principles.[119] Exoteric commentaries (*tafsīr* in the strict sense) are mostly confined to explaining the linguistic meaning of the text, the historical referents and occasional causes of the verses, and their legal and practical implications.[120] As Sulamī says in

[117] *En Islam iranien*, vol. 1, p. 22.

[118] Ibn ʿArabī, *Bezels of Wisdom—Fuṣūṣ al-ḥikam*, (tr. Ralph Austin), (New York: Paulist Press, 1980), p. 73.

[119] See, for one of the most comprehensive studies of Sufi *tafsīr*, the fine work by Gerhard Böwering, *The Mystical Vision of Existence in Classical Islam—The Qur'ānic Hermeneutics of the Ṣūfī Sahl al-Tustarī* (Berlin & New York: Walter de Gruyter, 1980); see also his helpful classification of the principal periods and personalities in the tradition of Sufi exegesis, in *Sufi Hermeneutics in Medieval Islam* (Tokyo: Sophia University, 1987). See also the comprehensive forthcoming article by Alan Godlas in the *Encyclopaedia Iranica*, 'al-Tafsīr al-Ṣūfī', now accessible on his website: www.arches.uga.edu/~godlas.

[120] See, for a standard work of typology and discussion of the different genres of commentary in the Islamic tradition, Muḥammad Ḥusayn al-Dhahabī, *Al-*

the introduction to his seminal commentary, *Ḥaqā'iq al-tafsīr* ("Realities of Exegesis"), he felt compelled to gather together the esoteric comments on the Qur'ān known to him, given his observation that the effort to comprehend the meaning of the text 'according to spiritual reality' was neglected by the scholars of the Qur'ān. They occupy themselves, writes Sulamī, with such sciences as 'styles of recitation, benefits, difficulties, legal rulings, syntax, lexicography, synthetic and analytic constructions, abrogating and abrogated verses.'[121]

To give a concrete example which illustrates the distinction between these two modes of exegesis, we can recall what Rūmī mentioned about Moses and Pharaoh not simply being historical personages, but expressions of spiritual tendencies that can be found also within oneself. Whereas it is the task of exoteric *tafsīr* to situate the story of the deliverance of the Jews from Egyptian oppression in outward, temporal terms, and to draw appropriate moral lessons from the story, it falls to the esoteric hermeneut to interiorize the human agents of the historical drama, and to thereby transfigure them into ever-present realities impinging upon the soul in its quest for spiritual realization. The temporal is transmuted into the timeless, the outward into the inward, the ethical into the spiritual. In terms of the latter distinction it is not so much a question of spirituality replacing morality, as providing the lessons of morality with an existential imperative, thus grounding them in spiritually transformative principles, and thereby rendering ethical values more, not less, meaningful.

Tafsīr wa'l-mufassirūn (Cairo: Dār al-Kutub al-Ḥāditha, 1961). While covering the field well enough, the author is not particularly sympathetic either to Sufi or to Shiʿi *tafsīr*. See also, for a comparable overview of the different genres, which, despite coming from an overtly Persian Shiʿi perspective, is less partial, generally, and more sympathetic to spiritual and philosophical commentary, in particular, Muḥammad Hādī Maʿrifat, *Tafsīr wa-mufassirān* (Qom: Mu'assisa Farhangī al-Tamhīd, 1379-1380 Sh./2000-2001), 2 vols. See vol. 2, pp. 333-445, for his discussion of Sufi commentaries, which comes under the heading of the *ʿirfānī* category.

121 *Tafsīr al-Sulamī* (Beirut: Dār al-Kutub al-ʿIlmiyya, 2001), vol. 1, p. 19.

We can turn to Kāshānī for a good example of how *ta'wīl* is performed upon the story of the deliverance of the Children of Israel. When God reminds the Jews in the Qur'ān: *And when We delivered you from the folk of Pharaoh* (II: 49), Kāshānī refers to the 'outward aspect' (*ẓāhiruhu*) of the deliverance and its *tafsīr* as relating to the remembrance of this divine blessing and the love that should be elicited as a result; by contrast, the 'inner aspect' (*bāṭinuhu*), and its *ta'wīl* is given as follows:

> '*And when We delivered you from the folk of* (the) *Pharaoh* of the soul that incites to evil, the soul that is veiled by its I-ness, and which reigns supreme over the kingdom of Being, and over the "Egypt"[122] of the city of the body which is enslaved, together with all its faculties, which are: conjecture, imagination, anger, evacuation and passion; and its spiritual faculties, which are the "tribes" of the sincere friend of God, the "Jacob" of the spirit; and the natural bodily faculties, such as the outward senses and the faculties of growth.'[123]

As a genre, the Sufis refer to their mode of interpretation of the Qur'ān in terms of 'allusions' (*ishārāt* sing. *ishāra*). Verses are deemed to allude to spiritual realities that may not be apparent at first sight, realities that are perceived by the Sufis in the measure of their contemplativity, their mystical states, their receptivity to the deeper meanings hidden within the text. In this connection, the following saying of the Prophet—designated as weak according to the criteria of *ḥadīth*—is often cited, in various versions: 'There is no verse of the Qur'ān which does not have an outward sense (*ẓahr*), an inward sense (*baṭn*), a limit (*ḥadd*)

---

[122] The word *miṣr* means both 'Egypt' and 'large city'.

[123] Kāshānī, *Tafsīr*, vol. I, pp. 33-34. This style of interpretation is given the name *taṭbīq*, 'microcosmic correspondence' whereby the outward meaning of the words come to denote inward realities of the soul. Lory shows that this kind of interpretation is not be seen in contrast to *ta'wīl* but as a particular type of *ta'wīl*. See his discussion in *Commentaires*, pp. 29-30.

and a place to which one ascends (*muṭṭalaʿ*).'[124] Ghazālī cites this saying, on the authority of Ibn Masʿūd, a companion and early authority on the Qur'ān, together with several other sayings attributed to such companions as ʿAlī ibn Abī Ṭālib,[125] then adds the following paragraph to justify the spiritual interpretations of the Sufis which differs so profoundly from ordinary, outward exegesis: 'Penetrating deeply into the explanation of the Qur'ān by stages amounts to the understanding of the Qur'ān; mere outward exegesis (*tafsīr al-ẓāhir*) does not lead to that. The truth is that to everything pertaining to reflective and intellectual matters which has become ambiguous to men of reflection and in which people have differed, there are indications (*ishārāt*) and implications in the Qur'ān which can be grasped by men of understanding. How can these indications and implications be completely conveyed by the translation of its outward meanings and by its [outward] exegesis?'[126]

The Sufis, according to Ibn ʿArabī, refer to their mystical commentaries as allusions partly in order to defend themselves against the attacks of exoteric scholars. They refer their interpretations 'back to their own souls', referring to the verses of the revealed text as 'signs'—the literal meaning of *āya* (pl. *āyāt*)—which are not only in the text but also, according to a verse of the Qur'ān itself, in the outer world and in the soul: *We shall show them Our signs on the horizons and in their own souls* (XLI: 53).[127] He continues:

---

[124] See for example, Kāshānī, *Tafsīr*, p. 3; Sulamī, *Tafsīr*, p. 21. In both of these instances, each verse is described as having a 'inward' and an 'outward' sense, but it is each 'letter' (*ḥarf*) that has a limit and a place of ascent.

[125] 'If I so will, I can certainly load seventy camels with the exegesis of the *Sūrat al-fātiḥa* [the opening chapter of the Qur'ān, consisting in just seven verses].' *The Recitation and Interpretation of the Qur'ān—Al-Ghazali's Theory* (Book 8 of the *Iḥyā' ʿulūm al-dīn*) (tr. Muhammad Abul Quasem), (London & Boston: Routledge & Kegan Paul, 1984), p. 87.

[126] *Ibid.*, p. 88.

[127] See Sayyid Ḥaydar Āmulī's commentary, *Al-Muḥīṭ al-aʿẓam wa'l-baḥr al-khiḍamm fī ta'wīl kitāb Allāh al-ʿazīz al-muḥkam* (Qom: al-Maʿhad al-Thaqāfī

> 'Every revealed verse has two senses (*wajh*): A sense which they [the 'Folk of Allah] see within themselves and a sense which they see outside of themselves. That which they see inside themselves they call an "allusion" in order that the jurist (*faqīh*)—the exoteric scholar—will be comfortable with it. They do not say that it is a "commentary". Thereby they defend themselves against the evil of the jurists and their vile accusations of unbelief.'

Then follows a partial justification of this 'vile' way of acting on the part of the jurists, for, on the one hand, they are 'ignorant of the modes in which the address of the Real descends'; and on the other, they 'follow the road of guidance, for God had the power to state explicitly the interpretation (*ta'awwul*) of the Folk of Allah in His Book, yet He did not do that. On the contrary, He inserted into those divine words which descend in the language of the common people the sciences of the meanings of election which He allows His servants to understand when He opens up the eye of understanding which He has provided for them.'[128]

In other words, Ibn ʿArabī does not blame the exoteric scholars for blaming the Sufis, for their understanding goes no further than the outward meaning of the text, and since this outward meaning was exactly what was intended by God to be derived from the words of the revelation by the people concerned. They cannot see that the Sufis base their interpretation upon a form of learning, just as their own interpretations derive from learning (*taʿallum*); but the Sufi mode of learning comes in the form of a divine bestowal, in which the exoteric scholars have no share. Moreover, the 'Folk of Allah' see that God has given power in this world to the exoteric scholars, and this they do not challenge:

Nūr ʿAlā Nūr, 1380 Sh./2001), vol. 1, pp. 206-257, for an extensive and illuminating exegesis of this verse.

[128] Chittick, *Sufi Path of Knowledge*, p. 247.

> 'He gave them [the exoteric scholars] domination over the creatures through the pronouncements they make, and He joined them to those "who know an outward significance of the present life, but of the next world they are heedless" (30: 7). In their denial of the Folk of Allah, "they think they are working good deeds" (18: 104). Hence, the Folk of Allah let them have their states, since they knew on what basis they are speaking. Then they protected themselves from these scholars by naming the realities "allusions", since the exoteric scholars do not deny "allusions".'[129]

This tolerant attitude even towards those who are intolerant towards oneself can only be properly understood in the light of one key principle of Ibn ʿArabī's hermeneutics, a principle which informs this study in a very particular way. The relevance of this principle for our purposes here can be seen more sharply against the background of the following fundamental statement by Ibn ʿArabī on the nature of being: 'Part of the perfection of existence is the existence of imperfection within it, since, were there no imperfection, the perfection of existence would be imperfect because of the absence of imperfection within it.'[130]

The word translated here as 'perfection' is *kamāl*, and this word also implies completeness, totality; taking note of these shades of meaning helps one to comprehend somewhat more easily this paradox, which plays a key role in the metaphysics of Ibn ʿArabī. The completeness/perfection of being is perfectly compatible with the existence of incompleteness/imperfection; indeed, its very completeness requires that it be affirmed by the existence of incompleteness. An apparent contradiction, in logical terms, is transformed into an ontological principle—one which, moreover goes a long way towards offering a satisfactory theodicy: the existence of a good and all-powerful God is not

[129] *Ibid.*, p. 248.
[130] *Ibid.*, p. 296.

brought into question by the existence of evil (a most intense form of 'imperfection' in being) in the universe.

This principle can be seen in relation to the divine nature itself, which is both one in itself and multiple in its expressions; in Ibn ʿArabī's perspective, this oneness in fact implies and requires multiplicity, rather than being contradicted by it. The divine Names or Qualities are multiple and they outwardly differ, while being inwardly identical; the ontological roots of all differentiation, hence conflict and contradiction are found in the very multiplicity of the Names of God.[131] But just as the Essence of God is unique in reality, while being diversified on the plane of the divine Qualities, so the assimilation of formal diversity in creation to essential unity is attained by one whose spiritual faculties are attuned to the higher reality.

The Qur'ān declares that *He is the First and the Last, and the Outward and the Inward* (LVII: 3); for Ibn ʿArabī, the divine outwardness does not contradict the divine inwardness, God's 'firstness' does not contradict His 'lastness'. His being incomparable (*tanzīh*) does not prevent His qualities from being comparable (*tashbīh*) to ours: *Nothing is like Him; and He is the Hearer, the Seer* (XLII: 11) The first part of the verse establishes *tanzīh*; the second, *tashbīh*.

> 'He is not declared incomparable in any manner that will remove Him from similarity, nor is He declared similar in any manner that would remove Him from incomparability. So do not declare Him nondelimited and thus delimited by being distinguished from delimitation! For if He is distinguished then He is delimited by His nondelimitation. And if He is delimited by His nondelimitation, then He is not He.'[132]

[131] This will be discussed further in the following chapter. See also the section entitled 'The Divine Roots of Hierarchy and Conflict', in Chittick, *Sufi Path of Knowledge*, pp. 47–58.

[132] Chittick, *Sufi Path of Knowledge*, p. 112.

Ibn ʿArabī often cited the words of a famous early Sufi, Abū Saʿīd al-Kharrāz, who answered, when asked how he came to know God: 'Through the fact that He brings opposites together (*jamʿuhu al-ḍiddayn*)'. He then recited *He is the First and the Last; and the Outward and the Inward.*[133]

These brief remarks on the transformation of formal contradiction into spiritual paradox, and outward diversity into inward unity, help one to see the importance of grasping the particular mode of knowledge proper to Sufism. Apparent contradictions are assimilated, resolved and transcended by modes of cognition that go beyond the formal categories of reason; these modes of cognition have been referred to above, in terms of the consciousness of the 'heart' (*al-qalb*),[134] of the imagination (*khayāl*), or the consciousness arising out of mystical 'unveiling' (*kashf*), 'direct witnessing' (*shuhūd*) or 'knowledge by presence' (*al-ʿilm al-ḥuḍūrī*).[135]

---

[133] *Ibid.*, p. 67. In addition to resolving these apparent contradictions between transcendence and immanence, similarity and incomparability, unity and multiplicity, Sufi spirituality also integrates and transcends such binary oppositions as: the miraculous and the natural; free will and determinism; the *Sharīʿa* and the *Ḥaqīqa*; matter and spirit; this world and the life hereafter; effort and Grace; action and contemplation, self and other, etc.

[134] The heart in turn is the 'envelope' of further degrees of what can be regarded as inward modes of consciousness, faculties of perception or ontological levels: *lubb* (kernel), *fu'ād* (inner heart), the *sirr* (the secret, or mystery). See al-Tirmidhī's fascinating quasi-physiological account of the process by which *maʿrifa* is realized. According to him, *maʿrifa* is a divine light residing in the heart from pre-eternity. It is realized when its light shines from the heart (*qalb*) through to the breast (*ṣadr*) and is there recognised by the eye of the heart (*fu'ād*) and then the intellect (*ʿaql*); this takes place only when the soul's vices—conceived as clouds of smoke welling up from the abdomen into the heart, thus obscuring the vision of the *fu'ād*—are overcome. See B. Radtke & J. O'Kane, *The Concept of Sainthood in Early Islamic Mysticism—Two Works by al-Ḥakīm al-Tirmidhī* (London: Curzon Press, 1996), pp. 46-51.

[135] One should take note of the work of one of the most important contemporary philosophers in the tradition of *ḥikmat* in Persia, Mehdi Ha'iri Yazdi. His book *The Principles of Epistemology in Islamic Philosophy—*

We can now situate against this background the following hermeneutical principle of Ibn ʿArabī; a principle which can be regarded as an expression, in exegetical mode, of the metaphysical principle expressed by the phrase, *al-jamʿ bayn al-ḍiddayn*, 'the coincidence of opposites', and of the ontological principle that completeness is not complete without incompleteness:

> 'As far as the Word of God is concerned, when it is revealed in the language of a certain people, and when those who speak this language differ as to what God meant by a certain word or group of words due to the variety of possible meanings of the words, each of them—however differing their interpretations may be—effectively comprises what God meant, provided that the interpretation does not deviate from the accepted meanings of the language in question. God knows all these meanings, and there is none that is not the expression of what He meant to say to this specific person.'[136]

Chodkiewicz adds this important comment: 'Given the extremely rich polysemy of Arabic vocabulary, rigorous fidelity to the letter of Revelation does not exclude but, on the contrary, it implies a multiplicity of interpretations.'[137] An important concomitant of this eirenic principle of exegesis is that nobody has the right to declare false or wrong an interpretation of a verse of the Qur'ān which can be supported by the literal meaning of the words of the verse; nonetheless one is not bound by an interpretation with which one does not agree. Thus, there is space for a multitude of interpretations, which dovetail perfectly with the receptivity—cognitive, moral, spiritual—of

Knowledge by Presence (Albany: State University of New York Press, 1992) offers an excellent presentation of the epistemology arising out of the mystical assimilation of the divine presence as the ultimate cognitive foundation of all knowledge.

[136] Cited in M. Chodkiewicz, *An Ocean Without Shore*, p. 30.

[137] *Ibid.*

the innumerable souls to whom the revelation is addressed, without this implying any abandonment of discernment as between the different interpretations, some being more subtle, exalted, universal, or galvanizing than others. Ibn ʿArabī explains:

> 'Every sense (*wajh*) which is supported (*iḥtimāl*) by any verse in God's Speech (*kalām*)—whether it is the Koran, the Torah, the Psalms, the Gospel, or the Scripture—in the view of anyone who knows that language (*lisān*) is intended (*maqṣūd*) by God in the case of that interpreter (*muta'awwil*). For His knowledge encompasses all senses... Hence every interpreter correctly grasps the intention of God in that word... Hence no man of knowledge can declare wrong an interpretation which is supported by the words (*lafẓ*). He who does so is extremely deficient in knowledge. However, *it is not necessary to uphold the interpretation nor to put it into practice*, except in the case of the interpreter himself and those who follow his authority.'[138] (emphasis added)

As will be seen in Chapter III, this principle is of particular relevance in situating one of the most important verses in connection with the universality being argued for here: *Truly religion with God is Islām* (III: 19).

The question as to whether 'Islam' is to be understood here universally—as religion as such,[139] as universal submission, as

[138] Cited in Chittick, *Sufi Path of Knowledge*, p. 244.

[139] As we shall discuss in more detail in Chapter III, Ibn ʿArabī refers to religion as such, in the singular, despite the fact that religious laws differ from one formal religious dispensation to the next. He writes as follows in connection with the words from V: 48 (*For each We have appointed from you a Law and a Way. And if God willed, He would have made you one nation*): 'Everyone is commanded to perform the religion and to come together in it... As for the rulings which are diverse, that is because of the Law which God assigned to each one of the messengers.' Here we have another example of the application of the bringing together of opposites: religious laws are diverse in one respect, but in another 'they are not diverse', for 'you have been

an ontological principle—or only as the particular religion revealed to the last Prophet, can be resolved without any need for mutual exclusion. Ibn ʿArabī's perspective on the nature of reality and of textual interpretation helps the 'universalist' to adopt a position which does not need to deny the validity of particularism. Indeed, the universalism that emerges from this perspective is one that simultaneously affirms and transcends particularism. From this angle of vision, the kind of universalism that denies particularism is itself particularist; an inclusivism that excludes exclusivism is itself exclusivist. A truly universalist understanding of the meaning of 'Islam', or of religion as such, both affirms and goes beyond the particular meaning, seeing the particular religion not just as an expression of the universal principle, but as a concrete embodiment of that principle. It is thus a pathway to that which is in its own essence; it is both distinct from the principle—by virtue of its form—and identical to it, by virtue of its essence. This universal principle, or religion as such, both comprises and surpasses all of its manifold religious expressions. Thus, the universalist/inclusivist perspective strictly implies and encompasses the particularist/exclusivist one, even if the exclusivist will exclude the point of view of the inclusivist.[140]

---

commanded to come together and to perform them', i.e. each community has been commanded to perform the Law revealed to it. Cited in Chittick, *Sufi Path of Knowledge*, p. 303. We will return to this important passage more than once in the following chapters.

[140] Those familiar with the metaphysics of Advaita in Hinduism will notice a similarity between this position and that of Shankara. In the confrontation between the dualist (the *dvaitin*) who believes in the absolute and unconditional reality of the distinction between the Absolute and the relative, and the non-dualist (*advaitin*) who holds that this distinction is real only from the viewpoint of relativity, Shankara says that 'the non-dualist does not conflict with the dualist'. This is because 'non-duality is the ultimate reality; . . . duality or multiplicity is only its effect'. Whereas the dualist perceives a duality composed of the Absolute and the relative, the non-dualist perceives duality only in respect of the relative, and from its vantage-point, knowing it to be unreal from the view-point of the Absolute. The key distinction here is between the Absolute (*paramarthika*) viewpoint and the

However, as will be argued later, the exclusivism of the exclusivist can be opened up, to some degree at least, to the inclusivist perspective. This is an aspect of intra-faith dialogue that will be discussed in Chapter IV.

Just as the divine principle is conceived in Ibn ʿArabī's metaphysics as transcendent in its very immanence, and immanent in its very transcendence, so the position on universality is one in which particularity is both embraced and surpassed: the universalist is particular in the very bosom of his universalism, and universal even within the confines of his particularism.

This inclusivist hermeneutic of Ibn ʿArabī has a place for exclusivism without being reduced to it, and also without being condescending towards it. For in this perspective, it is not so much a question of what particular interpretations are held, but rather, the degree to which the meaning understood by the mind transforms the inner consciousness, rendering it spiritually receptive to those realities of which the outward conceptual forms are but 'allusions', indications, sign-posts. So even if the universalist believes that his point of view is more profound than that of the exclusivist, there is no place for a sense of superiority, pride or arrogance; the priority given to spiritual realization, of *taḥqīq*, over conceptual comprehension precludes any such pretensions. A narrow point of view can be combined with the most profound inward piety and indeed sanctity, while the most broad-minded of people can be the most superficial, and indeed hypocritical. However, to realize, to whatever degree, the truths of other religious traditions cannot but contribute to one's receptivity to the Truth as such, which is above and beyond all those forms which both reveal and veil it; and cannot but enhance the basis for dialogue with, and respect for, the other.

It is against the background provided by this brief overview of some of the relevant principles of Sufi hermeneutics that the

---

relative (*vyavaharika*) one. Duality is real from the latter viewpoint and reduced to illusion from the former. See *The Mandukyopanisad with Gaudapada's Karika and Sankara's Commentary* (tr. S. Nikhilananda), (Mysore: Sri Ramakrishna Ashrama, 1974), p. 165.

ideas, interpretations, and principles contained in the following chapters can be situated. Thus, they ought to be viewed not as definitive and exclusive affirmations, but as possible openings to deeper levels of meaning; angles of vision aiming at 'disclosure' and not as 'closure'; themes for debate and dialogue, not hard and fast conclusions. It is hoped that the reflections offered will make manifest the relevance of spiritual exegesis of the Qur'ān to the on-going effort to articulate an appropriate Muslim approach to the other; to do so without undermining the integrity of the Islamic self-definition; and to do so in a manner that strengthens and complements all existing attempts to establish openness, tolerance, mutual respect and fruitful dialogue between believers in a world of religious plurality.

The following chapter begins, then, by setting in metaphysical context the relationship between plurality as such and the principle of oneness that, more than any other, characterises the way of Islam.

CHAPTER II

The Reality of the One and Dialogue with the Other

AT FIRST SIGHT, nothing could be simpler than the Qur'ānic message of *tawḥīd*. There is but one true or real God: *lā ilāha illa'Llāh*. All false gods are negated by this simple formula and by the mentality that it fosters. For the Sufis, however, the content of this simple message has no boundaries, for *tawḥīd* is not restricted to the plane of theology; it comes to embrace all that is. Consequently, the whole of Sufism—its speculative metaphysics, its transformative spirituality, its soul-searching psychology, its mystical practices and its ethical imperatives—can be seen as so much 'commentary' or elaboration upon this Qur'ānic message of *tawḥīd*. The most important shift effected by the Sufi assimilation of the message is that from theology to ontology, from the nature of God to the nature of Being.[1] As Kāshānī says, summing up this ontological perspective: 'There is no He but Him, and no existent apart from Him.'[2] Nothing exists apart from God or in addition to Him: we have here not only an affirmation of the oneness of God to the exclusion of

---

[1] This is the distinction which Āmulī makes, between *al-tawḥīd al-ulūhī*, and *al-tawḥīd al-wujūdī*, as will be further discussed below.

[2] Kāshānī, *Tafsīr*, vol. II, p. 17. The *tafsīr* in question was for centuries attributed to Ibn ʿArabī, on account of the evident fact that the essential approach, principles and even many of the specific interpretations found in this commentary are derived from the perspective of Ibn ʿArabī.

other gods, but also, and more fundamentally, the affirmation of a unique reality, which is exclusive of all otherness, or rather: in relation to which all otherness is, ultimately, unreal.

In relation to dialogue, one can then pose these questions: if nothing but God is real, and there is no 'otherness', in reality, what is the meaning of dialogue with the other? How can dialogue take place, and what can its purpose be, in a context defined by metaphysical oneness? What status can be attributed to the two agents of dialogue, the self, and the other, if nothing is real but God? Is dialogue in our actual world enhanced or undermined by such metaphysical perspectives? These are the questions that form the background against which the esoteric exegesis of the Qur'ānic concept of oneness will be presented in this chapter.

The starting point for these reflections will be a fairly lengthy exploration of the commentary given by Kāshānī on the chapter called *al-Ikhlāṣ* ('Sincerity'/'Purity'), also called *al-Tawḥīd*, a fundamental credal affirmation and one of the most oft-recited of all the chapters of the Qur'ān. The key theme here will be the relationship between unity and multiplicity, or between oneness in diversity and diversity within oneness. It will be seen that the oneness of reality, far from excluding multiplicity, implies it, embraces it and integrates it—the 'many' belong to the One, are projected by It into relativity, and return to It, this process manifesting to the One its own infinite richness: this, in essence, is the 'dialogue' constituted by existence itself, and which might be regarded as the ultimate 'prototype' or enlivening sap of all dialogues at the human level. Thus, the positive reason for diversity on the human plane, as indicated in the following words of verse XLIX: 13, can be situated within a universal context of divine Self-manifestation, whereby the One expresses and thus 'makes known' Its own inner infinitude: *O mankind, truly We have created you male and female, and have made you nations and tribes that ye may know one another.* (XLIX: 13)

The insights of other representatives of the Sufi tradition will also be considered, in order to explore and illustrate some of the concomitants of this metaphysical conception of *tawḥīd*, and its implications for dialogue. In relation to this divine Self-disclosure, the ontological status and cognitive function of the self, the human agent engaged in dialogue, is defined more clearly: on the one hand the human self will be seen to be integral to the divine Self-disclosure, being the most faithful reflection, within relative existence, of the unconditional being and manifold qualities of the divine nature; and on the other hand, the self-effacement required for the Sufi assimilation of *tawḥīd* will be seen to have potentially far-reaching consequences for effective dialogue with the other. Finally, the other will be examined in the light of the preceding discussion: as there is nothing in existence but the divine, and as multiplicity is affirmed as integral to the oneness of God, that divine Reality cannot but be present in the other, and it cannot but teach us something about that divine Reality, if we be sensitive to the divine 'Face' that is in the other, that is also in oneself, and, indeed, that is there, wherever we look: *And unto God belong the East and the West; and wherever ye turn, there is the Face of God.* (II: 115)

The One in the Many, the Many in the One

Before turning to Kāshānī's commentary on *Sūrat al-Ikhlāṣ*, it would be useful to bear the following point in mind. As was noted in the previous chapter, Sufi exegesis is characterised by its allusive (*ishārī*) character: the verses of the revealed text are seen to allude to realities and principles glimpsed, tasted, or fully realized by the Sufis in spiritual contemplation. In considering the commentaries below, some of which may appear to fly far from the evident or literal meaning of the words being commented upon, it would be wrong to infer that the vision of oneness presented by the Sufis is predicated solely on their own private, arbitrary inspirations and not on the text itself.

It is undeniable that the majority of the verses dealing with the oneness of God in the Qur'ān express this oneness in a manner which rigorously stresses the divine transcendence (*tanzīh*), incomparability and remoteness: *There is nothing like Him* (XLII: 11); *Glorified be thy Lord, the Lord of Glory, above what they describe* (XXXVII: 180). Such verses, however, give only one side of the picture, for there are others in which the immanence, similarity (*tashbīh*)[3] and proximity of God are stressed. These verses indicate that the divine Reality is not just exclusive but also inclusive, not just above and beyond all things, but also containing and thus penetrating all things. They reveal that the divine Presence, being infinite, is thereby inalienable—there is no space or time, where God is not present, even though He transcends all space and time. Such verses, albeit few in number, must be given an importance out of proportion to the frequency of their occurrence in the text, not only because they are so often invoked by the Sufis in their treatises; and not only because they resonate so profoundly with the experiential openings effected by the spiritual practices that are an inseparable part of Sufism understood as a living tradition;[4] but also because these verses define fundamental, metaphysical principles pertaining to the mystery of divine oneness. When Sufis therefore relate all sorts of verses—dealing with diverse subjects—to the all-pervading, immanent divine Presence, it is not a question of 'speculating in the void'. It is instead the expression of a vision of an all-embracing oneness evoked by particular verses, a vision which is experientially intuited, mystically anticipated or concretely realized. Verses such as the following, then, should be borne in

[3] It should be noted that *tashbīh*, though often translated as 'immanence' in contrast to *tanzīh*, 'transcendence', in fact means 'similarity', or 'making similar'. But similarity is not immanence, strictly speaking: divine immanence means the actual presence of God, not the presence of something similar; it is thus a mode of pure identity, and identity is not similarity. However, as will be seen below, the symbol of the mirror helps to show how it is that *tashbīh* can legitimately be used to refer to immanence, as well as to similarity.

[4] See the discussion in the previous chapter on the 'remembrance/invocation of God' (*dhikru'Llāh*).

mind, and meditated upon, as the background for the exegesis that will be presented in this and the following chapter:

Everything is perishing save His Face (XXVIII: 88)
Everything that is thereon is passing away; and there subsisteth but the Face of thy Lord, possessor of Glory and Bounty (LV: 26-27)
And unto God belong the East and the West; and wherever ye turn, there is the Face of God (II: 115)
He is with you wherever ye may be (LVII: 4)
We are nearer to him [man] *than the jugular vein* (L: 16)
And thou didst not throw when thou threwest, but God threw (VIII: 17)
We are nearer to him than ye are, but ye perceive not (LVI: 85)
God cometh in between a man and his own heart (VIII: 24)
Is He not encompassing all things? (XLI: 54)
He is the First and the Last, and the Outward and the Inward (LVII: 3)
God is the light of the heavens and the earth. The similitude of His light is as a niche wherein is a lamp. The lamp is in a glass. The glass is as it were a shining star. [The lamp is] *kindled from a blessed olive tree, neither of the East nor of the West, whose oil would almost glow forth though no fire touched it. Light upon light. God guideth to His light whom He will. And God striketh similitudes for mankind. And God knoweth all things* (XXIV: 35).

Turning now to Kāshānī's exegesis of *Surat al-Ikhlāṣ*, let us first cite the chapter itself:

Say: He is God,[5] *One;*
God, the eternally besought.

[5] I translate the word 'Allah' as 'God' here and in all translations of verses from the Qur'ān; retaining the Arabic can have, for some, the implication that what is in question is something other than the 'God' recognised in the Jewish and Christian traditions, whereas what is in question is the self-same deity. According to the Qur'ān: *And do not hold discourse with the People of the Book except in that which is finest, save with those who do wrong. And say: We*

He begets not, And He is not begotten;
And there is nothing similar to Him. (CXII: 1–4)

Say: He, God, is One—'The word *Say* (*qul*) is a command which issues from the essence of union (*ʿayn al-jamʿ*).'[6] The term *ʿayn al-jamʿ* refers here to the supreme, unconditioned level of the divine Essence, in which all things are contained in absolute non-differentiation; *jamʿ* can also be translated as 'synthesis', that which is 'gathered together'. The term also connotes a mystical state of absorption[7] within that 'essence', such that the individual is conscious only of being an instrument of the divine will. It is in this sense that it was used by Ḥallāj, with whom this term gained particular prominence.[8]

---

believe in that which hath been revealed to us and revealed to you. Our God and your God is one, and unto Him we surrender (XXIX: 46).

[6] Kāshānī, *Tafsīr*, vol. II, p. 423.

[7] This is one type of absorption; as will be seen below, there are other types and degrees of this state of absorption or extinction, the most radical being the one in which the individual is no longer conscious of anything—not even of his own unconsciousness.

[8] At his trial, the following 'incriminating' address in a letter, written by Ḥallāj, was read in court: 'From the Merciful, the Compassionate to X son of X.' Ḥallāj admitted it was his handwriting, but rejected the accusation that he was claiming divinity for himself: 'I do not claim omnipotence; that is what we call, between ourselves, *ʿayn al-jamʿ*... the mystical state in which [we ask]: who is it but God who writes, since I am no more than the hand that serves Him as an instrument?' See L. Massignon, *The Passion of al-Ḥallāj* (tr. H. Mason) (Princeton: Princeton University Press, 1982), vol. I, pp. 528–529. This position was defended by the Ḥanbalī jurist and Sufi, Khwāja ʿAbd Allāh al-Anṣārī (d. 481/1089): 'As for myself, I use the same words as he, but secretly, so that no uninitiated person may get hold of them. There is light in these words of mine, but does the one who hears me and gains access to it believe that it is mine as such? Indeed no. For this light is the (divine) Word which makes life flow through me. Ḥallāj was speaking in a state of essential union (*ʿayn al-jamʿ*); he was in it most of the time. Now, this state is delicate and difficult to grasp; essential union is part of the ocean of *tawḥīd*. In this state it is God Who expresses Himself, no longer I; it announces the annihilation of myself and the present permanence of God.' (*Passion*, vol. II, pp. 222–223).

To continue with Kāshānī's commentary: 'The word *Say* is a command which issues from the essence of union, and appears upon the plane of differentiated manifestation. The word *He* (*Huwa*) is an expression of the pure, unitive reality, that is, the Essence *per se*, without considering Its relationship with the Attributes; none knows It but Him. And the word "God (*Allāh*)" is a substitute for It, being a Name of the Essence together with all the Attributes. This substitution demonstrates that His Attributes are not super-added to His Essence; rather, they are identical to the Essence, there being no distinction between them and It. It is only from a conceptual point of view that they can be distinguished.'

In other words, the Names *Huwa* and *Allāh* are interchangeable precisely because the reality to which they refer is one; the two Names are distinct only in nominal terms, on the conceptual plane. This nominal distinction is to be regarded as a transparent veil over the essential identity of the two referents. The possibility of substituting one Name for the other thus 'demonstrates' the intrinsic or metaphysical oneness of the two conceptually distinct aspects of the divine nature—the supreme, unconditional Essence, above and beyond all Names and Attributes, on the one hand, and the Divinity or Lord, that which is the possessor of the Names and Attributes, on the other. When Kāshānī writes that the word *He* refers to the Essence 'without considering Its relationship with the Attributes (*bilā iʿtibār ṣifa*)', it is clear that the Essence does contain the Attributes, and thus does have a 'relationship' to them; but this is only so from a particular, conditioned, standpoint. In order to have a correct perception of the oneness of the Essence, one needs to conceive of the Essence, not as being deprived of the multiplicity it contains, but as being beyond it, and thus not conditioned by it. Only then can the oneness of the Essence be properly understood as unconditioned, undetermined, thus as absolutely one, with no taint of the relativity proper to multiplicity.[9]

[9] The transcendence of the One in relation to multiplicity is not, therefore, a privative condition; that is, the One is not conditioned by negation (*bi-sharṭ*

This discussion of the relationship between the multiplicity of the divine Names and the oneness of the divine Essence is of the utmost importance in the context of the ontological assimilation of *tawḥīd*, that is, if one is to grasp the meaning of the oneness of being. For the whole of creation is perceived by Kāshānī and the members of the Akbarī school in general, as being the traces or the effects (*āthār*) of the acts (*afʿāl*) of the Names of God: all outward multiplicity is thus reducible to the multiplicity of the divine Names.[10] If the Names are distinct, separate, ontologically autonomous entities then the vision of the oneness of being collapses. Hence the resolution of the multiplicity of the Names within the unity of the Essence lies at the core of the unitive vision of being, and of the vision of the One in the many and the many in the One. This is one reason why Kāshānī proceeds to stress the need for the negation of the multiplicity of the Names, to remove this 'stain' from

---

lā)—that is, by the non-existence of the multiple—for this very privation would undermine the principle of the infinitude of the One. Rather, the One is not conditioned by anything (*lā bi-sharṭ*), it is absolutely non-determined oneness, infinite Reality. It is not conditioned by the multiplicity or the relativity that it contains and manifests, nor is it conditioned by the simple negation of condition (*bi-sharṭ lā*); for, being beyond all condition, it must also be beyond that condition implied by the negation of condition. (I am grateful to Professor Hermann Landolt for his help in making this fundamental distinction clear to me.)

[10] Kāshānī refers repeatedly in the commentary to the degrees of *tawḥīd* pertaining to these three divine presences: Acts, Qualities and Essence; each has its spiritual station and each has its own types of veil. See for example, *Tafsīr*, vol. I, p. 7, the commentary on the opening of the first chapter, *al-Fātiḥa*; also, vol. I, p. 20; and vol. I, p. 78, where the Ḥajj is made to correspond to the manifestation of the Essence, and the ʿUmra, the lesser pilgrimage, to that of the Qualities; vol. I, p. 155; and vol. II, p. 8 which describes degrees of *taqwā*, that is pious 'protection' of the soul against not just vices and heedlessness, but also in respect of the 'veils' constituted by the divine Acts, Qualities and the Essence. This theme is taken up again at vol. II, p. 405 in an esoteric reading of a prophetic saying concerning seeking refuge in God. See also vol. II, p. 262, for the transcending of the consequences of *fanāʾ* in each of the three degrees.

the oneness of essential reality: 'For this reason, this chapter is named *al-ikhlāṣ* (purity, sincerity), for it is *ikhlāṣ* that removes all stain of multiplicity from the one reality.'

That is, it removes this 'stain' not from the One as such—since the One cannot by definition be affected by the multiple; rather, the removal or purification in question pertains to the human conception of the One. The purification of this perception paves the way for sincere or pure devotion, and, as will be seen below, for unitive extinction.

> 'As the Commander of the Faithful—upon whom be peace—says: "the perfection of *ikhlāṣ* in regard to Him is to divest Him of all Attributes[11] —because of the testimony of every Attribute that it is other than the object of attribution, and because of the testimony of every such object that it is other than the Attribute.'"

This famous sentence from the 'Commander of the Faithful' (*Amīr al-mu'minīn*) ʿAlī b. Abī Ṭālib—cousin and son-in-law of

[11] The word *ṣifa* can be translated either as 'attribute' or 'quality'. It is the *ṣifa* which is denoted by the 'Name' of God. A particular Name is understood as the Essence 'qualified' by a particular Attribute of the Essence. In classical Islamic theology there are ninety-nine divine Names; but in the school of Sufism we are considering here, all the phenomena in creation are also 'read' as so many divine 'words'. In Āmulī's commentary, the recurring theme of the concordance between the three 'books' containing 'verses' (*āyāt*) or 'signs'—that of the Qur'ān as a text, the cosmos as a text, and the soul as a text—is based on the following verse: *We shall show them Our signs* (āyāt) *on the horizons and in their own souls, so that it become clear to them that He is the Real* (XLI: 53). This is one of the central foundations of his esoteric exegesis, whereby 'reading' one's own soul is an integral part of reading correctly the 'sign' in the cosmos. See especially *Muḥīṭ*, vol. I, pp. 206 ff. where he expounds the relationship between the external, macrocosmic verses 'on the horizons' (*fi'l-āfāq*) and the inner, microcosmic verses 'within your souls' (*fī anfusikum*). It is only when one attains the inner realities denoted by both sets of verses/signs that one will have access to 'knowledge of the being of the Real, and gnosis thereof, by way of mystical disclosure (*kashf*), and direct witnessing (*shuhūd*), and taste (*dhawq*)...' *Muḥīṭ*, vol. I, p. 248.

the Prophet, fourth caliph of Islam, and the first Shiʿi Imam—comes in sermon number 1 of the *Nahj al-balāgha*, compiled by al-Sharīf al-Raḍī (d. 404/1016).[12] Given that this sentence on the meaning of *ikhlāṣ* has such prominence here, in the chapter named *ikhlāṣ*, we need to dwell a little upon it, and try and discern its implications for the relationship between unity and multiplicity within the divine nature. To begin with, one should note that this apparent negation of the Attributes is to be seen in the light of the phrase that occurs earlier in the same sermon: 'He Whose Attribute has no delimited boundary' (*alladhī laysa li-ṣifatihi ḥadd maḥdūd*). Thus, when the Imam says that *ikhlāṣ* requires divesting God of all Attributes (*nafy al-ṣifāt ʿanhu*), the negation here is not of the divine Attributes or Qualities as such, rather, it is a negation of them as separate, autonomous or super-added realities, conceived of as being substantially 'other than' or ontologically distinct from, the Essence of God. For the reality of God's *ṣifa*, or Attribute, is clearly affirmed in the earlier phrase: it is His Attribute which has no delimited boundary. What is denied is the possibility of confining the reality of any Attribute of God within any boundaries defined by human conception and language. Since no divine Attribute is separate from the divine nature, and since this nature is infinite, it follows that every Attribute is likewise of infinite scope and thus beyond all the limitations that are presupposed by formal conception and linguistic definition. This does not mean that the divine Attributes are mere names that tell us nothing about the divine nature; were this the case, the divine Names and Attributes

[12] It is important to recognise the importance of this sermon, and the *Nahj al-balāgha* as a whole in the formation of negative or apophatic theology in Islam, and of the role attributed to Imam ʿAlī in the Sufi tradition. See for a complete translation, *Peak of Eloquence*, by Sayed Ali Reza (New York: Tahrike Tarsile Qur'an, 1996). The following paragraphs are based upon the commentary accompanying my own translation of this sermon, due to be published in my forthcoming *Justice and Remembrance—Introducing the Spirituality of Imam ʿAlī* (London: I. B. Tauris/Institute of Ismaili Studies, 2006).

given in the Qur'ān would be redundant. The Qur'ān tells us, for instance, that:

> *He is God, other than Whom there is no god, the Knower of the hidden and the seen. He is the Infinitely Good, the All-Merciful. He is God, other than Whom there is no god, the King, the Holy, Peace, the Keeper of Faith, the Guardian, the Majestic, the All-Compelling, the Supreme. Glorified be God above all that they ascribe as partner* [to Him]. *He is God, the Creator, the Maker, the Fashioner. His are the Names most beautiful. All that is in the heavens and the earth glorifieth Him. And He is the Mighty, the Wise* (LIX: 22–24).

Needless to say, in the Imam's worldview and in the perspective of the Sufis, these Names and Attributes are of inestimable value in conveying something of the nature of divine Reality, and in providing objects of contemplation and invocation. But the type of apophatic discourse in question now is clearly intended to highlight the utter incommensurability between human *conceptions* of the divine Reality and that Reality *in itself*. This, it would appear, is what Kāshānī wishes to underline in quoting the Imam at this point of his commentary.[13]

To continue now with Kāshānī's commentary: 'This is what was meant by those who say, "His Attributes are neither He nor other than He"—that is, not He from the point of view of the intellect, and not other than He in respect of reality.'

---

[13] It is interesting to note what Ibn Maytham, author of a spiritual commentary on the *Nahj al-balāgha* says about this part of the sermon. It reflects, he writes, 'what is proven in the science of spiritual journeying to God' (*fī ʿilm al-sulūk ilā'Llāh*): the negation of all human, mental constructs is a pre-requisite for the realization of spiritual truth; human consciousness must first be shorn of all that is 'other than God' before the light of ultimate reality can be reflected in it. This principle, he says, is expressed in the very words of the first testimony of Islam, 'No god but God': the negation (*al-nafy*) precedes the affirmation (*al-ithbāt*). Kamāl al-Dīn b. Maytham al-Baḥrānī, *Sharḥ Nahj al-balāgha* (Beirut: Dār al-Thaqalayn, 1999), vol. 1, p. 144.

The oneness of the divine Essence does not so much negate the Names and the Attributes as comprise them within itself in undifferentiated mode; it is thus the aspect of plurality or multiplicity that is negated, not the intrinsic realities denoted by the Attributes themselves, for those realities are rooted in the one Reality. In this light, *ikhlāṣ* the process of 'purifying' devotion of the 'stain' of multiplicity, is seen as a reflection, on the plane of human conception, of this absolute oneness on the plane of metaphysical reality. To be 'pure' and 'sincere' in devotion and orientation means to negate all trace of metaphysical 'impurity'—that is, ontological alterity and autonomy, anything that can in any way be distinctively conceived apart from the one and only reality of God. Insofar as the Attributes are conceived apart from God, they are in that very measure, 'other than He', as Kāshānī says above. In other words, they are unreal if they are conceived by the mind as distinctive, separate, autonomous qualities.

Ibn ʿArabī sums up this point in the following words: '. . . the Names have two connotations; the first connotation is God Himself Who is what is named, the second that by which one Name is distinguished from another. . . As being essentially the other, the Name is the Reality, while as being not the other, it is the imagined Reality.'[14]

But from the viewpoint of Reality, which transcends the concepts proper to the mind, the Attributes are in fact nothing but God: in their intrinsic reality, they are absolutely identical to the Essence, while outwardly, they constitute so many pathways

[14] Austin, *Bezels*, p. 125. Also in the *Fuṣūṣ* we have the following important affirmation: 'the Cosmos is but a fantasy without any real existence. . . know that you are an imagination as is all that you regard as other than yourself an imagination. All existence is an imagination within an imagination, the only Reality being God, as Self and Essence, not in respect of His Names.' (*Ibid.*, pp. 124-125) On the subject of the divine Names, see Chittick, 'Divine Names and Theophanies' in M. Chodkiewicz (ed.), *Les Illuminations de La Mecque/The Meccan Illuminations* (Paris: Sindbad, 1988), pp. 77-116. And also Chittick, *Sufi Path of Knowledge*, pp. 33-77, for an important presentation of the different classifications of the Names adopted by Ibn ʿArabī.

by which this transcendent Essence enters into relationship with the created, relative order. That which 'relates' to the relative is single, but since relativity is multiple, the relationships become multiple.[15] Thus we have a resolution of the outward multiplicity of phenomena within the single reality of God by means of the relationships constituted by the divine Names: since all of these Names are relationships and not entities in themselves, they are nothing but the one Reality, intrinsically; thus, the vision of the oneness of being within the very multiplicity of the created order is maintained, and 'there is nothing in being but God' (*laysa fi'l-wujūd siwa'Llāh*) according to the Akbarī formula.

This vision implies a conceptual distinction, however, within the One: that is, between the One in itself and the One in relation to the many—it is the same One, but considered in different respects. When the One is considered in relation to the multiplicity of the created order, it appears as multiple—that is, it takes on or assumes the diverse qualities which constitute the ontological roots of created phenomena. This theme is addressed by Kāshānī in the following comment on the word *aḥad* and the difference between it and *wāḥid*:

> 'The word *aḥad* is a predicate of the subject (*Huwa, Allāh*). The difference between *al-Aḥad* and *al-Wāḥid* is that *al-Aḥad* is the unique Essence, without considering the multiplicity it contains, that is, it is pure Reality, the source of the Fountain of *Kāfūr*, or rather it is this Fountain itself.[16] It is Being *per se*, not determined by the general or the particular, nor conditioned by accidentality or non-accidentality.' As for *al-Wāḥid*, 'this is the Essence considered in relation to the plurality of Attributes, and

[15] Ibn ʿArabī writes that the Names designate relationships, which are intelligible, 'non-ontological realities'; therefore the Essence does not become multiple through them, since a thing can only become multiple through ontological entities, not through properties, attributions and relationships.' Chittick, *Sufi Path of Knowledge*, p. 52.

[16] This fountain is mentioned in LXXVI: 5, which will be discussed below.

it is the Presence of the Names (*al-ḥaḍra al-asmā'iyya*) for the reality of a Name is the Essence together with the Attribute. So the pure Reality—unknown to any but Him—is expressed by the word *Huwa*, and its substitution by (or equivalence to) the Essence together with all the Attributes shows that they (the Attributes) are identical to the one and only Essence in reality. And exclusive oneness (*aḥadiyya*) is predicated of this reality in order to show that the subjectively perceived plurality (*al-kathra al-iʿtibāriyya*) within it is nothing in reality.'

The meaning of this important passage can be elucidated by reference to what Kāshānī says in his commentary on another Qur'ānic chapter, named *al-Kawthar*. This word literally means abundance, and is from the same root as *kathra*, manyness or plurality. The chapter—the shortest in the Qur'ān—is addressed directly to the Prophet:

> *Truly We have bestowed upon you al-Kawthar.*[17] *So pray to thy Lord and sacrifice. Truly it is thine insulter who is cut off from posterity.* (CVIII: 1-3)

Kāshānī comments on the first verse by saying that *al-Kawthar* comprises 'the knowledge of multiplicity in oneness, and the science of differentiated *tawḥīd*, and the witnessing of oneness in the very midst of multiplicity, through the theophanic manifestation of the "multiple One" (*al-wāḥid al-kathīr*) and the "unique multiplicity" (*al-kathīr al-wāḥid*)... *So pray to thy Lord and sacrifice*, that is, when you witness the One in the midst of the multiple; *so pray* by establishing complete prayer, through

[17] In Bayḍāwī's commentary, we are told that *al-Kawthar* is described by the Prophet in a *ḥadīth* as being 'a river in the Garden which my Lord has promised me, one in which there is abundant (*kathīr*) good, which is sweeter than honey, whiter than milk, cooler than snow, smoother than cream; its banks are of chrysolite, its banks are of silver; whoever drinks from it shall never thirst.' *Tafsīr al-Bayḍāwī* (Beirut: Dār al-Fikr, 1996), vol. v, p. 536. (The saying is found in the collection of Tirmidhī.)

contemplation of the spirit, presence of the heart, submission of the soul, obedience of the body; by performing the motions [of prayer] in the temples of worship: that, truly, is perfect prayer, one which fulfils the obligations of synthesis and differentiation *(al-jamʿ wa'l-tafṣīl)*.[18]

Thus we are invited to contemplate the vision of the One in the many, and the many in the One. It is not a question of a simple alternative between oneness and multiplicity, for oneness is not absent from multiplicity, and for its part, multiplicity is contained metaphysically within oneness. Nor is it a question of an abstract unity opposing a concrete multiplicity of phenomena, nor of a real unity opposing a totally illusory multiplicity. A properly spiritual—as opposed to numerical, hence material—understanding of oneness does not need to negate the realm of multiple phenomena; rather, it fosters a perception of phenomena as so many projections or manifestations of oneness. From this perspective, one sees through the aspect of multiplicity to the real unity that each phenomenon replicates in its own way—to the oneness which gives it all its reality, and without which it is reduced to nothingness. To see the One in the many is thus to see the Real in the very heart of appearances, the Absolute in the relative: all relativities are thus so many projections of the one and only reality. And to see the many in the One is to perceive, on the one hand, that the One embraces all as *al-Muḥīṭ*, 'the All-Encompassing'; and on the other hand, it is to intuit the roots of all phenomena 'on high', that is, within the Absolute; it is thus to re-integrate[19] all phenomena within their unique source. The One is both absolute—hence exclusive of all relativity; and it is infinite—hence inclusive of all existence. As was observed in Chapter I, in connection with Ibn ʿArabī's fundamental statement on the completeness of being: the very infinitude or completeness of being requires finitude or incompleteness. The quality of absoluteness thus 'requires'

[18] *Tafsīr*, vol. II, p. 419.

[19] In the sense of to 'make one'—the literal meaning of *tawḥīd*, as was noted in Chapter I.

relativity if it is to be absolute, and to say relativity is to say multiplicity.

This implies that the initial denial of relativity/multiplicity (*lā ilāha*) in the face of absolute oneness must be followed by an affirmation of that same relativity/multiplicity within that oneness (*illa'Llāh*): one thus returns to phenomena, but no longer as simple expressions of finitude, rather, as so many loci of divine Self-disclosure—so many *maẓāhir* (sing. *maẓhar*) of the *ẓuhūr* or *tajallī* of the Real. We shall return to this central concept in the metaphysics of the school of Ibn ʿArabī below. At this point, discussion turns to the fountain of *Kāfūr*, mentioned above by Kāshānī in relation to the divine Name, *al-Aḥad: 'al-Aḥad* is the unique Essence, considered apart from the multiplicity it contains, that is, it is pure Reality, the source of the fountain of *Kāfūr*, or rather it is this Fountain itself.'

The fountain of *Kāfūr* is mentioned in a passage in the *Sūrat al-Insān*, one in which a distinction is made between the righteous (*al-abrār*) and the slaves of God (*ʿibād Allāh*): *Truly the righteous shall drink from a filled cup* [containing a drink] *flavoured with* Kāfūr—*A fountain from which the slaves of God drink, making it flow with greater abundance* (LXXVI: 5–6). Kāshānī interprets this fountain as a symbol of the divine Essence, beyond the divine Qualities. The righteous, he writes, 'are the joyous ones who have gone beyond the veils of traces and actions, and are now veiled by the veils of the divine Qualities. But they do not completely stop at this level; rather, their orientation is towards the Fountain of the Essence... they are midway along the Path.'

The slaves, on the other hand, who drink directly from the fountain itself, without diluting the drink at all, are distinguished by their exclusive devotion to the unity of the Essence. 'Their love is for the Fountain of the Essence beyond the Qualities, not differentiating between compulsion and kindness, gentleness and harshness... Their love abides in the midst of contraries, their joy remains in the face of graces and trials, compassion and distress...'[20]

[20] *Tafsīr*, vol. II, pp. 360–361.

Now it is important to see that these 'slaves' not only love the Fountain of the Essence: they are submerged in it. The words of the Qur'ān powerfully evoke this mystery: *A fountain from which the slaves of God drink, making it flow with greater abundance.* They make the fountain flow all the more abundantly, the more they drink from it, since, according to Kāshānī, the slaves 'are [themselves] the sources of this Fountain; there is no duality or otherness... were it otherwise, it would not be the Fountain of *Kāfūr*, because of the darkness of the veil of egoity (*anā'iyya*) and duality.'[21]

There is no ego-consciousness in the Essence, for there are no distinct egos, although all are nonetheless mysteriously contained by the Essence, in absolute non-differentiation; there is but the one Self, the *Nafs al-Ḥaqq*, the Self of the Real.[22]

The drinking of the 'slaves of God' at the fountain of the Essence—together with the fact that such drinking only increases the flow of the fountain—symbolises their inner identity with the Essence, but as individuals, they remain distinct in the various levels of Paradise. And, one might venture to add, in the spirit of Kāshānī's perspective, this is not just the case in the Hereafter, it is also the situation herebelow: the prophets and the saints are inwardly at one with the Essence, while outwardly, as slaves, they imbibe from this fountain, the source of essential identity,

---

[21] *Ibid.* Āmulī refers to a saying of Imam ʿAlī which mentions a special wine which God reserves for His 'friends': they drink it, and are taken through a series of states (inebriation, aspiration, finding, etc) finally culminating in the realization that 'there is no difference between them and their Beloved.' He proceeds to cite the verse above, together with others in which 'drinking' in the various Gardens are mentioned (LXXXIII: 28; LXXVI: 21; LXXXIII: 25-26). See also Abū Bakr Sirāj ad-Dīn, *The Book of Certainty* (Cambridge: Islamic Texts Society, 1996), pp. 85-89, for an insightful discussion of this passage in Kāshānī's commentary.

[22] On this Self of the Real, Ibn ʿArabī writes: 'The degree of the essential perfection is in the Self of the Real, while the degrees of accidental perfection are in the Gardens... Ranking according to excellence takes place in accidental perfection, but not in essential perfection.' Chittick, *Sufi Path of Knowledge*, p. 366.

the one and only Self of the Real. Now it is possible to see an analogy between the distinctiveness of the different souls and that of the divine Names and Attributes. Where the soul or the Attribute is affirmed as such, the Essence is infinitely 'other', the Attribute is reduced to an 'imagined' or relative reality; but where there is total effacement of the soul (or the inward negation of the Attribute—a negation which is in fact a sublimation, as it carries the Attribute 'inward' and 'upward' towards its source), then there is absolute identity with the Essence. Thus, the essential identity between 'pure Reality' and the Fountain of *Kāfūr*—asserted in the passage on the *Sūrat al-Ikhlāṣ*—mirrors the identity between the 'slaves of God' and this Fountain, as affirmed in the commentary on this passage in the *Sūrat al-Insān*.

Let us now return briefly to the phrase *al-kathra al-iʿtibāriyya*, used by Kāshānī in the passage cited above: exclusive oneness (*aḥadiyya*), he says, is predicated of ultimate Reality in order to show that the 'subjectively perceived plurality (*al-kathra al-iʿtibāriyya*) within it is nothing in reality.' The term *al-kathra al-iʿtibāriyya* is difficult to render concisely into English. The root of the word *iʿtibār* is *ʿabara*, to cross over. It comes to mean, among other things, to 'regard' or 'consider' a thing from a particular point of view. Thus it can mean 'relative to' a particular view-point. In the sentence above, the phrase *al-kathra al-iʿtibāriyya* can thus mean that plurality can be perceived within unity, from a certain relative and subjective point of view; but this plurality, *qua* plurality—that is, in its exclusively empirical, numerical, phenomenal aspect—is in fact an illusion, arising, precisely, out of the point of view of 'other' than God—and this 'other' is illusory, God's oneness being absolute. When, as seen above, plurality is viewed in its principial aspect, as expressing the unique principle, it is re-endowed with the reality that was veiled by the appearance of crude, empirical multiplicity, or of ontological plurality. This ontological plurality, in its purely phenomenal, empirical aspect, can thus be seen as 'polytheism' in the metaphysical, rather than simply theological sense; whereas theologically the false god is a human creation, metaphysically, the false god is each and every phenomenon which is abusively endowed with ontological self-sufficiency.

Kāshānī continues by asserting that as this subjectively posited plurality is nothing in reality, 'it does not negate the exclusive oneness (of the Real) nor does it leave a trace on its onliness (*waḥdatuhu*); for the presence of inclusive oneness (*al-wāḥidiyya*) is in its essence identical to the presence of exclusive oneness, in reality. This is akin to the illusion of drops of water in the ocean.'

The ocean is indivisible, the water constituting its identity is undifferentiated. But an illusion of separativity can be conjured up if one conceives of the ocean not as it is in itself, but as innumerable drops. Then, the reality of oneness is lost, and an imagined multiplicity takes its place. But the vision of oneness is regained as soon as one realizes that the imagined multiplicity is nothing other than the real unity—the drops are nothing other than the ocean, deriving their being from that unity, and only separable from it from a conceptual viewpoint. Viewed apart from the ocean, the drops are but drops, and thus utterly other than the ocean; but viewed in their totality, the drops are absolutely indistinguishable from it—they are the ocean, and the ocean is them.

This consubstantiality between the drops and the ocean, however, does not imply any equality[23] between multiplicity and unity, for the unity of the ocean can be conceived as

[23] An equality that would imply pantheism: the doctrine that everything in the cosmos is God, and God is the cosmos. The symbol of the ocean shows its inadequacy here, for the ocean is nothing more than the sum of its parts, whereas the cosmos in its entirety is but the manifestation of an infinitesimal dimension of the divine totality. The divine transcendence strictly implies that the whole of creation is reduced to nothing in the face of the Essence. The creature may be the Real, in one respect, but it never ceases to be a 'slave' in its own right: As Ibn ʿArabī says, the slave remains always the slave. It is interesting to note that Eckhart also uses the image of the drop and the ocean, doing so in order to evoke both the immanence and transcendence of God: 'If you were to cast a drop into the ocean, the drop would become the ocean, and not the ocean the drop. Thus it is with the soul: when she

such without need of any conception of the multiplicity of the drops; its reality is absolutely independent of any 'other'—whether real or imagined. But the converse is not true, for the multiple drops cannot be identified with reality—the ocean—except on condition of being 'dissolved' within that ocean; for as drops they are infinitesimally tiny units, only as the ocean are they one immeasurable vastness. Thus, the 'reality' pertaining to multiplicity is totally dependent upon the reality of unity, whereas the reality of unity is not contingent upon multiplicity, even if unity implies multiplicity.[24] When the drops are no longer viewed as such—that is, as determinate, individual, delimited and thus exclusive entities—they can rightly be referred to as the ocean. Viewed in its own right, then, or on its own account, multiplicity is an illusion; but viewed in its inner substance, it is not other than unity. It is for this reason that Kāshānī writes that the presence of inclusive oneness—multiplicity comprised within unity—is in reality identical to the presence of exclusive oneness.

Continuing with the commentary on the *sūrat al-Ikhlāṣ*: '*God, the eternally besought* (*al-Ṣamad*), that is, the Essence in the presence of inclusive oneness, in relation to the Names, is the absolute foundation of all things, because of the insufficiency of every contingent thing in relation to It; and because the very existence of things comes about through It. So It is the absolutely Rich (*al-Ghaniyy*), of which all things are in need, as He says

imbibes God, she is turned into God, so that the soul becomes divine, but God does not become the soul.' *Meister Eckhart*, vol. II, p. 323.

[24] In other terms: the Absolute is independent; but at the same time, its very absoluteness 'requires' the relative in order to be absolute. Ibn ʿArabī writes: 'Independence from creation belongs to God from eternity without beginning, while poverty toward God in respect of His Independence belongs to the possible thing in the state of its non-existence from eternity without beginning.' Chittick, *Sufi Path of Knowledge*, p. 64. But the very infinitude of God still requires finitude if it is to be infinite; hence, the oneness of the infinite 'requires' the multiplicity of the finite, such multiplicity bearing witness to that oneness in the same way that the finite bears witness to the infinite.

And God is the Rich and ye are the poor (XLVII: 38). Everything apart from Him is existent through His being, it is nothing in itself, because possibility (*imkān*)—which is the inseparable concomitant of every quiddity (*māhiyya*)—does not entail being, so no thing is of the same genus as being, nor is it similar to it.'

Kāshānī employs here an argument based on Avicennan ontology. The quiddity or essence (literally: what-it-is-ness) of every possible thing (*mumkin al-wujūd*) is distinct from the being of that thing. In God alone, or necessary being (*wājib al-wujūd*), quiddity and being are absolutely inseparable: God's being is His essence, and His essence is His being.[25] All other beings have specific, delimited quiddities, to which being is added, thus rendering them existent entities. But being is itself never entailed by any possible quiddity, it is bestowed upon it as a possibility, not as a necessity, hence Kāshānī's statement, 'possibility—which is the inseparable concomitant of every quiddity—does not entail being'. Thus the contingent possibility proper to every quiddity renders it 'poor' in relation to the source of its existentiation.

Ibn ʿArabī presents us with a metaphysical drama to express this 'poverty' of contingent beings in relation to the divine Names, and at the same time shows the paradoxical 'poverty' of the divine Names in relation to them:

> 'In the state of their nonexistence the possible things asked the divine Names—an asking through their state of abasement and poverty—as follows: "Nonexistence has blinded us, so we are not able to perceive one another or to know what God requires you to do with us. If you were to make manifest our entities and clothe them in the robe of existence, you would be doing us a favor, and we would undertake the appropriate veneration and reverence. Moreover, your sovereignty becomes genuine through our becoming manifest in actuality. Today you possess sovereignty over us only potentially and virtually.

[25] See, for an introduction to Avicennan ontology, S. H. Nasr, *Introduction to Islamic Cosmological Doctrines* (London: Thames & Hudson, 1978), pp. 197-214.

> What we seek from you is what you should be seeking to an even greater degree from us." The Names replied, "What the possible things have said is correct". So they fell to seeking the same thing.'[26]

Returning to the commentary: '*He begets not*, for His effects are not existent along with Him, but through Him, hence they are nothing in themselves. *And He is not begotten*, because of His absolute eternity; so He cannot have been in need of anything, in respect of being; and because His unique identity is subject neither to multiplicity nor division, nor can this essential oneness be conjoined to anything other than itself, for everything apart from absolute Being is but sheer nothingness, so nothing is similar to it: *And there is nothing similar to Him*, for pure nothingness is not similar to pure Being. It is for this reason that this chapter is [also] called 'the foundation' (*al-asās*), for *tawḥīd* is the foundation of religion, indeed, it is the foundation of being. . . '

Kāshānī's commentary demonstrates the vast gulf that separates the exoteric from the esoteric understanding of *tawḥīd*. It is not so much a question of the one being denied or contradicted by the other; it is rather a deepening of the meaning of the fundamental message of Islam, as summed up in its credal formula: no god but God. In this, the first testimony of Islam, false gods are negated and the one true God is affirmed. In the ontological application of the principle, it is not only false gods that are negated but the apparent and independent reality of all things—that is, all *appearances*—is denied, and the divine reality alone is affirmed—that which neither appears nor disappears, but always is, above and beyond all appearances.

If we were to stop here, we would have a view of reality as transcendent, surpassing and negating all relativities, all

[26] See Chittick, *Sufi Path of Knowledge*, pp. 52–54.

existent things, all appearances. In these terms, manifestation is unreal, the non-manifest Essence alone is real. But, in the context defined by Kāshānī, this is only part of the explicit metaphysical significance of the first *shahāda*. The second *shahāda*, *Muḥammadun rasūlu'Llāh*, completes the doctrinal formulation, making explicit what is implied in the affirmation *illa'Llāh*. In other words: form, appearance, the 'perfect man', the cosmos as a whole, is the manifestation of the Essence. That which appears in manifest form is thus re-endowed with reality: in theological terms the creature expresses something of the Creator; in metaphysical terms, manifestation is nothing but the Essence manifested. What emerges in this vision of oneness is a discernment between degrees of reality, all of which are encompassed by the one and only Reality. It implies going beyond appearances, in one respect, and also to return to them, but to return to them in depth and not on the surface. The transient, separative, illusory aspect of appearance, of manifestation, is sacrificed at the altar of transcendent Reality; but then the aspect of the Real that in-forms the appearance is, as it were, resurrected as immanent presence. The Absolute must be distinguished from the relative, in the first place; but the relative must also be grasped in the light of the Absolute, that is, as a ray projected by the sun of the Absolute. The Absolute is infinite, and as such projects itself within relativity, that relativity which is the dimension of finitude, which, in turn, is strictly implied by infinitude. In other words, the roots of the relative are in the Absolute—without this implying any elevation of relativity to the status of absoluteness; and on the other hand, the Absolute projects itself by means of relativity—without this in any way compromising its absoluteness.

So whereas a theological interpretation of the first testimony of Islam stops short at negating other 'gods' and affirming the one and only God; and whereas a partial ontological viewpoint goes further, by negating the multiplicity of outward phenomena, and affirming the one and only reality; an integral ontological conception goes further still: it both negates *and* affirms the multiple phenomena in the vision of the one and only Reality. The One, therefore, does not simply negate or transcend the many; rather, it projects, embraces, encompasses, penetrates and re-integrates the many: phenomenal multiplicity is thus not just the manifestation of the One, it is an integral dimension of it—'integral' here in the sense that the One integrates within itself all multiplicity.

Just as, on the plane of phenomena generally, the differentiated cosmos in its entirety is the outward manifestation of the infinite perfections of the One, so, in regard to humankind, human diversity is the expression of the immeasurable potentialities of the human soul: the soul is one in essence, but unlimited—and unrepeatable—in its expressions. Humanity is the defining reality of each human soul; every soul is thus humanity as such. Not only are all souls created from one single soul, (unity deploying multiplicity) but the resurrection of the whole of humanity after death, also, is akin to the resurrection of a single soul (multiplicity integrated within unity): *Your creation and your resurrection are but as a single soul* (xxxi: 28). Therefore, we are told that whoever kills a person unlawfully, *it is as if he had killed the whole of mankind, and whoever saves the life of a person, it is as if he had saved the whole of mankind* (v: 32).

While it is clear that the One, the unconditional Real, is infinitely greater than the sum of the parts of the cosmos, it is nonetheless also the case that the One is present within each and every part, each 'thing' in the cosmos, and this is what gives reality to each 'thing', rendering it unique, irreplaceable and sacred. Universal reality is more than the sum of all particulars; nonetheless, each particular makes present the Universal, embodying it concretely in a mode that distinguishes it from all other particulars. Thus, the other—in its very aspect of otherness, that is, its difference from the self—is to be respected, and accorded not just tolerance, but a dignity commensurate with its ontological status: the One and only Real is truly present in the other, and makes manifest therein a unique configuration of Its own infinite qualities.

Discussion now turns to themes more directly related to dialogue. It is hoped that this discussion can be appreciated in greater depth against the background of the metaphysics of oneness given above.

Self-Disclosure and Human Diversity

Turning now to other commentaries, both formal and informal, the concomitants of this ontological perspective on oneness can be articulated in terms more immediately relevant to the situation of human diversity. Specifically *religious* diversity, and its relationship to the essence of the religious phenomenon, will be addressed in the following chapter. The focus at present is on the philosophical implications of this *ontological* view of oneness for the theme of diversity and dialogue.

We can begin by referring to the perspective of Sayyid Ḥaydar Āmulī (d. 787/1385). The shift from 'theological' *tawḥīd* (*al-tawḥīd al-ulūhī*) to 'ontological' *tawḥīd* (*al-tawḥīd al-wujūdī*)[27] is one of the hallmarks of this important figure, in whose works one observes a remarkable synthesis between Shiʿi gnosis and Sufi metaphysics.[28] He refers to the 'folk of the outward (*ahl al-ẓāhir*) who pronounce the formula *lā ilāha illa'Llāh* in the sense conveyed by the following Qur'ānic verse, an exclamation by the polytheists of the strangeness of the idea of affirming one deity: *does he make the gods one God? This is a strange thing* (XXXVIII: 5). This monotheistic affirmation is, for Āmulī, the essence of the *tawḥīd* professed by the folk of the exterior, and is called 'theological' *tawḥīd* (*al-tawḥīd al-ulūhī*). In contrast, the 'folk of the inward (*ahl al-bāṭin*) negate the multiplicity of

[27] Sayyid Haydar Āmulī, *Kitāb jāmiʿ al-asrār wa-manbaʿ al-anwār* (*La philosophie Shi'ite*), eds. H. Corbin & O. Yahia (Tehran & Paris: Bibliothèque Iranienne, 1969), p. 72.

[28] Corbin writes that Āmulī's work 'constitutes one of those corpuses where one is able to see a Shiʿism conscious of being in its essence, the esoterism of Islam'. *En Islam iranien*, vol. II, p. 149.

existences, and affirm the sole reality of divine Being; their formula is: 'there is nothing in existence apart from God (*laysa fi'l-wujūd siwa'Llāh*)' and they cite the verse *Everything is perishing save His Face* (XXVIII: 88) in support of their comprehension of the principle. This, Āmulī, maintains, is 'ontological' *tawḥīd* (*al-tawḥīd al-wujūdī*).[29]

Despite the fact that the terms used here are original to Āmulī, the ontological shift in question is of course central to the earlier work of Kāshānī and the school of Ibn ʿArabī generally. What makes Āmulī's work interesting, and not a simple repetition of that of his forebears, is his application of the Akbarī perspective within the framework of central Shiʿi beliefs, on the one hand; and, on the other—more pertinent to the discussion in question—the manner in which he elucidates this perspective by means of his commentary on the Qur'ān, *al-Muḥīṭ al-aʿẓam*. In this section we shall briefly examine his commentary in relation to the theme of oneness and manyness; and in the following section, the radical implications of the idea of 'hidden polytheism' for dialogue will be discussed.

The Akbarī principle that the perfection of being requires imperfection has been discussed; but Āmulī brings to light a slightly different point, following on from this one: the creation itself manifests both the differentiation of phenomena *and* the non-differentiation of their unique source. This idea is given in connection with the words of the following verses: *They cease not differing... for this did He create them* (XI: 118-119).[30] He writes, in the passage preceding his citation of this verse, which is given as a kind of confirmation of the theme he is expounding: 'There is no differentiation in being itself, though the loci of theophanic manifestation differ, as do their degrees, in accordance with the perfections that are concomitants of the essence of Being. This is so because the Names are actualised in accordance with the divine Qualities, and these Qualities accord with the

[29] Āmulī, *Jāmiʿ al-asrār*, p. 72.

[30] Āmulī, *Muḥīṭ*, vol. 1, p. 407. The ellipse comprises the words *save him on whom thy Lord hath mercy.*

perfections, and the perfections are necessary concomitants of the Essence. Just as the Essence necessitates manifestation (*ẓuhūr*), so manifestation necessitates differentiation in the loci of manifestation (*maẓāhir* sing. *maẓhar*); and the differences among these loci of manifestation are identical to concordances among the realities (*ḥaqā'iq*).'[31]

The realities, being rooted in the perfections of the Essence, have but one ontological substratum, and are thus undifferentiated in essence; the loci or receptacles of manifestation, on the other hand, are differentiated, because the manifestations never cease to flow forth, in unrepeatable forms, from the infinite perfections of the Essence. 'The Real does not manifest Itself twice in one form, nor in a single form to two individuals.'[32] So there is no such thing as repetition in manifestation. But the point being made by Āmulī here is more subtle: Just as the perfections are unique in their inner infinitude, and become multiple when projected into finite existence, so this uniqueness is itself reflected in the very midst of the diversity of the cosmos in the fact that there is no repetition in manifestation: each manifestation is new, unique, and thus 'original', in the sense that it bears testimony to the uniqueness of its origin. But then, because this origin is infinite, it is infinitely varied and diverse in its manifestations. We return to the theme of spiritual paradox: a uniqueness which manifests infinite diversity, and a diversity which reproduces uniqueness. The One is thus revealed within the many, without ceasing to be One, and the many 'proves' or demonstrates oneness, without ceasing, outwardly, to be many. Diversity is thus integral to unity, and unity is perpetually affirmed in diversity.

The differences in creation arise, from the point of view of relativity, out of the different receptivities (*qawābil*, sing. *qābila*) and modes of preparedness (*istiʿdād*) on the part of the loci of manifestation; whilst from the point of view of the Absolute,

[31] *Ibid.*, vol. 1, p. 406–7.

[32] *Ibid.*, vol. 1, p. 407.

they arise out of the infinite perfections of the Essence, which call forth and fashion these receptivities.[33] The substance of that which is rendered manifest is one. Thus diversity in phenomena and oneness of Reality are not contradictory, but complementary, each being an aspect of the other. Āmulī proceeds with the following important point, in a further comment on the verses 118-119 in *Sūra Hūd* (XI), cited above: 'If being had only a single mode, there would be no differentiation within it, no ranking in degrees and levels, either in form or spirit. It would not be complete within itself, nor would it unite the outward with the inward: rather, it would be deficient in itself, in need of an "other". Therefore it would depart from the quality of being necessary by essence, and enter into that of being possible by essence, for the condition of being in need of an "other", together with that of deficiency, are concomitants of possibility, not necessity.'[34]

God cannot be in need of an 'other', His unity strictly precluding this condition. Yet the differentiation we observe in existence—which is identical to oneness in its essence—means that God *does* have an 'other', an 'other' that is paradoxically within His own oneness. It is thus an apparent otherness. This is clarified by what Āmulī writes in connection with the verses describing God as *al-Muḥīṭ*, the All-Encompassing: that which encompasses and that which is encompassed cannot be separate from one another. This important point comes in the commentary on the words of the following verses: . . . *Does not*

[33] This process is referred to in the Akbarī school as *al-fayḍ al-aqdas*, the 'most holy effusion'; following which—in ontological rather than temporal terms—comes the *al-fayḍ al-muqaddas*, the 'holy effusion', the manifestation in existence of the qualities of the Real, corresponding to the receptivities of the pre-existential possibilities. For a good discussion of these themes see Toshihiko Izutsu, *Sufism and Taoism—A Comparative Study of Key Philosophical Concepts* (Berkeley: University of California Press, 1983), pp. 152-158. See also *al-Muḥīṭ*, vol. 1, pp. 392-393, where Āmulī refers to the two levels of theophany.

[34] *Al-Muḥīṭ*, vol. 1, p. 407.

thy Lord suffice, since He is witness over all things? Are they yet in doubt about the meeting with their Lord? Verily, is He not encompassing every thing? (XLI: 53–54) 'And which *meeting*', Āmulī comments, 'is more tremendous than witnessing Him in every thing, by mystical disclosure and vision, and attainment of Him by way of "taste" (*dhawqan*) and "finding" (*wijdānan*)? He is the witnessed in every thing, and the object that is witnessed in every thing cannot be expected to be seen or encountered in one specific thing or in a specific moment; this would be impossible, for the Encompasser (*al-Muḥīṭ*) of every thing cannot be witnessed except in *every* thing; because the universal, *qua* universal, does not manifest except universally... And it is known also that the Encompasser cannot be disengaged from the encompassed, nor can the encompassed be disengaged from the Encompasser, so the witnessing of the one necessitates the witnessing of the other.'

Āmulī proceeds to write that this is the 'secret' of the words of the verse: *He is the First and the Last, and the Outward and the Inward* (LVII: 3). And also of the words: *and wherever ye turn, there is the Face of God* (II: 115). 'For the *Face* is the perfect Essence', Āmulī continues, 'encompassing everything, as is indicated in His speech: *Everything is perishing save His Face, His is the Command, and to Him they are brought back* (XXVIII: 88). His determining will is thus: that is every thing apart from Him is perishing in itself, not abiding in any time or place; *His is the Command*, that is, unto Him pertains eternal subsistence, and *to Him they are brought back*.'[35]

Here again, we are told that, though the Real in itself is utterly beyond all location, transcending time and space, it so penetrates everything that it encompasses, that no thing in time or space can be 'disengaged' from the Real: thus, God is witnessed in no particular thing to the exclusion of another, for He is witnessed in everything, excluding nothing. One cannot see 'the encompassed' without simultaneously 'seeing' the Encompasser,

[35] *Ibid.*, vol. I, pp. 330–331.

and *vice versa*; however, this 'vision' in the fullest sense can only be attained through mystical disclosure: the simple empirical vision of phenomena as such cannot be crudely equated with the concrete perception of the divine *Face* in all things. This does not preclude the possibility that outward vision of the cosmos can in fact be accompanied by a deeper intuition of the holiness that inheres therein, an intuition fostered by the initial conceptual or intellectual apprehension of the principle being proposed here. We shall return to this point below, in connection with Ghazālī's commentary on the verse of Light.

Within existence, then, there are degrees and levels of reality, but all of these are grounded in and encompassed by the one and only Reality, for 'there is nothing in being apart from God'. Now this formula in fact implies the following degrees within being, as we saw above: the Essence, the Qualities, the Names, the Acts and the effects or traces of these divine Acts—each degree of being constituting a locus of manifestation for the property of the degree superior to it, and the source of what is manifested within the degree inferior to it. Thus, the Qualities are at once the loci for the appearance of the perfections of the Essence, but they are also the veils that obscure the full reality of those perfections: they both reveal and veil the perfections of the Essence. And the same holds true for the Names in relation to the Qualities, the Acts in relation to the Names, and all created phenomena in relation to the Acts.[36] Thus we arrive at a vision of a hierarchy of veils and revelations, or, to use the words of a *ḥadīth* frequently quoted by Āmulī: 'God has seventy thousand veils of light and darkness.'[37]

---

[36] *Ibid.*, vol. 1, p. 321.

[37] See for example, *al-Muḥīt*, vol. 1, p. 311. It is found in a more complete form, where the following sentence is added: 'Were they to be removed, the glories of His Countenance would consume everything perceived by the sight of His creatures.' It is found in the *Sunan* of Ibn Māja, as noted by the editor (see note 70, p. 321). See Chittick, *Sufi Path of Knowledge*, pp. 217, 328, 364, 401 for Ibn ʿArabī's comments upon the saying. It is also

Understood in theological terms, this saying implies only that God is the Reality hidden behind these veils; but in Sufi metaphysics the saying is construed in a radically different manner: the veils themselves cannot be other than the Reality they apparently veil: so the veil not only hides, it also reveals. To appreciate this point more deeply, we can refer back to the verse cited above: *He is the First and the Last, and the Outward and the Inward* (LVII: 3). The whole of the external domain of existence is here understood as being nothing but the outward aspect of the divine nature: it is outward, but not ontologically 'other' than, or separate from, the other dimensions of the divine nature. Whereas God as *the First*, *the Last* and *the Inward* can be readily grasped, it is God as *the Outward*, the 'apparent' or 'evident' (*al-Ẓāhir*) that requires comment. For it is this outwardness that we need to understand as constituting not just the veil that hides God but also the revelation that discloses Him, failing which God cannot be regarded as 'the Outward'.

Let us turn to other informal 'commentaries' on the meaning of God's 'outwardness' or 'evidentness' provided by Sufi masters, before drawing out some of the implications of the divine Self-disclosure for dialogue and the other.

Mulay al-ʿArabī al-Darqāwī, founder of a major branch of the Shādhiliyya *ṭarīqa* in the nineteenth century, relates the following incident, which we can take as an indirect commentary on the verse, with a particular stress on the meaning of God's 'outwardness' or 'evidence'. He writes that he was 'in a state of remembrance' when he heard a voice recite the words of the verse.

> 'I remained silent, and the voice repeated it a second time, and then a third, whereupon I said: "As to *the First*, I understand, and as to *the Last*, I understand, and as to *the*

commented upon in detail by Ghazālī in his *Mishkāt al-anwār*, which will be discussed below.

> *Inwardly Hidden,*[38] I understand, but as to *the Outwardly Manifest*, I see nothing but created things." Then the voice said: "If there were any outwardly manifest other than Himself I should have told thee." In that moment I realized the whole hierarchy of absolute Being.'[39]

Insofar as being is one, the outward world, the manifest cosmos, created things, cannot be other than that being: they are manifestations of Being, therefore they are Being in manifest mode. We return to the dictum: there is nothing in being but God—but this oneness does not do away with hierarchy, for the 'traces' of being are not identical in every respect with being. Each drop may be water, we saw earlier, but water is not to be confined within any drop. Continuing with the theme of God's immanence within His manifestations, the following remarkable affirmations by Ibn ʿAṭā'illāh, an earlier Sufi master in the same *ṭarīqa* as Mulay al-ʿArabī, can also be read as an exegesis on the meaning of God's Name, *al-Ẓāhir*:

> 'How can it be conceived that something veils Him, since He is the one who manifests everything (*aẓhara kulla shay'*)?
> How can it be conceived that something veils Him, since He is the one who is manifest through everything (*ẓahara bi-kulli shay'*)?
> How can it be conceived that something veils Him, since He is the one who is manifest in everything (*ẓahara fī kulli shay'*)?
> How can it be conceived that something veils Him, since He is the Manifest to everything (*al-Ẓāhir li-kulli shay'*)?
> How can it be conceived that something veils Him, since He was the Manifest (*al-Ẓāhir*) before the existence of anything (*al-Ẓāhir qabla kulli shay'*)?

[38] This is the translation of *al-Bāṭin* in the text in which this report is translated by Lings; likewise, *al-Ẓāhir* is rendered as 'the Outwardly Manifest'.

[39] Cited in Lings, *Sufi Saint*, p. 131.

> How can it be conceived that something veils Him, since He is more manifest than anything (*aẓhar min kulli shay'*)? How can it be conceived that something veils Him, since He is the One (*al-Wāḥid*) alongside of whom there is nothing?'[40]

Nothing, then, can veil God; and yet, He *is* veiled—but only by a veil which is not other than Himself, for, in the words of the aphorism immediately preceding the above series, 'That which shows you the existence of His Omnipotence is that He veiled you from Himself by what has no existence alongside of Him.'[41] If, in one respect God veils Himself from His creatures by Himself, in another, more fundamental respect, He reveals Himself to Himself through His creatures. We return to the altogether pivotal function of self-disclosure, theophany, manifestation (*ẓuhūr, tajallī*) of divine Reality in, through, and as, the forms of created things, the cosmos in its entirety. Each phenomenon in creation cannot but constitute a locus of manifestation, a *maẓhar* for the *ẓuhūr* or *tajallī* of the Real; every created thing is grasped as a vehicle by which the Real discloses Itself to Itself, through an *apparent* 'other'. Thus we return to what was referred to above as at the ultimate metaphysical prototype of all 'dialogue'. What is in question is a kind of 'dialogue' or communication between different aspects of the Absolute, a dialogue mediated through relativity.

The idea of the self-disclosure of the Absolute to itself is implied in the verses noted so far; in particular, those proclaiming that God is both *the Outward and the Inward*, and that *wherever*

[40] *Ibn ʿAṭā'illāh's Sufi Aphorisms* (*Kitāb al-Ḥikam*) (tr. V. Danner), (Leiden: E. J. Brill, 1973), pp. 25-26.

[41] Cf. the Shaykh al-ʿAlawī's aphorism: 'It is not a question of knowing God when the veil be lifted, but of knowing Him in the veil itself.' Cited in Lings, *Sufi Saint*, p. 211. And also, the saying by Imam ʿAlī: 'Through things, their Creator manifests Himself to the intellects; and through things He is guarded from the sight of the eyes.' Al-Sharīf al-Raḍī, *Nahj al-balāgha*, ed. Shaykh ʿAzīzullāh al-ʿUtārdī (Tehran: Nahj al-Balāgha Foundation, 1993), p. 277; see Sayed Ali Reza's translation in *Peak of Eloquence*, p. 373.

ye turn, there is the Face of God. This *Face* is thus reflected in all things in the cosmos, including the most outward, material things in all their multiplicity, for, in the formula so often cited by Ibn ʿArabī, Kāshānī and Āmulī: 'in every thing is a sign (*āya*) showing that He is One'.[42] The idea here is clearly founded upon such verses as the following: *Truly, in the heavens and the earth are signs for the believers. And in your creation, and in all the beasts that He scattereth in the earth, there are signs for a people who are certain. And the difference of night and day, and the provision that God sendeth down from the sky and therewith revive the earth after its death, and the turning about of the winds—are signs for a people who comprehend* (XLV: 3–5).[43]

Every 'thing' is thus assimilated as a sign. Now whereas theologically this sign is totally and irreducibly distinct from that which is signalled—the creature is a sign of the creativity of its Creator—from the Sufi point of view, every sign in the cosmos functions both as a signal, pointing to something other than it, and as revealing in its own way, the *Face* of God that gives it all its reality. Thus, the sign is conceived from the point of view of the immanence as well as that of the transcendence of the divine Reality. The sign performs this double function inasmuch as it functions as a mirror that reflects the one and only *Face*—but doing so in a manner conforming to its own particularity, its own contours, its own colour and character. The Real thus discloses itself in a myriad ways: creation is seen as a magnificent, kaleidoscopic display of the reflections of the One—reflections that are, in one respect, infinitely diverse, and thus distinct, different from each other and from the Reality they reflect; but in another respect are nothing but that Reality. Self-

---

[42] *Al-Muḥīṭ*, vol. I, p. 226. The saying is attributed to Ibn ʿAtāhiyya (d. 310 AH). See note 21, pp. 226–7 by the editor of *Al-Muḥīṭ*, Sayyid Muḥsin Mūsawī al-Tabrīzī.

[43] There are many verses which refer to 'signs' (*āyāt*) in this all-encompassing sense. See XXX: 21–25 for another series of verses describing the phenomena of nature, each of which begins with the words, *And of His signs is this...*

disclosure thus gives rise to infinite variety and distinctiveness which, far from denying the oneness of what is revealed, are constitutive of the very process of the revelation of that oneness.

Self-disclosure, as we can see, lies at the very heart of the metaphysics of the school of Ibn ʿArabī.[44] The whole doctrine of this disclosure of God to Himself is summed up in the opening lines of Ibn ʿArabī's most commented text, *Fuṣūṣ al-ḥikam*.[45] The chapter entitled 'The Ringstone of the Wisdom of Divinity in the Word of Adam' begins:

> 'The Real willed, glorified be He, in virtue of His Beautiful Names, which are innumerable, to see their identities (*aʿyān*)—if you so wish you can say: to see His Identity (*ʿayn*)—in a comprehensive being that comprises the whole affair insofar as it is possessed of existence and His Mystery is manifest to Himself through it. For the vision a thing has of itself in itself is not like the vision a thing has of itself in another thing, which will be like a mirror for it. . .[46]

---

[44] 'The term *self-disclosure* (*tajallī*)—often translated as "theophany"—plays such a central role in Ibn ʿArabī's teachings that, before he was known as the great spokesman for *waḥdat al-wujūd*, he had been called one of the Companions of Self Disclosure (*aṣḥāb al-tajallī*).' Chittick, *The Self-Disclosure of God*, (Albany: State University of New York Press, 1998), p. 52.

[45] This text can also be seen as an esoteric commentary upon the Qur'ān inasmuch as most, if not all, of the important points are substantiated by Qur'ānic verses which abound in the work. See also Ronald L. Nettler, *Sufi Metaphysics and Qur'ānic Prophets—Ibn ʿArabī's Thought and Method in the* Fuṣūṣ al-Ḥikam (Cambridge: Islamic Texts Society, 2003) which demonstrates the centrality of the Qur'ān in Ibn ʿArabī's exposition. The same can be said for the *Futūḥāt*: see the large index of Qur'ānic verses provided by Chittick in his two books, *The Sufi Path of Knowledge*, and *The Self-Disclosure of God*.

[46] This is cited from a new translation of the *Fuṣūṣ al-ḥikam* by Caner Dagli, *The Ringstones of Wisdom* (Chicago: Kazi Publications, 2004), p. 3. This is the most accurate and reliable annotated translation of this seminal text in the English language. In this passage, the word *ʿayn* is translated as 'identity' whereas elsewhere in this text I have followed Chittick's translation, 'entity'.

Ibn ʿArabī continues with the above passage to refer to the cosmos as an 'unpolished mirror', and to the human being as the principle of reflection for that mirror, and as the spirit of its form. Man alone reflects back to the Absolute all, and not just some, of the divine Qualities; it is for this reason that man is the 'valid interlocutor', the receptacle and the most perfect mirror of the divine Qualities, the cognisant 'other' to whom and through whom these qualities are revealed. For not only does God make known to Himself His own perfections through man, He also sees through the eyes of those whom He created as contemplators, as witnesses. Ibn ʿArabī refers to this in terms of the very word *insān*, which means both 'human being' and 'pupil' of the eye.

According to Rūzbihān Baqlī (d. 606/1209), God sees Himself in the vision that the contemplator (*shāhid*) has of the divine Beauty, so the *shāhid* becomes also *mashhūd*, the object contemplated. God makes the individual soul the lover (*ḥabīb*) and the beloved (*maḥbūb*), the desirer (*murīd*) and the desired (*murād*), 'for God sees through the *shāhid* with the vision of eternity, His Attributes being bestowed upon the *shāhid*, but not by way of incarnation (*ḥulūl*), for the Real transcends all created, temporal things.'[47]

The difference between 'incarnation' and 'reflection' should be carefully noted in the passage quoted from Baqlī, as it points to a fundamental feature of the Sufi perception of the One in the many, a perception which does not in any way imply a reduction of the One to the many. Ibn ʿArabī's mirror-analogy helps one to understand better this perception, and at the same time furnishes us with an image by which the 'signs' of the

---

One feels that, in this passage at least, the word 'identity' conveys the sense intended by Ibn ʿArabī better than the word 'entity'.

[47] Rūzbihān Baqlī Shīrāzī, *Kitāb ʿabhar al-ʿāshiqīn*, eds. H. Corbin & M. Mo'in (Tehran: Intishārāt-i Manuchihrī, 1987), p. 134. See Corbin's excellent introduction to the Persian text and his translation into French of the first chapter of the work. Corbin also devotes one book to Rūzbihān in his magisterial *En Islam iranien*, *op. cit.*; this is book 3 in volume III.

cosmos can be seen, more profoundly, as so many 'faces' of God. For the divine Qualities are reflected in the cosmos in just the same way that an object is reflected on the surface of a mirror. It is the mirror that, in a sense, 'produces' the reflection—the object does not change, it remains what it is, it does not have to exert any influence other than that which derives from its *presence*: it simply has to be present before the mirror, and the mirror does the rest. Nothing is diminished from the object, nothing leaves it—there is no question here of incarnation; the substance of the mirror never comes to incorporate within itself anything of the material substance of the object it reflects: there is but one reality, for the reflection of that reality is not 'another' or separate reality, an existent entity in its own right, apart from the reality it reflects.[48]

This is a point which is made emphatically by the Sufis in order to avoid the accusation of *shirk*:[49] the presence of God really is 'in' the creature, but only in the sense that an image is really 'in' the mirror. There is no question of the glass of the mirror undergoing any material change as a result of the image that is present on its surface, nor is there any question of a material change or descent of the object into the mirror. Thus

[48] To the objection that there are in fact multiple realities, as the mirrors themselves are distinct from the object reflected, the Sufis of the *waḥdat al-wujūd* school would reply: the mirrors—the entities *aʿyān*—are defined essentially by their nonexistence, for 'they have never whiffed the scent of being'; their apparent existence is nothing but the being of God, which becomes defined by the receptivity (*istiʿdād*) of the entity in its immutable state of non-existence, wherein it abides solely within the knowledge of God. This mode of subsistence is compared to the 'existence' of ideas in the mind of a thinking person: they are intelligible to him, but have no existence in the objective world. See Chittick, *Sufi Path of Knowledge*, pp. 79-94; and his more extensive discussion of this theme in the chapter entitled '*Wujūd* and the Entities', pp. 3-47 in *Self-Disclosure*.

[49] The setting up of a 'partner' with God; idolatry, the worship of a false god. As will be seen shortly, this notion is treated by the Sufis with a particular nuance which renders the 'sin' in question very relevant to dialogue.

God remains absolutely transcendent, just as the object remains totally other than the mirror.

The analogy with the mirror combines perfectly the two principles of transcendence and immanence: the object and the mirror are totally separate, but the image seen in the mirror has no reality other than that of the object. The object is mysteriously one with the image, but the image is reduced to sheer nonexistence without the object: its reality is totally dependent upon the object, while the object is totally independent of the image. Just as God says in the Qur'ān that He is *nearer to him* [man] *than the jugular vein* (L: 16), so we can say that the object is closer to the reflected image than the image is to itself, in the sense that the image is more real as the object than it is in and as itself: its true identity is thus the object, not itself. Seeing things in this way helps us to grasp the meaning of the *ḥadīth qudsī* (a sacred utterance in which God speaks through the Prophet), which is so often quoted by the Sufis: 'My slave never ceases to draw near to Me through supererogatory acts until I love him. And when I love him, I am his hearing by which he hears, his sight by which he sees, his hand by which he grasps, and his foot by which he walks.'[50]

In terms of the mirror analogy, every property of the image is also and inescapably the property of the object, but the image remains what it is and the object remains what it is: 'It is impossible for realities to change, so the servant is servant, and the Lord Lord; the Real is the Real and the creature creature.'[51]

It should be stressed here that the function of an apparent 'other', within the process of the divine Self-disclosure of itself

---

[50] Kāshānī often cites this *ḥadīth*, which is strongly authenticated in terms of the traditional criteria; see for example vol. I, p. 15, where he uses it to illustrate the profound significance of the following verse, which indicates that the ultimate ontological agent in any act is God Himself: *And thou didst not throw when thou threwest, but God threw* (VIII: 17). The saying is found in Bukhārī, *Ṣaḥīḥ*, Riqāq, 38. See also no. 38 of *An-Nawawī's Forty Ḥadīth*, p. 118.

[51] Chittick, *Sufi Path of Knowledge*, p. 312.

to itself, is to make possible a particular mode of self-knowledge. Another Qur'ānic verse that can be given as a support for this perspective on the cognitive function of creation is the following: *I only created the jinn and mankind in order that they might worship Me.* (LI: 56)

Āmulī glosses this verse by simply saying 'that is, "in order that they might know Me".' This interpretation of the meaning of worship—and of the entire purpose of creation—dovetails with the *ḥadīth qudsī* so fundamental to Sufi spirituality: 'I was a hidden treasure, and I loved to be known (*fa aḥbabtu an uʿraf*), so I created the world.'[52] The interpretation found here is given also by several other prominent Sufi authorities, as well as some exoteric scholars.[53] The point to stress in connection with our theme of dialogue is this: If the creation of the world springs

---

[52] See *al-Muḥīṭ*, vol. I, pp. 324–325 where Āmulī connects this saying to a series of verses which are interpreted as allusions to the various levels of the disclosure of this 'treasure'. Kāshānī refers to this saying repeatedly in his commentary. See for example the way in which he relates the saying to his notion of the 'essential synthesis' (*ʿayn al-jamʿ*) in his comment on the beginning of *Sūrat al-ʿAnkabūt*, vol. II, p. 122. The *ḥadīth* of the 'hidden treasure' is not found in the canonical collections, its chain of transmission not being regarded as sound. This does not diminish its importance in the Sufi tradition, nor does it prevent various exoteric authorities from accepting its meaning, for the meaning harmonizes with the interpretation given by Ibn ʿAbbās to the verse, LI: 56, as mentioned in the following note. And this interpretation is accepted by the exoteric scholars.

[53] Abū Naṣr al-Sarrāj (d. 378/988), for example, reports the comment on this verse given by Ibn ʿAbbās (d. 68/688): the word 'worship' here means 'knowledge' (*maʿrifa*), so that the phrase *illā li-yaʿbudūni* (except that they might worship Me) becomes *illā li-yaʿrifūni* (except that they might know Me). *Kitāb al-lumaʿ*, ed. R. A. Nicholson, E. J. Gibb Memorial Series XXII (London: Luzac, 1963), p. 40 (of the Arabic text). See also Hujwīrī's *Kashf al-Maḥjūb*, p. 267; and Qushayrī's *Risāla*, translated by B. R. von Schlegell as *Principles of Sufism* (Berkeley: Mizan Press, 1990), p. 316. As regards exoteric scholars, Fakhr al-Dīn al-Rāzī, for example, cites the *ḥadīth* of the 'hidden treasure', as well as the interpretation *illā li-yaʿrifūni*, at the end of his commentary on LI: 56 (see *Tafsīr al-kabīr* (Beirut: Dār Iḥyā' al-Turāth al-ʿArabī, 2001), vol. 10, p. 194.

from a divine love for a distinct mode of self-knowledge, the Qur'ān indicates that the differentiation, within mankind, in respect of gender, tribe and race, likewise serves an essentially cognitive function. *O mankind, truly We have created you male and female, and have made you nations and tribes that ye may know one another. Truly the most noble of you, in the sight of God, is the most pious of you. Truly, God is Knowing, Aware.* (XLIX: 13)[54]

Distinction and difference are here affirmed, again, as divinely willed, but now with knowledge added as the reason for diversity: it is by means of this very differentiation—of gender, race and nation—that mutual knowledge is attained. One should note that the word used in the phrase *that ye may know one another* is *taʿārafū*; and the word for being 'known' in the *ḥadīth* of the 'hidden treasure' is *uʿraf*—both words being derived from the same root, *ʿarafa*. There is thus a clear connection here with *maʿrifa*, the essence of which is expressed in the famous *ḥadīth* attributed to the Prophet, 'Whoso knows himself knows his Lord' (*man ʿarafa nafsahu faqad ʿarafa rabbahu*).[55] Thus, knowledge of self, knowledge of the other and knowledge of God are all interwoven, and should be seen as complementary and mutually reinforcing, each element having a role to play in the plenary attainment of *maʿrifa*.

The verse cited above, XLIX: 13, is often given as a proof-text for the following: upholding the necessity of dialogue; establishing the principle of peaceful coexistence; eliminating all prejudice in respect of race, nation, or gender; affirming piety as the essential criterion for evaluating human beings;

[54] As will be noted in the following chapter, this verse also underlines the absolute spiritual equality between all believers: it is piety, alone, whatever be the 'nation' to which one belong, that determines one's worth in the eyes of God.

[55] The *ḥadīth* is not accepted as sound by the scholars of *ḥadīth* in the Sunni tradition, but is regarded as authentic in the Shiʿi tradition, where it is attributed to ʿAlī b. Abī Ṭālib. See the compendium of sayings compiled by Muḥammad Rayshahrī, *Mīzān al-ḥikma* (Tehran/Qom: Maktab al-Iʿlām al-Islāmī, 1362 Sh. /1983), vol. 6, p. 142.

and indicating the divine ordainment of human and religious diversity. Let us also note the following verses, the profound spiritual implications of which should be clearer in the light of the presentation of the meaning of ontological *tawḥīd* by the Sufis:

> *And of His signs is the creation of the heavens and the earth, and the differences of your languages and colours. Indeed, herein are signs for those who know* (XXX: 22)
> *For each We have appointed from you a Law and a Way. Had God willed, He could have made you one community. But that He might try you by that which He hath given you* [He hath made you as you are]. *So vie with one another in good works. Unto God ye will all return, and He will inform you of that wherein ye differed* (V: 48)
> *Unto each community We have given sacred rites* (mansakan) *which they are to perform; so let them not dispute with thee about the matter, but summon them unto thy Lord* (XXII: 67)
> *He hath ordained for you of the religion* (min al-dīn) *that which He commended unto Noah, and that which We reveal to thee* [Muḥammad],*and that which We commended unto Abraham and Moses and Jesus, saying: Establish the religion, and be not divided therein. . .* (XLII: 13)
> *Truly those who believe, and the Jews, and the Christians, and the Sabeans—whoever believeth in God and the Last Day and performeth virtuous deeds—surely their reward is with their Lord, and no fear shall come upon them, neither shall they grieve* (II: 62)
> *And whoso doeth good works, whether male or female, and is a believer, such will enter paradise, and will not be wronged the dint of a date-stone* (IV: 124–125)
> *Say: We believe in God, and that which was revealed unto Abraham, and Ishmael, and Isaac, and Jacob, and the tribes, and that which was given unto Moses and Jesus and the prophets from their Lord. We make no distinction between any of them, and unto Him we have submitted* (II: 136)

> *Call unto the way of thy Lord with wisdom and fair exhortation, and hold discourse with them* [the People of the Book] *in the finest manner* (XVI: 125)
> *And do not hold discourse with the People of the Book except in that which is finest, save with those who do wrong. And say: We believe in that which hath been revealed to us and revealed to you. Our God and your God is one, and unto Him we surrender* (XXIX: 46).[56]

Such verses confirm—indeed, celebrate—diversity, they evidently promote dialogue, and they do foster mutual acceptance and tolerance, but the import of the verses is deepened, their message is made the more compelling, and their scope more far-reaching, insofar as they are consciously related, on the one hand, to the metaphysical principle of self-knowledge through divine self-disclosure; and on the other hand, to the ontological conception of the reason for diversity, that is, of the vision of the One in the many, and the many in the One. Indeed, the verses above, and others of similar import, when understood in the deepest spirit of *tawḥīd*, lead to something far more precious than mere 'tolerance': they invite the sensitive reader to contemplate divine 'signs' in the other, thus to learn more about the divine Reality—and about themselves—through the other, and not simply tolerate the other because of the legal requirement to do so. A spiritual appreciation of these verses ensures that the Muslim's attitude to the other will not be based upon expedient toleration or superficial tolerance, but will rather be oriented towards transformative contemplation, for the divine One is really present in the other: therefore the other must be seen in the light of the One.

Thus, dialogue here-below—a dialogue rooted in the sincere desire for greater knowledge and understanding both of the other and of oneself—can be seen as a reflection of, and participation in, the very process by which God knows Himself in distinctive, differentiated mode; that is, not in respect of His unique, eternal

[56] These and other verses of similar import will be discussed in Chapter IV.

essence, but in respect of the manifestation of the 'treasure' comprised or 'hidden' within that essence, a process yielding the perpetually renewed theophanies of Himself to Himself through an apparent 'other', the 'seeing of Himself as it were in a mirror'. Each phenomenon in creation—and not just each tribe or nation—reveals something of that divine treasure, manifests something of the divine Face, demonstrates in its own unique and original way the oneness of its origin. For, on the one hand: *And there is not a thing but that with Us are its treasuries, and We send it not down save in appointed measure* (XV: 21). And on the other: *He hath created the heavens and the earth with the Real* (XVI: 3).

In this process of divine self-disclosure, the human being has a crucial, but not exclusive, role to play. While it is true that it is man, alone, who consciously manifests and reflects aspects of the divine treasure, there is nothing in creation that does not obey the ontological imperative of 'making known' the divine treasure: *We shall show them Our signs on the horizons and in their own souls, so that it become clear to them that He is the Real.* (XLI: 53)

As regards the objective signs *on the horizons*, the Qur'ān refers repeatedly to the universal law of 'making known' the hidden treasure, doing so in reference to a broadly conceived notion of praise and glorification:

> *All that is in the heavens and the earth glorifieth God; and He is the Mighty, the Wise* (LVII: 1)
> *The seven heavens and the earth and all that is therein praise Him, and there is not a thing but hymneth His praise, but ye understand not their praise* (XVII: 44)
> *Hast thou not seen that God—He it is Whom all who are in the heavens and the earth praise; and the birds in flight: each verily knoweth its prayer and its form of glorification* (XXIV: 41)
> *He is God, the Creator, the Maker, the Fashioner. His are the most beautiful Names. All that is in the heavens and the earth glorifieth Him, and He is the Mighty, the Wise* (LIX: 22–24).[57]

[57] This theme is expressed in several other verses. See for example, XIII: 13; LIX: 1; LXI: 1; LXII: 1; LXIV: 1, *et passim*.

Thus we see that in the Qur'ānic perspective, every single thing, by dint of its very existence, 'praises' and 'glorifies' its Creator: its existence constitutes its praise. Every created thing bears witness to, and thus 'praises', its Creator; the existence of every existent 'glorifies' the bestower of existence.[58] But, more fundamentally, the existence of every existing thing is not its own; this existence 'belongs' exclusively to that reality for which it serves as a locus of theophany (*maẓhar*), there is no 'sharing', 'partnership' or 'association' in being—no ontological *shirk*, in other words. Thus we return to the metaphysics of oneness: nothing is real but God. Each thing in existence has two incommensurable dimensions: in and of itself—it is pure nothingness; but in respect of that which is manifested in it, through it, by means of it—it is real. This leads us to the relationship between extinction and contemplation: between knowledge of one's nothingness and truly witnessing the divine 'Face' in the other, and in Itself.

Self-Effacement and the Face of God

Despite appearing to be the concern only of mystics with an otherworldly and introspective orientation, such metaphysical perspectives on the central Qur'ānic message of *tawḥīd* are in fact highly pertinent to the theme of dialogue. In particular, the implications of *tawḥīd* in respect of notions of 'self' and 'other' are potentially of considerable value in helping to overcome one of the key obstacles to authentic and fruitful dialogue in today's multi-religious world. This obstacle consists in a notion of 'identity' or 'selfhood' that has become opaque, congealed, or reified. This obstacle has been formulated as follows by Mohamed Talbi, a prominent Muslim scholar engaged deeply in interfaith dialogue, and who is to be highly commended

[58] Ibn ʿArabī asserts that 'glorification' essentially means to declare the incomparability (*tanzīh*) of God. Chittick, *Sufi Path of Knowledge*, p. 71.

for all that he has done to promote the cause of tolerance and moderation in Islamic discourse:

> 'After all, is it possible to understand the Other as he or she really is? "The Other", in fact, is always perceived through the distorting eyes of the individual "I" or the social "we"... We are—all of us—prisoners of our own egos and our own group mentality, and it is probably impossible for us to free ourselves completely from our own prison bars... "The Other" is always "shaped" or "constructed". "The Other" is the image that is projected on the screen of my individual "I" through the filtering lens of our social "we". This constraint is inherent in our individual being, which is the bearer of endogenous values. It constitutes a natural blockage, a kind of immunizing code that preserves our identity.'[59]

This may be true to a certain extent, and for certain individuals, but one must nevertheless be alert to the danger of allowing oneself to be imprisoned by this apparently inescapable 'natural blockage'. For one risks inadvertently transforming this blockage into an insuperable barrier, and remaining complacently and uncritically within the boundaries of the 'identity' defined by the 'immunizing code'. Spiritual attitudes arising out of meditation upon Sufi perspectives can help considerably in preventing this kind of unconscious reification of the self, and in opening up a horizon which situates the self 'objectively', that is, seeing the self itself as an 'other'. When, however, the self is regarded as a kind of absolute criterion for engaging with the other, there arises a suffocating notion of identity which feeds directly into chauvinism, bigotry and fanaticism—qualities that are expressed by the Arabic word

[59] Mohamed Talbi, "Possibilities and Conditions For a Better Understanding Between Islam and the West", in Leonard Swidler, ed., *Muslims in Dialogue: The Evolution of a Dialogue* (Lewiston/Queenston/Lampeter: The Edwin Mellen Press, 1992), p. 134.

taʿaṣṣub. In its root meaning, this word graphically conveys the self-indulgence that constitutes the life-blood of all forms of fanaticism: the verb *taʿaṣṣaba* primarily signifies binding a cloth around one's head.[60] One becomes literally self-enwrapped, each fold of the cloth compounding the initial preoccupation with one's own congealed frame of identity; one becomes imprisoned within a mental 'fabric' woven by one's own prejudices; as the head swells, the mind narrows.

If the 'I' be identified in a quasi-absolute manner with the ego, the family, the nation or even the religion to which one belongs, then the other—at whatever level—will likewise be given a quasi-absolute character. It is precisely such exclusivist notions of 'self' and other that contribute to the dynamics of suspicion and fear, fanaticism and conflict. The metaphysics, or science, of oneness, in contrast, does not so much abolish as attenuate, not equalize but situate, all limited conceptions of identity. It serves to relativize every conceivable degree of identity in the face of the Absolute; in other words, it ensures that no determinate, formal conception of 'self' be absolutized, or 'worshipped', however unconsciously, as 'idol'.

The metaphysics of integral *tawḥīd* can be regarded as the most complete and effective antidote to fanaticism insofar as it undermines this idolatry of selfhood, a type of idolatry tersely summed up in the Qur'ānic question: *Hast thou seen him who maketh his desire his god?* (XXV: 43; almost identical at XLV: 23)[61]

This elevation of one's own desire to the status of God is identified by the Sufis as 'hidden polytheism' (*al-shirk al-khafī*),

---

[60] Lane, *Arabic-English Lexicon* (Cambridge: Islamic Texts Society, 1984), vol. 2, p. 2058. Needless to say, in the Islamic tradition, the turban is also, and pre-eminently, endowed with a positive value, indicating nobility, dignity and grace, as attested by numerous sayings of the Prophet.

[61] The word translated here as 'desire' is *hawā*; it contains also the sense of whim, caprice, arbitrariness, subjectivism. The revelation granted to the Prophet, we are told, has nothing to do with his own *hawā*: *Your companion has not erred, nor gone astray. And he speaks not from caprice* (hawā). *It* [the Qur'ān] *is nothing but a revelation revealed.* (LIII: 2–4)

a term referred to in a saying of the Prophet: 'The creeping of *shirk* in my community is more hidden (*akhfā*) than the creeping of a black ant on a hard rock on a dark [moonless] night.'[62]

According to Āmulī, overt *shirk* (*al-shirk al-jalī*) characterises disbelievers and polytheists. While hidden *shirk* can only pertain to believers; in other words, it is a form of *shirk* that, even while affirming theological *tawḥīd*, violates ontological *tawḥīd*. Overt, evident or legalistically defined *shirk* means simply associating other gods with God, attributing 'partners' to Him in divinity; while hidden, subtle and spiritually defined *shirk* means implicitly attributing to God a 'partner' in being: namely, oneself.

Āmulī cites these words from the Qur'ān: *Whoever hopeth for the meeting of his Lord, let him act virtuously, and not associate anyone with the worship of his Lord* (XVIII: 110). The literal meaning of the verse is clear: when one worships God, there should not be any associate or 'partner' (*sharīk*) taking a share in that worship; there must be no other object of worship or devotion, no other 'god' but God. But Āmulī points out that the *shirk* in question here must pertain to 'hidden' *shirk*, rather than to the overt *shirk* of polytheism or paganism. 'What is meant here,' he writes, 'is hidden *shirk*, for if it were overt *shirk* that is in question, the following would have been said: ". . . and not associate anyone with his Lord". Since this was not said, and instead God said "*with the worship of his Lord*", we understand that the meaning here is hidden *shirk*. For the polytheist in overt *shirk* has no worship nor obedience [to God], as is established in the principles [of the faith] such that he should be virtuous or otherwise.' [63]

Hidden *shirk* therefore is the danger that believers have to guard against. This warding off of hidden idolatry is one of the meanings of *taqwā*, which one can translate as 'piety' or 'God-wariness', but which is related to the meaning of

---

[62] The saying is found in slightly differing versions in *Musnad* Ibn Ḥanbal, vol. 4 p. 403; *al-Mustadrak*, vol. 1, p. 113; and Tabarsī in his comment on verse VI: 108—these references are given by the editor of *al-Muḥīṭ*, vol. 1, p. 284, n. 54.

[63] *Al-Muḥīṭ*, vol. 1, p. 284.

'protection': one who has *taqwā* is one who 'protects' himself against the punishment brought about by sin, vice, inadvertence and ignorance.

Āmulī lists ten things to 'guard' against, beginning with the most obvious—the avoidance of all prohibited actions—and finishing with the following two: one must guard against 'seeing' the soul along with one's witnessing of the Lord; and against the witnessing of existent, determined entities along with unconditional being. The reality, or 'due' (*ḥaqq*), of *taqwā* lies in guarding against the witnessing of alterity in one's contemplation and knowledge of God. He cites the following verses: *O ye who believe, fear God* (ittaqū'Llāh) *as He ought to be feared* (ḥaqq tuqātihi), *and die not save as those who have submitted* (muslimūn) (III: 102). *And most of them believe not in God, except that they associate partners with Him* (XII: 106).

These verses refer, according to Āmulī, to the fact that the majority of 'Muslims' fall prey to hidden *shirk*: they die outwardly as Muslims, but inwardly as polytheists, in the very measure that they 'associate' outward existent things with absolute being, or the vision of their own souls with the contemplation of God.

From this perspective, the remedy for this hidden *shirk*, or this tendency to deify one's own *hawā*, is to deepen one's consciousness of the Absolute; it is from this orientation that there emerges the possibility of seeing the self and its desires in an objective light, and in engaging in what the Prophet called the 'greater' *jihād*: the war against the soul, which we can call in the present context, the war against the idolator within.[64]

As we saw earlier: *God is the Rich and ye are the poor* (XLVII: 38). God is described here as the 'Rich', the absolutely 'Independent';

[64] See S. H. Nasr, 'The Spiritual Significance of Jihād' in his *Traditional Islam in the Modern World* (London & New York: Kegan Paul International, 1987); S. A. Schleifer, 'Jihād and Traditional Islamic Consciousness' in *Islamic Quarterly*, vol. XXVII, no. 4, 1983, pp. 173-203; and our 'From the Spirituality of Jihad to the Ideology of Jihadism', in *Seasons—Semiannual Journal of Zaytuna Institute*, Spring-Summer Reflections, 2005, vol. 2, no. 2, 2005, pp. 44-68.

all that is other than Him is 'poor' not just in comparative terms but in respect of being as such: for all things are existentially indigent, possessing no reality on their own account. Man, though, is described as rebellious inasmuch as he *deemeth himself independent* (XCVI: 6–7), that is, he attributes the divine quality of sufficiency, of independence, to himself. It is this illusory self-sufficiency, source of all pride and arrogance, that must be uprooted in the 'greater' *jihād*. The 'I', on its own account, in its own terms, is pure negation: it negates all that falls outside of its narrow confines. Hence it is the negation of this negation that constitutes pure affirmation, pure positivity.

In other words, only God can say 'I' in an absolutely unqualified way. Such is the interpretation given by Jaʿfar al-Ṣādiq[65] (d. 148/765) to the words of God to Moses at the theophany of the burning bush, *Innī anā rabbuka*; that is, *Truly I, I am thy Lord* (XX: 12). This extremely important comment comes in a *tafsīr* that was to have a profound influence both on the unfolding of the genre of esoteric exegesis, and on the articulation and diffusion of Sufi metaphysical doctrines:

> 'It is not proper for anyone but God to speak of himself by using these words *innī anā*... I [that is Moses, according to al-Ṣādiq's commentary] was seized by a stupor and annihilation (*fanā'*) took place. I said then: "You! You are He who is and who will be eternally, and Moses has no place with You nor the audacity to speak, unless You let him subsist by your subsistence.' "[66]

[65] Shiʿi Imam, regarded also in the Sufi tradition as one of the 'poles' (*aqṭāb*, sing. *quṭb*) or supreme authorities of the early generations.

[66] Quoted in C. W. Ernst, *Words of Ecstasy in Sufism* (Albany: State University of New York Press, 1984), p. 10. The commentary of al-Ṣādiq, especially in the recension transmitted through the commentary of Sulamī, plays an important role in the unfolding of the tradition of esoteric commentary in Islam, Sunni and Shiʿi alike. It should also be noted that Dhū'l-Nūn made an edition of al-Ṣādiq's esoteric commentary on the Qur'ān, which had a highly significant impact both on the science of esoteric hermeneutics and Islamic spirituality generally, given the centrality of the Qur'ān therein.

This expresses a theme of fundamental importance in Sufi metaphysics, or in that dimension of the Sufi tradition that pertains directly to gnosis, *maʿrifa*.[67] The primary focus of *maʿrifa* is God conceived of as *al-Ḥaqq*, the True or the Real,[68] in the face of which the individual 'I', on its own account, is reduced to naught. Human subjectivity is strictly speaking nothing when juxtaposed with the divine 'I'.

Kāshānī makes this point in relation to the important verse in which Moses asks to see God, and God discloses Himself (*tajallā*)[69] to the mountain:

> *And when Moses came to Our appointed tryst and his Lord spoke to him, he said: My Lord, show me [Thy Self] that I may behold Thee. He said: thou wilt not see Me, but behold the mountain. If it stand still in its place, then thou wilt see Me. And when His Lord manifested Himself to the mountain He sent it crashing down. And Moses fell down, senseless. And when he arose, he said: Glory be to Thee, I turn to Thee repentant, and I am the first of the believers* (VII: 143).

'. . . it was al-Ṣādiq who played the most important role in the whole history of esoteric commentaries upon the Qur'ān in both its Shīʿite and Sufi facets.' Abdurrahman Habil, 'Traditional Esoteric Commentaries on the Quran', in Nasr (ed.), *Islamic Spirituality*, vol. 1 Foundations, pp. 29-30.

[67] See our article 'The Notion and Significance of *Maʿrifa* in Sufism', *Journal of Islamic Studies*, vol. 13, no. 2, 2002, pp. 155-181.

[68] As regards the increasing use by Sufis of the Name *al-Ḥaqq* for God, which is of profound significance for the shift from 'theological' to 'ontological' oneness, Massignon argues, in his essay on the lexicography of Islamic mysticism, that 'it was from the *tafsīr* of Jaʿfar and the mystic circles of Kufah that the term *al-Ḥaqq* spread, through Dhū'l-Nūn al-Miṣrī and others, to become the classic Name for God in *taṣawwuf*.' Cited in John Taylor, 'Jaʿfar al-Ṣādiq: Forebear of the Sufis', in *Islamic Culture*, vol. XL, no. 2, 1966, p. 110.

[69] This is the only instance of this term occurring in connection with the self-revelation of God. In the *Sūrat al-Layl* (XCII: 2) we find the word *tajallā* used in reference to the 'shining forth' of the day, in contrast to the dark 'enshrouding' of the night.

Kāshānī writes: '*And when he arose, he said: Glory be to Thee, I turn to Thee repentant* of the sin of manifesting I-ness (*min dhanbi ẓuhūri 'l-anā'iyya*).'[70]

Another important early Sufi, mentioned above, Kharrāz, defines *ma'rifa* in relation to this principle of the one-and-only 'I-ness' of God: 'Only God has the right to say "I". For whoever says "I" will not reach the level of gnosis.'[71]

It is difficult to over-emphasize the importance of this perspective in both the speculative metaphysics and the spiritual realization proper to Sufism. If the Qur'ānic presentation of the principle of *tawḥīd* predominantly stresses the objective truth of the message, Sufi spirituality finds its apotheosis in the realization of the subjective concomitant of this message: this subjective element being, paradoxically, the very extinction of individual subjectivity, expressed by the term *fanā'*.[72] One might almost

---

[70] Kāshānī, *Tafsīr*, vol. II, p. 8. It is interesting to note Ibn ʿArabī's visionary dialogue with Moses as regards this Qur'ānic episode. In the chapter on Ibn ʿArabī's own spiritual ascent through the heavens, one finds the following dialogue with Moses, in the sixth heaven: '. . . I said to him. . . you requested the vision (of God), while the Messenger of God [Muhammad] said that "not one of you will see his Lord until he dies"? So he said: "And it was just like that: when I asked Him for the vision (of God), He answered me, so that '*I fell down stunned*' (Kor., 7: 143). Then I saw Him in my '(state of) being stunned'." I said: "While (you were) dead?" He replied: "While (I was) dead. . . I did not see God until I had died."' Cited by James Morris, 'Ibn ʿArabī's Spiritual Ascension' in *Les Illuminations de La Mecque*, p. 375.

[71] Cited in Schimmel, *Mystical Dimensions*, p. 55. Also, Abū Naṣr al-Sarrāj, in the chapter on *tawḥīd* in his *Kitāb al-lumaʿ*, makes the statement that none can say 'I' but God, because 'I-ness' pertains only to God; p. 32 (of the Arabic text).

[72] It ought to be said that in fact the ultimate 'apotheosis' of Sufism is not *fanā'*, but *baqā'*, or subsistence, which follows the state of extinction, as is indicated in the sentence quoted above from al-Ṣādiq's commentary. This 'return' of consciousness to the world of phenomena, and to the individual condition, after the realization, through the state of *fanā'*, of the 'nothingness' of the ego apart from God—this 'return'is deemed to be a 'higher' or more complete attainment than the state of *fanā'*. Ibn ʿArabī distinguishes between those 'sent back' (*al-mardūdūn*) and those 'absorbed' or effaced (*al-mustahlikūn*);

say that the truth of *tawḥīd* is realized in direct proportion to the realization of *fanā'*, or to the realization of the realities that flow from the attainment of this state;[73] inversely, to the extent that one falls short of the realization of one's nothingness, one cannot escape the 'sin' of idolatry (*shirk*): the setting up of 'another' as a 'partner' or 'associate' of the one-and-only Reality, the 'other' being one's own self.

The truth which *tawḥīd* declares is thus, from this perspective, radically different from the 'truth' of dogmatic theology, of propositional logic, or of empirical fact: this truth is the intelligible face of an infinite Reality, which cannot be exhaustively defined or confined by any words, and in the face of which the individuality as such is extinguished.[74] No dogma, no formula, no words can exhaustively express 'the truth', even though some formulations might reflect the truth more accurately than others. Nonetheless, inasmuch as they are formal expressions, they are all equally far removed from the Reality that can be fully realized or 'made real' only

---

the former are deemed 'more perfect' and are in turn sub-divided into those who return only to themselves, and those who return with the mandate to guide others to the Truth, these latter being the higher of the two. See his *Journey to the Lord of Power—A Sufi Manual on Retreat* (this being the translation of his treatise entitled *Risālat al-anwār fī mā yumnaḥ ṣāḥib al-khalwa min al-asrār*, literally 'Treatise on the lights in the secrets granted to the one who enters the spiritual retreat'), tr. R. T. Harris (New York: Inner Traditions International, 1981), p. 51.

[73] Ghazālī mentions various gnostic sciences (*maʿārif*, pl. of *maʿrifa*) that are revealed only in the state of *fanā'*: the operations of the individual faculties act as obstacles to this mode of inspired disclosure, being tied to the sensible world which is 'a world of error and illusion'. See no. 56 of his treatise *al-Arbaʿīn*, quoted in Farid Jabre, *La notion de la maʿrifa chez Ghazali* (Paris/Beirut: Librarie Orientale, 1958), p. 124. He also speaks of the ultimate degree of *maʿrifa*, the revelation of the sole reality of God, that only comes about through the state of *fanā'*. See *Ibid.*, p. 65.

[74] The Arabic root *ḥā'-qāf-qāf* represents very clearly this relationship between truth and reality: *ḥaqq* means both true and real (as well as 'right', 'due', 'worth', etc.), with the emphasis on truth; while *ḥaqīqa* means both reality and truth, with the emphasis on reality.

on the plane of consciousness which utterly transcends the individual. However, the individual receives traces of this supra-individual consciousness, one such trace consisting, precisely, in the knowledge that this consciousness does not 'belong' to him, nor can it be appropriated by the soul; rather, access to it is possible in strict proportion to the degree of effacement realized by the soul. Attainment of 'the truth', then, far from being a simple act of verbal affirmation or mental appropriation, is rather a process of spiritual assimilation—an ever-deepening process which has no terminus, in that the reality assimilated is infinite.

For the Sufis, then, the sin of *shirk* is identified not in theological but ontological terms: it is the sin of one's own separative existence. 'Separative' rather than simply 'separate', because the individual cannot be blamed on account of merely existing as a separate entity; the latter becomes a 'sin' inasmuch as it is endowed with an autonomous ontological status. It is the false consciousness of this autonomy, rather than the objective fact of individual existence, that is implied—albeit highly elliptically—by Kāshānī when he comments as follows on the words of the Qur'ān which describe the qualities of the believers, *those who avoid the worst of sins* (XLII: 37), 'those sins constituted by their existences (*wujūdātihim*), and this is the most despicable of the qualities of their souls.'[75] In relation to the plea for forgiveness at II: 286, Kāshānī comments, 'forgive us the sin of our very existence, for truly it is the gravest of the grave sins (*akbar al-kabā'ir*).' He then cites the following lines of verse, referring, without actually naming her, to the great woman saint, Rābiʿa al-ʿAdawiyya:

> 'When I said I have not sinned, she said by way of response
> Thine own existence is a sin to which none can be compared.'[76]

---

[75] Kāshānī, *Tafsīr*, vol. II, p. 213.

[76] *Ibid.*, vol. I, p. 100. For a valuable discussion of this theme of 'ontological sin' in the context of the doctrine of *waḥdat al-wujūd*, see the chapter 'Oneness of Being' (pp. 121–130) in Lings, *Sufi Saint*. The statement attributed to Rābiʿa

The 'repentance' incumbent on the soul is, not outward self-destruction but an inward effacement, which opens consciousness up to the sole Reality of God, there being no end to the assimilation of this Reality. The relationship between the 'truth' of *tawḥīd* and the soul of the individual is thus elevated beyond the spheres of morality, theology and all formal thought as such. The soul does not 'acquire' some cognitive content that is called 'knowledge of divine unity'; rather, its very manifestation as soul precludes or contradicts the full, mystical realization of that unity. Ibn ʿArabī quotes Junayd: 'When He is there, thou art not, and if thou art there, He is not.'[77]

The exoteric notion of a conceptual truth that, *qua* notion, is appropriated by the individual is here inverted: according to Sufi gnosis, it is the reality alluded to by conceptual truth that assimilates the individual to it.[78] On the one hand, there is the effacement of the individual before a truth whose fulgurating reality infinitely transcends all conceptually posited notions, principles and dogmas; and on the other, there is the entrenchment of the individuality brought about by the appropriation of a truth whose very conceptual form can become a veil over the reality it is supposed to reveal, and which is its *raison d'être*.

---

is found at p. 125, n. 2. See also the discussion of Kāshānī's treatment of evil by Pierre Lory in Chapter 8, 'La Nature du Mal' (pp. 88–97) of his *Commentaires ésotériques*. He cites the reference to Rābiʿa at p. 90, but translates the words *mā adhnabtu* as a question, *quelle faute ai-je commise*? ('what sin have I committed?') instead of as an affirmation, 'I have not sinned'. Whereas both are possible readings, the context favours the latter, to which Rābiʿa's words are a fitting riposte: you have indeed sinned, inasmuch as your very existence is a sin.

[77] In *Tarjumān al-Ashwāq*, p. 90.

[78] It is difficult to refrain from mentioning in this connection the words of a Christian mystic whom most Sufis would have little difficulty in recognising as an *ʿārif bi'Llāh*, a 'knower of God', namely, Meister Eckhart. He said in one his sermons: 'The bodily food we take is changed into us, but the spiritual food we receive changes us into itself'. *Meister Eckhart, Sermons and Treatises*, tr. and ed. M. O'C. Walshe (Longmead: Element Books, 1987), vol. 1, p. 50.

In relation to the words of the verse describing the 'hypocrites' as those who are *wandering blind in their rebellion* (II: 15), Kāshānī refers to one of the characteristic properties of hypocrisy as being 'the acquisition of gnoses (*maʿārif*) and sciences (*ʿulūm*) and realities (*ḥaqā'iq*) and words of wisdom (*ḥikam*) and divine laws (*sharā'iʿ*), only in order to adorn the heart with them, so that the soul might be embellished thereby.'[79] All knowledge and wisdom, even if divine in origin, can be so many veils if they contribute not to the effacement but to the glorification of the individual soul. Conceptual or dogmatic knowledge is therefore to be seen as an opening and starting point and not as the goal; as 'dis-closure' and not closure, as aspects of truth and not truth itself.

It is not only the different sciences but also the different virtues that can become veils over the Real; even the supreme virtue of *ikhlāṣ*, sincerity, purity of devotion, can be a veil insofar as the individual appropriates it to himself rather than attributing its presence in the soul to the grace of God, the Object of devotion. In his comment on the verse *Assuredly We purified them with a pure quality—remembrance of the Abode* [of the Hereafter] (XXXVIII: 46), Maybudī (d. 530/1135) quotes the following sentence: 'The defect of every *mukhliṣ* (pure, sincere person) in his *ikhlāṣ* lies in the vision of his *ikhlāṣ*. So when God desires to purify (*akhlaṣa*) his *ikhlāṣ*, He negates from his *ikhlāṣ* the vision of his own *ikhlāṣ*, so that he becomes *mukhlaṣ* (*rendered* pure, sincere) and not *mukhliṣ* (pure, sincere).'[80]

In the very measure that the soul attributes to itself the properties—or the virtues, let alone the existence—that God bestows upon it, ontological, as opposed to theological, *tawḥīd* is violated: the soul is guilty of hidden *shirk*. The only fully effective remedy for this subtle form of polytheism is *fanā'*. It is *fanā'*, ultimately, that enables one to see through the artificial walls—

[79] Kāshānī, *Tafsīr*, vol. I, p. 17. Cf. the saying of ʿAlī: 'Know that even the smallest hypocrisy (*riyā'*) is like believing in more than one God.' *Peak of Eloquence*, Sermon 85, p. 216

[80] Cited by Maʿrifat, *Tafsīr wa'l-mufassirān*, vol. II, p. 405.

individual and collective—that surround the ego; and allows one to perceive—with one's very being, or with the divine 'eye' and not the human 'I'—the 'truth' that there is nothing real but God. It is not difficult to appreciate the implications of this principle in relation to the requirements for effective dialogue with the other. The spiritual awareness which arises out of this conception of *tawḥīd* engenders the following important transformation in regard to oneself and the other: for the ego itself acquires something of the quality of 'otherness'. In the brilliant light of the Absolute, the ego appears only as a veil or as a kind of darkness. A genuine opening to the Absolute renders difficult, if not absurd, the act of shutting oneself up within the evident relativity of one's ego, or of preferring individual 'closure' within oneself to divine 'dis-closure' in the other. The resulting diminution of egocentricity and the corresponding humility before God enhance the basis for truly engaging with, and opening oneself up to, the other—defined both in terms of the human and the divine.

It might however be objected here that such sublime metaphysical ideals and the spiritual states they call forth can only be the concern of a small number of mystics, and highly accomplished ones, at that. Can ordinary people concerned with dialogue and coexistence in the modern world, really benefit from such perspectives? We would readily answer in the affirmative. For not only do the principles in question—even on the discursive plane—help dissolve the fixations on selfhood that give rise to pride and arrogance, on the individual and collective levels. But also, more directly, the key Qur'ānic verses from which these principles and perspectives flow can bring about, in the heart of the receptive reader, a penetrating sense of the ephemerality of all things, including, crucially, the ego and its manifold extensions. Two of the most important of these verses, cited earlier, are the following: *Everything is perishing save His Face* [or essence] (XXVIII: 88), and *Everything that is thereon is passing away; and there subsisteth but the Face of thy Lord, possessor of Glory and Bounty* (LV: 26-27).

It should be noticed here that the words indicating the ephemeral nature of all things—*hālik*, 'perishing', and *fān*, 'passing away' or 'evanescing'—are both in the present tense: it is not that things will come to naught or perish at some later point in time, they are in fact, here and now, 'extinguishing', before our very eyes. In the treatise entitled *Kitāb al-fanā' fi'l-mushāhada* ('The Book of Extinction in Contemplation') Ibn ʿArabī writes that the elimination of 'that which never was' is tantamount to realization of 'that which never ceased to be'.[81] That which will not be is already 'not', in a certain sense, and one grasps this not only in the ineffable moments of mystical experience, but also in the very measure that one understands the following principle: Reality is not subject to finality, cancellation, extinction, non-being. That which is absolutely real is that which is eternal: it is the *Face of thy Lord* that, alone, *subsisteth*. Conversely, all that which is impermanent is, by that very fact, unreal in the final analysis.

Reflection on the verses above, then, can heighten the sense of the relativity of all things—and, pre-eminently, the ego with all its pretensions and extensions—in the face of the one, sole, exclusive Reality. Instead of allowing an egocentric conception of selfhood to be superimposed onto religion and even onto God—both of which are then 'appropriated' by the ego[82]—such a perspective helps to engender the opposite tendency:

---

[81] This pinnacle of contemplation which is predicated on extinction is discussed in relation to the prophetic definition of *iḥsān*, or spiritual excellence: 'that you should worship God as if you could see Him, and if you see Him not, He sees you.' By effecting a stop in the phrase, 'if you see Him not' (*in lam takun tarāhu*), the phrase is changed into: 'if you *are not*, see Him.' See pp. 48-49 of the French translation of Michel Valsan, *Le Livre de l'Extinction dans la Contemplation* (Paris: Les Editions de l'Œuvre, 1984).

[82] This is one meaning of Ibn ʿArabī's daring term, 'God created in beliefs', (*al-ḥaqq al-makhlūq fi'l-iʿtiqādāt*); see p. 224 of *Bezels*. What is in question here are conceptions of God that are pre-determined by the contours of an inherited confessional faith; as such they are more indicative of the believer's own mind than the reality of God. See the chapter entitled 'Transcending the Gods of Belief', pp. 335-356 in Chittick, *Sufi Path of Knowledge*.

to see the ego itself *sub specie aeternitatis*, from the aspect of eternity. What results from this perspective on the ego is a more concrete apprehension of its essential limitations: the contours that delimit and define the ego are more vividly perceived against an infinite background. Thus, what is in question here is not so much a vaguely mystical notion of universal illusion but a concrete, realistic and effective sense of spiritual proportions. The limitations—existentially—and the pretensions—psychologically—of the ego are cut down to size, and a consciously theocentric focus replaces the all too often unconsciously egocentric one: nothing is absolute but the Absolute. Herein, one might say, lies a major lesson given by Sufi gnosis to those engaged in dialogue, a negative one, that is, the negation of egocentricity as source of pride, exclusivity, and fanaticism.

There is a complementary lesson: this arises from the positivity which flows from the inclusive or affirmative aspect of gnosis. For, as we saw earlier, the verses quoted above do not only assert the exclusive reality of God; they also contain a subtle allusion to the *inclusive* reality of God. The *Face* of God which alone subsists is not only the transcendent, divine Essence, in relation to which all things are nothing; it is also the immanent Presence which pervades and encompasses all things, constituting in fact their true being. Before focussing on the verse *Everything perisheth except His Face*, and in particular on the important and illuminating interpretation of it given by Ghazālī, let us remind ourselves of some verses quoted earlier, which refer to this complementary, inclusive dimension of the divine Reality:

> *And unto God belong the East and the West; and wherever ye turn, there is the Face of God* (II: 115)
> *He is with you wherever ye may be* (LVII: 4)
> *We are nearer to him* [man] *than the jugular vein* (L: 16)
> *God cometh in between a man and his own heart* (VIII: 24)
> *Is He not encompassing all things?* (XLI: 54)

He is the First and the Last, and the Outward and the Inward (LVII: 3).

We can now turn to Ghazālī to help us draw out the implications, as regards our perception of the other, of this vision of the divine transcendence and immanence. In particular, his commentary on the verse cited above, *Everything is perishing except His Face* (XXVIII: 88), should be noted. It is worth dwelling on the commentary he provides upon this verse; for it contains, arguably, some of the most radically esoteric ideas of his entire corpus, and also sums up many of the themes expressed thus far. The commentary comes in his treatise entitled *Mishkāt al-anwār* ('The Niche of Lights'), which takes as its point of departure the famous 'light verse':

> *God is the light of the heavens and the earth. The similitude of His light is as a niche wherein is a lamp. The lamp is in a glass. The glass is as it were a shining star.* [The lamp is] *kindled from a blessed olive tree, neither of the East nor of the West, whose oil would almost glow forth though no fire touched it. Light upon light. God guideth to His light whom He will. And God striketh similitudes for mankind. And God knoweth all things.* (XXIV: 35)

Ghazālī's commentary on this verse identifies the one, true light of God as the one, true being: darkness is not just 'other than God' it is strictly nonexistent, for that very reason. The following statement on the nature of existence forms the backdrop for the commentary on XXVIII: 88, which is our focus here:

> 'Existence can be classified into the existence that a thing possesses in itself, and that which it possesses from another. When a thing has existence from another, its existence is borrowed and has no support in itself. When the thing is viewed in itself, and with respect to itself, it is pure non-existence. It only exists inasmuch as it is ascribed to

> another. This is not a true existence... Hence the Real Existent is God, just as the Real Light is He.'[83]

Then comes the section entitled *Ḥaqīqat al-ḥaqā'iq* (the Reality of realities), which describes the ascent of the gnostics, the knowers of God, 'from the lowlands of metaphor to the highlands of reality'. They are given direct vision of the truth 'that there is none in existence save God, and that *everything is perishing except His Face.* [It is] not that each thing is perishing at one time or at other times, but that it is perishing from eternity without beginning to eternity without end. It can only be so conceived since, when the essence of anything other than He is considered in respect of its own essence, it is sheer nonexistence. But when it is viewed in respect of the "face" to which existence flows forth from the First, the Real, then it is seen as existing not in itself but through the face turned to[84] its giver of existence. Hence the only existent is the Face of God. Each thing has two faces: a face toward itself, and a face toward its Lord. Viewed in terms of the face of itself, it is nonexistent; but viewed in terms of the Face of God, it exists. Hence nothing exists but God and His Face.'[85]

Ghazālī then makes an important distinction within the category of these gnostics who 'see nothing in existence save the One, the Real.' One group are said to arrive at this vision *ʿirfānan ʿilmiyyan*, that is, as a mode of cognitive knowledge; and another group possess this vision *dhawqan*, that is, as a mystical

---

[83] *Al-Ghazālī—The Niche of Lights*, tr. David Buchman (Provo, Utah: Brigham Young University Press, 1998), p. 16.

[84] We are following Hermann Landolt's translation of *yalī* as 'turned to' rather than Buchman's 'adjacent to'. See Landolt, 'Ghazali and "*Religionswissenschaft*"—Some Notes on the *Mishkāt al-Anwār* for Professor Charles J. Adams', *Etudes Asiatiques*, XLV, no. 1, 1991, p. 60. Kāshānī likewise refers to two faces of the heart: the *ṣadr* and the *fu'ād*. The *ṣadr* is the 'face of the heart which is turned to (*yalī*) the soul, just as the *fu'ād* is the face of the heart which is turned to the spirit.' *Tafsīr*, vol. 1, p. 17.

[85] *Niche of Lights*, pp. 16–17.

state of 'tasting'.[86] The essential vision is the same, but there is a difference as regards the depth of assimilation, the mystical attunement to the reality perceived. This distinction helps to underscore the epistemological value of affirming principles of a metaphysical and mystical order, even if the plenary realization of those principles eludes the rational faculty. Reflection and meditation on the principles alluded to can bring about at least some degree of cognitive apprehension of the ultimate realities in question. To understand this principle more fully, and to help place it in the context of Ghazālī's overall perspective on the hierarchy of knowledge, the following points should be noted.

In his ranking of the faculties of knowledge he distinguishes sharply between the intellect and prophecy: 'Just as intellect is one of the stages of human development in which there is an "eye" which sees the various types of intelligible objects which are beyond the ken of the senses, so prophecy alone is the description of a stage in which there is an eye endowed with light such that in that light the unseen and other supra-intellectual objects become visible.'[87]

Despite the fact that the intellect is transcended in principle by the prophetic faculty, the gap between the two is diminished by the intuition that lies at the root of states analogous to prophecy, such as dream-states: 'In the dream-state a man apprehends what is to be in the future, which is something of the unseen; he does so either explicitly or else clothed in a symbolic form whose interpretation is disclosed.'[88]

However, what is important is not only the fact that the dream-state 'reveals' something akin to prophecy in man; what confirms the truth of prophetic revelation much more strongly—even in the absence of any empirical instance of a 'prophetic' dream—is the presence within human consciousness

---

86 *Ibid.*, p. 17

87 *Al-Munqidh min al-ḍalāl* ('Deliverance from Error'), tr. W. Montgomery Watt in *The Faith and Practice of al-Ghazālī* (London: George Allen & Unwin, 1953), p. 65.

88 *Ibid.*, p. 64.

of a faculty that is in principle analogous to prophecy; a faculty that remains dormant in most souls, one that can produce veridical dreams for some, mystical experiences for others, but is above all else the properly epistemic foundation for all belief in prophetic revelation 'from without': that is, belief in the claim by prophets to having received revelation from God. This faculty, analogous to prophecy, is cultivated and brought to fruition by the mystics, who thereby point the way to the attainment of personal, experiential certainty of revelation, beyond that kind of preliminary belief based on reason, sentiment, tradition or other contingent factors: 'If the Prophet possessed a faculty to which you had nothing analogous and which you did not understand, how could you believe in it? Believing presupposes understanding. Now that analogous experience comes to a man in the early stages of the mystic way.'[89] Thus we return to *dhawq*, which can now be seen as a 'taste' pertaining to a 'sense' that goes beyond the ordinary faculties of sense; it is a 'sense of the sacred', one might say, a kind of quasi-prophetic sense which, despite being unable to perceive the total extent of the realm of the unseen that is revealed to the Prophet, is nonetheless able to affirm all that the Prophet revealed about that realm, this affirmation being founded upon personal immediate experience. This initial *dhawq* not only confers upon the mystic a certainty in respect of all that falls within the realm opened up by the experience, but also a certainty that goes infinitely beyond this realm: 'Thereby he attains to a kind of immediate experience, extending as far as that to which he has attained, and by analogy to a kind of belief (or assent) in respect to that to which he has not attained.'[90]

---

[89] *Ibid.*, p. 66.

[90] *Ibid.* He says further that anyone can verify for himself the truth of the Prophet's revelation and urges his reader: 'Convince yourself... by trying out what he said about the influence of devotional practices on the purification of the heart—how truly he asserted that "whoever lives out what he knows will receive from God what he does not know"... "if a man rises up in the morning with but a single care (*sc.* to please God), God most high will

To return to the *Mishkāt*, what is in question at the higher stages of *tawḥīd* goes beyond the individual as cognitive agent, even though the imprint left on the soul by undergoing extinction from self can be described as a 'taste' of that extinction, and, more importantly, of the oneness of the Reality realized ineffably, supra-cognitively, and supra-individually, within the very bosom of that state of extinction. Ghazālī continues with a description of those who experience this transcendent extinction: Plurality disappears for them, as they are plunged in 'sheer singularity' (*al-fardāniyya al-maḥḍa*).

'They become intoxicated with such an intoxication that the ruling authority of their rational faculty is overthrown. Hence one of them says, "I am the Real!" (*anā'l-Ḥaqq*), another, "Glory be to me, how great is my station!"[91] . . . When this state gets the upper hand, it is called "extinction" in relation to the one who possesses it. Or rather, it is called "extinction from extinction", since the possessor of the state is extinct from himself and from his own extinction. For he is conscious neither of himself in that state, nor of his own unconsciousness of himself. If he were conscious of his own unconsciousness, then he would [still] be conscious of himself. In relation to the one immersed in it, this state is called "unification" (*ittiḥād*) according to the language of metaphor, or is called "declaring God's unity" (*tawḥīd*) according to the language of reality.'[92]

---

preserve him from all cares in this world and the next." When you have made trial of these in a thousand or several thousand instances, you will arrive at a necessary knowledge beyond all doubt.' *Ibid.*, p. 67.

[91] See Carl Ernst, *Words of Ecstasy*, for a good discussion of these *shaṭḥiyyāt*, or theopathic utterances, by Ḥallāj and Bāyazīd al-Basṭāmī respectively.

[92] *The Niche of Lights*, pp. 17–18. Kāshānī also refers to the 'veil' constituted by the vision (*ru'ya*) one might have of one's own state of *fanā'*. Commenting on the words of the Qur'ān '*ittaqi'Llāh*', (be wary of God/literally: 'guard yourselves' against [sinning against God, or: the punishment of God) he writes: '[Take refuge] in His Essence, from the affirmation of your existence, and make of It a protection (*wiqāya*) for yourselves against the manifestation of remnants from yourselves in the state of *fanā'* in *tawḥīd*, so that you shall not be veiled by your vision of [the state of] *fanā'*.' *Tafsīr*, vol. 1, p. 144.

We return to the relationship between *fanā'* and *tawḥīd*, between extinction and, not only 'declaring God's unity', which is but one aspect of *tawḥīd*, but, more essentially, the 'making one', or 'the realization of oneness', the 'making real' of the actual reality of oneness, through the elimination of all multiplicity.

Earlier, the divinely willed plurality within the human race was referred to—God divided mankind into *nations and tribes* so that *ye may know one another*. Is there not a contradiction, it might be asked, between the extinction of phenomenal multiplicity presupposed by the deepest level of *tawḥīd*, and the affirmation of human plurality called forth by the will of God? Addressing this question helps to situate the relevance of the Sufi conception of *tawḥīd* for dialogue in today's multi-religious context. One answer that can be given here helps to transform the apparent contradiction into an expression of spiritual profundity. The key lies in the idea of the 'face' within each thing that constitutes the real being of that thing.

Those Sufis who are extinguished to their own particular 'face'—extinguished from their own non-existence—come alive to the divine 'Face' that constitutes their true reality, the immanence of God's presence within them, and also within all that exists: *Wherever ye turn there is the Face of God*. Now it is precisely that divine aspect, in all things, and in all other *nations and tribes*, that comes into focus when this level of *tawḥīd* is grasped aright. The innate holiness of the 'neighbour'—at all levels—is seen more clearly in this light, this holiness emerging as a reflection of the 'Face' of God in all things. Now, one does not have to experience the grace of mystical annihilation to comprehend this principle; as Ghazālī put it, one can arrive at this principle not only *dhawqan*, by way of 'taste', or mystical experience, but also *ʿirfānan ʿilmiyyan*, as a mode of cognitive knowledge. If the mystical realization of this principle bestows a 'taste' of *tawḥīd*, one might say, following on from Ghazālī, that an intellectual assimilation of the principle bestows a 'scent' of *tawḥīd*. As Ibn ʿArabī puts it: 'The gnostics cannot explain their spiritual states (*aḥwāl*) to other men; they can only indicate them symbolically to those who have begun to experience the like.'[93] Although it is clear that Ibn ʿArabī has in mind those who have 'begun to experience' states of a mystical nature, one can extend this somewhat and argue that even a certain kind of conceptual grasp of these deeper aspects of *tawḥīd* might constitute—at a stretch—just such a 'beginning'. If the ultimate, mystical degree of *tawḥīd* is only realized through extinction, the lower, conceptual degrees imply at least that 'beginning' or prefiguration of mystical extinction which consists in self-effacement, or truly spiritual and not merely sentimental humility, which can be understood as the concrete concomitant—and the gauge—of an effective intellectual grasp of *tawḥīd*. In other words, an intellectual assimilation of this vision of unity, together with a moral attunement to the humility that it demands, is not to be disdained as something 'merely' theoretical, and moralistic, falling short of mystical realization and thus of little value. For such a perspective on oneness, integrating the higher reaches of the intellect with the deeper wellsprings of self-effacing virtue, is certainly sufficient, in principle, to dissolve the egocentric knots that constitute the stuff of *taʿaṣṣub*, of all forms of fanaticism.

Elsewhere, Ghazālī gives this telling description of *taʿaṣṣub*. He writes that it 'usually comes together with man's disregard of his neighbour, and of his opinions, and the taking root in his heart of certain ideas which become so much a part of him that he fails to distinguish between right and wrong.'[94]

What results, on the contrary, from an apprehension of the deeper implications of *tawḥīd* is a heightened, spiritual discern-

[93] We have slightly modified this sentence, which Nicholson translates in *The Tarjumān al-Ashwāq*, p. 68. See note 39 of the previous chapter for why Nicholson's translation of *ḥāl* as 'feeling' is unsatisfactory. The sentence quoted is part of Ibn ʿArabī's commentary on one of the poems in the *Tarjumān*.

[94] Quoted by H. Lazarus-Yafeh, *Studies in Ghazālī* (Jerusalem: Magnes Press, 1975), pp. 197-198.

ment: that is, not just a moral judgement between right and wrong, but also a presentiment both of one's own nothingness before the divine Reality, and also, of the innate holiness, the divine *Face*, within the 'neighbour'. The transcendent, divine Reality before which one is extinguished is known to be mysteriously present within the other. One observes here the spiritual underpinning of that crucial relationship, so often stressed in Sufi ethics, between humility and generosity, between self-effacement and self-giving; the first being a foreshadowing of *fanā'*, and the second being a moral application of *tawḥīd*. Respect for one's neighbour is thus deepened in the very measure that one is aware of the divine Presence which is at once within and beyond oneself, and within and beyond the neighbour. This might be seen as one of the spiritual foundations of *adab*, or 'courtesy', understanding by this word the profound respect for the other that constitutes the true substance of all outward, socially conditioned forms of etiquette, good manners, and propriety towards the neighbour. One sees here that it is not so much 'religious pluralism'[95] as 'metaphysical unity' that establishes a deep-rooted and far-reaching tolerance, one that is not only formulated as a rule, to be obeyed or broken as one wills, but a mode of tolerance that is organically related to a reverential awareness of the divine Presence in all things, an apprehension of the inner holiness of all that exists.[96]

---

[95] In Chapter IV a critique of the kind of pluralism associated with John Hick will be given.

[96] This kind of 'tolerance' evidently goes far beyond the boundaries implicit in the restrictive meaning that is derived from the etymology of the word. As Omid Safi notes, the term 'tolerance' is derived 'from medieval toxology and pharmacology, marking how much poison a body could "tolerate" before it would succumb to death.' *Progressive Muslims: On Justice, Gender and Pluralism* (Oxford: Oneworld, 2003), p. 23. This was cited by Jeremy Henzell-Thomas in his valuable paper, 'Identity and Dialogue: Spiritual Roots and Educational Needs', delivered at the Tenth Annual International Conference on Education, Spirituality and the Whole Child: Faith, Feeling and Identity; University of Surrey, June 26-28, 2003.

CHAPTER III

Islam: Quintessential and Universal Submission

IN THE PREVIOUS CHAPTER it was observed that, from a Sufi metaphysical perspective, oneness and diversity imply rather than contradict each other. The whole of creation, in all its variegated multiplicity, is the deployment, or self-disclosure, of the one and only Reality. In this perspective, the One transcends multiplicity but also embraces it, manifests and penetrates it, in such a manner that it is immanent within it; every phenomenon is both a unique manifestation of that oneness and at the same time shares with other phenomena the function of revealing something of the infinite riches of that oneness, the inexhaustible beauty of the 'hidden treasure': *and there is not a thing but hymneth His praise* (XVII: 44).

In this chapter we shall keep this ontological perspective on *tawḥīd* firmly in mind while turning to the religious phenomenon, and to Islam, in particular. It will be argued, on the basis of Qur'ānic verses and Sufi commentary, that there is something unique about each revealed religion, conceived as a particular phenomenon, and at the same time that all revelations are expressions of one and the same religious essence. From this point of view, Islam can be conceived both as a particular religion, unique in its form, and as universal religion; or rather: the particular religion defined as Islam is one unique expression of the quintessential and universal religion, defined as submission to the revealed will of the Absolute.[1] Each religion is a unique expression of this quintessence, and for this very reason, each differs from the others in fundamental, irreducible ways, and yet all are identical in their essence. Such is the picture that emerges from reflection upon Sufi exegesis of key Qur'ānic verses pertaining to the religious phenomenon. As in the previous chapter, our chief source of exegesis will be Kāshānī's *tafsīr*; but other commentaries, formal and informal, will also be cited to illuminate and illustrate certain principles and themes. The decisive influence of Ibn ʿArabī will, again, be apparent, even when he is not being cited directly.

The Religion of God

Seek they other than the religion of God (dīn Allāh), *when unto Him submitteth whosoever is in the heavens and the earth, willingly or unwillingly?* (III: 83) The word 'submitteth' in this verse translates *aslama*, the verb from which is derived the noun, *islām*. The verse thus clearly identifies *the religion of God* with the act of submission—an act accomplished by all of creation. However,

[1] The two definitions of Islam offered here are by no means intended to be exclusive. As with all of the fundamental concepts of religion viewed from the Sufi perspective, an inner metaphysical suppleness goes hand in hand with the basic polyvalence of the Arabic language to produce multiple levels of meaning that are mutually inclusive. In the case of 'Islam', the classical prophetic definition, as seen in chapter one, focuses upon acts that manifest submission, the five 'pillars' of the formal religion: the double testification, the daily prayers, the alms-tax, fasting in Ramadan and the pilgrimage to the Kaʿba. It is the definition of 'faith' (*īmān*) that focuses on inner belief, and that of 'spiritual excellence' or 'virtue' (*iḥsān*) that defines the essential nature of the devotional attitude of the believer: 'to worship God as if you could see Him; and if you see Him not, then [know that] He truly sees you.' See above p. 7. As will be seen below, the definition of Islam as quintessential submission does not so much contradict as encompass the outward acts which are deemed to demonstrate formal submission.

even if it be true that all things submit to God, there are two key qualities which transform that submission into *the religion of God* in the full sense: one is the voluntary nature of the submission; and the other is the form taken by that submission. On the one hand, if all of creation submits to God ontologically, it is only a certain number of human souls that consciously, freely and willingly submit to God; and on the other hand, the form taken by that submission is active adherence to God's revelation, and not simply the fact of passively existing. The free will of the individual submits to the revealed Will of God, and in that very submission participates, to some degree, in the absolute freedom proper to God. Thus, what occurs on the universal plane—inescapable submission to God—is faithfully reflected and transcribed on the plane of religion by voluntary submission to God's revealed Will. There is no mutual exclusion here: on the contrary, for *the religion of God* comprises both the ontological and the religious planes:[2] the human soul is fully at one with the deepest nature of things in submitting wholeheartedly to the religion by means of which God reveals His will—and through which is revealed something of the 'hidden treasure' of the divine Essence.

This submission to revelation, then, rather than being seen in opposition to the principle of submission to God, should be regarded as complementary to it. However, from a different point of view, the two are to be kept distinct, in order to avoid the danger of religious formalism. This difference between the two kinds of submission is overcome, though, in the very measure that submission to divine revelation is enacted as a means, rather than as end, a path rather than the goal. It is when religion *per se* is endowed with an absolute value that there arises the risk of engaging in a form of subtle idolatry: the mistaking of the means for the end. When, on the other hand, the revelation of God is seen as delineating the path that leads back to God,

[2] These two aspects of the divine Will are referred to in the school of Ibn ʿArabī as *takwīnī* (ontological or 'existentiating') and *tashrīʿī* (religious or 'legislative').

and when fidelity to that revelation is motivated by fidelity to the Absolute, then the translation of the universal, ontological principle of submission to God into the specific, religious act of submission to His revelation will be untainted by any religious 'idolatry'.

Before entering into the exegesis proper, it is important to stress here the distinction between the literal meaning of the word 'Islam' and the acquired, institutional or communal meaning. According to a highly respected translator of the Qur'ān into English, Muhammad Asad,[3] the word 'Islam' would have been understood by the hearers of the word at the time of the revelation of the Qur'ān in terms of its universal/linguistic meaning, and not in its communal or acquired meaning. In a note on the first use of the word *muslim* in the chronological order of the revelation (LXVIII: 35), he writes: 'Throughout this work, I have translated the terms *muslim* and *islām* in accordance with their original connotations, namely, "one who surrenders [or "has surrendered"] himself to God", and "man's self-surrender to God"... It should be borne in mind that the "institutionalized" use of these terms—that is, their exclusive application to the followers of the Prophet Muḥammad—represents a definitely post-Qur'ānic development and, hence, must be avoided in a translation of the Qur'ān.'[4] He asserts in his introduction to the translation that when the Prophet's contemporaries heard the words *islām* and *muslim*, they would have understood them in this original sense, 'without limiting these terms to any specific community or denomination—for example, in III: 67, where Abraham is spoken of as having "surrendered himself unto God (*kāna musliman*), or in III: 52, where the disciples of Jesus say, "bear thou witness that we have surrendered ourselves to God (*bi-annā muslimūn*)". In Arabic,

[3] Asad had a fine grasp of the subtleties of the Arabic language, and his translation incorporates many of the linguistic principles he learnt first-hand during his many years with the Bedouin.

[4] *The Message of the Qur'ān*, translated and explained by Muhammad Asad (Bristol: The Book Foundation, 2003), pp.1011-1012, n. 17.

this original meaning has remained unimpaired, and no Arab scholar has ever become oblivious of the wide connotation of these terms. Not so, however, the non-Arab of our day, believer and non-believer alike: to him *islām* and *muslim* usually bear a restricted, historically circumscribed significance, and apply exclusively to the followers of the Prophet Muḥammad.'[5]

This helps one to situate the deeper and wider implications of all the verses in the Qur'ān which contain this word and its derivatives; and is also important in situating those verses which describe all previous prophets—and their followers—as 'Muslims'.[6] For example, the disciples of Jesus proclaim: *We believe in God; and bear thou witness that we have submitted* [or: *we are Muslims*] (V: 111). Abraham likewise declares that *I am first of those who submit* [or: *of the Muslims*] (VI: 163). Just as all prophets are 'Muslim' in this universal sense, so the revelations received by them, though outwardly diverse, are one in substance; in the following verse, it is this unique revelation—*the Book*—that should be noted as the means by which fragmented and divided humanity is restored to its original unity: *Mankind were one community* (umma wāḥida)*, and God sent [unto them] prophets as bearers of good tidings and as warners, and revealed with them the Book that it might judge between mankind concerning that wherein they differed. . .* (II: 213)

[5] *Ibid.*, p. xi.

[6] One should also note that the Qur'ān refers to 'those who have faith' (*al-mu'minūn*) as having a higher status than those who have only submitted: *The wandering Arabs say: We believe. Say: Ye believe not, but rather say, 'We submit', for faith has not yet entered into your hearts* (XLIX: 14). One sees here the distinction between formal, outwardly compliant submission and essential, inwardly vibrant faith. However, the deeper meaning of Islam, as understood by Kāshānī and the Sufis, eminently comprises this dimension of faith, while going beyond it, inasmuch as the extinction that constitutes the ultimate degree of 'Islam' entails not just faith or certainty, but gnosis: that is, realized knowledge of *tawḥīd*, which, as seen in the previous chapter, surpasses and comprises the duality implicit in faith—the duality, that is, which consists of the believing soul, on the one hand, and the object of belief, on the other.

This theme of the unity of divine revelation is closely connected to the contestation over the meaning of the verse quoted at the outset: *Truly religion with God is Islām* (III: 19). How one understands this verse is of fundamental significance for determining one's attitude towards religions 'other than' Islam, when this refers to one among several faith-communities. Does it mean that the only religion, in God's eyes, is the particular religion revealed to the last Prophet—in which case all other religions are invalidated—or does 'Islam', understood in its literal sense, mean the principle of quintessential submission which, as such, encompasses and thus validates all previous revelations? And if it does validate earlier revelations, to what extent does this imply the continuing validity of the religious traditions that have developed on the basis of those revelations? As this and the following chapter unfold, one hopes that the exegesis presented will shed light on such questions. As regards the contestation over the meaning of verse III: 19, the hermeneutic principle of Ibn ʿArabī, noted in Chapter I, allows the interpreter to uphold the universalist interpretation without necessarily having to deny the validity, on its own plane, of the particularist interpretation. This nuanced approach to the apparently irresolvable antinomy between a particularist and a universalist perspective should become clearer as the argument unfolds, and as the commentaries on such verses as the above are brought into the picture. The conception being articulated here is not so much a 'qualified' or diluted universality as an uncompromising, all-embracing universality, encompassing even that which apparently negates itself.[7] In this connection, one should recall the principle of *al-jamʿ bayn al-ḍiddayn*, the ability of the Sufis to synthesise apparent contradictions, discussed in Chapter I.

both.

---

[7] This universality being a reflection of the principle by which the 'completeness' (*kamāl*) of being requires incompleteness (*naqṣ*) in order to be complete: the apparent negation of completeness/universality is in fact an aspect—albeit extrinsic—of that very completeness/universality.

Kāshānī comments on *Truly the religion with God is Islām* (III: 19) as follows: '*The religion* is the religion of submission of all *faces* (*wujūh*, sing. *wajh*)';[8] he then quotes the following verse in which Abraham says, *Truly I have turned my face to Him Who created the heavens and the earth, with unswerving devotion*[9] ... (VI: 79). Kāshānī then adds these words by way of comment on the submission in question: 'that is, my soul and my entirety, being divested of my selfhood, thus being extinguished in Him.'[10] The deepest meaning, then, of 'Islam' is extinction of selfhood within God,[11] the prefiguration of this extinction being submission. The quintessence of religion here is expressed in universal terms—the fact that it is Abraham—in whose person the three Semitic monotheisms are at one—who is used to exemplify the meaning of the verse proclaiming 'Islam' as *the* religion with God is to be noted. This quintessence is also expressed mystically in terms of an existential imperative, that of extinction: an imperative which is likewise of a universal order, transcending as it does all the

[8] It is in the face of a person that the character of a person is most fully expressed, thus *wajh* denotes not simply 'face', but also one's innermost disposition.

[9] The word *ḥanīfan* is translated here in accordance with the note by Asad on it, which first comes at II: 135, in connection with Abraham, the epitome of pure, monotheistic faith, the *ḥanīf* par excellence. Asad writes: 'The expression *ḥanīf* is derived from the verb *ḥanafa*, which literally means "he inclined [towards a right state or tendency]". Already in pre-Islamic times, this term had a definitely monotheistic connotation, and was used to describe a man who turned away from sin and worldliness and from all dubious beliefs, especially idol-worship; and *taḥannuf* denoted the ardent devotions, mainly consisting of long vigils and prayers, of the unitarian God-seekers of pre-Islamic times.' Taking due note of this explanation, it seems preferable to translate the word in a manner which accords with its positive, literal meaning, thus by the words 'with unswerving devotion', rather than following Asad's rather negative expression, 'turning away from all that is false'. One might thus translate *al-ḥanīf*, as 'the unswervingly devout', one who 'inclines' to nothing but God.

[10] Kāshānī, *Tafsīr*, vol. I, p. 105.

[11] And, as pointed out in the previous chapter, the 'subsistence' (*baqā'*) that follows this extinction.

relativities and particularities entailed by outward laws, social conventions, systems of theology, and so on. The extinction of individuality strictly implies the transcendence of all the factors presupposed by the ontological state of individuality.

To return to the path of submission that leads to this summit of extinction, Kāshānī helps to situate with the utmost clarity the nature of this quintessential religion. Of particular interest in this connection is his esoteric exegesis on two sets of verses. First, in relation to a verse which declares that the religion bestowed upon the Prophet Muḥammad was the very same religion as that which was bestowed upon his predecessors: *He hath ordained for you of the religion* (min al-dīn) *that which He commended unto Noah, and that which We reveal to thee* [Muḥammad]*, and that which We commended unto Abraham and Moses and Jesus, saying: Establish the religion, and be not divided therein...* (XLII: 13).

Kāshānī comments: '*He hath ordained for you of the religion,* [that is] the absolute religion (*al-dīn al-muṭlaq*),[12] which God charged all the prophets to establish, and to be unanimous, not divided, with regard to it. This is the principle and root of religion (*aṣl al-dīn*), that is, *tawḥīd*, justice, and knowledge of the Resurrection, as expressed by [the term] "faith in God and the Last Day". This is other than the details of the revealed Laws, by which they [the prophets] differentiate this [root of religion]; this differentiation occurs according to the needs of welfare [in the different situations]—such as the prescription of acts of obedience, worship and social intercourse. As God Most High says, *For each We have appointed from you a Law and a Way.*' (V: 48)[13]

The difference between the 'absolute' or unconditional religion (*al-dīn al-muṭlaq*) and the various forms it may take is then described by Kāshānī in terms of permanence and immutability. He continues: 'So the right religion (*al-dīn al-*

[12] This word can also be translated as 'unconditional', 'non-delimited', 'un-determined', 'unrestricted'; it is largely used in contradistinction to the term *muqayyad*, 'delimited', 'determined', etc.

[13] Kāshānī, *Tafsīr*, vol. II, p. 209.

qayyim) is tied to that which is immutable within knowledge and action; while the revealed Law is tied to that which alters in respect of rules and conditions.'

The nature of this unchanging religion, together with its essential connection with the primordial nature of the human soul, the *fiṭra*, is expounded by Kāshānī in an illuminating commentary on the following crucial verse: *So set thy purpose for the religion with unswerving devotion—the nature [framed] of God* (fiṭrat Allāh), *according to which He hath created man. There is no altering God's creation. That is the right religion* (al-dīn al-qayyim), *but most men know not.* (XXX: 30)

Kāshānī comments: '*So set thy purpose for the religion* of *tawḥīd*, and this is the path to the Real... or religion in the absolute sense (*al-dīn muṭlaqan*). That which is other than this is not "religion", because of its separation from the [way which leads to] attainment of the goal. The "face" refers to the existent essence, with all its concomitants and accidental properties; and its being set for religion, is its disengagement from all that which is other than the Real, its being upright in *tawḥīd*, and residing with the Real, without heeding its own soul or others, so that his way will be the way of God; and his religion and his path will be the religion and path of God, for he sees nothing but Him in existence.'[14]

Then comes this comment on the word *ḥanīfan*, the epithet applied to Abraham, the *ḥanīf* par excellence: '*Ḥanīfan*, tending and inclining away from false religions (*al-adyān al-bāṭila*),[15] which are paths of alterities and rivals (*ṭuruq al-aghyār wa'l-andād*),

[14] Kāshānī, *Tafsīr*, vol. II, p. 131.

[15] It is of interest to note how the Persian poet Maḥmūd Shabistarī uses the image of the *ḥanīf* to convey detachment from all of the constraints of formal religion, and relates this to the vocation of the monk, who disengages from all worldly distraction. These lines are from Shabistarī's masterpiece, the *Gulshan-i rāz* (The Garden of Divine Mysteries):

'Detach thyself, be *ḥanīfī*,
And from all faiths' fetters free;
So come, like the monk, step up into religion's abbey.'

these paths being followed by whoever affirms [the reality of] that which is other than Him, thereby associating it with God.' This intrinsic inclination away from false deities and towards what was described earlier as 'ontological *tawḥīd*' is intimately connected to the primordial nature of the soul, the *fiṭra* fashioned by God, which is now referred to: 'That is, they cleave to the *fiṭrat Allāh*, which is the state in accordance with which the reality of humanity was created—eternal purity and disengagement, and this is the right religion (*al-dīn al-qayyim*) in eternity without beginning or end. There can be no alteration or transformation in respect of that original purity and this intrinsic, primordial *tawḥīd*.'[16]

The *fiṭra* is then described as being the result of the 'most holy effusion' (*al-fayḍ al-aqdas*)[17] of the divine Essence; and nobody who remains faithful to this original nature can deviate from *tawḥīd*, or be veiled from God's reality by the presence of phenomena. Kāshānī cites the saying of the Prophet, 'Every baby is born according to the *fiṭra*; its parents make it a Jew, a

---

Quoted by Leonard Lewisohn in his 'The Transcendent Unity of Polytheism and Monotheism in the Sufism of Shabistarī', in L. Lewisohn (ed.), *The Heritage of Sufism*—Vol. II, *The Legacy of Medieval Persian Sufism (1150-1500)*, (Oxford: Oneworld, 1999), p. 402.

[16] *Tafsīr*, vol. II, p. 132.

[17] In his commentary on Ibn ʿArabī's *Fuṣūṣ al-ḥikam*, Kāshānī refers to this 'most holy effusion' as the first degree of divine self-disclosure, or essential self-manifestation (*al-tajallī al-dhātī*); at this level of theophany there is no plurality. The 'presence' of exclusive unity (*aḥadiyya*) has descended to that of inclusive unity (*wāḥidiyya*), without its unity having been differentiated by the fact that it is at this stage that the 'immutable archetypes', or 'entities' (Chittick's preferred translation of *al-aʿyān al-thābita*) of all things are expressed as such, in supra-manifest mode, by virtue of the 'most holy effusion'. It is only at the second degree of self-disclosure, the 'holy effusion' (*al-fayḍ al-muqaddas*), also referred to as the 'perceptible self-disclosure' (*al-tajallī al-shuhūdī*), that differentiated forms are manifested in outward existence. See the useful discussion of this theme by Izutsu, *Sufism and Taoism*, pp. 152-158.

Christian. . . '[18] But then he adds this important point: 'It is not that this underlying reality changes in itself, such that its essential state be altered, for that is impossible. This is the meaning of His words *there is no altering God's creation. That is the right religion, but most men know not* (XXX: 30).'

The 'impossibility' of altering the essential state of the *fiṭra* should be noted here. The meaning of the inalterability of *God's creation* is tied firmly to the immutability of the *fiṭra*. The underlying and inalienable spiritual substance of the soul subsists whatever religion is superimposed upon it. It 'in-forms' the soul in a more fundamental way than any 'formal' religious affiliation. All forms of confessional religion are seen here as so many superimpositions on the basic spiritual 'infrastructure' of the soul—that innate faith, that pre-personal knowledge of supernal realities, that 'breath' of God—which is ingrained in the deepest substance of the human soul. The fact that Islam, in the particular sense, would be seen as resonating most harmoniously with this inner substance would of course be asserted by Kāshānī; but what should be stressed at this point is that this inner substance of faith precedes, both temporally and ontologically, *all* subsequent confessional denominations and religious orientations. The identity articulated by primordial human nature takes precedence over all other affiliations, religious or otherwise; indeed, as will be seen below, it is on the basis of this primordial substance that the soul is able not simply to identify the truth revealed by religion, but, more fundamentally, to identify *with* that truth, and thus to strive to realize it existentially rather than simply understand it mentally.

The following verse (XXX: 31) reads: *Turn to Him; and do your duty to Him, and establish worship and be not of those who ascribe partners.* The 'turning' to God implies for Kāshānī turning away from all other-ness, from the 'demons of fancy and imagination' and from 'false religions'; it implies also the disengagement and

[margin note: our humanity is bare.]

---

[18] See *Ṣaḥīḥ al-Bukhārī* (Chicago: Kazi Publications, 1977), tr. M. M. Khan, vol. II, p. 247, no. 4440. The saying appears here in a slightly different version from that cited by Kāshānī.

detachment from the 'shrouds of created nature, bodily accidents, natural forms, psychic properties.' As regards the last part of the verse, he comments as follows: be not of those who ascribe partners [or: be not of the polytheists] '... through the remnant of the *fiṭra*, and the manifestation of I-ness in its station (*ẓuhūr al-anā'iyya fī maqāmihā*).'[19]

Here, the ontological limitation of the *fiṭra* and its 'station' is indicated by Kāshānī: for the *fiṭra* presupposes an individual soul, of which it is the most fundamental model, pattern or prototype; to remain in its 'station' means, ineluctably, remaining within that 'I-ness' or egoic nucleus which must be transcended if ultimate oneness is to be realized; and it is only transcended by *fanā'*. Despite this ontological shortcoming attendant upon the operative presence of the *fiṭra*, it is clear that for Kāshānī, it is only through fidelity to the *fiṭra* that one can open oneself up to that ultimate form of Islam which is constituted by—or rather sublimated within—*fanā'*.[20]

At the level of human knowledge, though, the *fiṭra* is conceived positively as the substratum of the soul, that by virtue of which there is a fundamental—or 'constitutional'—affinity between the essence of humanity and the nature of ultimate reality. Thus the innermost substance of the soul resonates harmoniously with the transcendent truths conveyed by the revealed Word. It is on the basis of this reverberation, together with the imponderables of divine grace and human effort, that spiritual affinity is transformed into mystical unity: the realization, through *fanā'*, of the deepest meaning of Islam, as described above by Kāshānī. This extinction is the condition *sine qua non* for the realization of the ultimate degree of *tawḥīd*, as was affirmed by Ghazālī in his exegesis of *Everything is perishing save His Face* (XXVIII: 88), noted in the previous chapter.

It is also important to note Kāshānī's comment on the words following those commented upon above: *For each We have*

[19] Kāshānī, *Tafsīr*, vol. II, p. 132.

[20] Although, as was seen in the last chapter, extinction is but the beginning of a subsistence (*baqā'*) on a higher plane of consciousness.

appointed from you a Law and a Way (v: 48). The verse continues: *Had God willed, He could have made you one community. But that He might try you by that which He hath given you* [He hath made you as you are]. *So vie with one another in good works. Unto God ye will all return, and He will inform you of that wherein ye differed.* Kāshānī comments: '*Had God willed, He could have made you one community* realizers of oneness, in accordance with primordial nature, being in agreement upon a single religion. *But* He willed to manifest to you that which He gave you, according to your preparedness, and in the measure of the receptivity of each one of you, so that the perfections may become variegated. *So vie with one another in good works*, that is, those things which connect you with your perfection, which have been measured out for you according to your preparedness, causing you to attain nearness to Him, by bringing perfection from latency into actuality.'[21]

Although the *fiṭra* is one, the 'perfections' latent within this primordial human nature are diverse. These human perfections can thus be understood as so many modes of receptivity to the effusion of divine Being, which Itself comprises all possible perfections. In coming to realize his or her particular mode of perfection, the 'perfect human being' (*al-insān al-kāmil*) thus mirrors and partially constitutes[22] the process by which the 'hidden treasure' of the divine Essence comes to manifest—in relative existence—its own hidden perfections. The diversity of religious communities can thus be seen as a formal prolongation of the diversity of human receptacles, the ontological necessity of which was discussed in the previous chapter. Just as the

[21] Kāshānī, *Tafsīr*, vol. I, p. 183.

[22] We say 'partially constitutes' because the process of Self-disclosure involves not just the human realm, but the whole of the cosmos. But it is in the human being, alone, that all of the divine Qualities are reflected. Insofar as the cosmos itself is perceived as 'The Great Man' (*al-insān al-kabīr*) and man is perceived as 'The Small World' (*al-ʿālam al-ṣaghīr*), the microcosmic perfection of man and the macrocosmic perfection of the universe are mutually reflecting mirrors. For a discussion of Ibn ʿArabī's conception of the 'Perfect Man', see the four chapters on the theme in Izutsu, *Sufism and Taoism*, pp. 218–283.

phenomena of creation make manifest something of the 'hidden treasure', so the forms of religion make manifest particularly striking 'jewels', one might say, within that treasure: each religion can be conceived of as being, from the point of view of the 'descent' of revelation (*nuzūl*), a refulgent light emanating from the divine treasure; and from the point of view of the 'ascent' of the soul (*ṣuʿūd*), as a vehicle by which the latent perfections of human souls are realized.[23] Religion as such is thus revelation and reintegration, radiance and attraction. Just as human souls are infinitely varied, while sharing the attribute of humanity, so the forms of the religions vary, but they are as one in respect of the fact that the divine intention behind their diversity is that the latent perfections within the soul—and the community or communion of souls—be brought to fruition.

This conception of religious diversity is closely related to that of Ibn ʿArabī, which will be discussed below. At this juncture it suffices to take note of the following important passage, in which Ibn ʿArabī affirms the identity of the 'roots' of different revelations, despite outwardly divergent 'rulings' emerging therefrom:

> '... messengers were sent according to the diversity of the times and the variety of the situations. Each of them confirmed the truth of the others. None of them differed whatsoever in the roots by which they were supported and of which they spoke, even if rulings differed... The governing property belonged to the time and the situation, just as God has declared: "To every one of you We have appointed a right way and a revealed law" (5, 48). So the roots coincided, without disagreement on anything.'[24]

[23] See Kāshānī's commentary on these two 'arcs' (*qāb qawsayn*, 'the two bows' length' in *Sūrat al-Najm*, (LIII: 9), *Tafsīr*, vol. II, pp. 270–271.

[24] W. C. Chittick, *Imaginal Worlds—Ibn ʿArabī and the Problem of Religious Diversity* (Albany: State University of New York Press, 1994), p. 134.

Even though in this passage the 'governing property' of the diversity of revealed religions is said to be 'time' and 'situation', elsewhere Ibn ʿArabī gives primacy to the diversity of divine relationships (or Names or Qualities) as being the immediate cause of the diversity of revealed religions. But there is no contradiction here, for each apparent cause—diverse religions, divine relationships, states, times, movements, attentivenesses, goals, self-disclosures—is itself an effect of a prior cause which leads back, finally, to itself again, in a complex circle of interlocking causes and effects that closes in on itself perpetually.[25] This point of view does not prevent the ultimate cause of religious diversity—the cause of this chain of causality—from being the divine mercy, described by Ibn ʿArabī as the 'root' of the diversity of beliefs, as will be seen below.

Just as the divine Qualities are diverse, and yet are rooted in a unique Essence, so is primordial human nature unique, while comprising innumerable modes of perfection; each revelation can thus be understood as the expression of a particular configuration of divine Qualities which awaken, galvanise and perfect the human qualities prefigured within the *fiṭra*. It is thus that the Muslim can, in principle, identify as realized human beings all those prophets and saints belonging to religious traditions rooted in revelations that preceded the Qur'ān; they are all 'Muslim' in this deepest sense. It is not possible to confine the category of realized souls only to those who are 'Muslim' in the specific sense. In other words, wherever there is spiritual realization, there is Islam, in the universal sense; this, as opposed to the exclusivist notion: only where there is Islam, in the particular sense, is there spiritual realization.

In his commentary, Sayyid Ḥaydar Āmulī makes the same basic points, while adding other valuable insights. He draws attention to the inevitability of differences between the religions as regards outward forms, while equally stressing the underlying unity of principles. He writes: 'It is evident that there is definitely

[25] See *Ibid.*, chapter 9 'Diversity of Belief', pp. 137-160.

no difference between the prophets and the saints as regards the principles of religion, and the foundations of the revealed Law, as is shown in His words: *He hath ordained for you of the religion* (min al-dīn) *that which He commended unto Noah, and that which We reveal to thee* [Muḥammad], *and that which We commended unto Abraham and Moses and Jesus, saying: Establish the religion, and be not divided therein* ... [XLII: 13]. And likewise in His words: *We make no distinction between any of His Messengers* [II: 285].'

He then proceeds to make essentially the same point as Kāshānī and Ibn ʿArabī in regard to the reconciliation between outwardly different legal rulings and the essential unity of underlying principles. He makes this point, however, in an interesting way. He claims that the prophets 'say nothing from themselves; rather, they speak not except with His permission and according to His command, as is shown by His words: *And he speaks not from caprice. It* [the Qur'ān] *is nothing but a revelation revealed* [LIII: 2–4].'

All of the prophets are brought into the category of those who 'speak not from caprice', and the diversity of their pronouncements as regards commandments and prohibitions are thus expressions of the divine Will in response to particular requirements of different communities; this diversity is governed by a unitive and universal principle, that of establishing spiritual wholeness and perfection. We see here again a clear application of *tawḥīd* in its ontological aspect, as discussed in the previous chapter: oneness is expressed in diversity, and diversity is comprised within oneness. Āmulī then introduces this useful analogy with medicine. 'Analogous to this [diversity of rulings expressing a single principle] is the case of physicians dealing with diseases. The aim of the physicians is one, though there be a hundred thousand of them, and that aim is health.'[26]

[26] *Al-Muḥīṭ*, vol. I, p. 373. It is interesting to note that, in one of his sermons, Imam ʿAlī b. Abī Ṭālib compares the Prophet to 'a physician roving with his medicine, having fortified his remedies, and heated up his implements, ready to place them at the disposal of those who need them: hearts which are blind, ears that are deaf, tongues that are mute. With his medicines he seeks out

The different remedies and potions administered are determined by the different diseases that need to be cured. Those who are treated argue amongst themselves about the different remedies and physicians, claiming some to be better than others, without realizing that the aim of the physicians is one and the same, and that their remedies are precisely what are needed by those who are afflicted with particular diseases. 'So the opinions and whims differ, according to what is appropriate or inappropriate; however their aim is one in actual fact... so compare this to the physicians of the soul, and to spiritual diseases, and the differences between the souls as regards receptivity and intractability, and their inclination to some physicians as opposed to others. Then you will understand the mystery of disagreement as you have understood the mystery of concordance.'[27]

It is important at this stage to flesh out this conception of universal Islam through reference to more explicit Qur'ānic verses describing or alluding to this quintessential religion. We can begin with the following credal affirmation: *Say: We believe in God and that which is revealed unto us, and that which is revealed unto Abraham and Ishmael and Isaac and Jacob and the tribes, and that which was given unto Moses and Jesus and the prophets from their Lord. We make no distinction between any of them, and unto Him we have submitted* (III: 84). Then comes this verse: *And whoso seeketh a religion other than Islam, it will not be accepted from him, and he will be a loser in the Hereafter* (III: 85).

Whereas this last verse is understood, from a theological point of view, as upholding the exclusive validity of 'Islam', defined as the religion revealed to God's last Prophet, and, as will be discussed below, as abrogating other verses which point to a different conclusion, it can also be seen as confirming the intrinsic validity of all the revelations brought by all the prophets mentioned in the previous verse. From the inclusive

the domains of heedlessness (*ghafla*) and the homelands of perplexity.' *Nahj al-balāgha*, p. 120. See the English translation of the whole sermon, which I have not followed, in *Peak of Eloquence*, p. 251–2.

[27] *Al-Muḥīṭ*, vol. I, p. 374.

point of view, 'Islam' encompasses all revelations, which can thus be seen as so many different facets of one principle: the self-disclosure of the divine Reality. Before elaborating further upon the implications of this conception of Islam, it is important to repeat what has been stated earlier: what will be put forward as a universalist, inclusivist, metaphysical vision of Islam need not be articulated in such a way as to exclude altogether the particularist, exclusivist and theological perspective or 'reading' of the Qur'ān. For, recalling the hermeneutical principle of Ibn ʿArabī: it is not tenable to exclude the validity of an interpretation of a verse, or series of verses, which is clearly upheld by the literal meaning of the words. It is one of an indefinite number of meanings that are all 'intended' by God to be derived from the words of the verse. No one interpretation can therefore be put forward as right and true to the exclusion of all others. One must repeat: to exclude the exclusivist reading is in turn to fall into a mode of exclusivism. Thus, a truly inclusivist metaphysical perspective must recognize the validity of the exclusivist, theological perspective, even if it must also—on pain of disingenuousness—uphold as more compelling, more convincing, and even more 'true', the universalist understanding of Islam.

In the process of presenting this case, an attempt will be made to underline one of the points made in the previous chapter: religious chauvinism, bigotry, fanaticism—indeed, all forms of *taʿaṣṣub*—are alien to the spirit of these verses. On the contrary, these verses, and indeed the Qur'ān as a whole, can be seen as providing a unique, all-inclusive spiritual vision of pre-Qur'ānic revelations, and an extraordinarily fecund source for the articulation of that 'transcendently ordained tolerance'[28] which is so urgently needed today.

This universalist conception of religion is closely linked to the principle that knowledge of God is innately within

[28] To quote Winter again ('Islam and the Threat of Europe'); see the discussion in the Introduction.

all human souls, and to the universal function of revelatory 'remembrance'—the means by which that innate knowledge is re-awakened within the forgetful soul by divine revelation. This is closely related to the *fiṭra*, as discussed earlier; at this stage, it is a question not of transcending the *fiṭra* through extinction, but of fathoming the depth of the *fiṭra*, and stressing its quintessential cognitive content: knowledge of the Absolute.

The following verse establishes with the utmost clarity the fact that knowledge of God is inscribed in the very substance of the human soul at its inception, and is thus an integral dimension of the *fiṭra*: *And when thy Lord brought forth from the Children of Adam, from their reins, their seed, and made them testify of themselves* [saying], '*Am I not your Lord?' They said: 'Yea, verily. We testify.'* [That was] *lest ye say on the Day of Resurrection: 'Truly, of this we were unaware.'* (VII: 172)

At the dawn of creation, then, knowledge of the divine lordship, the reality of the Absolute, and all essential truths deriving therefrom, is infused into the human soul—into all human souls, all *Children of Adam*, without exception. No human soul is bereft of this essential, salvific truth. Another way of presenting this universal fact, with the stress on the spiritual substance of these principial truths, is given in these verses: *And when thy Lord said unto the angels: Verily I am creating a mortal from clay of black mud, altered. So, when I have made him and have breathed into him of My Spirit, fall ye down, prostrating yourselves before him.* (XV: 28–29)[29]

Thus, it is this Spirit of God, breathed into man, that constitutes, according to the Qur'ān, the fundamental, irreducible substance of the human soul. It is for this reason that the angels are commanded to prostrate to him: the act not only proceeds from obedience to the command of God, but also out of acknowledgement of the breath of God that articulates the Adamic substance—the very reason for the command, one might say.

[29] Identical to XXXVIII: 72. Cf. also the verse, *Then He fashioned him and breathed into him of His Spirit. . .* (XXXII: 9).

One can understand the truths comprised within the divine Spirit, which is 'breathed' into the soul, in terms of the 'names' taught to Adam by God, in virtue of which his knowledge transcends that of all other beings, including the angels. The story of the creation of Adam, the transcendent knowledge proper to the human soul, the Fall, and the means of overcoming the consequences of the Fall—all of these fundamental principles are given in the following verses in a manner which succinctly presents both the necessity and the universality of divine revelation:

> *And when thy Lord said unto the angels: Verily I am placing a viceroy* (khalīfa) *on earth, they said: Wilt Thou place therein one who will do harm therein and will shed blood, while we, we hymn Thy praise and sanctify Thee? He said: Surely I know that which ye know not.*
> *And He taught Adam all the names, then showed them to the angels, saying: Inform Me of the names of these, if ye are truthful.*
> *They said: Be Thou glorified! We have no knowledge save that which Thou hast taught us. Truly Thou, only Thou, art the Knower, the Wise.*
> *He said: O Adam, inform them of their names, and when he had informed them of their names, He said: Did I not tell you that I know the secret of the heavens and the earth? And I know that which ye disclose and that which ye hide.*
> *And when We said unto the angels: Prostrate yourselves before Adam, they fell prostrate, all save Iblis. He refused and waxed proud, and so became a disbeliever.*
> *And We said: O Adam, dwell thou and thy wife in the Garden, and eat freely thereof where ye will; but come not near this tree lest ye become wrong-doers.*
> *But Satan caused them to slip therefrom, and expelled them from the state they were in. And We said: Fall down, one of you a foe unto the other! There shall be for you on earth a habitation and provision for a time.*
> *Then Adam received words from his Lord, and He relented*

> *toward him; verily He is ever-Relenting, all-Merciful.*
> *We said: Go down, all of you, from hence; but verily there cometh unto you from Me a guidance; and whoso followeth My guidance, no fear shall come upon them neither shall they grieve.*
> *But they who disbelieve, and deny Our revelations, such are rightful owners of the Fire. They abide therein.* (II: 30–39)

Adam is therefore not just the first man, but also the first prophet, the first to have *received words from his Lord*. The *guidance* promised by God—the means by which the primordial human condition is restored to its plenary state—is immediately defined in terms of *Our revelations*, or *Our signs*, that is, *āyātinā*. One is again given the sense of a single religion—divine guidance—which comprises diverse forms of expression—different 'signs'.

The universality of this guidance through revelation is clearly stressed in the following verses: *For every community* (umma) *there is a Messenger* (X: 47). As noted above (III: 84), the Qur'ān makes explicit reference to several prophets, but the scope of prophetic guidance extends far beyond those mentioned, for *Verily We sent Messengers before thee; among them are those about whom We have told thee, and those about whom We have not told thee* (XL: 78). The various modes of revelation granted to the different prophets, together with their underlying unity of essence, are linked in the following verses with the idea that all of the revealed messages together constitute an 'argument' against which there is no appeal.

> *Truly We have revealed unto thee as We have revealed to Noah and the prophets after him, as We revealed to Abraham and Ishmael and Isaac and the tribes, and Jesus and Job and Jonah and Aaron and Solomon, and as We bestowed upon David the Psalms;*
> *And messengers We have mentioned to thee before and messengers We have not mentioned to thee; And God spoke directly to Moses;*
> *Messengers giving good tidings and* [also] *warnings, so that*

mankind might have no argument against God after the messengers. God is ever Mighty, Wise (IV: 163–165).

Moreover, that which was revealed to the Prophet in the Qur'ān does not differ in essence from what was revealed to all the prophets:

> *And We sent no Messenger before thee but We inspired him* [saying]: *There is no God save Me, so worship Me* (XXI: 25)
> *Naught is said unto thee* [Muḥammad] *but what was said unto the Messengers before thee* (XLI: 43)
> *Say: I am no innovation among the messengers. . .* (XLVI: 9).

This single, unique message of guidance is always revealed to the messenger *in the language of his folk* (XIV: 4). All of the different ways in which God has revealed His will to mankind through the prophets (their number is given as 124,000 by tradition) convey a single essential message; but this unity of the essence of the message, far from implying a uniformity of the mode of its communication, on the contrary makes itself compelling to the different communities by having the messenger convey it *in the language of his folk*; thus, in accordance with the very particularity and specificity of the community addressed. Needless to say, the distinction in question is not to be understood as relating to a merely linguistic difference with identical semantic content, but rather, by 'language' should be understood the whole gamut of factors—spiritual, psychological, cultural and linguistic—that go to make the message of the supra-formal Truth intelligible to a given human collectivity. Herein, indeed, lies an important aspect of the message conveyed by Ibn ʿArabī's *Fuṣūṣ al-ḥikam*: the nature of the jewel (Revelation) is shaped according to the receptivity—conceptual, volitive, affective—of the bezel (*faṣṣ*, sing. of *fuṣūṣ*)—that is, the specific mode of prophetic consciousness as determined by the particular human collectivity addressed by the Revelation. In this perspective, the receptivity of the collectivity itself is determined by God, inasmuch as the hearts—the spiritual receptacles—of all souls are fashioned by the 'most holy effusion', the stage of divine self-disclosure at which the immutable entities (*al-aʿyān al-thābita*) are specifically articulated as such, albeit in supra-manifest mode.[30]

The oneness of the message thus implies a diversity of formal expressions, these expressions not being reducible to each other on the formal plane, even if they are considered, in their formal aspect, as 'accidental' in relation to the 'necessary' import of the supra-formal substance. One may assert, in accordance with Ibn ʿArabī's hermeneutical principles, that any attempt to abolish or ignore the formal differences between the revelations violates the divine intentionality; the diversity of revelations is divinely willed, and thus deploys rather than contradicts the unity of the message.

The diversity of laws, paths, and rites, however, must not obscure the fact that the religion ordained through the last Prophet is nothing other than the one religion that was ordained through all previous prophets. The oneness of this religion is brought home forcefully by Ibn ʿArabī. He quotes XLII: 13, cited above, then refers to a passage in which God 'mentions the prophets and the messengers'. It is worth citing this passage in full, in order to place in context the sentence which Ibn ʿArabī quotes and upon which he makes an important comment:

> *Those who believe and obscure not their belief by wrongdoing, theirs is safety* (al-amn), *and they are the rightly guided. That is Our argument. We gave it to Abraham against his folk. We raise up through degrees of wisdom whom We will. Truly thy Lord is Wise, all-Knowing. And We bestowed upon him Isaac and Jacob; each of them We guided; and Noah We guided aforetime; and of his seed* [We guided] *David and Solomon and Job and Joseph and Moses and Aaron. Thus do we reward the good. And Zachariah and John and Jesus and Elias. Each one was of the righteous. And Ishmael and Elisha and Jonah and Lot. Each one did We prefer above the creation, with some of their forefathers and their offspring and their brethren; and We chose them and*

[30] See note 17 above.

> *guided them to a straight path. Such is the guidance of God wherewith He guideth whom He will of His slaves... Those are they unto whom We gave the Scripture and the command and prophethood...* (VI: 82–89)

Then comes verse VI: 90, the opening words of which Ibn ʿArabī cites: *Those are they whom God guideth, so follow their guidance.* He comments, as partially cited earlier: 'This is the path that brings together every prophet and messenger. It is the performance of religion, scattering not concerning it and coming together in it. It is that concerning which Bukhārī wrote a chapter entitled, "The chapter on what has come concerning the fact that the religions of the prophets is one". He brought the article which makes the word "religion" definite, because all religion comes from God, even if some of the rulings are diverse. Everyone is commanded to perform the religion and to come together in it... As for the rulings which are diverse, that is because of the Law which God assigned to each one of the messengers. He said, "To every one (of the Prophets) We have appointed a Law and a Way; and if God willed, He would have made you one nation" (V: 48).[31] If He had done that, your revealed Laws would not be diverse, just as they are not diverse in the fact that you have been commanded to come together and to perform them.'[32]

Again we have a clear reference to the substantial content of religion which both transcends and invests the various revelations; the two key dimensions of this substance indicated here are divine command and human submission, or divine revelation and human conformation. In other words, however diverse may be the particular rulings pertaining to the different

---

[31] We quote here Chittick's rendition of the verse. Our preferred translation of the first part of the verse is: *For each We have appointed from you a Law and a Way.* The importance of translating the phrase literally, together with the mysterious phrase *minkum*, 'from you', will be discussed below, in connection with Rūmī's illuminating comment on this verse.

[32] Quoted in Chittick, *Sufi Path of Knowledge*, p. 303.

'religions', the substance or principle of these rulings remains the same: to submit to that which has been divinely instituted, to conform as best one can to what is revealed, and more fundamentally, to actualise within oneself the truths and realities that are bestowed from on high. These spiritual depths of religion are thus unfolded for the individual—of whatever religion—in the course of submission to God, such submission implying not just obedience to the Law, but also practice of the worship enjoined by the faith, intellectual penetration of the principles of the religion, and the sincere orientation towards the values enshrined in its moral precepts.

The above considerations, together with the earlier discussion of Kāshānī's conception of the 'absolute' or 'unconditional' religion, lead one to posit the distinction between religion as such, on the one hand, and such and such a religion, on the other. While such and such a religion is distinct from all others, possessing its own particular rites, laws and spiritual 'economy', religion as such can be discerned within it and within all religions; religion as such being the exclusive property of none, as it constitutes the inner substance of all. Given the misunderstandings that can so easily arise when one contrasts 'essential' with 'formal' religion, it must be carefully noted here that this view of a religious essence that at once transcends and abides within all religions does not in the least imply a blurring of the boundaries between them on the plane of their formal diversity. Rather, the conception of this 'essential religion' *presupposes* formal religious diversity, regarding it not so much as a regrettable differentiation but a divinely willed necessity. This necessary diversity flows forth as a natural consequence of the ontological principle of *tawḥīd* discussed in Chapter II. Just as the whole of existence is integrated—made one—by the unitive principle of *tawḥīd*—on the very basis of the diversity of its deployment, and not at the expense of this diversity, or the particularity of each existent thing; so, on the religious plane, the totality of the pre-Qur'ānic revelations are integrated—made one—on the very basis of their formal diversity, and not at the expense of this diversity, or at the expense of the uniqueness of each of the revelations. Each revealed religion is totally unique—totally 'itself'—while at the same time being an expression of a single, all-encompassing principle which integrates it within religion as such. Each is thus different from all the others, in form, and also identical to all the others in essence.

It is worth repeating here verse v: 48 as it is indispensable for correctly situating the following practical concomitant of this calibrated conception of the religious phenomenon: a recognition of the inner substance of religion inherent in all revealed religions implies the formal necessity of abiding by the dictates of one particular religion. *For each We have appointed from you a Law and a Way. Had God willed, He could have made you one community. But that He might try you by that which He hath given you* [He hath made you as you are]. *So vie with one another in good works. Unto God ye will all return, and He will inform you of that wherein ye differed.* (v: 48)

Of similar import is the following verse: *Unto each community We have given sacred rites* (mansakan) *which they are to perform; so let them not dispute with thee about the matter, but summon them unto thy Lord* (XXII: 67). Likewise: *And each one hath a goal*(wijha) *toward which he turneth. So vie with one another in good works...* (II: 148)

We noted earlier the importance of the verse which tells us that, *wherever ye turn, there is the Face of God* (II: 115). The ubiquity of the divine Face, however, does not imply that, in one's formal worship,[33] the direction in which one turns to pray does not matter. For the Qur'ān also says: *Turn thy face toward the Sacred*

[33] We say 'formal worship' here in order to distinguish the canonical prayer, (*al-ṣalāt*), from the remembrance of God, *dhikru'Llāh*, which is described as 'greater' than the canonical prayer in the following verse: *Truly prayer keepeth* [one] *away from lewdness and iniquity, and the remembrance of God is greater* (XXIX: 45). As noted in Chapter I, the *dhikr* is to be performed at all times, in all places, and in all postures—it is not restricted, as is the formal prayer, to designated times and movements. Not only does the Qur'ān describe the *dhikr* as an unconditional, permanent 'practice', it also clearly indicates that, understood as the principle of the awareness of God, the *dhikr* constitutes the

Mosque, and ye [O Muslims], *wheresoever ye may be, turn your faces* [when ye pray] *toward it.* (II: 144)

For Ibn ʿArabī, this apparent contradiction is assimilated as another example of the bringing together of opposites. Nondelimitation is not contradicted by delimitation; if nondelimitation were devoid of delimitation it would be delimited—by the absence of delimitation. On the one hand, the instruction to turn in a specific direction 'does not eliminate the property of God's Face being wherever you turn.' On the other, the fact that God is there wherever one turns does not preclude the bestowal of a specific 'felicity' (*saʿāda*) as the consequence of turning in a particular direction for prayer. 'Hence for you He combined delimitation and nondelimitation, just as for Himself He combined incomparability and similarity. He said; "Nothing is like Him, and He is the Hearing, the Seeing" (42: 11).'[34]

This combination between the universality of the divine Presence and the particularity of man's orientation thereto is an important aspect of the universalism being expounded here. Just as, ontologically, there is no contradiction between asserting the uniqueness of each human soul, on the one hand, and affirming the all-encompassing unity of being which transcends and thus negates the distinctions between all human souls, on the other; so, on the religious plane, there is no contradiction between asserting the uniqueness—and abiding by the specific dictates—of a particular religion, on the one hand, and affirming the all-encompassing principle of religion which transcends and negates the distinctions between religions, on the other. The point is that this negation by way of transcendence leaves intact the formal differences of the religions; it is thus very different from the kind of 'religious pluralism' which embraces the religions only at the expense of the uniqueness of each, pretending to attain the quintessence of the religious phenomenon on the plane of form—thus aiming at a kind of 'uni-formity'—rather

---

very *raison d'être* of the formal prayer:... *Establish the prayer for the sake of My remembrance.* (XX: 14)

[34] Chittick, *Sufi Path of Knowledge*, p. 111.

than perceiving this unity in terms of the spiritual realization of the intended essence of religious forms, and in the transcendent, unique origin of all religions.

We shall return to this difference between universalism and the kind of pluralism associated with John Hick in the next chapter. At this point, however, attention should remain focused on the ramifications of Islam understood as quintessential and universal submission.

To recapitulate the argument so far: The 'Islam' revealed to the Prophet Muḥammad is unique, and thus *a* religion; but at the same time, it is identical in its essence to all religions, and is thus *the religion*—in other words, it is both such and such a religion, and religion as such: *Establish the religion, and be not divided* (XLII: 13), for: *Naught is said unto thee* [Muḥammad] *but what was said unto the Messengers before thee.* (XLI: 43)

In another verse germane to this discussion, we are given a succinct definition of what constitutes this inner, essential religion. The verse also stands out as one of the most significant proof-texts in the Qur'ān for upholding the principle that access to salvation is not the exclusive preserve of the particular religion of Islam, that is, the specific Law and Way ordained through the last Prophet. On the contrary, the description given in this verse of that which is necessary for salvation gives substance to the universal definition of Islam which is being presented here: *Truly those who believe, and the Jews, and the Christians, and the Sabeans*[35]*—whoever believeth in God and the Last Day and performeth virtuous*

[35] The identity of the Sabeans is somewhat contested in the sources, but those 'Sabeans' with whom the Muslims came into contact historically constituted a community centred in Ḥarrān, which claimed to trace its origin back to the Prophet Enoch (in Islamic terms, Idrīs), 'who is also regarded in the Islamic world as the founder of the sciences of the heavens and of philosophy, and who is identified by some with Hermes Trismegistus. The Sabaeans possessed a remarkable knowledge of astronomy, astrology and mathematics; their doctrines were in many respects similar to those of the Pythagoreans.' S. H. Nasr, *Science and Civilization in Islam* (Cambridge: Islamic Texts Society, 1987), p. 31. See also J. D. McAuliffe, 'Exegetical Identification of the Ṣābi'ūn', in *The Muslim World*, vol. 72, 1983, pp. 95–106.

deeds—surely their reward is with their Lord, and no fear shall come upon them, neither shall they grieve (II: 62).

A great deal hinges on the meaning attributed to this verse. We need to digress from our main theme for a moment to consider briefly the question of its supposed abrogation. For, despite the fact that its literal meaning is clear enough, it is held by many of the classical commentators, based on a report from Ibn ʿAbbās, that this verse is abrogated by III: 85: *And whoso seeketh a religion other than Islam, it will not be accepted from him, and he will be a loser in the Hereafter.* Among these commentators, however, it is noteworthy that Ṭabarī (d. 310/923) and the Shiʿi commentator, Ṭabarsī (d. 548/1153) both reject the idea that the verse can be subject to abrogation. In general, as regards the principle of abrogation (*naskh*) Ṭabarī writes, in his commentary on verse II: 106: *We abrogate no verse, nor do We cause it to be forgotten, but that We bring one better than it or like it.* 'Thus, God transforms the lawful into the unlawful, and the unlawful into the lawful, and the permitted into the forbidden, and the forbidden into the permitted. This only pertains to such issues as commands and prohibitions, proscriptions and generalizations, withholding and granting authorization. But as for reports (*akhbār*), they cannot abrogate nor be abrogated.'[36]

In regard to verse II: 62, he writes that the literal meaning of the verse should be upheld, without being restricted in its scope by reference to reports of its abrogation, 'because, in respect of the bestowal of reward for virtuous action with faith, God has not singled out some of His creatures as opposed to others.'[37] Ṭabarsī, for his part, argues in his commentary, *Majmaʿ al-bayān fī tafsīr al-Qur'ān*, that 'abrogation cannot apply to a declaration of promise. It can be allowed only in respect of legal judgements which may

[36] *Jāmiʿ al-bayān ʿan ta'wīl ay al-qur'ān* (Beirut: Dār Iḥyā' al-Turāth al-ʿArabī, 2001), vol. 1, p. 546.

[37] *Ibid.*, vol. 1, p. 373.

be changed or altered with any changes in the conditions of general welfare.'[38]

Returning now to our theme, it was seen above that, although several prophets are explicitly mentioned by name, their number is given indefinite extension by the verse which says, *We sent Messengers before thee; among them are those about whom We have told thee, and those about whom We have not told thee* (XL: 78). Likewise, in II: 62, those who attain salvation are not restricted to the adherents of the four groups explicitly named—*those who believe* referring to Muslims in the particular sense, as a group, alongside the Jews, the Christians and the Sabeans; for there is the additional, universal category comprising *whoever believeth in God and the Last Day and is virtuous*. We shall return in a moment to this crucial, and controversial, principle which extends the possibility of salvation beyond the confines of Islam *qua* particular religion.

The following verse is akin to a veritable credal affirmation: *The Messenger believeth in that which hath been revealed unto him from his Lord, and* [so do] *the believers. Every one believeth in God and His angels and His scriptures and His Messengers—we make no distinction between any of His Messengers...* (II: 285)[39] What should be underscored here is the fact that belief in all the revealed scriptures is followed by the declaration that no distinction can be made between any of God's Messengers. Again, there is the recognition of the formal diversity of revelation combined with the affirmation of a unique message.

---

[38] Quoted by M. Ayoub, *The Qur'ān and Its Interpreters* (Albany: State University of New York Press, 1984), vol. I, p. 110. In the contemporary period, both Rashīd Riḍā and ʿAllāmah Ṭabāṭabā'ī likewise uphold the literal meaning of the verse, and reject the possibility that it is subject to abrogation. See the discussion of this issue in Farid Esack, *Qur'ān, Liberation and Pluralism*, pp. 162-166; and in Abdulaziz Sachedina, *The Islamic Roots of Democratic Pluralism* (Oxford: Oxford University Press, 2001), pp. 29-34.

[39] The phrase *we make no distinction between any of His Messengers* also comes earlier in the same Sūra, at II: 136, which we cite below.

The following description of rain and its effects can be seen as a poetic image of this mystery whereby a unique cause or substance engenders multiple forms: *And in the earth are neighbouring tracts, and gardens of vines, and fields sown, and palms in pairs, and palms single, watered with one water. And we have made some of them to excel others in fruit. Surely herein are signs for a people who understand.* (XIII: 4)

All the latent perfections, lying in seed-form within the 'earth' of the soul, are thus brought to fruition by one and the same 'water' of revelation. But there is another mystery here, which was broached in relation to the *fiṭra*: that which is revealed from above is in essence identical to that which is most deeply hidden within. This affinity between prophetic revelation and the human faculty—common to all human beings—that is analogous to prophecy was discussed in the previous chapter, in relation to al-Ghazālī's epistemology. This can be understood in the present context as the harmonious relationship between primordiality and revelation—between the knowledge divinely embedded, *a priori*, within the soul, and the knowledge divinely bestowed, *a posteriori*, upon the soul. It is this relationship that appears to be alluded to the literal wording of the first part of verse V: 48: *For each We have appointed from you a Law and a Way*. One also has the following verse: *Truly there hath come unto you a Prophet from yourselves* (IX: 128).

The literal meaning here, as addressed to the immediate recipients of the revelation, is that the Prophet is one of you, a man, not an angel, an Arab, not a foreigner, and so forth. But the word *minkum*, 'from you', also carries a deeper significance. One also has this verse: *The Prophet is closer to the believers than their own selves* (XXXIII: 6). Again, the literal meaning refers to the precedence of the Prophet, to the fact that he has a greater right or claim over the believers than they have over themselves. But a mystical meaning emerges as a different, and equally legitimate, reading of the word *minkum*. Not only the Prophet, but the revealed Law and the spiritual Way he brings—all seem already to be, in essence, within the human soul. To follow the Prophet, to abide by the Law, to follow the Way he traces out, is to follow, not some rules arbitrarily imposed from without, but a call from within; it is to follow one's own deepest nature. It is for this reason that the Qur'ān refers to itself in several places, as a 'reminder' or as a remembrance (*dhikr*): *And it is nothing but a reminder to creation* (LXVIII: 52 and LXXXI: 27); *We have not revealed unto thee this Qur'ān that thou shouldst be distressed, but as a reminder unto him that feareth* (XX: 2–3); *Nay, verily this is a reminder, so whoever will, shall remember it* (LXXIV: 54–55).

This understanding of the meaning of the word *minkum* is a possible but by no means exclusive one. It does flow naturally, however, from a fundamental principle of Sufi spirituality. For our purposes here it suffices to cite the engaging simile offered by Rūmī, by which he explains verse IX: 128:

> 'In the composition of man all sciences were originally commingled so that his spirit might show forth all hidden things, as limpid water shows forth all that is under it... and all that is above it, reflected in the substance of water. Such is its nature, without treatment or training. But when it was mingled with earth or other colours, that property and that knowledge was parted from it and forgotten by it. Then God Most High sent forth prophets and saints, like a great, limpid water such as delivers out of darkness and accidental colouration every mean and dark water that enters into it. Then it remembers; when the soul of man sees itself unsullied, it knows for sure that so it was in the beginning, pure, and it knows that those shadows and colours were mere accidents. Remembering its state before those accidents supervened, it says, *This is that sustenance which we were provided with before.*[40] The prophets and the saints therefore remind him of his former state; they do not implant anything new in his substance. Now every dark water that recognises that great water, saying,

[40] II: 25. This verse is given as the words uttered by the souls in Paradise upon being given fruits of the heavenly garden.

> "I come from this and I belong to this", mingles with that water... It was on this account that God declared: *Truly there hath come unto you a Prophet from yourselves.*'[41]

Near the end of the *Discourses*, this theme is expressed again, this time in more intimate terms:

> 'Those who acknowledge the truth see themselves in the prophet and hear their own voice proceeding from him and smell their own scent proceeding from him. No man denies his own self. Therefore the prophets say to the community, "We are you and you are we; there is no strangeness between us".'[42]

It is clear from these passages that Rūmī, referring to the prophets in the plural, regards the prophetic mission as one and the same, despite the different forms taken by that message. In the *Mathnawī*, this principle is expressed in many different places. One striking example is his poetic comment upon the words of the Qur'ānic verse, *we make no distinction between any of them* (God's prophets) (II: 136; and at III: 84). Under this verse as a heading come the following couplets:

> 'If ten lamps are present in (one) place, each differs in form from the other:
> To distinguish without any doubt the light of each, when you turn your face toward their light, is impossible...
> In things spiritual there is no division and no numbers; in things spiritual there is no partition and no individuals.'[43]

---

[41] We have slightly modified Arberry's translation of II: 25 and of IX: 128, which concludes the paragraph from Rūmī's *Discourses*, pp. 44-45.

[42] *Ibid.*, p. 227. Note the similarity between this idea and that expressed by Ghazālī in the previous chapter.

[43] *Mathnawī*, I, verses 678-679, 681. Nicholson does not include the heading, consisting of the verse, which is, however given in the Persian edition. See the edition by ʿAbd al-Ḥamīd Mashāyikh Ṭabāṭabā'ī, published by Nashr-i Ṭulūʿ, in Tehran (n.d.), p. 35.

A few lines later, we are returned to the image of water:

> 'Simple were we and all one substance; we were all without head and without foot yonder.
> We were one Substance, like the Sun; we were knotless and pure, like water.'[44]

For Rūmī, the theme of a unique message expressed through diverse revelations has, as its counterpart, the principle of a unique goal, toward which all are oriented. In his *Discourses*, Rūmī makes this point through a series of reflections on religious diversity. These reflections are of the utmost importance in connection with the theme of religious universality and warrant being cited *in extenso*. To place these reflections in context, it would be useful to begin with Rūmī's comment on the Qur'ānic verse, *God hath fulfilled the vision of His Messenger in very truth. Ye shall indeed enter the Holy Mosque...* (XLVIII: 27). 'Now the literalists take *the Holy Mosque* to be that Kaaba (sic) to which people repair. Lovers, however, and the elect of God, take *the Holy Mosque* to mean union with God.'[45]

Against this esoteric understanding of mystical union as the 'point' towards which the prayer is oriented, and as the goal of pilgrimage, his comments below can be more clearly appreciated. The following passage helps further underscore the idea that all religious paths are so many radii leading from the circumference of the circle of being to the centre, at which point the paths are no longer distinguishable one from the other:

> 'Though the ways are various, the goal is one. Do you not see that there are various roads to the Kaaba? For some the road is from Rūm, for some from Syria, for some from Persia, for some from China, for some by sea from India and Yemen. So if you consider the roads, the variety is great and the divergence infinite; but when you

[44] *Mathnawī*, I, verses 686-687.

[45] *Discourses*, p. 111.

> consider the goal, they are all of one accord, and one. The hearts of all are upon the Kaaba. The hearts have an attachment, an ardour, and a great love for the Kaaba, and in that there is no room for contrariety. That attachment is neither infidelity nor faith; that is to say, that attachment is not confounded with the various roads which we have mentioned. Once they have arrived there, that disputation and war and diversity touching the roads—this man saying to that man, "You are false, you are an infidel", and the other replying in kind—once they have arrived at the Kaaba, it is realized that that warfare was concerning the roads only, and that their goal was one.'[46]

Certain implications of this perception of religious diversity will be addressed in the following chapter, in connection with the theological critique of the universalist reading of the Qur'ān. For now, it should be noted that Rūmī's view does not deny the multiplicity of religious paths; rather, he is asserting that this multiplicity is transcended. The paths remain intact, as paths—and as absolutely necessary paths—but they are relativized in view of their goal. This is affirmed by Rūmī in the following passage: 'How do you want me to make the religions one? It will be one only in the next world, at the resurrection. As for this present world, here it is not possible, for here each one has a different desire and design.'[47]

What is being stressed here, again, is that diversity and difference here below is divinely willed; it is not mere human accidentality: for each religion 'has a different desire and design', a difference reflecting that of the different communities upon

[46] *Ibid.*, p. 109.

[47] *Ibid.*, p. 39. The fact that this passage refers not just to Muslim pilgrims to Mecca but also religious believers of all denominations is indicated by the context; these lines follow on from a description of how non-Muslims 'register emotion and ecstasy' upon hearing a discourse of Rūmī, from which they derive a 'scent of their Beloved and their Quest.' This passage will be discussed below.

whom revelation is bestowed: *For each We have appointed from you a Law and a Way.* (v: 48)

* * *

The conception of essential or absolute religion, explicitly affirmed by Kāshānī and implicit in so much of Rūmī's writings, is predicated on a clear vision of the spirit of faith which transcends all the forms that religious traditions assume. In this connection, it would not be out of place to mention briefly the Qur'ānic account of the encounter between Moses and the mysterious personage, not mentioned by name in the Qur'ān, but identified by tradition with the saint, al-Khiḍr.[48] Even in its literal aspect, the story alludes to the distinction between the form of religion and its transcendent essence, between exoteric and esoteric knowledge. In this encounter certain forms of the law and social convention are violated by al-Khiḍr, who is questioned and criticised as a result by Moses. After committing three acts that flout outward norms—the destruction of a ship, the slaying of a youth, and the building up of a wall in a city whose inhabitants had refused the two of them food—al-Khiḍr tells Moses of the realities hidden beneath the surface of each of the situations in which the acts take place, realities revealed to al-Khiḍr by direct, divine inspiration:

> *As for the ship, it belonged to poor people plying the river, and I wished to mar it, for there was a king behind them taking every ship by force.*
> *And as for the youth, his parents were believers, and we feared lest he should oppress them by rebellion and disbelief.*
> *And we intended that their Lord should exchange him for them for one better in purity and nearer to mercy.*
> *And as for the wall, it belonged to two orphan boys in the city, and there was beneath it a treasure belonging to them, and their*

[48] See the article "Al-Khaḍir (al-Khiḍr)" by A. J. Wensinck in *Encyclopedia of Islam*, 2nd ed.

> *father had been righteous, and thy Lord intended that they should come to their full strength and should bring forth their treasure as a mercy from their Lord...* (XVIII: 79-82)

One of the uses to which Ibn ʿArabī puts this story reinforces its already esoteric nature. Al-Khiḍr becomes the personification of the station of nearness (*maqām al-qurba*) a station which is identified with plenary sanctity (*walāya*);[49] while Moses personifies the law-giving prophet, or prophecy as such (*nubuwwa*). In Ibn ʿArabī's perspective, sanctity as such is superior to prophecy as such, because, as he explains in the chapter of the *Fuṣūṣ* under the heading of Seth, 'the message (*risāla*) and prophecy (*nubuwwa*)—that is, law-giving prophecy and its message—come to an end, but sanctity (*walāya*) never comes to an end.'[50]

Sanctity is higher because the knowledge proper to it is universal, and prophecy is lower insofar as the knowledge comprised within it is delimited by a particular message: 'Know that *walāya* is the all-encompassing sphere, thus it never comes to an end, and to it belong [the assimilation and communication of] universal tidings; but as for law-giving prophecy and the message, they terminate...'[51] But it is a question of principial priority and not personal superiority: sanctity is more universal than prophecy, but the prophet is always superior to the saint. For, on the one hand, the prophet's sanctity is the source of the sanctity of the saint; and on the other, every prophet is a saint, but not every saint is a prophet:

[49] See the French translation of the chapter on the 'station of nearness' (chapter 161 of the *Futūḥāt*) by Denis Gril in 'Le terme du voyage' (pp. 339-347) in M. Chodkiewicz (ed.) *Les Illuminations de La Mecque*. This station 'represents the ultimate point in the hierarchy of the saints...' M. Chodkiewicz, *Seal of the Saints—Prophethood and Sainthood in the Doctrine of Ibn ʿArabī* (tr. Liadain Sherrard) (Cambridge: Islamic Texts Society, 1993), p. 58.

[50] *Fuṣūṣ*, p. 34. See R. Austin's translation, *The Bezels of Wisdom*, p. 66.

[51] *Fuṣūṣ*, p. 167; in *Bezels*, p. 168.

'When you observe the prophet saying things which relate to what is outside the law-giving function,[52] then he does so as a saint (*walī*) and a gnostic (*ʿārif*). Thus his station as a knower and a saint is more complete and more perfect than [his station] as a messenger or as a legislative prophet... So if one says that the saint is above the prophet and the messenger, he means that this is the case within a single person, that is: the messenger, in respect of his being a saint, is more complete than he is in respect of his being a prophet or messenger.'[53]

According to Ibn ʿArabī, then, the encounter between Moses and al-Khiḍr is understood microcosmically: al-Khiḍr represents a mode of universal consciousness within the very soul of Moses, one which surpasses his consciousness *qua* prophet, whence the disapproval by the 'prophet' of the antinomian acts of the 'saint': 'He [al-Khiḍr] showed him [Moses] nothing but his [Moses's] own form: it was his own state that Moses saw, and himself that he censured.'[54]

Kāshānī clarifies the distinction between *walāya* and *nubuwwa* in many places in his commentary. To give just one example, he comments as follows on the verse, *and We sent no Messenger* (rasūl) *except that he be obeyed, by God's permission* (IV: 64): 'The difference between the messenger (*rasūl*) and the prophet (*nabī*) is that the content of the message of the messenger is the conveyance of rulings, *O Messenger, convey* (balligh)... (V: 67). As for *nubuwwa*, its function is to convey tidings related to gnostic sciences and spiritual realities, pertaining to the articulation of the different

[52] Kāshānī comments on this domain that is said to lie beyond the scope of the law-giving function: '... the explanation of "assimilating the character-traits of God" (*takhalluq bi-akhlāq Allāh*), the proximity [attained through] supererogatory and obligatory devotions; and the stations of trust, contentment, submission, realizing oneness, attaining singularity, extinction, union and separation, and the like... '. *Fuṣūṣ*, p. 168.

[53] *Fuṣūṣ*, p. 168; *Bezels*, pp. 168–169.

[54] Cited by Gril, 'Le terme du voyage', p. 342 (from the *Futūḥāt*, vol. II, p. 261).

aspects of the [divine] Qualities and Acts. *Nubuwwa* is, indeed, the outward aspect of *walāya*, which, for its part, consists in the various dimensions of drowning in the essence of union (*ᶜayn al-jamᶜ*)[55] and extinction in the Essence. So the knowledge proper to *walāya* is knowledge of the *tawḥīd* of the Essence and the effacement of the [divine] Acts and Qualities. Thus every *rasūl* is a *nabī* and every *nabī* is a *walī*, but not every *walī* is a *nabī*, nor is every *nabī* a *rasūl*—even though the spiritual degree of *walāya* is more noble than that of *nubuwwa* and that of *nubuwwa*, more noble than that of *risāla*.'[56]

This Akbarī conception of *walāya* is a complex and controversial one, but it does shed light upon the esoteric implications of the Qur'ānic narrative of the encounter between the prophet Moses and the saint al-Khiḍr; and it also helps to demonstrate the relevance of this encounter to the discussion in hand. For it clearly alludes to the relativity of the outward law in the face of its inner spirit, and the limitations proper to the law-giving function as opposed to the universal dimensions of sanctity. There is a clear and important relationship between this universal view of sanctity and the 'absolute' or 'unconditional' religion referred to above, that religion which is above

---

[55] See Chapter II for discussion of this concept in Kāshānī's commentary on the *Sūrat al-Ikhlāṣ*.

[56] Kāshānī, vol. I, p. 153. See also Kāshānī's commentary on the first verses of the *Sūrat al-Inshirāḥ* ('The Expansion', XCIV: 1–3: *Have We not expanded for thee thy breast, and removed from thee thy burden, which weighed down upon thy back*), where the relationship between the station of sanctity and that of prophecy is presented in terms of the return from absorption in the Essence to the realm of differentiation, a return which is strictly required for the prophetic function of commanding and prohibiting. The 'burden' thus acquired is that of being deprived of the unitive vision by the phenomena of creation. The removal of this burden for the Prophet is his being granted 'stability in the station of *baqā'* so that he is no longer veiled by multiplicity from unity, and he witnesses synthesis in the bosom of differentiation, and his invitation [to people to accept his message] does not cause him to be absent from contemplating Him—and this is the "expansion of the breast" and the very essence of "removing the burden"...' Kāshānī, vol. II, p. 401.

and beyond all the particular forms—legal, confessional, social, cultural, and psychological—that it may assume. In the measure that one fails to see the relativity of these forms, there arises the danger of falling into an implicit idolatry—worshipping one's religion instead of God—and into an explicit confessional chauvinism—belief that membership in one's religion, alone, holds out the prospect of salvation. It is to this tendency and the strong Qur'ānic denunciation thereof, that the following section is addressed.

The Vanity of Chauvinism

In the Qur'ān, the universal religion, or religion as such, which resists any communal specification, is often referred to as the religion of Abraham, *al-ḥanīf*, 'the unswervingly devout'. Abraham stands forth as both the symbol and the concrete embodiment of pure, monotheistic worship—*he was not one of the idolators.* In the following verses we read: *And they say: Be Jews or Christians, then ye will be rightly guided. Say: Nay but* [we are of] *the religious community* (milla) *of Abraham, the devout* (ḥanīfan), *and he was not one of the idolators.* (II: 135)

Then there follows a description of what affiliation to this *milla*, or religious community entails, in the verse immediately following this one (this verse is almost identical to III: 84, cited above): *Say: We believe in God, and that which was revealed unto Abraham, and Ishmael, and Isaac, and Jacob, and the tribes, and that which was given unto Moses and Jesus and the prophets from their Lord. We make no distinction between any of them, and unto Him we have submitted.* (II: 136)

After this comes another important verse, which reinforces the interpretation of religion as universal submission: *And if they believe in the like of that which ye believe, then they are rightly guided. But if they turn away, then they are in schism...* (II: 137)

The next verse is also highly relevant to our theme. It begins, mysteriously, simply with the words, *colour of God* (*ṣibghat Allāh*).

Pickthall renders the verse thus, making explicit what he sees as intended by the ellipse: [We take our] *colour from God; and who is better than God at colouring? And we worship Him* (II: 138). The last words of the verse are *naḥnu lahu 'ābidūn*, which can also be translated as 'we are His worshippers'; the strong implication, in both senses of the phrase, is that God is the sole object of worship, and, as such, true worshippers 'belong' to God, alone, only they take on His 'colour'. The following verses give one a sense of what this 'colour' of God might be:

> *Say: Dispute ye with us concerning God, when He is our Lord and your Lord? Ours are our works, and yours your works. We are devoted purely to Him . . .*
> *Or say ye that Abraham, and Ishmael, and Isaac, and Jacob, and the tribes were Jews or Christians? Say: Do you know best or doth God?* (II: 139–140)

Here, we are given a clear expression of the need to view religious affiliation in the light of absolute values, rather than allowing religious affiliation to determine the 'colour' or nature of the Absolute: *We are devoted purely to Him—naḥnu lahu mukhliṣūn.* This last phrase strongly connotes the combination of the notions of sincerity and purity; one is sincere (*mukhliṣ*) only if one's orientation to God is 'purified' (*mukhlaṣ*) of all taint of otherness: that which is absolutely pure is that which is totally itself, there being no extraneous matter, no impurity, altering its essential nature. Thus, 'to be purely for God' is to refuse access to any other 'colouring' than that of the object of devotion, it is to take on only His 'colour'. So it is not religion, but God Who is worshipped: *And we worship Him.*

The meaning and implications of verses II: 135–140 are clear enough; but the commentary given by Kāshānī on this passage helps to reinforce the distinction between confessional formalism and spiritual essentiality, between attachment to religious form and orientation to the divine Reality, and between the inevitable differentiation on the plane of religion and the unifying force proper to integral *tawḥīd*. To put his commentary in context, we need to go back a few verses. II: 130 begins *And who turns away from the religion of Abraham except one who fooleth himself*; Kāshānī identifies this 'religion' as that of *tawḥīd*. The passage continues (II: 131–2): *When his Lord said unto him: Submit* (aslim)! *He said: I have submitted* (aslamtu) *to the Lord of the worlds. The same did Abraham enjoin upon his sons, and also Jacob* [saying]: *O my sons, God hath truly chosen for you the religion; therefore die not except as those who have submitted* (muslimūn). Kāshānī glosses the words *the religion* as follows: 'that is, His religion, which is followed by the realizer of *tawḥīd* (*al-muwaḥḥid*), for whom there is no religion apart from this, and no essence; so his religion is the religion of God, and its essence, the essence of God. . .'[57]

Verses 133–134 read: *Or were ye present when death came to Jacob, when he said to his sons: What will ye worship when I have passed away? They said: We shall worship thy God, the God of thy fathers, Abraham and Ishmael and Isaac, One God, and unto Him we have submitted. Those are a people who have passed away. Theirs is that which they earned and yours is that which ye earn. And ye will not be responsible for what they did.* Kāshānī comments: 'That is, do not be imitators (*muqallidūn*), do not be content with mere imitation in religion, for one cannot rely upon transmitted knowledge. One only acquires that which one has earned—from one's knowledge and action, from one's belief and conduct. No one is rewarded for the belief or actions of another. So conduct yourself in accordance with your own insight, and aspire to certainty, and act thereupon.'

We now arrive at verses 135–140; in the passage that follows Kāshānī does not cite the verses in their entirety, only certain words, which are given in italics to mark them off from his commentary:

> '*And they say: Be Jews or Christians*—each is veiled by his religion, claiming that the Real is identified with their religion and none other. *Say Nay but* [we are of] *the religious community* (milla) *of Abraham*, for truly, absolute

[57] *Tafsīr*, vol. I, p. 59.

guidance (*al-hudā al-muṭlaq*) is *tawḥīd*, which comprises all religions, and lifts every veil, as He says in His words: *Say: we believe in God...* (verse 136, to the end:) *We make no distinction between any of them* [the prophets], by negating the religion of some, rejecting the validity of their community, while affirming the other religion and its truth. Rather, we declare that all of them are brought together within the Real, and they are all concordant with *tawḥīd*; and that all religions are transcribed by *tawḥīd*, which comprises all of them.[58] *And if they believe in the like of that which ye believe*, that is, in *tawḥīd*, which brings together every religion and creed, *then they are rightly guided*, in the absolute [or non-delimited] state of right guidance, that is, according to every manner of right guidance. *But if they turn away, then they are* taking sides in religion, splitting up the guidance, causing you to be divided with regard to it. *The colour of God*, that is, we believe in God, and take God as our colour, for the inward dimension (*bāṭin*) of every one who possesses a belief and creed is coloured with the colour of his belief, his religion and his creed. Thus the worshippers of the different religious communities are coloured by the colour of their intentions; those who follow a particular school of law, by the colour of their *imām* and their leader; the philosophers, by the colour of their intellects; the folk of caprice and schismatic innovation, by the colour of their whims and their souls; and the realizers of oneness, by the colour of God alone, than which no other colour is more excellent...'[59]

One is reminded here of Junayd's dictum, which Ibn ʿArabī so often repeats: 'Water takes on the colour of the cup'.[60] Ibn ʿArabī

[58] It is important to note here that *tawḥīd* is said to comprise all religions within itself (*al-shāmil li-kullihā*). This aspect of 'integration' proper to *tawḥīd* must not be overlooked.

[59] *Ibid.*, p. 60.

[60] See Chittick, *Sufi Path of Knowledge*, pp. 149, 229, 341–344.

refers to the need to go beyond the 'God created in beliefs', that is the restriction on the reality of the divine constituted by the form of one's own beliefs. The sage is the one who sees God both within all such beliefs, and also above and beyond them. The transcendence of the divine Reality vis-à-vis beliefs does not imply that such beliefs are devoid of value: they are vehicles of salvation insofar as they are all rooted in divine revelation, and insofar as the divine Reality is truly present in these beliefs that are 'created' by God, even if the conception of God within them is, in a certain sense, 'created' by man. That is, it is the product, in one respect, of man's faculty of conception. The essential content of the belief—the 'water' in the cup—is divine, while the conceptual form taken by it—the 'cup'—is human. On the one hand: 'Since God is the root of every diversity in beliefs... everyone will end up with mercy. For it is He who created them (the diverse beliefs)...'[61] On the other: 'Beware of being bound up by a particular creed and rejecting others as unbelief! Try to make yourself a prime matter for all forms of religious belief. God is greater and wider than to be confined to one particular creed to the exclusion of others. For He says *To whichever direction you turn, there is the face of God.*'[62]

This warning by Ibn ʿArabī elucidates the meaning of the *colour of God*. It reaffirms the need to go beyond the 'colour' imparted by religious dogma or affiliation to the pure Absolute, which, for its part, is beyond all colour in the ordinary sense.

---

[61] *Ibid.*, p. 388

[62] Quoted by T. Izutsu, *Sufism and Taoism*, p. 254. We have modified somewhat Izutsu's translation of this passage from the *Fuṣūṣ* (pp. 135-136). In particular, the word *ʿaqīda*, should, we believe, be translated as 'creed' and not, as Izutsu has it, 'religion'. Izutsu's translation nonetheless adequately conveys the clear intention behind this warning to believers not to restrict God to the form of their own belief, whether this be a doctrinal form vis-à-vis other possible forms within the same religion, or a religious belief vis-à-vis the beliefs of other religions. But, as has been discussed earlier, for Ibn ʿArabī, there is but one religion, which comprises diverse modes of revelation and different rulings, according to the requirements of the different human collectivities addressed by the one and only divinity.

Hence, God's true 'colour' might in fact be referred to as colourlessness, that which transcends all manifestation. It is interesting to note in this connection that Rūmī refers to colour as a metaphor for manifestation, in contradistinction to 'colourlessness', standing here for the Absolute, which is untainted by any 'shade' of manifestation: 'Since colourlessness (pure Unity) became the captive of colour (manifestation in the phenomenal world), a Moses came into conflict with a Moses. When you attain unto the colourlessness which you possessed, Moses and Pharaoh are at peace.'[63]

When he refers directly to the Qur'ānic term *ṣibghat Allāh*, as in the following verses, the deepest mystical meaning of 'taking on the colour of God' is brought to our attention, and we return to *fanā'* as the consummation of true Islam:

'*The baptism*[64] *of Allāh* is the dyeing-vat of *Hu* (He, the Absolute): therein (all) piebald things become of one colour.
When he (the mystic) falls into the vat, and you say to him, "Arise," he says in rapture, "I am the vat: do not blame (me)."
That "I am the vat" is the (same as) saying "I am God": he has the colour of the fire, albeit he is iron.
The colour of the iron is naughted in the colour of the fire: it (the iron) boasts of (its) fieriness, though (actually) it is like one who keeps silence.'[65]

In these lines Rūmī takes his reader to the ultimate metaphysical implication of taking upon oneself the 'colour of God': it is not just one's religion that is transcended by this colour, but also, and essentially, one's very individuality. That individuality perforce remains—the 'iron' remains iron—but it is transfigured in the very measure that it gives itself up to the fire, and thereby assumes its fiery 'colour'. The true *muwaḥḥid* thus rises above all particularities that can in any way 'tinge' the colour of the Absolute with its own nature; he focuses on nothing but the Absolute, so that all relative things are perceived in Its light,

[63] *Mathnawī*, I, verses 2467–8.

[64] Nicholson translates *ṣibgha* as 'baptism'.

[65] *Ibid.*, II, verses 1345–1348 (partially modified).

rather than It being perceived through the prisms of relativity.[66] It is worth repeating here the couplet of Rūmī which sums up the perspective being expounded here:

> 'The religion of Love is separate from all religions.
> For lovers, the religion and creed is—God.'[67]

* * *

As will be seen in the next section, even such universalist mystics as Rūmī show their particularism on the plane of religious forms, and believe in the normativity and uniqueness of Islam as the final revelation. This belief, however, does not necessarily imply chauvinism, and still less, intolerance. For the metaphysical vision of the religious essence that transcends all forms leads directly to an appreciation of the possibility of salvation and sanctification through diverse—and unequal—religious forms. The importance of highlighting the spirit of universality thus shows itself here not only in regard to those who are already sensitive to the truth and holiness present in other religions, but also in respect of those who adhere to a more narrowly circumscribed particularism. For a belief in the superiority of Islam, while it certainly can lead to exclusivism and fanaticism, need not necessarily do so. This belief can be aerated, opened up, and rendered receptive to alien religious forms, through dialogue with the other, on the one hand; and through the efforts of Muslim scholars and thinkers to valorise and bring into sharper focus the universal aspects of the Qur'ānic discourse, such as has been attempted here.

---

[66] See the discussion of this point in connection with our critique of postmodern hermeneutics in Chapter I.

[67] *Mathnawī*, II, verse 1770. The following line from Rūmī's *Dīwān-i Shams al-Dīn Tabrīzī* is also pertinent here: 'O lovers! The religion of love is not found in Islam alone.' Quoted by Ashk Dahlen, 'Transcendent Hermeneutics of Supreme Love: Rumi's Concept of Mystical Appropriation' in *Orientalia Suecana* (vol. 52, Uppsala, 2003).

Another way of making this point to those who regard other religious forms as less 'complete' than Islam, or in a certain sense superseded by it, is to stress that, according to the Qur'ān, all believers in God can and must be regarded as belonging to the same community, the same *umma* defined in terms of essential faith, rather than as a confessionally delimited community.[68] There is evidence in the Qur'ān to indicate that within this single community of mankind there is absolute spiritual equality: for each person is judged strictly according to his or her own state of soul, not on the basis of formal religious affiliation, nor on the basis of conforming outwardly to a set of formal legal rules. Salvation—and, *a fortiori*, sanctification—is the consummation, through grace, of a fundamental spiritual orientation; it is not the automatic reward bestowed upon one simply for belonging to one community rather than another, or for acting in certain ways as opposed to others. In the Sūra entitled 'The Prophets', the following verse is given, after mentioning several prophets and finishing with a reference to the Virgin Mary: *Truly, this, your umma, is one umma, and I am your Lord, so worship Me* (XXI: 92).

Just as *our God and your God is one*,[69] so, all believers, whatever be the outward, denominational form taken by their belief, are judged strictly according to their merits, and not according to some artificial formal label: *And those who believe and do good works, We shall bring them into Gardens underneath which rivers flow, wherein they will abide forever—a promise of God in truth; and who can be more truthful than God in utterance?* (IV: 122)[70] Lest one think that the category *those who believe and do good works* refers

[68] The term *umma* is used in several different contexts. For example, Abraham is described as an *umma* (XVI: 120); all creatures form their own *umma* (VI: 38).

[69] The verse in which these words are given is as follows: *And only discourse with the People of the Book in a way that is most excellent, save with those who do wrong. And say: We believe in that which hath been revealed to us and revealed to you. Our God and your God is one, and unto Him we surrender* (XXIX: 46).

[70] This is reinforced by the verse, cited in the last chapter, which declares piety to be the sole criterion of honour with God: *O mankind, truly We have created you male and female, and have made you nations and tribes that ye may know*

only to the Muslims in the specific sense—one possible reading, admittedly—the following verse establishes the universal scope of the *promise*. This verse, indeed, is of the utmost importance for the perspective or the 'reading' being expounded here: *It will not be in accordance with your desires, nor the desires of the People of the Scripture. He who doth wrong will have the recompense thereof*. . . (IV: 123)

One can read this verse as implying that insofar as the Muslim 'desires' that salvation be restricted to Muslims in the specific, communal sense, he falls into exactly the same kind of exclusivism of which the Christians and Jews stand accused: *And they say: None entereth paradise unless he be a Jew or a Christian. These are their own desires* (II: 111). It should be noted that the very same word is used both for the 'desires' of the Jews and the Christians, and the 'desires' of the Muslims, *amāniyy* (sing. *umniyya*).[71] As noted above, the logic of these verses clearly indicates that one form of religious prejudice, or chauvinism is not to be replaced with another form of the same, but with an objective, unprejudiced recognition of the inexorable and universal law of divine justice. This universal law is expressed with the utmost clarity in the following two verses which complete this important passage from the *Sūrat al-Nisā'*: *And whoso doeth good works, whether male or female, and is a believer, such will enter paradise, and will not be wronged the dint of a date-stone. Who is better in religion than he who submitteth his purpose to God* (aslama wajhahu li'Llāh), *while being virtuous, and following the religious community of Abraham the unswervingly devout?*. . . (IV: 124-125)

In these four verses, taken together as a whole (IV: 122-125), the divine 'promise' of salvation is starkly contrasted with confessional 'desires'; on the one hand there is an objective and

one another. Truly the most noble of you, in the sight of God, is the most pious of you. Truly, God is Knowing, Aware. (XLIX: 13)

[71] Note the negative connotation of this word in the Qur'ān; it is even applied to the personal desire of the prophets, into which Satan casts his insinuation. See XXII: 52.

universal criterion of wholehearted submission to God, and on the other, a subjective and particularistic criterion of formal attachment to a specific community. To return to the verse cited above, one should note the riposte that follows the unwarranted exclusivism of the People of the Book: *And they say: None entereth paradise unless he be a Jew or a Christian. These are their own desires. Say: Bring your proof if ye are truthful. Nay, but whosoever submitteth his purpose to God, and he is virtuous, his reward is with his Lord. No fear shall come upon them, neither shall they grieve.* (II: 111-112)

Verse 112 thus comes as a concrete rebuttal of this kind of religious exclusivism. It does not contradict the exclusivist claims of the Jews and the Christians with an exclusivism of its own, that is, with a claim that only 'Muslims', in the specific sense, go to paradise. Access to salvation, far from being further narrowed by reference to the privileged rights of some other 'group', is broadened, and in fact universalized: those who attain salvation and enter paradise are those who have submitted wholeheartedly to God and are intrinsically virtuous. Faithful submission, allied to virtue: such are the two indispensable requisites for salvation.[72] Thus, it is perfectly justified to argue that the verse does not respond 'in kind' to the exclusivism of the People of the Book: rather, it pitches the response on a completely different level, a supra-theological or metaphysical level, which surpasses all reified definitions, confessional denominations, communal allegiances and partisan affiliations.[73] One receives heavenly reward not for having a particular label, but on account of

[72] From another point of view, even these two quintessential elements of religion are inadequate; that is, they are necessary but not sufficient conditions for salvation, given that, according to the Prophet, 'no one is saved by their deeds'. When asked: 'Not even you, O messenger of God?', he replied that not even he was saved by his deeds, 'unless God embraces me with mercy (*illā an yataghammadanī Allāh bi-raḥma*)'. See Bukhārī, *Ṣaḥīḥ*, vol. VIII, p. 313.

[73] In his article 'Christianity in the Qur'ān' (*Encounter—Documents for Muslim-Christian Understanding*, no. 81, 1982), Reverend J. M. Richie points out that these verses (II: 111-113), 'remind us of what our dogmatism tends to obscure, that a man's faith can only be judged from his behaviour: we cannot judge his behaviour from the faith or belief he professes.'

that submission and virtue that flow forth from one's faith. Islam, then, denotes, from the strictly Qur'ānic perspective, submission of self to God, and from the point of view of Sufi spirituality, includes also that pinnacle of self-submission: self-annihilation in the Reality of God, *al-fanā' fī'Llāh*, the former being, as mentioned earlier, a prefiguration or anticipation of the latter.

The following verse, II: 113 should also be noted here: *And the Jews say the Christians follow nothing, and the Christians say the Jews follow nothing; yet they are readers of the Book. Even thus speak those who know not. God will judge between them on the Day of Resurrection concerning that wherein they differ.* Kāshānī comments as follows: '*And the Jews say the Christians follow nothing*—because they are veiled by their religion from their [the Christian] religion; likewise, the Christians say the same, because they are veiled by the inward (*al-bāṭin*) from the outward (*al-ẓāhir*), just as the Jews are veiled by the outward from the inward.'[74] Then Kāshānī adds an important self-critical comment from which today's Muslims can derive considerable benefit: the state of being veiled from the inward reality by the outward form is, he says, precisely the condition into which 'the followers of the legal schools of thought (*ahl al-madhāhib*) in Islam today' have fallen. The criticism, then, that is made of the 'People of the Book' extends, according to Kāshānī, to the Muslims also, in the very measure that they lapse into the outwardness that enshrouds the inner reality of the faith—a reality that is universal and inclusive—with the forms of the religion—forms that are particular and thus exclusive.[75]

---

[74] *Tafsīr*, vol. I, pp. 53–54.

[75] Lory also makes the point that the description of the 'Muḥammadans' given by Kāshānī, that is, those who have attained the full plenitude of spiritual realization, are not just the Sufis of the Islamic tradition, but all of those saints in other traditions who have attained this highest degree of spirituality. Conversely, the archetypes of the 'Jew' and the 'Christian'—one who is veiled by the divine Acts, and one veiled by the Qualities, respectively—are found also amongst Muslims. See Lory, *Commentaires*, p. 124, n. 2; see also pp. 122–135 for discussion of this question.

His commentary continues: '. . . *yet they are readers of the Book*—within which is that which guides them aright, to the lifting of the veil and to the vision of the truth of every religion and school of thought.' He then proceeds to criticise those who remain in the state of *taqyīd*, that is, fettered or 'tied up', by the forms of their own beliefs. This criticism is not just made of the Christians and the Jews, but extends to all of those who are restricted and confined within their own beliefs. It is important to observe here the etymology of the word 'belief': *ʿaqīda* or *iʿtiqād* derive from the root *ʿaqada*, the primary meaning of which is 'to tie a knot'. The mass of ordinary believers are 'tied up' into the 'knot' of their belief; only the *muwaḥḥid*, the realizer of oneness, 'is not bound by the form of his belief (*lam yataqayyad bi-ṣūrati muʿtaqidihi*)'.[76] Kāshānī goes so far as to say that it is a form of *kufr*, disbelief, to be veiled by the 'blessing of religion' from 'the one who bestows blessing' (*al-munʿim*).[77] This relates of course to the root meaning of the word, *kafara*, 'to cover'. From this point of view, the individual thus enshrouds the Absolute with the veil of the blessings of the Absolute, in the very measure that adherence to religion distracts from, instead of leading to, the source and goal of religion: [We take our] *colour from God; and who is better than God at colouring? And we worship Him.* (II: 138)

Particularism within Universalism

It might be objected here that the Qur'ānic verses commented on above (II: 135–140) could just as easily be interpreted as an affirmation of Islamic particularism, the 'Islam' revealed by the Qur'ān being the purest form of that primordial religion of

[76] *Ibid.*, I, p. 54. He makes reference here to a well-known *ḥadīth* in which God, unrecognised in a particular form by a group of believers, transforms Himself in order to be recognised by them. See Muslim, *Ṣaḥīḥ*, *kitāb al-īmān*, 302; see also the discussion of this saying by Ibn ʿArabī in Chittick, *Sufi Path of Knowledge*, pp. 38, 100, 336–7.

[77] *Ibid.*, I, p. 65.

Abraham that was subsequently distorted by the Jews and the Christians. It will readily be conceded that such a view would be upheld, in differing degrees, and with varying implications, not only by traditional theological/exoteric authorities but also by mystical/esoteric ones—including those cited here, Ibn ʿArabī, Rūmī, Kāshānī and Ghazālī. For all such Sufis—those belonging to what one might call the 'normative' Sufi tradition, in which the Shariʿa is scrupulously upheld—Islam in the particular sense would indeed be regarded as the most complete religion, *qua* religion, the final, comprehensive and universally binding revelation.

Indeed, it would be pointed out that Kāshānī continues his commentary on the verses above not only with a reference to Islam as the 'truth of truths', 'the most tremendous and manifest truth', but also with criticism of the People of the Book for their failure to recognise the spiritual reality and 'conclusive finality' of Islam.[78]

In other words, the 'universalists', whose insights and readings of the Qur'ān are being presented here appear also to be 'particularists' in that they all affirm the superiority of Islam in the particular sense. That is, they give precedence, theologically, to Islam, even while affirming the holiness, virtue and truth which are present in principle within other revealed traditions. Does this return to particularism vitiate the conception of the universal religious essence that has been presented above? Not at all. This universal conception is not undermined for two reasons, one principial and the other practical. As regards the principial reason: the particular, as has been repeatedly stressed, is to be embraced and 'comprehended' by a perspective that is truly universal. Secondly, on the practical level, it is precisely

[78] *Ibid.*, I, p. 60–61. This comes in his commentary on the words *the foolish ones among people* (II: 142). Rūmī also says, in a statement quoted fully below, that one who sees that God has sent 'a Prophet superior to Jesus, manifesting by his hand all that He manifested by Jesus' hand and more, it behoves him to follow that Prophet, for God's sake, not for the sake of the Prophet himself.' *Discourses*, p. 136.

this ability to comprehend and include the particular that makes the 'universalists' of Islam so relevant to the religion as a whole, and prevents them from being dismissed as individualist free-thinkers on the margins of the faith. In other words, it is this very particularism that opens up the mainstream of the faith to some degree of universalism. This point will be developed in the following chapter, dealing as it does with different levels of dialogue.

The rest of this section will explore the paradoxical combination of particularism and universalism in Ibn ʿArabī's perspective, with particular reference to the distinction between the universal 'religion of love' (or what we might call 'ontological religion') and 'revealed religion', presenting this theme in relation to its foundations in the text of the Qur'ān in order to integrate it within the larger argument of this chapter. In so doing the intention is to make clear the distinction between the universal 'ontological religion' and the specifically religious form of universality; and to see that upholding Islamic particularism does not contradict the principle of a religious essence residing at the core of all revealed religions. Each apparent 'limitation' should be grasped in the light of the ontological principle of Ibn ʿArabī: that the completeness of being requires limitation, the infinite presupposes finitude, the universal is present within the particular. And this principle is expressed in the hermeneutical axiom underlying this exposition: that inclusivism must include exclusivism, even while going beyond it.

We can begin this discussion by citing again the following lines from Ibn ʿArabī's *Tarjumān al-ashwāq*, which contain the most famous reference to the 'religion of love' (*dīn al-ḥubb*) in Arabic Sufi poetry:

> My heart has become capable of every form: it is a pasture for gazelles and a convent for Christian monks,
> And a temple for idols and the pilgrim's Kaʿba and the tables of the Tora and the book of the Koran.

> I follow the religion of Love: whatever way Love's camels take, that is my religion and my faith.[79]

It should be clear that such declarations as these are rooted in the 'ontological' perception of *tawḥīd* that was discussed in the first part of Chapter II above. The principle whence such a vision springs is not only clearly related to 'ontological *tawḥīd*', but also to the Qur'ānic perspective on the universal 'praise' accomplished by all things, by dint of their very existence, as noted also in the previous chapter. It is in this spirit that Ibn ʿArabī interprets the following verse not as a formal injunction but as an ontological decree: *Thy Lord has decreed that you shall not worship any but Him.* (XVII: 23)

In other words, for Ibn ʿArabī, this is not a religious command that can be obeyed or disobeyed, but an all-encompassing principle, from which no thing is excluded: whatever be the ostensible object or subjective focus of worship it is only God that is in fact worshipped in reality. From this point of view, even the polytheistic idol-worshipper cannot, objectively, worship anything other than God; it is God, alone, who 'receives' the worship of whatever is worshipped. From the point of view of the oneness of being, the 'religion of love' is conceived as the ontologically inescapable 'praise' offered up to God by all the phenomena of the cosmos without exception. The 'sin' of the idolator consists, on the one hand, in viewing his object of worship as being separate from its divine source; and, on the other hand, in the fact that it is he, rather than God, who instituted this form of worship. It is not divinely revealed but humanly 'constructed' religion. But this cannot detract from the ontological truth that 'in every object of worship it is God who is worshipped.'[80]

The issue of provenance, though, is of fundamental importance in Ibn ʿArabī's perspective; it constitutes the criterion for evaluating true religion and discriminating between it and its

[79] *Tarjumān*, p. 67.

[80] *Bezels*, p. 78.

counterfeit. This is the import of the following visionary event experienced by Ibn ʿArabī:

> 'I saw in an Incident a spring of fresh milk. I had never seen milk so white and pleasant. I entered into it until it reached my breast, while it was gushing forth, and I marveled at that. I heard a strange divine speech saying, "He who prostrates himself to other than God by God's command seeking nearness to God and obeying God will be felicitous and attain deliverance, but he who prostrates himself to other than God without God's command seeking nearness will be wretched. God says, *The places of prostration belong to God, so call not upon anyone with God.*" (LXXII: 18).'[81]

This echoes the point made earlier: though God's *Face* is there wherever one turns, the Muslim has been instructed to turn in a particular direction in prayer. Here, despite the fact that nothing can be worshipped except God, it is only that form of worship ordained by God which is acceptable to Him, and it is obedience to this divine decree which results in felicity and deliverance. Wretchedness is the lot of one who 'associates' others with God, inasmuch as he has 'set up for himself a special road of worship which was not established for him by a revealed Law from the Real'.[82] However, this wretchedness is not eternal, since 'all will end up in mercy', according to a fundamental theme of Ibn ʿArabī's eschatology.[83] He takes as absolutely unconditional the Qur'ānic verse which says, *My Mercy encompasseth all things* (VII: 156). Eternal suffering would be a 'thing' not encompassed by God's Mercy, therefore there can be no such 'thing' as eternal suffering.[84] However, the reality of heaven and hell, together with the force of the distinction

[81] Chittick, *Sufi Path of Knowledge*, p. 365

[82] *Ibid.*, p. 343.

[83] *Ibid.*, p. 338.

[84] See Corbin, *Creative Imagination in the Sufism of Ibn ʿArabī* (tr. R. Mannheim), (Princeton, Princeton University Press, 1969), pp. 105–135 for one

between 'felicity' and 'wretchedness' in the Hereafter, is by no means attenuated by this ultimate metaphysical consummation of all things in the divine Mercy. On their own plane, these distinctions remain real; it is the plane itself that is ultimately engulfed by the inescapable, ultimate reality of Mercy.[85]

Ibn ʿArabī tells us that whatever be given as the 'names' of the gods worshipped as idols, all of these idols, together with all objects in creation, cannot but be theophanies of the one divinity, the one Reality:

> 'The perfect gnostic is one who regards every object of worship as a manifestation of God in which He is worshipped. They call it a god, though its proper name might be stone, wood, animal, man, star or angel. Although that might be its particular name, Divinity presents a level that causes the worshipper to imagine that it is his object of worship. In reality, this level is the Self-manifestation of God to the consciousness of the worshipper of the object in this particular mode of manifestation.'[86]

The Essence of God cannot be defined, conceived, meditated upon or worshipped; it is only His Names and Qualities that make accessible to human consciousness something of the divine nature. This is because there is no common measure

---

of the most illuminating expositions of the theme of mercy in Ibn ʿArabī's doctrine.

[85] One sees an allusion to this subtle metaphysical truth in XI: 107–108, which tell us that the wicked abide in hell for *as long as the heavens and the earth endure, except as thy Lord willeth*; whereas in the case of the paradisal abode this same double limitation is immediately followed by the words: *a gift never to be cut off*. That which brings paradise to an end can only therefore be something of even greater beatific magnitude, an idea which evokes the verse: *God promiseth to the believing men and believing women Gardens underneath which rivers flow, wherein they will abide—blessed dwellings in Gardens of Eden. And the Good Pleasure* (riḍwān) *of God is greater.* (IX: 72)

[86] *Bezels*, p. 247.

between the created individual as such and the supra-manifest transcendence of the divine Essence. Thus, Ibn ʿArabī asserts that the individual's worship does not reach the One (*al-Aḥad*), but only relates to the personal Divinity, that is, the Lord (*al-Rabb*), that 'level' of the divine Reality at which the relationship between God and the world is mediated, through the divine Names and Qualities. This important, and radical, point is made by Ibn ʿArabī by means of an esoteric interpretation of the following words of the Qur'ānic verse: *Let him not associate one with his Lord's worship.* (XVIII: 110)[87]

The literal meaning of the verse relates to the legal prohibition of *shirk*; but Ibn ʿArabī makes the 'one' in question refer to 'the One', *al-Aḥad*, the unique and unattainable Essence, and thus says:

> 'He is not worshipped in respect of His Unity, since Unity contradicts the existence of the worshipper. It is as if He is saying, "What is worshipped is only the 'Lord' in respect of His Lordship, since the Lord brought you into existence. So connect yourself to Him and make yourself lowly before Him, and do not associate Unity with Lordship in worship... For Unity does not know you and will not accept you..."'[88]

Even the divine scriptures do not reach the divine Essence, but only reveal aspects of the divine Names and Qualities; each scripture, being itself a revelation, and thus distinct from the essence of that which is revealed, can only disclose other manifestations—other 'revelations'—of the Essence and not the Essence itself. In another of his poems, Ibn ʿArabī refers to the beautiful maiden Niẓām, as symbol of the ultimate Reality (*al-ḥaqīqa*): 'She has baffled everyone who is learned in our religion, every student of the Psalms of David, every Jewish doctor and

---

[87] See Āmulī's commentary on this verse, given in the previous chapter.

[88] Chittick, *Sufi Path of Knowledge*, p. 244.

every Christian priest.'[89] In his own commentary on these lines, the following explanation is given: 'All the sciences comprised in the four Books [Qur'ān, Psalms, Torah and Gospel] point only to the Divine Names and are incapable of solving a question that concerns the Divine Essence.'[90]

This perspective is of course entirely in accordance with the principle of divine transcendence. The Qur'ān repeatedly declares *Exalted be God above what they describe.* If descriptions and words relate only to the Attributes of God, not His Essence, the worship ordained by the scriptures—all of them, it should be noted—relates only to the 'Lord', not the Essence, the Lord that is the immediate source of the Names and Attributes, that 'level' (*martaba*) of the divine Reality which receives worship and responds to it. Hence, all that is worshipped, by the idol-worshipper and the monotheist alike, is not God in His Essence, or God as such, but God such as He reveals Himself in a particular mode of self-disclosure. Now formal religion is one mode of this manifestation; but so is the whole of the created order. So when the idolator worships some created object as 'God' what is being worshipped is nothing but the divine Presence within the object. There is thus a mysterious, ontological link between idolatry and monotheistic religion; both fall short of the Essence, in the most metaphysically rigorous perspective, and are focused on the self-manifestation of God, on some theophany of the divine Reality, however much the one may lead to 'felicity' and the other to 'wretchedness'. It is in the light of this link, or this common ontological 'infrastructure', that one can appreciate the following lines of Shabistarī's poetic masterpiece, *Gulshan-i rāz* (The Garden of Divine Mysteries); lines that are so shocking to the exoteric mentality:

> 'O Muslim, if you knew what the idol is,
> You would know that religion is in idol-worship.'[91]

---

[89] *Tarjumān*, p. 49.

[90] *Ibid.*, p. 52.

[91] Translated from the text of the poem as contained within the commentary of Shams al-Dīn Muḥammad Lāhījī, *Mafātīḥ al-iʿjāz fī sharḥ-i*

Religion is 'in' idol-worship firstly because the idol, being an existent entity, cannot but be a locus of the divine self-manifestation, for everything that exists is a receptacle for the effusion of the one and only being, that of God; secondly, what is worshipped is in fact the theophanic dimension of the object, that is, the element of divinity that, alone, receives worship, according to the Qur'ānic verse quoted above: nothing can be worshipped but God; thirdly, 'religion is in idol-worship' in that all religious devotion relates, not to the Essence of God, but to a determinate level of the divine nature, that is, to God as Lord and not as Essence; and finally, because the conception of God, even in revealed, monotheistic religion, is inescapably the product of two elements, one human, the other divine: the conception is mentally articulated, on the one hand, and divinely revealed, on the other. There is the human 'container' and the divine 'content'.[92] One is again reminded of the image given by Junayd cited earlier: 'Water takes on the colour of the cup'.[93]

The ubiquity of the divine Presence, then, leaves room for nothing but Ibn ʿArabī's universal religion of love, a kind of

---

gulshan-i rāz (Tehran: Intishārāt-i Zuwwār, 2000) p. 538. Lāhījī writes in his commentary: 'Behind the curtain of the individuation of every single atom, the sun of the oneness of the Real lies veiled and hidden.' *Ibid.*, p. 538. See Leonard Lewisohn, *Beyond Faith and Infidelity—The Sufi Poetry and Teachings of Mahmud Shabistarī* (London: Curzon Press, 1995), p. 292 for discussion of these lines in the *Gulshan-i rāz*. Lewisohn's book is the most comprehensive appraisal and contextualization of Shabistarī's doctrines available in the English language. (It should be noted that Shabistarī's poem is widely regarded as one of the most profound poetic expressions in Persian of the Akbarī doctrine of *waḥdat al-wujūd*.)

[92] Needless to say, from this point of view, the divine content takes precedence over the mental container, and this for two reasons: firstly, because the content is absolute and the container is relative; and secondly, the container, human consciousness, is itself moulded by God—the preparedness of the heart being fashioned by the 'most holy effusion (*al-fayḍ al-aqdas*)' in the Akbarī perspective. The human container itself is therefore also an aspect of the divine self-manifestation, and thus a property of the divine content. We return to the theme of the 'hidden treasure' that loved to be known.

[93] See Chittick, *Sufi Path of Knowledge*, pp. 149, 229, 341-344.

religion which burns up all forms in its quest for that which transcends all forms; this transcendence having been glimpsed, intuited or realized as being above all forms, it is then grasped within and through all forms. Thus, when the Sufi poets sing of their having adopted all forms of religious devotion, including idol-worship, one can understand this as being, among other things, an expression of their having transcended not just forms as such, but also formalism—the hypocrisy that consists in reducing the intended essence of worship to its outward forms, and pretending that adherence to these forms suffices to prove one's piety or sanctity.

The distinction between the two levels—spiritual vision and theological exposition—helps explain many puzzling juxtapositions, within one and the same author's work, of spiritual universality and theological specificity. Returning to Ibn ʿArabī, one can see this combination of universalism and particularism as an expression of the principle derived from his hermeneutics and his ontology: true universalism must contain particularism. That he, too, is capable of shifting from the plane of universal reality to that of confessional partiality is clear from, among other things, the commentary he provides on his own verses, cited above, on the 'religion of love':

> 'No religion is more sublime than a religion based on love and longing for Him whom I worship and in whom I have faith... This is a peculiar prerogative of Muslims, for the station of perfect love is appropriated to Muḥammad beyond any other prophet, since God took him as His beloved.'[94]

One might also draw attention here to the paradoxical contrast between the profound universality expressed in Shabistarī's poetry and his vehement denunciations of, not just other religions, but also all those schools and sects in Islam that did not

[94] *Tarjumān*, p. 69

conform to his own strict Ashʿarism.[95] Likewise with Rūmī, we see that, though he declares that the religion of Love is separate from all religions, this religion being nothing but God Himself, he still chides the Christian, Jarrāḥ, for adhering to the mistaken belief that Christ is God; and urges him to adopt the superior religion brought through the last of the prophets. When Jarrāḥ says that he believes that Jesus is God because this is what 'our books' tell us, Rūmī replies:

> 'That is not the action or the words of an intelligent man possessed of sound senses. God gave you an intelligence of your own, other than your father's intelligence, a sight of your own other than your father's sight, a discrimination of your own. Why do you nullify your sight and your intelligence, following an intelligence that will destroy you and not guide you?... Certainly, it is right that... the Lord of Jesus, upon whom be peace, honoured Jesus and brought him nigh to Him, so that whoever serves him has served his Lord, whoever obeys him has obeys his Lord. But inasmuch as God has sent a Prophet superior to Jesus, manifesting by his hand all that He manifested by Jesus' hand and more, it behoves him to follow that Prophet, for God's sake, not for the sake of the Prophet himself.'[96]

[95] A paradox well brought out by Leonard Lewisohn, *Beyond Faith and Infidelity*, pp. 24-38.

[96] *Discourses*, pp. 135-136. Muhammad Legenhausen cites this passage in his *Islam and Religious Pluralism* (London: Al-Hoda, 1999), pp. 108-109, in order to show that Rūmī 'was by no means a reductive religious pluralist of the sort Hick makes him out to be'. Legenhausen's critique of Hick's presentation of religious pluralism, from a strictly orthodox Muslim point of view, is incisive and irrefutable. Despite the positive features of this book, certain aspects of the critique of Nasr, whose 'pluralism' differs radically from that of Hick, are not justified. We will return to this point in the next chapter. Also in the following chapter reference will be made to other passages in Rūmī's *Discourses* which must be read in conjunction with the one under consideration here.

In other words, a poetic vision *can* inspire a form of specifically religious—as opposed to ontological—universality, but it should not be equated with it, *grosso modo.* A careful distinction must be made between clear universalist openings to the other revealed religions, based on a spiritual assimilation of their message, on the one hand; and an ontological embrace of any and all forms of worship, on the basis of the principle which affirms that 'none is worshipped but God'. To give a clear instance of the former, whereby a dogma of a foreign religion is interpreted in a way which universalizes its meaning and thus renders it spiritually assimilable, Shabistarī's poetic rendition of the meaning of Christ's 'sonship' can be cited here.[97] The following verses are given as a kind of commentary on the words of Jesus in the Gospel of St John, 'I go to the Father' (XVI: 16):

'First the suckling infant,
bound to a cradle, is sustained on milk.
Then, when mature, becomes a wayfarer,
and if a man, travels with his father.

The elements of nature for you
resembles an earthborn mother.
You are a son whose father
Is a patriarch from on high.

So Jesus proclaimed up in ascension
"I go to my Father alone."
You too, O favourite of your father,
Set forth for your father!'[98]

Likewise, one is given the following altogether remarkable affirmation of religious universality, the uncompromising nature of which leaves no room whatsoever for any religious partiality. In his *Dīwān*, Manṣūr al-Ḥallāj writes the following verse:

---

[97] See the following chapter also for Ibn ʿArabī's treatment of the 'disbelief' (*kufr*) of the Christians in asserting the Sonship of Christ.

[98] Leonard Lewisohn, *Beyond Faith and Infidelity*, p. 90.

'Earnest for truth, I thought on the religions:
They are, I found, one root with many a branch.
Therefore impose on no man a religion,
Lest it should bar him from the firm-set root.
Let the root claim him, a root wherein all heights
And meanings are made clear for him to grasp.'[99]

As we have seen above, one can definitely discern within the Qur'ānic discourse a warrant for this supra-confessional perspective, even though it is extremely rare for the full metaphysical implications of this perspective to have been as boldly stated as they were by Ḥallāj. What is important here is that Ḥallāj's radical verse is not 'un-Qur'ānic'; the 'meditation' which gives rise to his evaluation is in complete harmony with *one* aspect of the Qur'ānic discourse, even if this supra-confessional aspect is so dazzling as to eclipse, for Ḥallāj, the exclusivist aspect of that same discourse, and thus the 'invitation' to the other to enter Islam that derives from that aspect of the Qur'ān's message. This is not so much a question of selectivity as of essentiality: Ḥallāj is drawing our attention here to the most essential, metaphysical implication of the supra-confessional dimension of religion, that to which reference was made in terms of the *fiṭra*, on the one hand, and the spiritual as opposed to merely conceptual realization of *tawḥīd*—or of 'the principle' as Ḥallāj refers to it here—on the other. When aspiration is focused upon this ultimate degree of realization, the limitations of all confessional perspectives are apparent but, by the same token, one also comes to perceive the possibilities of realization present within the confessional limitations of the religion of the other.

Such openings to other revealed religions, on the plane of universal spirituality, though, must be kept distinct from an indiscriminate acceptance of all modes of worship, such acceptance flowing forth as a concomitant of one's perception of the oneness of being. The two perspectives are certainly

[99] This is the translation of Martin Lings, taken from his book, *Sufi Poems—A Mediaeval Anthology* (Cambridge: Islamic Texts Society, 2004), p. 34.

compatible, and can in fact be mutually reinforcing, but one should not automatically assume a universalist approach to other religions on the part of one who poetically or rhetorically proclaims the oneness of being through extolling alien religious—and anti-religious—symbols.[100] One should carefully note that for Ibn ʿArabī, and for Shabistarī, who faithfully reflected the Akbarī perspective, the distinction between true religion—that which is revealed by God—and false religion—that which is instituted by man—remains real at its own level; it is this level, precisely, that is transcended by means of the realization of the oneness of being, the realization proper to 'the religion of love'.

It is by virtue of its rigorously theocentric focus, its view of religion as a means to this divine end, and not an end in itself, that this conception of the 'religion of love' is deemed to embrace all forms of religion, both those which are true and those which are false. From this point of view, though, no religion is 'false': all of existence is 'religion' inasmuch as *The seven heavens and the earth and all that is therein praise Him, and there is not a thing but hymneth His praise...* (XVII: 44). However, on the specifically religious plane, the criterion for evaluating true from false religion remains valid. For Ibn ʿArabī and his school, this criterion is divine revelation: 'The road to felicity is that set down by revealed religion, nothing else.'[101]

Even though all things are thus 'religious' in their inescapable ontological 'praise' of God, only those religions rooted in divine revelation can be regarded as true and valid in a specifically religious sense. The objection that would be made at this point by the conventional Muslim exclusivist is this: while previous

---

[100] Legenhausen makes this point effectively by quoting the following lines from the *Dīwān* of the late Ayatollah Khomeini:

> 'At the door of the tavern,
> temple, mosque and monastery,
> I have fallen in prostration,
> As though You had glanced upon me.'

Islam and Religious Pluralism, p. 115.

[101] Quoted by Chittick, *Imaginal Worlds*, p. 146.

revelations *were* true and valid in a specifically religious sense, they are no longer so, inasmuch as Islam, in the particular sense, has abrogated them all. From the time of the revelation of the Qur'ān and the promulgation of the Shariʿa by the last Prophet, all previous religious dispensations are rendered invalid. We shall turn to Ibn ʿArabī in the following chapter for one possible means of resolving this specific question.[102] In principial terms, however, the following passages from his corpus can be cited; this resonates deeply with the anti-chauvinist tone of the Qur'ānic discourse that we have been presenting in this chapter.

First, as noted earlier, Ibn ʿArabī explicitly warns against dogmatic chauvinism: 'Beware of being bound up by a particular creed and rejecting others as unbelief! Try to make yourself a prime matter for all forms of religious belief. God is greater and wider than to be confined to one particular creed to the exclusion of others. For He says *To whichever direction you turn, there is the face of God*.'[103]

This witnessing of the Divine in the diverse forms of religion can be seen as entirely congruent with the perception of ontological *tawḥīd*, or with what Ibn ʿArabī calls elsewhere the perception proper to the 'heart' of the 'Muḥammadan' saint, who witnesses the divine 'withness' (*maʿiyya*) in every moment and in every form, according to the verse: *He is with you* (maʿakum) *wherever ye may be* (LVII: 4). The consciousness proper to this kind of saint is not exhausted by the content of any specific revelation, but is receptive to the divine manifestation in all forms of revelation. This relates back to the distinction drawn above between the consciousness of the prophet and that of the saint:

> 'The perfect friend [*walī*, or saint] calls upon God in every station and tongue, but the messengers [*rusul*,

[102] The whole question of *naskh* (abrogation) is extremely complex; its theological/juridical aspects will not be broached here. It is the Sufi approach to the question, represented by Ibn ʿArabī, that will be of concern to us in the following chapter.

[103] Quoted by Izutsu, *Sufism and Taoism*, p. 254.

sing. *rasūl*]... stop with that which was revealed to them.[104] What has been revealed to one of them may not have been revealed to another. But the Muḥammadan gathers together through his level every call that has been dispersed among the messengers. Hence he is non-delimited because he calls with every tongue. For he is commanded to have faith in the messengers and in that which was sent down to them.'[105]

Here Ibn ʿArabī clearly intends us to have in mind the words of the verse cited above: *The Messenger believeth in that which hath been revealed unto him from his Lord, and* [so do] *the believers. Every one believeth in God and His angels and His scriptures and His Messengers—we make no distinction between any of His Messengers...* (II: 285)

As was said earlier, this is a credal affirmation, and while every exoteric Muslim will readily affirm belief in the messages brought by all previous messengers, in practice, this amounts to a belief only in those aspects of the previous religions that are identical to the Islam constituted in their own specific belief-system.[106] For Ibn ʿArabī, on the other hand, believing in the previous revelations implies that one 'does not stop with a specific revelation'[107] in terms of spiritual content. It is only in respect of specific commandments pertaining to what is lawful and unlawful that he does 'stop' with Islam in the particular sense. Here, again, we see the combination between an inwardly unbound spirituality—hence an innate receptivity

[104] One must remember here that the prophet only 'stops' with what is revealed to him insofar as he is a prophet, and in respect of his specific function of transmitting the message entrusted to him. But insofar as the prophet is also, and pre-eminently, a saint, his consciousness of the ultimate realities surpasses the limits proper to the particular contents of the message relayed by him.

[105] Chittick, *Sufi Path of Knowledge*, pp. 377-378.

[106] Ibn ʿArabī refers to this kind of restriction, as seen above, in terms of the 'God created in beliefs'.

[107] Chittick, *Sufi Path of Knowledge*, p. 378.

to the divine *Face* in the other—and an outwardly circumspect legality—hence fidelity to the *praxis* of one's own tradition. Such a combination of points of view, in addition to flowing forth organically from Ibn ʿArabī's basic approach, has the merit of rendering this kind of universal spirituality more accessible—or at least less unpalatable—to the formal scholars or the legally-oriented Muslims in general. In other words, this instance of 'bringing together opposites' permits the mentality governed by legal propriety to feel more secure about acknowledging, tolerating, and respecting the beliefs of the other. Legal formality is thus enlivened by the spirit, in the very measure that the spirit is itself grounded in the Law, this kind of interplay between the two apparently opposed dimensions of the letter and the spirit of the Law being constantly repeated in Ibn ʿArabī's perspective.

Finally, let us note the following practical advice Ibn ʿArabī gives to his readers:

> 'He who counsels his own soul should investigate during his life in this world, all doctrines concerning God. He should learn from whence each possessor of a doctrine affirms the validity of his doctrine. Once its validity has been affirmed for him in the specific mode in which it is correct for him who upholds it, then he should support it in the case of him who believes in it. He should not deny it or reject it, for he will gather its fruit on the Day of Visitation... So turn your attention to what we have mentioned and put it into practice! Then you will give the Divinity its due... For God is exalted high above entering under delimitation. He cannot be tied down by one form rather than another. From here you will come to know the all-inclusiveness of felicity for God's creatures and the all-embracingness of the mercy which covers everything.'[108]

The relationship between the all-encompassing mercy of God and the exaltation of God beyond all beliefs concerning Him

[108] *Ibid.*, p. 355–356.

should be noted here. On the one hand, we are urged by Ibn ʿArabī to make an effort to explore the root of 'all doctrines concerning God'; and on the other, we are told that this will lead us to see the felicity that embraces all creatures, thanks to divine Mercy, which as the Qur'ān tells us, and which Ibn ʿArabī continuously reminds us, *encompasseth all things*. The link is crucial: for God leads His creatures back to Himself by means of 'doctrines' that He mercifully reveals, even though these doctrines cannot, as it were, 'tie Him down'. No doctrine, no form of words, can delimit the Divine, for *Exalted be God above what they describe*. This very transcendence of Reality above all doctrines and beliefs, one's own included, should engender in the soul of the sensitive seeker not only a proper humility in regard to one's own beliefs, but also a respectful attitude towards the beliefs of the other, even if they differ fundamentally from one's own. For 'God is the root of every diversity in beliefs', and thus 'everyone will end up with mercy', as Ibn ʿArabī affirms.

When, therefore, Ibn ʿArabī warns us, 'beware of being bound up by a particular creed and rejecting others as unbelief!', this is not only on account of the objective truth that the divine reality cannot be 'confined to one particular creed to the exclusion of others'; it is also because in restricting God to the form of one's own belief, one is diminishing receptivity to the Mercy that *encompasseth all things*, one ignores the grace inherent in perceiving that *to whichever direction you turn, there is the Face of God*. The religions can be appreciated in this perspective as so many marvellous—and unique—expressions assumed by this one and only Face. As was stressed in the previous chapter, the 'truth' of God is not some empirical fact, but the intelligible face of an infinite Reality; not the terminus of a formal doctrine but the genesis of an endless spiritual journey. The initial human conception of the divine Reality begins, but cannot complete, the process of authentic transformation, for it is divine grace and spiritual effort that bring to fruition the seeds of reality sown by the limited conceptions of the human mind, seeds that are fashioned by the Self-disclosure of the Absolute, not by the speculations of the relative. Therefore all conceptions of God, of the self and of the other should be accompanied by the two key virtues stressed in the last chapter: humility and generosity, both of which express the self-effacement demanded by 'Islam', understood in the universal sense of this term.

Such a view of the transformative function of religious doctrine is indirectly alluded to by the verse of the Qur'ān which refers to those who 'carry' Scripture without putting it into practice: *The likeness of those who are entrusted with the Torah and then apply it not is as the likeness of the ass carrying books* (LXII: 5). This verse is commented upon by Rūmī in the following moving passage from the *Mathnawī*, with which this chapter is brought to a close:

> 'When knowledge strikes on the heart, it becomes a helper; when knowledge strikes on the body, it becomes a burden.
> God hath said (*Like an ass*) *laden with his books*: burdensome is the knowledge that is not from Himself.
> . . . Beware! Do not carry this burden of knowledge for the sake of selfish desire (but be effaced), so that thou may ride on the smooth-paced steed of knowledge. . .
> How wilt thou be freed from selfish desires without the cup of *Hu* (He, the Absolute), O thou who hast become content with no more of *Hu* than the name of *Hu*?
> From attribute and name what comes to birth? Imagination;[109] and that imagination shows the way to union with Him.
> . . . Hast thou ever seen a name without the reality? Or hast thou plucked a rose (*gul*) from the (letters) *gāf* and *lām* of (the word) *gul*?

[109] The word translated here as imagination is *khayāl*; Nicholson's 'phantasy' seems rather inappropriate. Human imagination is not simply a subjective fantasy; its objective character is indicated by Rūmī here in the fact that it 'shows the way to union'—it provides an orientation towards spiritual reality and thus participates positively in the process whereby that reality is assimilated.

Thou hast pronounced the name: go, seek the thing named.
Know that the moon is on high, not in the water of the stream.
If thou wouldst pass beyond name and letter, oh, make thyself wholly purged of self.'[110]

[110] *Mathnawī*, I, verses 3447–3448; 3451–3454; 3456–3458 (Nicholson's translation partially modified).

CHAPTER IV

Dialogue, Diatribe, or *Daʿwa*?

THIS CHAPTER is concerned with *intra*-faith dialogue as much as *inter*-faith dialogue. The approach to the other that has been developed in the previous two chapters, based on the themes of divine unity and of religious universality, needs to be presented in a manner that renders it appealing to, or at least worthy of consideration by, the internal other, including those referred to as religious exclusivists. For this is a key requirement if such an approach is to have anything more than theoretical value in the actual world of religious dialogue. This, however, remains a secondary concern, for the primary purpose here has been to demonstrate the way in which Sufi exegesis of the Qur'ān can help to articulate a positive spiritual approach to the religious other.

At the end of the last chapter, it was argued that the universality being presented here on the basis of Sufi exegesis is perfectly compatible with upholding the normativity of Islam, conceived in specific terms as the final revelation of God to man. But what it is not compatible with is an *a priori* denial of the possibility of truth, salvation, and spiritual efficacy in religions other than Islam, in the specific sense. The aim of the universalist in this intra-faith dialogue is to promote attitudes that might result, at least, in the movement from one, 'harsh' form of exclusivism to a 'mild' form thereof; that is, one which, while still upholding the normativity of Islam, is open to and respectful of the values enshrined within other religions. The extent to which those values remain operative and effective can remain an open-ended question in this intra- and inter-faith dialogue; this question would then be studied in the light of the concrete contexts within which the dialogues take place.

For the universalist, the aim of such dialogues would be to bring to light the evidence of the beauty and the truth, the piety and the sanctity present within the religions of the other; and doing so on the basis of that aspect of the Qur'ānic discourse from which the universalist approach is derived, one form of which has been presented in the previous two chapters.

This would seem to be a more realistic way of trying to achieve, in the Islamic context at least, the goals of 'religious pluralism': tolerance, respect and openness vis-à-vis the religious other. The kind of pluralism associated with John Hick, however, based on a certain kind of theological revisionism, radically undermines a central tenet of conventional religious belief—the conviction that one must 'bear witness' to one's faith, by inviting people to it as the one, true faith; it thus vitiates in advance its own credibility in the eyes of the majority of the adherents of any given religion. A universalist approach to the same goals, based on a supra-theological, metaphysical perspective, can uphold this central tenet of belief without detriment to its universalism. Whereas religious pluralism excludes all exclusivists—and thus excludes itself in the eyes of all exclusivists—universalism within Islam is able to include the exclusivists, at least to a certain extent, and might thus be 'included' by them—again, with the caveat: to some extent at least—as a legitimate possibility within the framework of the faith, one which is worthy of consideration, rather than being beyond the pale.

This will be argued in the second part of this chapter, after situating the response to theological exclusivism on a metaphysical plane, and demonstrating some practical advantages of conducting dialogue on this plane, in respect of one particularly thorny set of issues in Muslim-Christian dialogue. The contrast between the kind of pluralism championed by John

Hick and the universalism espoused by Seyyed Hossein Nasr—taken as a representative of the kind of universalism articulated in the previous two chapters—will then be presented. Finally, discussion turns to the question of how best to respond to the Qur'ānic injunction to engage with the other in terms of that which is *aḥsan*—most fine, excellent and beautiful.

From Theological Exclusivism to Metaphysical Inclusivism

Despite the evidence adduced in the previous chapters in support of a universal understanding of the meaning of 'Islam', and the warnings found in the Qur'ān against religious chauvinism, the following objection might well be made by those opposed to the idea of religions other than Islam (in the specific sense) being valid paths to piety, salvation and the Real: first, the religion of Islam abrogates the previous religions and second, the Qur'ān contains a considerable number of strident and polemical-sounding denunciations and refutations of the dogmas, actions and attitudes of pre-Qur'ānic faith communities. Abrogation will be addressed briefly in a moment. We should look first, however, at the larger question of how our proposed Sufi reading of the Qur'ān deals with a certain kind of religious exclusivism that is based on a theological reading of the text. Verses such as the following would be cited in support of Islamic exclusivism:

> *They surely disbelieve who say: Verily, God is the third of three; when there is no God save the One God. If they desist not from so saying a painful doom will fall on those of them who disbelieve* (V: 73)
> *And the Jews say: Ezra is the son of God, and the Christians say: The Messiah is the son of God. That is their saying with their mouths. They imitate the saying of those who disbelieved of old. God fighteth them. How perverse are they!* (IX: 30)
> *O ye who believe, take not the Jews and the Christians as*

guardians.[1] *They are guardians one for another* (V: 51)
Fight against such of those who have been given the Scripture as believe not in God and the Last Day, and forbid not that which God and His messenger have forbidden, and follow not the religion of truth, until they pay the tribute readily, being brought low (IX: 29)
O People of the Book, do not exaggerate in your religion, nor utter anything concerning God save the truth. The Messiah, Jesus son of Mary, was only a messenger of God, and His Word which He conveyed unto Mary, and a Spirit from Him. So believe in God and His messengers, and say not 'Three'—Cease! [it is] better for you. God is only one divinity. Glorified be He above having a son. Unto Him belong whatever is in the heavens and whatever is in the earth... (IV: 171)
They have disbelieved who said: Truly God is the Messiah Son of Mary... (V: 17).

Also, verses such as the following would be cited as evidence that the Qur'ān invites the People of the Book to give up their existing religion and to embrace the new revelation: *O ye unto whom the Book hath been given, believe in what We have revealed, confirming that which ye possess, before We destroy countenances and turn them back to front, or curse them as We cursed the people of the Sabbath...* (IV: 47)

If the Muslims' attitude to other faiths were based on such verses alone, the result would be more diatribe than dialogue.

---

[1] The Arabic is *awliyā'* (plural of *walī*) often wrongly translated as 'friends'. The context of the verse, and the supporting 'occasional causes of the revelation' (*asbāb al-nuzūl*) make it clear beyond question that what is being referred to here is a prohibition on making political alliances with particular Jewish and Christian tribes, at a particular moment in the history of the Muslim community, rather than 'friendship' with Jews and Christians as a principle. See the useful discussion of this verse, and traditional commentaries upon it, by David Dakake, 'The Myth of a Militant Islam', in J. Lumbard (ed.), *Islam, Fundamentalism and the Betrayal of Tradition* (Bloomington: World Wisdom Books, 2004), especially pp. 5-8.

The first response to such a critique is to accept the fact that there are indeed numerous verses which uphold an exclusivist perspective in the Qur'ān. As has been repeated throughout this book, there is a place in Ibn ʿArabī's hermeneutical framework for the kind of exclusivism which emerges not only out of such verses, but also from a narrower interpretation of all the verses cited earlier in support of the principle of Qur'ānic universalism. For a truly inclusivist/universalist attitude must tolerate the exclusivist/particularist position, without which it becomes exclusivist and intolerant itself. However, even if from such a universalist vantage point both positions correspond to aspects of a truth that, in its essence, goes beyond all perspectives, the question remains: which of the two perspectives is the most persuasive, the most compelling, the one which appears to pertain to more essential truth? It is clear what our answer to this is. But what is important is the way one presents the answer.

The proponent of a certain type of theological pluralism would be challenged with the task of systematically refuting every exclusivist interpretation of all verses that might be seen as promoting polemical or antagonistic attitudes towards other faith communities, and insisting that there is no basis whatsoever for exclusivism. It would also have the task of showing that the verses in question are context-specific, and cannot be applied as universal principles pertaining to other religions. While a well-intentioned exercise of this kind is certainly not without its merits, and can go far in dissipating tensions between the different faith communities, it would nonetheless suffer from a lack of credibility, both within its own terms and extrinsically, in the eyes of traditional practising Muslims. It would have little or no chance of influencing those who uphold current majoritarian opinions regarding the non-Muslim other if it makes no effort to assimilate and situate the exclusivist perspective. Another type of pluralism would simply ignore these verses, and concentrate instead on the more positive evaluation of the non-Muslim faith communities found in the 'universalist' verses. Such an approach, however, being so obviously selective in this way, and thus ducking the issue, would likewise not be ascribed much value by orthodox Muslim circles.

The approach favoured here, however, deriving from the perspective of Ibn ʿArabī, is not to engage in a head-on confrontation with the theological or *ẓāhirī* position, but to recognize its correspondence with an incontrovertible aspect of the Qur'ānic discourse—and thus its correspondence with a given degree of divine 'intentionality'—while at the same time pointing out countervailing tendencies within that same discourse, tendencies opening up other horizons, or vantage points, which should not be overlooked, marginalized or disdained. The question of priority or precedence as regards the two approaches will always perforce remain, but this can be an open-ended aspect of the intra-faith dialogue that should always accompany authentic inter-faith dialogue.

The promotion of effective inter-faith dialogue, for Muslims, is enhanced by striking the right balance between two principles: opening up towards the other on the basis of spiritual perspectives within the Qur'ānic discourse; and maintaining fidelity to the traditional community of interpretation—to the community that one is ostensibly representing. If no effort is made to balance these two principles, and one merely presents a universalist understanding of the text, then whatever intellectual merit such a presentation may possess, it will not necessarily be contributing to inter-faith dialogue in the actual world—a world that is not made up only of pluralists, inclusivists or universalists already convinced of the need for dialogue, but also, and predominantly, of communities upholding conventional exclusivist attitudes towards the non-Muslim other.[2] Those who need to be convinced of the need for dialogue, its propriety, and most importantly, its Qur'ānic sanction, are the representatives of these communities. Given that these representatives are for the most part conservative and exclusivist, any form of universalism or pluralism that

[2] See the point made by Richard Neuhas, cited in the introduction, p. xxi.

too radically excludes the exclusivist mentality does so to the detriment of its own efficacy in the practical domain, the actual world of interfaith dialogue.

In a different context, Peter Donovan makes the following point, which is not without relevance to our discussion here. Partially acknowledging the claims of conservative Christians like D'Costa—which will be discussed shortly—that pluralism is in practice intolerant of the religious other, he goes so far as to argue that 'unshakeable conservatism may well be far better placed than fallibilist liberals to engage effectively in practical co-operation with those holding different beliefs. Mutual concerns can be dealt with more congenially when there is no question of the parties involved being expected to reconsider their deepest traditional convictions and commitments. As conservative folk-wisdom has always said, "Strong fences make good neighbours.' "[3]

While agreeing to some degree with this point, we would argue that the proposed alternative between the two opposed positions is too 'exclusive' in its turn. That is, there is a third option, one which surpasses the opposition between conservative upholders of exclusivism and liberal upholders of pluralism, and at the same time combines the best of both positions: the commitment and conviction of the exclusivist can be combined with the most radical 'pluralist' conception of the other by

[3] Peter Donovan, 'The Intolerance of Religious Pluralism', *Religious Studies*, vol. 29, 1993, p. 225. He sums up well the critique made of pluralism by traditional Christian thinkers who see in Hick's pluralist project nothing less than a covert form of coercion. 'It does not allow others simply to be themselves. To play the pluralist game properly, parties are expected to countenance quite radical reinterpretations and amendments being made to their own positions.' (p. 218) The crux of this critique is that the central presupposition of pluralism—liberalism—is assumed rather than expressed as such. 'Pluralism presupposes liberalism, which involves compromise, accommodation and the dismantling of distinctive traditional convictions. The common features and agreed truths it purports to arrive at through embracing a wide range of viewpoints, are in fact simply reinforcements for the political and economic interests of a dominant ideology.' (*Ibid.*)

the kind of universalism proffered here. This combination, rare though it be, is precisely what characterises the nuanced approach of the Sufis considered in this book. (We shall return to this argument in the next section).

The second response to the exclusivist citing the verses above is to point out that these verses do demonstrate the formal contradictions between different theological perspectives, and the consequent difficulties attendant upon the effort to engage in effective dialogue on the basis of such theological perspectives alone. By that very token, however, they also indicate, albeit negatively, the value of the esoteric perspectives outlined here, which help to elevate the mode of discourse to a metaphysical, supra-theological level, from the vantage point of which those formal contradictions are not so much removed as rendered less decisive as determinants of dialogue.[4] The contradictions remain on their own plane; but the more challenging question is to determine the significance of that plane, and to make an effort to discern within the text of the Qur'ān itself those openings that warrant the transition to a higher plane. This is what has been attempted in the two previous chapters.

But one must also respond, if briefly, to the specific question: in the concrete context of contemporary inter-faith dialogue, how is one to relate to the verses of the Qur'ān that severely criticise the errors of the 'People of the Book'? In terms of theological discourse, one would need to examine, among other factors, the wording of each such verse, its context (*maqām*) and 'occasional cause'[5] (*sabāb al-nuzūl*), and the degree to which the

[4] Leaving aside for now the possibilities of existentially transcending the plane on which those contradictions arise, possibilities deriving from mysticism in its practical aspect. On this question see the essay, 'Inter-faith Work Needs Its Mystics', by Marcus Braybrooke in *World Faiths Encounter*, no. 16, 1997.

[5] The *asbāb al-nuzūl* are the specific circumstances within which a particular verse or set of verses were revealed, even if the principle embodied in the verse transcends the particularities of the historical context.

error in question is attributable to the non-Muslim theologies apparently being censured.[6]

This is not the place to enter into this theological mode of systematic enquiry. What will be addressed shortly is how dialogue can be practised on the basis of some esoteric openings to the other within one particular area of Muslim-Christian dialogue. The difficulties attendant upon a formal theological approach to these issues can be gauged from the conclusions reached by a study of the theological exegesis, not of such polemical verses as those cited above, but the very opposite: verses which apparently depict Christians in a positive light. Jane McAuliffe, in her important work *Qur'ānic Christians*, carefully analysed the formal exegesis by standard exoteric commentators[7] of seven verse-groups 'that make ostensibly positive remarks about the Christians'—that is, II; 62; III: 55; III: 199; V: 66; V: 82-83; XXVIII: 52-55; LVII: 27. Somewhat surprisingly, the conclusion of the study is that 'ultimately, exegetical circumscription prevails. Within the commentary tradition on these seven verse groups,

[6] See, for a good example of this approach in regard to the Qur'ānic criticism of the doctrine of the divine sonship, Mahmoud Ayoub, 'Jesus the Son of God: A Study of the Terms *Ibn* and *Walad* in the Qur'ān and *Tafsīr* Tradition' in *Christian-Muslim Encounters*, eds. Yvonne Y. Haddad & Wadi Z. Haddad (Gainesville: University Press of Florida, 1995), pp. 65-81. Ayoub calls on contemporary Muslims concerned with overcoming obstacles to dialogue with Christians to reflect on the historical circumstances in which the Qur'ānic critique of the Christian dogma of divine sonship was expressed. 'If, as we may well discover, the historical situation which the Qur'ān presupposed in its primary address no longer obtains, then the challenge for us all is to go beyond that situation and seek other, and deeper, meanings of God's Word to our own existential situation.'(p. 66) See also 'The Christianity criticized in the Qur'ān', W. Montgomery Watt, *Early Islam: Collected Articles* (Edinburgh: Edinburgh University Press, 1990); and also Giulio Basetti-Sani, *The Koran in the Light of Christ* (Chicago: Franciscan Herald Press, 1977); and Geoffrey Parrinder, *Jesus in the Qur'an* (Oxford: Oneworld, 1996).

[7] The following commentators were studied: Ṭabarī, Abū Jaʿfar al-Ṭūsī, Zamakhsharī, Ibn al-Jawzī, Fakhr al-Dīn al-Rāzī, Ibn Kathīr, Fatḥ Allāh Kāshānī, Rashīd Riḍā, Ṭabāṭabā'ī.

delimitation and specification clearly control the emerging depiction [of Christians]. The centuries-long testimony of commentary sunders the category of Christians, reserving to but a very limited number the application of divine approval and award... The commentators understand the Qur'ān to make a clear distinction between true Christians, a tiny minority, and those who have appropriated and propagated a corrupted form of the religion of Jesus.'[8] Thus 'true Christians' are defined in this exegetical tradition as those who, having kept intact the original, uncorrupted Gospel (the *Injīl*), make the appropriate response to the revelation of the Qur'ān, and enter Islam—Salmān al-Fārsī being held up as paradigmatic.[9]

McAuliffe rightly concludes that any effort to present these positive verses as proof-texts 'to demonstrate unrestricted Muslim toleration of Christians would be to ignore the decisive impact of both classical and modern *tafsīr*'. This being the case in connection with the *positive* verses, the problems connected with articulating, on the theological/exoteric level of exegesis, a positive evaluation of the *negative* verses can well be imagined. Rather, what can be given here is a demonstration of how a Sufi approach to such questions can cast a different light on theologically abstruse issues that so bedevil interfaith dialogue. It is possible to envisage a mode of discourse which, while still being 'theological', in a certain sense, incorporates transformative insights derived from a mystical or metaphysical appreciation of the dogmas censured in the Qur'ān, and thus, help us arrive at a more subtle understanding of the verses which castigate the religious other. The lines that separate the theological from the metaphysical perspective are real enough,[10]

[8] Jane D. McAuliffe, *Qur'ānic Christians—An Analysis of Classical and Modern Exegesis* (Cambridge: Cambridge University Press, 1991), p. 286.

[9] *Ibid.*, p. 287.

[10] In Chapter II, the distinction between ontological and theological *tawḥīd* was drawn. In opening out to the whole of being, rather than restricting itself to the dogmatic definition of the nature of God, ontological *tawḥīd* is thus metaphysical rather than theological: this does not mean taking God

but this does not preclude altogether the possibility of the one influencing the other, and producing something akin to a 'mystical theology' of the religious other.

Turning then to Muslim-Christian dialogue, we can address one of the verses cited above: *They have disbelieved who said: Truly God is the Messiah Son of Mary...* (V: 17). This brings into question two highly charged themes in the debate, the divine nature of Christ and the description of Christians as *kāfirs*, disbelievers.[11] It is possible to uphold the Qur'ān's criticism, on both questions, and at the same time interpret this criticism in such a way as to reveal its universal significance, and thus transcend the plane of theological controversy. Ibn ʿArabī refers to this verse in his chapter on Jesus in the *Fuṣūṣ*. He points to the literal meaning of the word *kufr*, that is, 'covering up' or

out of being, but the contrary, refusing to take being out of God—refusing to see oneness only in respect of the divine principle, and affirming that this oneness embraces all that is. Although theology is 'metaphysical' and metaphysics is concerned with 'theology', the distinction between the two terms is an important one. Theology can be somewhat summarily defined as follows: a formal system of interrelated concepts concerning God, elaborated within a clearly defined confessional framework, using reason as its central analytical tool, which is applied exclusively to the data provided by revelation. This can be distinguished from metaphysics, understood in this context not as a branch of philosophy as in its current usage, but as the 'science of the Real', the focus of which is universal truths that are not confined by any confessional framework, a 'science' in which knowledge and being are ultimately united, and which is therefore predicated not on reason alone but also, and more fundamentally, on spiritual intuition and inspiration. See Kenneth Oldmeadow, 'Metaphysics, Theology and Philosophy', in *Sacred Web*, no. 1, July 1998, pp. 31-51 for a good overview of this distinction from the point of view of the perennialist school. It should also be pointed out that metaphysics, according to this school, goes beyond ontology, insofar as the Real is conceived as that which is 'beyond Being'. See René Guénon, *The Multiple States of Being* (New York: Larson Publications, 1984), (tr. J. Godwin), especially Ch. 3, 'Being and Non-Being', pp. 43-49.

[11] Two other contested themes, that of 'alteration' (of scripture by the People of the Book, *taḥrīf*) and abrogation (of the previous religions by Islam, *naskh*) will be briefly discussed in the following section.

'concealing', and writes that the Christians are called *kāfirs* in that they conceal God in the form of Jesus: the divine reality is 'covered over' by the human manifestation. He writes: 'The real error and unbelief in the full sense of the word is not in their saying "He is God" nor "the son of Mary," but in their having turned aside from God by enclosing [God within one particular human form].'[12]

In his commentary on this sentence, Kāshānī elucidates the import of this interpretation: the *kufr*, or concealment, in question arises because of the 'confinement of the Real in the ipseity of the Messiah, son of Mary, and their [the Christians'] imagining that God is incarnate in him. But God is not confined within anything, rather, He is the Messiah and He is the entire universe.'[13] In other words, one must affirm, simultaneously, the divine transcendence and the divine immanence; this is well expressed in the poem of Ibn ʿArabī in the same chapter.

> I worship truly, and God is our Master;
> and I am His very identity, so understand.
> When I say 'man', do not be veiled by man,
> for He has given you proof.
> So be the Real and be a creature.
> You will be, by God, compassionate.[14]

---

[12] Austin, *Bezels*, p. 177 (modified translation). 'Enclosing' translates *taḍmīn*.

[13] *Fuṣūṣ*, p. 177. One might also mention in this connection the interpretation given by Shabistarī of the aim of Christianity. In an 'allusion to the Christian faith' he writes:

> 'In Christianity I have perceived the goal of detachment
> [from the self],
> Deliverance from the servitude of imitation;
> The majesty of blessed oneness is the monastery of the soul,
> The eternal *Sīmorgh* is its nest.
> This matter was brought to light by the Spirit of God
> [*rūḥu'Llāh*, that is, Jesus],
> Who arose from the Holy Spirit.'

Shabistarī, *Gulshan-i rāz*, pp. 564–5.

[14] *Fuṣūṣ*, p. 180. See the translation in *Bezels*, p. 179, which I have not followed.

This paradoxical combination between 'being' the Real and also 'being' a creature goes to the heart of Ibn ᶜArabī's spirituality. To be a 'creature' means to be a slave, and this helps us to situate the Qur'ānic description of Christ as a 'slave'.[15] From this metaphysical perspective, Christ's slavehood can be interpreted as affirming the realized divinity or Selfhood of Christ, rather than simply being used as a basis for the theological rejection of the Christian conception of Jesus. In Ibn ᶜArabī's perspective, only he who knows in an absolute sense that he is a 'slave' of God knows that God is the only true Self of all. In his description of the climax of his own spiritual ascension, Ibn ᶜArabī makes clear the relationship between slavehood and Selfhood. After ascending through different exalted degrees and states, he proclaims:

> 'God removed from me my contingent dimension (*imkānī*). Thus I attained in this nocturnal journey the inner realities of all the Names, and I saw them all returning to One Subject (*musammā wāḥid*) and One Entity (*ᶜayn wāḥida*): that Subject was what I witnessed and that Entity was my being. For my voyage was only in myself and pointed to myself, and through this I came to know that I was a pure "slave" without a trace of lordship in me at all.'[16]

One observes with the help of these metaphysical principles, a universalisation, rather than rejection, of the divinity of Christ. That is, one discerns a distinction between a mystical Islamic conception of universal theophany and the theological Christian conception of the unique incarnation.[17] It is the difference between seeing the whole of creation as so many mirrors

---

[15] Christ is described as a slave in several places, for example: *The Messiah disdaineth not to be a slave of God* (IV: 172); Jesus refers to himself as *the slave of God* (XIX: 30).

[16] *Futūḥāt*, III 350.30; what I cite here is the translation given by James Morris, 'Ibn ᶜArabī's Spiritual Ascension', p. 380 in *Les Illuminations de La Mecque.* See also the spiritual interpretation of the divine 'paternity' by Shabistarī in the previous chapter.

[17] See the discussion of this distinction in Chapter II.

reflecting the one and only Divinity, and seeing the whole of that Divinity incarnate in the unique Person of Christ. While this Sufi conception of Christ would not of course satisfy those Christian theologians who insist on the manifestation of God in Christ, alone, a metaphysical appreciation of the meaning of theophany would at least narrow the gap significantly between the Islamic and the Christian position on this question, and enable each to see something of value in the conception of the other.

In addition, it should help one to take note of the complementary aspects of this distinction between the Christian doctrine of the unique Incarnation and the mystical Islamic doctrine of universal theophany. On the one hand, the uniqueness of Christ in Islam is by no means denied: he alone is described as the Word of God, and *a spirit from Him* (IV: 171); as healing the leper, curing the blind, raising the living from the dead, by God's permission (V: 110); as being conceived in and born of a virgin (XIX: 16–34, *et passim*). On the other hand, we observe something of the 'Islamic' perspective within the Christian mystical tradition. Meister Eckhart universalizes the function and status of Jesus as follows: 'All that God the Father gave His only-begotten Son in human nature He has given me: I except nothing, neither union nor holiness. . .'[18] In one of his sermons he proposes and answers the key question implicit in the condemnation of such an idea: if we have everything that Christ was given 'why then do we praise and magnify Christ as our Lord and our God?' He answers: 'That is because he was a messenger from God to us and has brought our blessedness to us. The blessedness he brought us was our own.' (I: 116)[19]

Such mystical assimilations of religious dogma harmonises well with some of the more thoughtful theological approaches to dialogue that one observes in such contemporary writers as Robert Fastiggi. In an article on the Incarnation, he offers

[18] *Meister Eckhart*, vol. I, p. xlviii.

[19] *Ibid.*, vol. I, p. 116.

an extremely valuable interpretation and explanation of the doctrine in theological terms, responding to the Qur'ānic critique of the doctrine in a manner which upholds what he perceives as the thrust of that critique and simultaneously affirms the traditional Christian understanding of the Incarnation.[20] He succeeds in demonstrating that, within Christian-Muslim dialogue, 'discussion of the Incarnation can lead to a clearer understanding of how the two traditions differ and why. Such a dialogue might help Christians come to a deeper appreciation of the Islamic faith through the realization that the Muslim rejection of the Incarnation is based on deeply felt convictions that emerge from theological concerns that Christians also share in common. Such a dialogue might also increase the Muslim respect for the Christian faith through the recognition that the Christian articulation of the Incarnation has always tried to be sensitive to the same theological concerns that cause Muslims to reject the doctrine.'[21]

One impressive point made by Fastiggi here concerns the shared concern between Muslims and Christians over the inviolability of the divine transcendence. Just as the Qur'ān declares that God is neither begotten nor begets (CXII: 3), so the Fourth Lateran Council (1215) affirms, 'the divine essence or nature is not generating, nor generated, nor proceeding.' The kind of filiation/incarnation/generation/begetting that is attacked by the Qur'ān (*How can He have a son when He hath no consort?* VI: 101), he asserts, is thus exactly the kind of carnal relation that is explicitly rejected by Christianity.[22] He also refers to the rigorous distinction between the two natures within Christ, as established by the Council of Chalcedon (451), arguing

[20] Robert L. Fastiggi, 'The Incarnation: Muslim Objections and the Christian Response', *The Thomist*, vol. 57, no. 3, July 1993, pp. 456–493.

[21] *Ibid.*, p. 460.

[22] *Ibid.*, pp. 489–490. One might also note here that most of the dogmatic positions criticised in the Qur'ān are in fact early heresies, rejected by the orthodox Church Councils. See G. Parrinder, *Jesus in the Qur'ān*, for further discussion.

that the divine transcendence is not in any way compromised by the 'union without confusion' between the human and the divine nature of Christ.[23]

This theme is taken up in more detail and with greater metaphysical elaboration in another fine article, not explicitly to do with Christian-Muslim dialogue, but which nonetheless is of potential significance for this dialogue.[24] James Cutsinger, basing himself upon Frithjof Schuon's esoteric understanding of Christology, makes the somewhat abstruse theological doctrine of the 'divinity' of Christ metaphysically intelligible and thus universalizable. In his article Cutsinger shows conclusively that the earliest conception of Christ's 'divinity' envisaged the subordination of his divine personhood within the divine nature, and not just the subordination of his created personhood to the divine nature. In other words, it is not just Jesus the man, but Christ the second Person of the Trinity that is distinct from, and subordinate to, God as such, or the Godhead, principle of the unity of the divine nature. Moreover, the 'divinity' proper to Christ is the very divinity that is proper to all of humanity, insofar as it was not a particular man, Jesus, alone that the Word assumed, but human nature as such.

Cutsinger's elucidation of these important metaphysical principles allows the Muslim with some receptivity to the notion of the 'Muḥammadan Reality' to see certain parallels between the Christian and the Muslim conception of the cosmic principle (and divine root) of the historical founders of their respective religions. It thus transforms an apparently exclusivist dogma into a universal truth: 'It is true that *no man cometh unto the Father* (John 14: 6) except by way of the Logos, but what this means metaphysically is that there is no entry into the Divine Essence

[23] Hence, the 'divinity' of Christ does not detract from the fact that *No man hath seen God at any time.* (John 1: 18)

[24] James S. Cutsinger, 'The Mystery of the Two Natures' *Sophia—The Journal of Traditional Studies*, vol. 4, no. 2, 1998, pp. 111–141.

except through the Divine Person—however or wherever that Person may choose to be present on earth.'[25]

This helps the Muslim to read with greater appreciation the words of the Gospel: *In the beginning was the Word, and the Word was with God, and the Word was God. The same was in the beginning with God. All things were made by him; and without him was not any thing made that was made* (John, 1: 1-3). For, in like manner, Ibn ʿArabī tells us that the Muḥammadan Reality or Light is not identical with God nor different from Him, and that what God makes manifest in the cosmos is already contained in undifferentiated mode by this Muḥammadan Reality. Kāshānī makes the parallel with the Johanine conception of the Logos striking when he writes that the Prophet Muḥammad was 'the first self-determination with which the Essence at the level of Unity determined itself before any other forms of self-determination. So all the infinite self-determinations became actualized through him... [the Muḥammadan Light] comprises in itself all these self-determinations without leaving anything. He is in this sense unique in the whole world of Being... there is above him only the Essence, at the level of its absolute Unity...'[26]

In the same order of ideas, one could mention here the remarkable interpretation given by Ibn ʿArabī to one of his own lines of poetry in the *Tarjumān al-ashwāq*. This gives us one possible way of understanding the meaning of the Christian Trinity from within the Islamic faith. The line is as follows: 'My Beloved is three although He is One, even as the Persons are made one Person in essence.' The interpretation: 'Number does not beget multiplicity in the Divine Substance, as the Christians declare that the Three Persons of the Trinity are One God, and as the Qur'ān declares: *"Call upon God or call on the Merciful;*

[25] *Ibid.*, p. 134.

[26] Quoted by Izutsu, *Sufism and Taoism*, p. 237. See also Chittick, *Self-Disclosure of God*, pp. xxvii, 368-370.

however ye invoke Him, it is well, for to Him belong the most excellent Names" [Qur'ān, 17: 110].'[27]

✻ ✻ ✻

Even if the perspectives proposed in this book may have a limited impact on inter-faith dialogues conceived within narrow theological boundaries, they can have a significant impact on the effort to reach mutual understanding on the spiritual and metaphysical level, especially for those in the Christian tradition who have some knowledge of its mystical dimensions. The possibilities of dialogue at this deeper level were vividly demonstrated at an inter-faith conference entitled *Paths to the Heart: Sufism and the Christian East*, at the University of South Carolina in October, 2001, justly described by its organiser, Dr James Cutsinger, as 'without precedent'.[28] The conference brought together 'some of the world's leading authorities on the mystical and contemplative dimensions of Islam and Eastern Christianity' in an effort to overcome the conventional theological barriers to dialogue and to plumb the dimension of depth—of the 'heart'—which brings the two traditions so close together. As Cutsinger notes in his foreword, while the dogmatic beliefs and normative practices of the two religions are mutually exclusive, being situated on the horizontal plane alone, 'each of the great traditions also has a third "dimension", a spiritual heart, in which the deeper meaning of those beliefs and practices comes alive, and where the spiritual pilgrim may discover, beyond the level of seemingly contradictory forms, an inner commonality with those who follow other paths.' [29] The contributions by such authorities as Bishop Kallistos Ware and Seyyed Hossein Nasr,[30] in particular, certainly brought to light

[27] *Tarjumān*, p. 70.

[28] *Paths to the Heart*, p. vii.

[29] *Ibid.*

[30] Kallistos Ware, 'How Do We Enter the Heart?', *Ibid.*, pp. 2-23; S. H. Nasr, 'The Heart of the Faithful is the Throne of the All-Merciful', pp. 32-45.

the remarkable commonalities on this level of spiritual discourse and mystical orientation.

In this connection, it is important to mention Thomas Merton (d. 1968), the famous Cistercian monk at the Abbey of Gethsemani, Kentucky, whose writings, teachings and example have been of considerable importance to those seriously pursuing a spiritual life in Christianity in recent decades. It is well known that he was extremely interested in other spiritual paths, and in Sufism in particular.[31] The extent of the influence of Sufism upon his own contemplative life is difficult to measure, but what is clear is that his study of Sufism and his profound affinity with its mystical and intellectual principles deepened considerably his commitment to his own monastic path within Christianity. What we see in the life of this remarkable monk is dialogue being conducted at the highest level: a perception of the truth made accessible through the spiritual path of the other, an intellectual engagement with the forms expressing that truth, a deepened spiritual aspiration to realize the Truth as such, but by continuing to follow one's *own* path—a path to the One, a path now immeasurably enriched by the spiritual vistas opened up by the insights of the other.[32] The following poem of Merton can be given here as an indication of the way in which Sufi

The essay by Peter Samsel, 'A Unity With Distinctions: Parallels in the Thought of St Gregory Palamas and Ibn ʿArabī', pp. 190–224, highlighted the extraordinary similarities between these two seminal figures on the plane of mystical theology.

[31] See the remarkable volume *Merton and Sufism—The Untold Story*, eds. R. Baker & G. Henry, (Louisville: Fons Vitae, 1999). This contains, in addition to essays on the relationship between Merton and Sufism, the transcripts of the lectures on Sufism given by Merton to Cistercian monks between 1966 and his death in 1968; the correspondence between Merton and a Sufi, Abdul Aziz; and the Sufi poems written by Merton.

[32] One should mention here such figures as Louis Massignon and Charles de Foucault who were also brought to a more profound understanding of and commitment to their own path within Catholicism, as a result of their encounter with Islam.

spirituality concretely entered into his own perception of his contemplative discipline:

> To belong to Allah
> Is to see in your own existence
> And in all that pertains to it
> Something that is neither yours
> Nor from yourself,
> Something you have on loan;
> To see your being in His Being,
> Your subsistence in His Subsistence,
> Your strength in His Strength:
> Thus you will recognize in yourself
> His title to possession of you
> As Lord, And your own title as servant:
> Which is Nothingness.[33]

The fruits of this spiritual dialogue with Sufism can be gauged by the following passage in one of his lectures on Sufism to his fellow monks at the Abbey in Gethsemeni:

> 'And there's one ground for everybody, and this ground is the Divine Mercy... The people of the unveiling, that is to say the Sufis, ask the Mercy of God to subsist in them. This is a totally different outlook. It is the outlook whereby the Mercy of God is not arranged on the outside in events for me—in good and bad events—but it is subsisting in me all the time... The opposition between me and everything else ceases, and what remains in terms of opposition is purely accidental and it doesn't matter... it is arriving at a unity in which the superficial differences don't matter. It doesn't mean that they're not real, it doesn't mean that they're not there. They still subsist...'[34]

---

[33] *Merton and Sufism*, p. 290-291.

[34] *Ibid.*, pp. 144-145.

Differences still remain, but it is the significance attributed to those differences that fundamentally alters when one is receptive to the one and only reality that transcends and embraces all such differences. The discourses of someone like Merton, and the exchanges in conferences such as *Paths to the Heart*, go far in reducing the antagonisms that all too often follow from a perspective that stresses the formal differences between religions. As was evident at the conference, however close to each other the two traditions appeared on the mystical level, the participants did not pretend that the differences on the formal level were non-existent; but this recognition did not prevent them, either, from 'searching for a unified truth beneath their dogmatic differences', as Cutsinger noted.[35]

One way of ensuring that these theological differences do not result in hostility is to acknowledge them openly, and not pretend that they are negligible; for when the distinctive features of deeply held doctrines are dismissed as negligible, that is when defensive reflexes set in. As regards the verses in the Qur'ān which affirm the distinctiveness of the Islamic perspective, often in harsh contrast to others, while it may be possible to interpret favourably many polemical-sounding verses and attenuate their impact, it is neither possible nor desirable to ignore the fact that, understood according to their literal and obvious meaning, and read in conjunction with numerous other verses of similar import, these verses do uphold and express a theologically exclusivist perspective. And the Qur'ān is not, to say the least, unique among the world's scriptures in containing such a perspective.[36]

The words of Christ: 'I am the Way, the Truth and the Life' is thus the scriptural foundation for the exclusivist theological

[35] *Paths to the Heart*, p. ix.

[36] As was noted in the introduction, the Qur'ān is in fact unique among world scriptures for the very opposite reason: no other scripture refers in such explicit fashion to other religions, granting them not just a recognised status, but also presenting the very diversity of religions as divinely-willed.

principle of the Church: *extra ecclesiam nulla salus*.[37] To say 'theology', in the ordinary sense of the term, is to imply 'specificity', it is to imply the application of reason to the data of a specific revelation, and it is thus to imply 'exclusivism'; for reason 'defines',[38] separates, analyzes, and in so doing 'excludes': it is intuition, mystical 'taste', inspiration or disclosure that performs the opposite function: it unites, synthesizes, and thus 'includes' by way of integration—'making one', or *tawḥīd*. Of course, the two functions are not mutually exclusive; it is a question of accentuation of the one or the other in a cognitive framework which always contains the two elements in differing combinations.[39]

Needless to say, the universality expounded here derives not so much from reason as from intellectual intuition, initially, and from mystical inspiration, ultimately. The fruits of the intuitions and inspirations of the mystics, however, have been communicated in rational and linguistic terms and are thus available to all; so even if the spiritual 'taste' of such fruits requires some degree of mystical realization, one can still benefit spiritually, intellectually, and morally from reflecting upon the ideas and principles expounded by the Sufis—using one's reason, intuition and imagination, as was argued in the previous chapter in relation to Ghazālī's approach to knowledge.

The aim of the universalist, then, is not to undermine or denounce exclusivism, but to challenge some of its concomitants, probe its assumptions, point out the dangers inherent in

[37] 'No salvation outside the Church'.

[38] To define is to set a limit (de-fine); likewise the Arabic word for definition, *taḥdīd*, is derived from the word *ḥadda*, to establish a boundary, to delimit, or demarcate.

[39] As noted in Chapter I, Sufism as a whole has been characterized by Sachiko Murata in her *The Tao of Islam*, as the 'feminine' or Yin aspect of Islam, in contrast to the 'masculine' or Yang aspect of the legal and theological sciences in Islam. In the former, it is intuition that predominates, thus the stress is on the divine beauty (*jamāl*) and the divine resemblance (*tashbīh*); whereas in the latter, it is reason that predominates, and thus the stress is on the divine majesty (*jalāl*) and divine transcendence (*tanzīh*).

exaggerating its application in a world of religious diversity—thus, to engage it in an internal dialogue, but doing so in a manner that does not threaten its intrinsic foundations, thereby causing its partisans to react in violent self-defence. In this way, intra-faith dialogue will mirror and help to replicate the most fruitful examples of inter-faith dialogue in the past. Commenting on the history of such mutually enriching contacts between representatives of Sufism and the Orthodox Church, Cutsinger notes that most masters in the two traditions would have still insisted 'on the superiority of their own religions.'[40] This kind of exclusivism is thus not to be seen as a totally negative factor in dialogue, but as an entirely legitimate point of view which can, on the contrary, give rise to the most spiritually rewarding exchanges, as well as to the most beneficial outcomes on the practical plane of mutual tolerance and peaceful co-existence.

The exclusivist perspective on the Qur'ān, then, rather than being wished away or derided, should be accepted by the true inclusivist, the degree of such acceptance depending on the way in which its implications are presented. Universalism does not deny the Qur'ānic basis of exclusivism; but it does seek to eliminate the negative repercussions that can ensue from an ill-considered or totalitarian emphasis upon this aspect of the Qur'ānic discourse alone, ignoring altogether the countervailing aspects of the same discourse, which, as we have seen in the previous chapter, point to the vanity of chauvinism and religious prejudice. This universalism is based on the assumption that exclusivism need not necessarily be fanatical;[41] it can also be

[40] *Paths to the Heart*, p. viii.

[41] James Smith, having successfully demonstrated the exclusivism proper even to the most 'enlightened' form of postmodern, ostensibly 'structure-less', 'content-free' religion, argues that the traditional exclusivist religions, which are overtly 'determinate and contentful', should not be disregarded on this score alone. Rather, they should be evaluated according to their actual performance, and not regarded as intrinsically violent or prone to injustice towards the other, simply because of their exclusivism. Instead, 'we must address how particular, determinate religious faith plays a role in the call for

attenuated and enriched by being opened up, to some degree at least, to the universal dimensions of the Qur'ānic message. It will remain exclusivist, if by exclusivism be understood the belief that one's own religion is the *best* religion; but, insofar as it is open to the truth and salvific value of other religions, such a perspective will no longer be harshly exclusivist: that is, it will no longer be defined by the belief that historical, particular Islam is the *only* true religion, and that all others are irremediably false.

This milder form of exclusivism is in fact what has characterised the historical experience of classical Islam, and has been the basis of the tolerance which, likewise, has so clearly marked the normative traditions of Islam.[42] As was pointed out in the introduction to this book, the normative piety of Islam was deeply influenced by Sufism. Just as, traditionally, the spiritual values championed by the Sufis helped to forge the foundations of tolerance,[43] so, one can argue, Sufi perspectives today can help transform tolerance into respect, and defensive theological reflexes into fruitful spiritual dialogue.

The following sections look at some of the possible ways in which their example can help to define an approach to the other which, if not convincing in every respect for the traditional exclusivist, might at least succeed in not alienating too severely

justice, and how it can be kept from violence.' James Smith, 'Determined Violence', p. 211.

[42] The fact that systematic religious persecution was virtually unknown in the traditional Islamic world is attested not only by Muslim apologists and historians generally, but also by western scholars not known for their sympathetic attitude to Islam, such as Bernard Lewis, who admits in his book *The Jews of Islam* (New Jersey: Princeton University Press, 1984) that persecution of Jews and Christians by Muslims, 'that is to say, violent and active repression, was rare and atypical' in Islamic history (p. 8). He also makes the following 'important point': 'There is little sign of any deep-rooted emotional hostility directed against Jews—or for that matter any other group—such as the anti-Semitism of the Christian world.' (*Ibid.*, p. 32)

[43] This aspect of the Sufi tradition has not received the attention it merits. We thus eagerly await the series of books being prepared on this theme by Professor James Morris.

the upholders of conservative norms within contemporary Muslim communities.

Given the extent to which universalism is perceived exoterically as undermining the normativity of Islam, one way of introducing universalism into the intra-faith dialogue is to present it as, in fact, one of the bases upon which the normativity of Islam is upheld: to present it, in other words, as one of the best ways to issue the 'call' (*daʿwa*) to Islam.

Universalism: A Form of *Daʿwa*?

An obvious question that imposes itself in the practical domain of contemporary inter-faith dialogue is this: To what extent, if at all, can exoterically-minded Muslims (*ahl al-ẓāhir*) accept the need to engage in dialogue at all? For such Muslims, what matters is not so much dialogue as *daʿwa*—the call or invitation to embrace Islam, 'bearing witness' to the truth of the religion. There appears to be an irreconcilable opposition between the conditions and aims of dialogue, as understood in contemporary discourse, and the imperatives and goals of *daʿwa*, as traditionally conceived. But there is a way of resolving this outward incompatibility, for some at least: dialogue is more likely to be welcomed insofar as it is conceived and conducted as a form of *daʿwa*. While this clearly goes against the contemporary conceptual underpinnings of the notion of dialogue,[44] and appears to be a major concession to those whose aim is only

[44] Mohamed Talbi, for example, writes that dialogue must be kept altogether separate from *daʿwa* in order to avoid the 'restoration of the age of polemics'. See the summary of his position on dialogue in Ataullah Siddiqui, *Christian-Muslim Dialogue in the Twentieth Century* (London: Palgrave MacMillan, 1997), p. 146. The kind of *daʿwa* intended here is expressed by Nasr when he said in an interview with Siddiqui, published in the same work, that the aim of *daʿwa* should not be to convert others, but to 'present the message of Islam and the message of *tawḥīd* wherever possible'; in the course of thus 'bearing witness' to one's faith, some 'may receive the call of God and enter Islam'. (*Ibid.*, pp. 158-159)

to convert non-Muslims to Islam, it is nevertheless a realistic way of introducing a note of universality into what otherwise might remain a closed system of exoteric dogma, in which dialogue is either reduced to conflictual forms of discourse, or else regarded as a regrettable necessity, occasioned by a world in which power and wealth just happen to be concentrated in the hands of non-Muslims.

In other words it should be possible to present an 'invitation' to study the universality that is undoubtedly present in the Qur'ān, together with the profound Sufi perspectives on key Qur'ānic verses, as a most—possibly the most—effective and appropriate manner in which to 'call' people to Islam.[45] In an age dominated by the opposition between atheism and religion, when 'religion' often appears as but another form of bigotry, chauvinism, and exclusivism, and when secularism appears on the contrary as the only ideological antidote to such narrowness—in such a context, the explicit universality of the Qur'ānic revelation stands out as a brilliant *spiritual* corrective to religious bigotry. It is a revealed 'invitation' to combine depth of conviction with breadth of spiritual vision; a depth of conviction that calls out to be plumbed intellectually and spiritually, rather than just defined dogmatically, and a truly panoramic scope of spiritual perception, one which encompasses all revealed faiths, without dissipating, in the name of tolerance, into an unthinking acceptance of all ideas as equally 'true'.

---

[45] Syed Vahiduddin sees a parallel between the Sufi approach to Qur'ānic universality and the attitude of one of the most influential religious scholars of India, Abul Kalam Azad (1888-1958), thus demonstrating the positive influence that Sufi exegesis can have upon exoterically-minded authorities. 'We may readily give credit to the Sufis for having bravely carried to its utmost limit the spirit of tolerance which the Qur'ān inculcates', on the one hand; and on the other, Abul Kalam Azad 'sought support in some of the crucial Qur'ānic verses which assume the diversity of religions as well as their unity in essence.' Syed Vahiduddin, 'Islam and Diversity of Religions' in *Islam and Christian-Muslim Relations*, vol. 1, no. 1, 1990, pp. 5, 6.

An effort must be made, then, to include within the ranks of those who are open to dialogue and co-existence not just Muslim universalists or liberals but also those who feel conscience-bound to uphold the normativity and superiority of Islam vis-à-vis other religions—that is to say, the overwhelming majority of practising Muslims. For this majority, as we have argued above, a belief in Islam as the most complete and perfect religion need not translate into a denigration of the other faiths, or into a denial of their validity, and still less into intolerance or persecution of non-Muslims. On the contrary, belief in Islam's completeness can go hand in hand with a recognition of the abiding value of all genuine faiths, this very recognition being itself an expression of that completeness. As Ismail Raji Faruqi, one of the most important spokespersons for scholarly Islam in the West, puts it: 'In this Islam is unique. For no other religion in the world has yet made belief in the truth of other religions a necessary condition of its own faith and witness.'[46]

Such is also the import of the following discourse by a mysterious, unnamed Sufi of Marrakesh, widely regarded in the region as a saint. It is related in an anecdote recounted by Titus Burckhardt (d. 1984), the late scholar of Sufism and sacred art.[47] The Sufi entered a gathering of disciples of Sīdī Muḥammad Mejedlī, while the latter was in the middle of giving a commentary on a traditional text; the Sufi closed the book, saying 'these texts are too elevated for you, so I will speak to you about something else', and then gave the following brief address:

[46] Ismail Raji Faruqi, 'Toward a Critical World Theology' in *Towards Islamization of Disciplines*, as cited in Adnan Aslan, *Religious Pluralism in Christian and Islamic Philosophy—The Thought of John Hick and Seyyed Hossein Nasr* (Richmond: Curzon Press, 1998), p. 193.

[47] In addition to the collection of essays noted above, *The Mirror of the Intellect*, see his excellent, concise exposition of the most profound aspects of Sufism in his *Introduction to Sufi Doctrine* (tr. D. M. Matheson), (Wellingborough: Thorsons, 1976); and his unrivalled works on the principles of sacred art, *Sacred Art East and West* (Louisville: Fons Vitae, 2002); and *The Art of Islam—Language and Meaning* (London: World of Islam Festival Trust, 1976).

> 'You consider yourselves superior to the Jews and the Christians simply because you adhere to the Muḥammadan Sharīʿah; you are making a mistake, because the same Sharīʿah is also found among the Jews and the Christians, otherwise it would not be possible to have any understanding between the members of the different faiths, not even on the level of a commercial contract. What could make you superior to a Jew or a Christian is only the fact that one or the other of these two believes exclusively in the revelation to Moses or to Christ, while you recognize the same truth in the Torah, the Gospels, and the Muḥammadan Sharīʿah, as well as in every sacred book.'[48]

To this position many Muslims would of course respond by asserting the unreliability of the 'sacred books' revealed before the Qur'ān, and the abrogation of other religions by Islam. As regards the first, referred to as the doctrine of *taḥrīf* (alteration), the Qur'ān refers to the People of the Book having taken words out of context, in such verses as the following: *They* [the Jews who broke the Covenant] *change words from their context and forget a part of that whereof they were admonished* (v: 13).[49]

While the Qur'ān gives only a single actual instance of actual alteration (iv: 46), it also tells us, in an unconditional way, that in the Torah there is *guidance and light*. In the verse preceding that in which these words are used to describe the Torah, it is clear that it is not simply the original Torah that is intended, but also

[48] Cited by J.-L. Michon, 'Titus Burckhardt and the Sense of Beauty', in *Sophia—The Journal of Traditional Studies*, vol. 5, no. 2, 1999, p. 139.

[49] Cf. iv: 46 and v: 41. While many Muslim scholars have in the past accused the People of the Book of having actually distorted the revealed texts (*taḥrīf al-naṣṣ*), a far from negligible minority—including such eminent authorities as Ṭabarī, Masʿūdī, Ibn Qutayba, and Bāqillānī—refer to the distortion in question as being one of interpretation (*taḥrīf al-maʿnā*). See Camilla Adang, *Muslim Writers on Judaism and the Hebrew Bible from Ibn Rabban to Ibn Hazm* (Leiden: E. J. Brill, 1996), which, despite its often tendentious nature, offers a useful discussion of the particular issue of *taḥrīf*.

the Torah in the hands of the Jews in the Prophet's time: *How do they* [the Jews] *come unto thee for judgement when they have the Torah, wherein is God's judgement?...* (v: 43). Then comes verse 44, in which the Torah is referred to in terms of *guidance and light, by which the prophets who submitted judged the Jews, and the rabbis and the priests* [judged] *by such of God's Scripture as they were bidden to observe, and to which they bore witness* (v: 44).

Similarly, as regards the Christian Scripture, we have one verse telling us that there is *guidance and light* in the revelation, and another which indicates that the revelation in question has not lost those qualities: for the Christians are urged to continue to judge according to it, which would be illogical if it were deprived—due to 'alteration'—of its *guidance and light*:

> *And We caused Jesus, son of Mary, to follow in their footsteps, confirming that which was* [revealed] *before him in the Torah, and We bestowed upon him the Gospel wherein is guidance and light, confirming that which was* [revealed] *before it in the Torah—a guidance and an admonition unto those who are pious. Let the People of the Gospel judge by that which God hath revealed therein. Whoso judgeth not by that which God hath revealed, such are the miscreants* (v: 46–47).

The continuing validity of the revealed Scriptures of the People of the Book is likewise upheld, implicitly, in the following verse: *Say: O People of the Book, ye have nothing until ye observe the Torah and the Gospel and that which was revealed to you from your Lord...* (v: 68)

Furthermore, the Qur'ān refers to its own function as being one of confirmation, guardianship and preservation, not of refutation, denial and subversion in respect of the Scriptures preceding it. This comes in verse v: 48, the second part of which we have had occasion to cite several times, given its immense importance. Citing it in full below, in the present context, can help one to appreciate the subtlety of the position being articulated by the Qur'ānic discourse: a position which at once recognises the legitimacy of the diverse paths revealed by

God before the advent of the Qur'ān, and upholds the primacy of the particular path revealed by the Qur'ān.

> *And unto thee We have revealed the Scripture with the truth, confirming whatever Scripture was before it, and as a guardian over it. So judge between them by that which God has revealed, and follow not their desires away from the Truth which hath come unto thee. For each We have appointed from you a Law and a Way. Had God willed, He could have made you one community. But that He might try you by that which He hath given you* [He hath made you as you are].*So vie with one another in good works. Unto God ye will all return, and He will inform you of that wherein ye differed.* (v: 48)[50]

While, as we have seen above, the Qur'ān certainly castigates some of the People of the Book for some attitudes, this criticism does not extend to the sources of their tradition, sources which retain their value: otherwise the legal recognition and formal protection granted to them would be devoid of meaning, and their being referred to as 'People of the Book' would be both inaccurate and illogical. In other words, it would be illogical to tolerate, protect and defend (with the Muslims' own lives, if necessary) the 'People of the Book' if the 'Book' in question were deprived of spiritual value, not to mention the even more stark absurdity of the Muslim man allowing his children to be brought up by his Christian or Jewish wife, if the 'Book' revered and acted upon by the mother of his children were fundamentally and irremediably flawed.[51]

---

[50] As Issa Boullata notes, the majority of the exoteric commentators interpret the words *li-kullin* (for each) to mean 'each umma'. See his fine article, '*Fa-stabiqū'l-khayrāt*: A Qur'anic Principle of Interfaith Relations', in Haddad & Haddad, *Christian-Muslim Encounters*, *op. cit.*, pp. 45–53.

[51] One might also mention in this regard that one of the very last verses to be revealed tells the Muslims that *the food of the People of the Book is lawful* for them (v: 5). In other words, the rites of the Jews and Christians that accompanied animal slaughter remain acceptable to God: if their religions

As regards the doctrine of abrogation (*naskh*), this, too, is a complex subject and we do not pretend to offer anything more than a spiritual perspective on it, the juristic and theological dimensions of the question being beyond the scope of this work, not to mention the competence of this writer.[52] Insofar as the idea of the abrogation of other religions by Islam constitutes a considerable obstacle to wholesome dialogue between Muslims and members of other faiths, however, we cannot simply ignore it in this context.

In terms of the specifically juristic point of view, it is conventionally upheld that Islam 'abrogates' the previous religious dispensations, in the sense that its revealed law supersedes the laws promulgated in pre-Qur'ānic revelations, with the concomitant that it is no longer permissible for Muslims to abide by those pre-Qur'ānic revealed laws, the Shariʿa brought by the Prophet being henceforth normative and binding.[53] How, then, can a Muslim today, concerned with dialogue, reconcile the idea of piety, holiness, and truth being present in other religions, on the one hand, with the principle that Islam abrogates or supersedes all previous religions, on the other? One answer is given by Ibn ʿArabī, for whom the fact of abrogation does not imply the nullification of those religions which are superseded, nor does it render them inefficacious, in salvific terms. In a brilliant dialectical stroke, Ibn ʿArabī transforms the whole doctrine of abrogation from being the ground upon which other religions are rejected into an argument for the continuing validity of the other religions: because one of the reasons for the pre-eminence (the 'supercession', literally, the quality of

---

were abrogated and thereby rendered null and void, this divine acceptance would be unimaginable.

[52] See Abdulaziz Sachedina, 'Is Islam an Abrogation of Judeo-Christian Revelation?' in *Concilium: International Review of Theology*, no. 3, 1994, pp. 94-102.

[53] See al-Ghazālī *al-Mustaṣfā min ʿilm al-uṣūl* (Cairo, 1904) vol. I, p. 111, as cited in the article 'Abrogation', by John Burton in *Encyclopedia of the Qur'ān*, ed. J. D. McAuliffe (Leiden: E. J. Brill, 2001), p. 13.

being 'seated above') of Islam is precisely the fact that Muslims are enjoined to believe in all revelations and not just in that conveyed by the Prophet of Islam. We thus return to the idea conveyed by the Sufi of Marrakesh:

> 'All the revealed religions are lights. Among these religions, the revealed religion of Muhammad is like the light of the sun among the lights of the stars. When the sun appears, the lights of the stars are hidden, and their lights are included in the light of the sun. Their being hidden is like the abrogation of the other revealed religions that takes place through Muhammad's revealed religion. Nevertheless, they do in fact exist, just as the existence of the lights of the stars is actualized. This explains why we have been required in our all-inclusive religion to have faith in the truth of all the messengers and all the revealed religions. They are not rendered null (*bāṭil*) by abrogation—that is the opinion of the ignorant.'[54]

Thus it is quite possible to practise the religion of Islam, believing sincerely that this religion is the most complete, the one which is most 'fresh' from the hands of the Revealer, at the same time as believing that other religions retain their enlightening function and their spiritual efficacy for their adherents. How much this function and efficacy remain will be a question to be determined by intellectual evaluation and spiritual sensibility, rather than by a priori rejection based on prejudice.

The imperative of fully abiding by one's religion even while recognising its inevitable particularity and hence relativity, and even while recognising the sacred values of other religions, and their particularities may appear somewhat challenging, if not contradictory. But in fact, we have here yet another example of the resolution of antinomies so characteristic of the Sufi

[54] Cited by Chittick, *Imaginal Worlds*, p. 125. See below for our discussion of the lines in the *Futūḥāt* which follow on from this passage that Chittick cites.

perspective: the need to follow one's own path is absolute; but the path itself is not absolute. Only the Absolute is absolute: *lā ilāha illa'Llāh*. Therefore, for Ibn ʿArabī there is no contradiction between following the dictates of one's own 'way'—in terms of which certain things may be forbidden—and accepting the intrinsic validity of another 'way' which permits those same things.

He illustrates this point by way of referring to the Qur'ānic story of how Moses, as a baby, was made by God to refuse the milk of all but his own mother; by this means the mother was eventually re-united with her son.[55] Ibn ʿArabī recounts the story, and then adds the verse quoted several times above, V: 48, to which he imparts a subtle connotation, saying that the word *minhāja* ('way') can be understood in terms of the words of which it appears to be composed: *minhā* ('from her') *jā'a* ('he came').[56] This means 'that it came from that way, this being an allusion to the source from which it came, which is sustenance for the law-abiding servant, just as the branch of a tree feeds only from its root. Thus, what is forbidden in one Law is permitted in another, from the formal standpoint.'[57]

One's own 'milk' can be fully satisfactory as a means of sustenance, without this needing to imply that the 'milk' of other mothers lacks nutritional value. For Ibn ʿArabī, the fact that one's own religious Law sustains the traveller upon the path does not signify that other Laws are intrinsically incapable of

---

[55] See XXVIII: 3-13.

[56] The root of the word *minhāj* is *nahaja*, to follow a path.

[57] Austin, *Bezels*, p. 255. This is similar to the analogy made by Āmulī: the different revealed Laws and the prophets are likened to different physicians treating different diseases of the spirit. See the previous chapter. See also Ronald Nettler, *Sufi Metaphysics and Qur'ānic Prophets—Ibn ʿArabī's Thought and Method in the* Fuṣūṣ al-Ḥikam (Cambridge: Islamic Texts Society, 2003), chapter 3, 'The Wisdom of Exaltedness in the Word of Mūsā', pp. 25-37, for other esoteric aspects of the Qur'ānic account of the story of Moses, which reveal well the principal aim of Nettler's analysis, namely, to demonstrate the way in which Ibn ʿArabī's metaphysics are woven into a particular method of scriptural exegesis.

sustaining other communities in their spiritual journey—even if all other religions are deemed to be eminently comprised within Islam, seen as the final, all-comprehensive way. In other words, such a position does not preclude belief in the superiority of one's own way, as was noted in the previous chapter.

Ibn ʿArabī continues with the passage quoted above, regarding abrogation, by referring to the superiority of the Law brought by the last Prophet over all previous revealed Laws, that of the Prophet himself over all previous Prophets, and that of the Muslim *umma* over all other religious communities. 'For he [the Prophet] was given the "all-comprehensive Word" (*jawāmiʿ al-kalim*); [and the verse] *and that God may help thee with a mighty victory*[58] (*naṣr ʿazīz*)—"the Almighty" (*al-ʿAzīz*) is one who is aimed at, but cannot be reached. So when the messengers sought to reach him, he was exalted beyond (*ʿazza*) their reach, for he was sent for all, and he was given the "all-comprehensive Word", and the authority of *the praiseworthy rank*[59] in the Hereafter, and for God's having appointed his community *the best community brought forth for mankind*.[60] And the community of each Prophet is valued according to the rank of their Prophet, so know this!'[61]

We observe again here that combination of universalism and particularism which renders the latter receptive to the influx of the former, and thus helps to minimise the negative consequences that might otherwise flow from a particularism left entirely to its own resources. The universalist perceives the continuing validity of the religion of the other—which is not rendered null (*bāṭil*) by abrogation—without this perception necessarily translating into a source of antagonism between him

[58] The context of this verse is as follows: *Truly We have given thee a clear victory, That God may forgive thee thy of thy sin which is past and which is to come, and may perfect His favour for thee, and may guide thee on a straight path, And that God may help thee with a mighty victory.* (XLVIII: 1–3)

[59] XVII: 79.

[60] III: 110.

[61] *Al-Futūḥāt al-makkiyya* (Cairo: Dār al-Kutub al-ʿArabiyyat al-Kubrā, 1911), vol. III, p. 153, lines 17–20.

and the particularist, insofar as a mode of particularism is still being upheld by the universalist alongside his universalism; and, for his part, the particularist will not feel so deeply threatened by a universalism that retains a belief in the normativity of Islam, that is, by a universalist who 'keeps one foot', as it were, on the common ground constituted by belief in Islam's superiority over other religions.

This attitude of superiority, while it can of course lead to arrogance and chauvinism, need not necessarily do so: and it will not, in the very measure that the indisputably universalist verses considered earlier, together with the interpretations thereof by the Sufis, are assimilated spiritually. If left to their own devices, narrow-minded, or what was called above, 'harsh' exclusivists would pay no more than lip-service to such verses; but if presented with intelligence and sensitivity by one who speaks 'the same language', as it were, there is a much greater likelihood that the profound import of these verses will be brought into the conceptual and existential frame of reference of Muslim exclusivists. Moreover, as observed earlier, the Sufi understanding of the *fiṭra* translates into the most radically conceivable spiritual equality between all human beings; a belief in the superiority of one's religion cannot therefore imply the superiority of oneself over other individuals. As was argued in the previous chapter, certain verses in the Qur'ān make it absolutely clear that each person is judged strictly according to his or her own state of soul. Salvation is not bestowed as the automatic reward for merely belonging to a particular religion.

One can put forward, therefore, a nuanced universalism that will evince a degree of solidarity with the exclusivist, not only by upholding the normativity of the particular religion, Islam, but also by maintaining the 'invitation' to others to consider and to study this religion, such an invitation being made, precisely, on the basis of Islam's universalism, its affirmation of the continuing validity of pre-Qur'ānic religious traditions. This position can be strengthened by the following argument, based on one particularly convincing, and well-researched version of the history of the spread of Islam, that of Thomas Arnold; an argument which might also go some way towards allaying the suspicions of the exclusivists that this kind of universalism lacks credibility as a basis for *daʿwa*. That is, it might be objected that an 'invitation' to Islam cannot be very compelling when it is based, partly or wholly, on the belief that the other religions retain their salvific power even after the advent of Islam. What kind of *daʿwa*, the exclusivist might ask, is it that says to people of other faiths: join our religion, because it is the most complete, and because it, alone, affirms the validity of all faiths, including your present one? Without pretending that the universalism presented here will satisfy every kind of exclusivist, one can argue forcefully that it holds out a more realistic chance of being accepted as a valid position than the kind of universalism/inclusivism/pluralism that excludes *a priori* the exclusivist position, and denies altogether the right of the believer to 'bear witness' to his or her faith.

The argument here[62] is based on the principle that *There is no compulsion in religion* (II: 256), which is absolutely fundamental to the Islamic spirit, both as regards the sincerity of commitment to religion and as regards the preaching or spread of the religion. The religion of Islam was not spread by force; examples of forced conversion were rare and completely atypical, as attested by numerous sources. Suffice to mention here the still unsurpassed work of Thomas Arnold, *The Preaching of Islam*,[63] which remains one of the best refutations of the idea that Islam was spread by the sword. In fact, as Arnold shows conclusively, while Muslims did of course fight in numerous wars, the military campaigns and conquests of the Muslim armies were on the whole carried out in such an exemplary manner—measured against the standards of the time—that the conquered peoples became attracted by the religion which so impressively disciplined its armies, and whose adherents so scrupulously respected the principle of freedom of

[62] The following paragraphs are based on my article, 'From the Spirituality of Jihad to the Ideology of Jihadism', *op. cit.*

[63] Thomas Arnold, *The Preaching of Islam* (London: Luzac, 1935).

worship. Paradoxically, the very freedom and respect given by the Muslim conquerors to believers of different faith-communities—based on the tolerance of the other that, as was noted above, characterised the religion from its very inception—this very respect intensified the process of conversion to Islam.

Arnold's comprehensive account of the spread of Islam in all the major regions of what is now the Muslim world demonstrates beyond doubt that the growth and spread of the religion was of an essentially peaceful nature, the two most important factors in accounting for conversion to Islam being Sufism and trade. The mystic and the merchant, in other words, were the most successful 'missionaries' of Islam. This fact alone should give today's exclusivists some cause to consider more seriously the question of what it is that attracts people of other religions to Islam.

One telling document cited in his work sheds light on the nature of the mass conversion of one significant group, the Christians of the Persian province of Khurasan; and may be taken as indicative of the general conditions under which Christians, and non-Muslims in general, converted to Islam. This is the letter of the Nestorian Patriarch, Isho-yabh III to Simeon, Metropolitan of Rev-Ardashir, Primate of Persia:

> 'Alas, alas! Out of so many thousands who bore the name of Christians, not even one single victim was consecrated unto God by the shedding of his blood for the true faith... [the Arabs] attack not the Christian faith, but on the contrary, they favour our religion, do honour to our priests and the saints of our Lord and confer benefits on churches and monasteries. Why then have your people of Merv abandoned their faith for the sake of these Arabs?'[64]

This honouring of Christian priests, saints, churches and monasteries flows directly from the practice of the Prophet, as will be discussed below; and it is likewise rooted in clear verses

[64] *Ibid.*, pp. 81–82.

relating to the inviolability of all places of worship. Indeed, in the verse giving permission to the Muslims to begin to fight back in self-defence against the Meccans, the need to protect all holy places, and not just mosques, is tied to the reason for the necessity of warfare:

> *Permission* [to fight] *is given to those who are being fought, for they have been wronged, and surely God is able to give them victory; those who have been expelled from their homes unjustly, only because they said: Our Lord is God. Had God not driven back some by means of others, monasteries, churches, synagogues and mosques—wherein the name of God is oft-invoked—would assuredly have been destroyed.* (XXII: 39–40)

We shall return to this verse below, in connection with the Bosnian experience and the lesson it teaches all Muslims concerned with dialogue, tolerance and religious diversity.

The universalist, then, in his response to the exclusivist, can point to the effectiveness of such exercises in tolerance in attracting the other to the religion of Islam, without overt preaching in the ordinary sense; and he would be justified in arguing that, in the contemporary context, a call to Islam that is based on its universalism, while appearing somewhat contradictory from the particularist point of view, is nonetheless not to be dismissed either as hopelessly inefficacious, nor as mere subterfuge behind which the universalist disguises his true, unmitigated universalism. On the contrary, this combination of universalism and particularism permits those practising Muslims who are aware of the presence of holiness, truth, beauty, and virtue in religions other than Islam to do justice to what is perceived in the religion of the other, without compromising fidelity to one's own religion.

For there are many believers in today's multicultural world who cannot, in good conscience, believe that the right to salvation and the realization of spiritual truth is the preserve of one religion only, and that all other religions are intrinsically false. Islam caters for such individuals precisely through its universality, a universality that ensures that it also caters for those who, on the contrary, cannot commit themselves to Islam unless they believe it to be the best, and, for yet others, the only true, religion. As Frithjof Schuon observes: 'Every religion by definition wants to be the best, and "must want" to be the best, as a whole and also as regards its constitutive elements; this is only natural, so to speak, or rather "supernaturally natural"'.[65]

A truly universal Islam must find room for both types of mentality, the universalist/inclusivist and the particularist/exclusivist—and there is room for both types in the measure that the tolerance which is so central to the Islamic message is recognized. Just as the universalist is asked to accept the validity of the point of view of the exclusivist—this being the gauge of his metaphysical as opposed to notional or cosmetic inclusivism; so, for his part, will the exclusivist be asked to respect the right of the universalist to his opinion on the religious other, an opinion which, far from deriving from some idle speculation, is on the contrary firmly grounded in the Qur'ānic revelation, and reinforced by the inspired and inspiring spirituality of the Sufi tradition. The

[65] Frithjof Schuon, 'The Idea of "The Best" in Religions', p. 151 in his *Christianity/Islam—Essays on Esoteric Ecumenism* (Bloomington: World Wisdom Books, 1985). Recent writings in religious philosophy in the West have been re-evaluating the intellectual credibility of religious exclusivism. See for example, David Basinger, *Religious Diversity—A Philosophical Assessment* (Aldershot: Ashgate, 2002). The most salient point made in this book seems to be the following, which develops some powerful arguments made by Kelly James Clarke in 'Perils of Pluralists' (*Faith and Philosophy*, vol. 14, no. 3, 1997, pp. 303-320): exclusivism is justified insofar as the grounds for affirming the truth and validity of one's own tradition are stronger than those for affirming the 'transformational parity'—the equality of the power to transform and re-centre consciousness, the central function of religion—posited by the pluralists as the premise for their acceptance of all religions as equally true and valid. Basinger proceeds to argue that 'while an exclusivist can never justifiably deny that there is actual transformational parity among diverse religious perspectives on the basis of experience alone, she [sic] can justifiably deny such parity if the denial follows from (or is required by) other beliefs within her perspective that she justifiably affirms.' (p. 64)

universalist, in other words, should be allowed, at the very least, to have a 'good opinion' (*ḥusn al-ẓann*) of faiths other than his own.

Nasr's Universalism vs Hick's Pluralism

In this section we turn to a point raised briefly in the last chapter, namely, the importance of distinguishing carefully between the type of religious pluralism associated with John Hick and the esoteric universalism espoused by Seyyed Hossein Nasr. This is relevant to the argument here in that we consider Nasr's approach to be a faithful contemporary application of the perspectives outlined in the previous chapters: his type of universalism is articulated without detriment to his fidelity to his own tradition, in contrast to the pluralism of John Hick, whose well-intentioned pluralism is propounded at the expense of the unique characteristics of his own—and of all—religious traditions. To bring home the contrast between the two perspectives, and to relate the intra-faith dialogue between the universalist and the exclusivist within Islam to a wider framework, we will enter to some extent into the interesting and illuminating debate between the pluralist and the exclusivist within Christianity.

The difference between Hick and Nasr revolves around the axis that connects the principle of unity to the particularity of each religion. In contrast to Hick's approach, the type of 'pluralism'[66] upheld by Nasr is founded upon a belief in the

[66] I would prefer to use the more neutral term 'plurality'. Pluralism has too many overtones of an intolerant nature, because of its close identification with John Hick's version thereof. See, though, the version of pluralism presented by Diana Eck, which comes closer to the kind of universalism being expressed in this book. Eck's expression of pluralism does not appear to imply or require that commitment to one's religious tradition be diminished. She does, however, insist on moving from 'inclusivism' to 'pluralism'—that is, from viewing the other through the prism of one's own religion, accommodating the other within one's own frame of reference (inclusivism), to viewing the other in the other's own terms, doing justice to it in all its otherness

transcendent unity of religions, upon the complementarity between the particular forms and the universal essence of religion, and thus upholds the irreducible character—the divinely willed uniqueness—of each of the revealed religions. This approach is thus much more respectful of real difference—in the face of an essential unity which transcends forms—than Hick's pluralism which, on the contrary, seeks to eliminate these differences for the sake of a unity which is envisaged on the non-transcendent plane of the forms themselves.

It is true that Hick does perceive a kind of unity on the transcendent plane also, but this oneness of the 'ineffable Real' is in practice less important than the unity aimed at on the plane of forms, for the transcendent Real is utterly unknowable, and has no intrinsic relation to the variegated 'cognitive responses' that constitute, for Hick, the foundations of the different religions. The unity on the level of these cognitive responses is therefore far more significant for Hick, this unity being found in the principle of 're-centering' the soul from the ego to the Real. While one can agree with the profound need for this re-centering—as discussed in Chapter II—one cannot go along with Hick when he reduces the totality of the religious quest to this single function, and then seeks to eliminate anything that, inconveniently, does not quite fit into this unitive mould. As discussed in Chapter III, one can indeed speak of a religious essence subsisting within diverse forms, but the Sufi conception of this essence does not abolish diversity of expression; it celebrates it, even while seeing through it. On the one hand, its root in metaphysical necessity and in the divine will is perceived: *For each We have appointed from you a Law and a Way* (v: 48); and on the other, the plane on which religious diversity unfolds is

---

(pluralism). See her book, *Encountering God: A Spiritual Journey from Bozeman to Banares* (Boston: Beacon Press, 1993). See also Jeremy Henzell-Thomas, *The Challenge of Pluralism and the Middle Way of Islam*, Occasional Papers, no. 1, (Richmond: The Association of Muslim Social Scientists (UK), 2002), for a thoughtful appraisal of this question.

transcended: *Glorified and exalted be He above what they describe* (VI: 100).

Nasr is completely at one with this Sufi conception of the religious essence which is at once transcendent vis-à-vis all religions and immanent within each. This is but one of several points at which the perspectives of Nasr and Hick diverge significantly,[67] but perhaps the most important one is this: whereas Hick sees the religions as being so many 'cognitive responses', on the part of man, to the ineffable Real, Nasr sees the religions as so many Self-revelations of the ineffable Real to man. This fundamental difference in conceiving the origin of the religious phenomenon translates into radically divergent perceptions as regards the relationship between the particular religious form and the universal spiritual essence. For Nasr, there is no contradiction whatsoever between upholding the uniqueness, the integrity—the *particularity*—of the religious forms, and affirming the universality of the spiritual essence residing within but also surpassing those forms. For Hick, there is a fatal contradiction here: for his putative universal essence abolishes all claims to uniqueness made on behalf of particular religious forms—whence his need to refer to the doctrine of the Incarnation within Christianity as a 'myth', in the negative sense of this word.[68] Hence, transposed to Islam, the 'problem' for Hick is the Muslim claim that the Qur'ān is the final revelation,

[67] See Aslan, *Religious Pluralism*, for a good comparison between the two thinkers; though Aslan seems not to have fully grasped Nasr's position on certain points, and to have misinterpreted some of the 'aims' of perennial philosophy. See pp. 126-129, where one of these aims is curiously described as 'the complete religious transformation of the culture.' See Nasr's chapter, 'Knowledge of the Sacred as Deliverance', in his *Knowledge and the Sacred* (Albany: State University of New York Press, 1989), pp. 309-333, for the actual aims of this perspective, which are summed up in the word 'deliverance', precisely.

[68] Hick edited a book entitled *The Myth of God Incarnate* containing essays which elaborate upon the basic idea expressed in his own work, *The Metaphor of God Incarnate—Christology in a Pluralistic World* (London: SCM Press, 1993): 'If Jesus was God incarnate, the Christian religion is unique in having been

for this would make Islam unique, and thus bestow upon it a privileged status in terms of transformational and salvific efficacy. As Aslan notes, 'This for Hick is one of the biggest obstacles that prevents Islam from being integrated into his pluralism.'[69]

It is ironic that what is most attractive and powerful about any particular religion—its most dazzling proof, its most compelling 'argument'—translates for Hick into its central 'problem'. The problem, for us, is that there are Muslims who appear to take on this reductionist view of their own religion in order to conform to this model of pluralism. Hasan Askari, a notable Muslim scholar associated with Hick, accepts Hick's definition of the 'problem', and thus provides the solution most obligingly: for Askari, Islam, in the sense of primordial and universal submission abolishes 'the particular and the historical Islam'.[70] Askari thus undermines, not so much the claim that the Qur'ān is the final revelation, but the very ground upon which such a claim rests; that is, the particularity and historicity of the religion of Islam itself, which is to be sacrificed at the altar of 'primordial and universal submission'. This mutual exclusion between the particular religion of Islam and the principle of universal submission totally contradicts the view of harmonious integration between the two effected by the metaphysical principles of the Sufis studied here. It is a pale caricature of the Sufi conception of the relationship between the One and the many, the universal and the particular, the principle and its manifestations, in terms of which the latter is a unique expression of the former, and is by no means 'abolished' by it. Askari's position also radically contradicts the self-definition of observant Muslims. All Muslims who take as axiomatic the belief in the finality of the Qur'ānic revelation, and the uniqueness of this

founded by God in person.' (p. 87; cited by Aslan, *Religious Pluralism in Christian and Islamic Philosophy*, p. 250).

[69] Aslan, *Religious Pluralism*, p. 183.

[70] Hasan Askari, 'Within and Beyond the Experience of Religious Diversity', in *The Experience of Religious Diversity*, eds. J. Hick & H. Askari (Aldershot: Gower Press, 1985), p. 199.

revelation, together with the belief that God has truly revealed His will by means of this revelation, at a particular time and place, as the final instance of the universal religion of *islām*, would thus reject Hick's pluralism; and they would agree with Gavin D'Costa, Hick's chief critic in the debate within Christianity, when he writes:

> 'It is claimed [by Hick] that the Real cannot be known in itself and when any religion claims that the Real has revealed itself, then such claims are false. Such pluralism cannot tolerate alternative claims and is forced to deem them mythical. The irony about tolerant pluralism is that it is eventually intolerant towards most forms of orthodox religious belief.'[71]

It is interesting to note that, in his reply to this criticism, Hick does not actually deny the truth of the claim; he only points out that 'people in glass houses shouldn't throw stones'. That is, D'Costa's own conservative Catholicism contradicts the self-definition of every religion except his own, and continues with the claim that D'Costa's 'difference from the religious pluralist is that he regards his own tradition as the sole exception to the general principle that claims to be the one and only "true" religion are mistaken!'[72] However, D'Costa's critique of this

[71] Gavin D'Costa, 'The Impossibility of a Pluralist View of Religions', in *Religious Studies*, no. 32, 1996, p. 223.

[72] John Hick, 'The Possibility of Religious Pluralism: A Reply to Gavin D'Costa', in *Religious Studies*, no. 33, 1997, p. 165. D'Costa's reply to this is elaborated in his important recent work, *The Meeting of Religions and the Trinity* (Edinburgh: T & T Clark, 2000), a fascinating attempt to demonstrate that an approach to other religions based on trinitarian theology can achieve more successfully the goals of pluralism—openness, tolerance, equality, etc.—than pluralist approaches themselves. He argues: 'Within a Roman Catholic trinitarian orientation the other is always interesting in their difference, and may be the possible face of God… Furthermore, the other may teach Christians to know and worship their own trinitarian God more truthfully and richly. Trinitarian theology provides the context for a critical, reverent

central, intolerant tenet within Hick's pluralism stands, and this is asserted even more forcefully in his response to Hick's reply.

Hick's pluralism is more exclusivist than orthodox exclusivism, according to D'Costa, for it asserts that *all* religions make false, mythological claims, 'except for the pluralists who possess a non-mythological set of ontological assumptions to sustain their tradition (liberal modernity).'[73] The exclusivist, on the other hand, 'is at least faithful to the self-description of *one* of the religions (their own), rather than undermining all the religions' self-descriptions. On this point, dialectically, exclusivists emerge as the winners of this debate, showing that pluralists fail to solve their own problem, but more so, that exclusivism solves it better.'[74]

Without going any further into this interesting debate, its significance for the discussion here is clear. What is in question is, on the one hand, the manner in which fidelity to the particularities—including the exclusivist particularities—of one's own faith determine one's ability to open up to the other with tolerance and respect; and, on the other, the degree to which a pluralist approach to all faiths implies a contradiction of the self-definition of each. The point to be made here is that a *universalism* which upholds the particularities of one's own faith is, by virtue of that very universalism, able to grant the other the right to uphold the particularities of his or her faith. In identifying, first and foremost, with the innermost substance of

and open engagement with otherness, without any predictable outcome.' (p. 9) The crux of his approach is expressed in chapter 4, 'Trinitarian Theology: An Invitation to Engagement', pp. 99–142. This is a laudable attempt to relate an exegesis of the verses of the Gospel regarding the Holy Spirit, which *bloweth where it listeth* (John III: 8), to interfaith dialogue, tolerance and respect for the other.

[73] D'Costa, *The Meeting of the Religions*, p. 46.

[74] *Ibid.*, p. 47. He argues that the trinitarian approach 'attains pluralist goals in taking difference and otherness utterly seriously. Trinitarian exclusivism can acknowledge God's action within other traditions without domesticating or obliterating their alterity, such that real conversation and engagement might occur.' (p. 47)

one's own faith, the Muslim universalist such as Nasr identifies, likewise, with the inner substance—not all the outward forms—of all the revealed faiths, without this in any way detracting from his own initial self-identification as a Muslim, that is, his *particular* identity.

It is thus that, despite Legenhausen's claim that Nasr's universalism is not firmly rooted in Islamic spirituality,[75] one can indeed present Nasr as a *Muslim* universalist, one who can justifiably be regarded as a valid representative of Islam, at the same time as being a Muslim representative of the school of thought known as *sophia perennis*, which, conceived in Islamic terms is nothing other than the timeless religion of the *fiṭra*,[76] underlying and enlivening all the subsequent religions that are superimposed thereupon.

Nasr expresses this nuanced approach to identity in the following way: 'Although, being a Muslim, I naturally have my roots in the Islamic tradition which I know better than others, my exposition of the perennial philosophy is not personal and individualistic and has its roots in an anonymous wisdom

---

[75] Legenhausen thinks that the source of Nasr's pluralism might not be found 'in the sufi [sic] tradition at all, but in the European romantic tradition'. *Islam and Religious Pluralism*, p. 122.

[76] Nasr also refers to such terms as *al-ḥikma al-ʿatīqa* (ancient wisdom) and *al-ḥikma al-laduniyya* (divine wisdom) in connection with the *ishrāqī* philosophy of Suhrawardī, according to whom 'this wisdom is universal and perennial', and that 'it existed in various forms among the ancient Hindus and Persians, Babylonians and Egyptians, and among the Greeks up to the time of Aristotle, who for Suhrawardī was not the beginning but rather the end of philosophy among the Greeks, who terminated this tradition of wisdom by limiting it to its rationalistic aspect.' *Three Muslim Sages—Avicenna, Suhrawardī, Ibn ʿArabī* (Delmar: Caravan Books, 1976), p. 61. It is of interest to note what Nasr says about Suhrawardī in his 'Reply to Hossein Ziai': 'To understand fully my synthesis of the perennial philosophy in its contemporary expression and traditional Islamic philosophy, the role of Suhrawardī and the School of Illumination remains of great importance.' *The Philosophy of Seyyed Hossein Nasr*, The Library of Living Philosophers, vol. XXVIII, (eds. Lewis Edwin Hahn, Randall E. Auxier, Lucian W. Stone Jr.), (Chicago & La Salle, Ill.: Open Court, 2001) p. 776.

to be found wherever tradition has flourished.' He then adds the following point, which demonstrates the practical value of dialogue conducted on the basis of this form of universalism: 'I have known many Christian, Jewish, Hindu and Confucian scholars and thinkers of note who have found my exposition to be applicable to their own tradition as well, and I have carried out many dialogues on the basis of my understanding of the perennial philosophy with those belonging to other religious traditions. Among them the scholars who have accepted the traditional point of view have been able to identify themselves with my perspectives while they remain firmly rooted in their own traditions.'[77]

In this kind of dialogue one observes that the integrity of each tradition is respected, and this concern with the particulars of each tradition, far from contradicting the principle of universalism, emerges as the concomitant of one's very receptivity to the universal realities transcending each tradition, and of which each tradition is a vehicle and embodiment. Scholars and thinkers of different traditions who have come to accept Nasr's exposition are not thereby diluting their commitment to their own traditions: 'they remain firmly rooted in their own traditions.' Indeed, one may go further and assert: they become even more firmly rooted in their own traditions inasmuch as a genuine receptivity to the underlying, universal substance of religion results in the strengthening of the roots of one's own particular tradition.[78]

In other words, a belief in the universal and primordial substance of religion—which is both beyond one's own particular religion, but also accessible only by means of practising it faithfully—intensifies, and does not dilute or diminish, commit-

[77] S. H. Nasr, 'Reply to Sallie B. King' in *The Philosophy of Seyyed Hossein Nasr*, p. 231. See our review of this important elucidation of the essential elements of Nasr's philosophy in *Sophia—The Journal of Traditional Studies*, vol. 8, no. 2, Winter, 2002, pp. 155–180; the following paragraphs are based upon this review.

[78] This is a major point overlooked by Legenhausen in his critique of Nasr.

ment to that religion. Such a belief enhances one's intention to plumb the depths of one's religion, reaching down, as it were, into the existential root of one's own religious roots, or into what Rūmī calls, in his subtitle for the *Mathnawī*, 'the roots of the roots of the roots of religion'. These ultimate 'roots' penetrate beyond the 'earth' and open out into the underlying 'ground' of the divine nature: thus one arrives at a penetration in 'depth' and an ascent in 'height', for the immanent is also the transcendent. One observes the paradox: there is both a greater degree of 'rootedness' in one's own religion—for one is more 'grounded' in the deeper, universal realities underpinning it—*and* a greater degree of detachment from it, for it is seen, *sub specie aeternitatis*, as a religious form in the face of the formless, as a limitation in the bosom of the infinite. Hence, to repeat the lines from Rūmī:

> 'The religion of Love is separate from all religions,
> For lovers, the religion and creed is—God.'

The paradox observed here between depth of affiliation to one's religion and metaphysical 'independence' from it is well expressed by Martin Lings in his comment on the symbol often used to explain the way in which the mysticisms of the different religions are one in essence: the symbol of multiple radii connected to a single centre. 'Our image as a whole reveals clearly the truth that as each mystical path approaches its End, it is nearer to the other mysticisms than it was at the beginning. But there is a complementary and almost paradoxical truth which it cannot reveal, but which it implies by the idea of concentration which it evokes: increase of nearness does not mean decrease of distinctness, for the nearer the centre, the greater the concentration, the stronger the "dose".'[79]

One is thus more deeply engaged with the particular essence—whence the 'dose'—of one's religion, the closer one comes to its centre, a centre which also comprises the essence of all religions, or religion as such. For it is only at that centre—that ungraspable

[79] Lings, *What is Sufism?*, pp. 21-22.

'point' from which the inner infinitude of the divine Essence unfolds—that the particularities of the religions can be said to be extinguished in the bosom of the unitive state of *fanā'*. On the one hand, according to Sufi metaphysics, religious forms are transcended through the consummation of the practices enjoined by those religious forms; and on the other, according to the pluralistic vision, religious forms are to be levelled, if not 'abolished', through the application of a purely theoretical evaluation of what constitutes the essence of religion. One can observe clearly the contrast between a metaphysical appreciation of a unity which transcends forms, and a speculative attempt to establish unity on the basis of an abolition of forms.

Nasr's way of presenting the theme of 'the transcendent unity of religions', following in the footsteps of Schuon, helps ensure that the perception of truth in other religions, instead of translating into a dilution of commitment to one's own religion, in fact heightens and deepens orientation towards those elements of one's own tradition that lead to the ultimate reality, 'the one thing needful', without pretending that this reality can be the product or the prisoner of any conceptual schema whatsoever. By being receptive to universal realities that go beyond the confines of one's own faith, one is not thereby diminishing that faith, but bestowing upon it 'a compass that touches the very roots of Existence' in the words of Schuon.[80] In other words, an orientation towards the timeless and universal principles does not negate, but infinitely enriches, one's appreciation of the revealed manifestations of those principles in time and space. One's love of the universal deepens, and does not diminish, one's love for

[80] Schuon makes this statement in connection with the particular and universal aspects of Christianity, but the principle enunciated applies, *mutatis mutandis*, to each of the revealed traditions: 'The Christ of the gnostics is he who is "before Abraham was" and from whom arise all the ancient wisdoms; a consciousness of this, far from diminishing a participation in the treasures of the historical Redemption, confers on them a compass that touches the very roots of Existence.' F. Schuon, *Light on the Ancient Worlds* (Bloomington: World Wisdom Books, 1984), p. 70.

the particular; conversely, one's love for the particular does not stop at the particular, it flows all the way to the universal.

The Muslim universalist, then, is able to view the orthodox dogmas of other religions—even those perceived as erroneous—from two different points of view. What is perceived in these dogmas from the universal point of view is a series of points of reference, conceptual orientations opening out to, or 'intending'[81] realities that transcend the dogmas. What can be affirmed is thus the consummation of the orientations, practices, and aspirations set in motion by the beliefs in question: they are 'true' insofar as they can lead one to the 'real'. From the point of view of the universalist *qua* Muslim, however, there will be no need to identify, on the level of formal belief, with any of the dogmas of other religions. This combination between metaphysical universality and Muslim specificity—which, as we have seen, characterises the perspectives of Sufis such as Rūmī and Ibn ʿArabī—permits one to maintain openness to the other without undermining the normativity of one's own tradition; and at the same time it ensures that fidelity to this normativity does not compromise one's openness to the other.

From this point of view, universal Islam transcends particular Islam whilst simultaneously affirming it, not 'abolishing' it as Askari believes. The two dimensions of Islam ought to be seen as complementary and not contradictory, just as, in terms of ontological *tawḥīd*, the particular does not contradict the universal, nor does the universal contradict the particular: each is not only a corollary of the other, but also present within the other, even if the particular is reduced to nothing without the universal. It is true, of course, that the particularist will contradict the universalist; but the universalist will not totally contradict the particularist. We say not *totally*, for the universalist evinces solidarity with the particularist in two respects: he upholds and practises Islam in all its uniqueness, its *particularity*—even

[81] One should note the etymological sense of the word 'intend': tending inwards.

while recognising the truth and holiness in other religions; and the universalist also grants the particularist the right to this exclusivism, seeing it as rooted in the exclusivist aspect of the Qur'ānic discourse, thus as corresponding to one dimension of the divine intentionality consecrated within the revelation. This type of inclusivism emerges naturally out of the principles of Ibn ʿArabī's hermeneutics.

The contrast between this kind of Muslim universalism and Hick's pluralism is made clear in a recent book by Abdulaziz Sachedina, which, though making a number of extremely important points with which one can readily agree, unnecessarily weakens the impact of these ideas on those who most need to think about and implement them. His approach to religious exclusivism seems close to that which Hick would expect from a good Muslim pluralist. That is, he engages in what appears to be a somewhat gratuitous confrontation with the conservative upholders of religious tradition in Islam, excluding their exclusivism totally, in the name of inclusive pluralism. In his book *The Islamic Roots of Democratic Pluralism*, Sachedina rails against the 'abhorrently exclusivist monotheistic religions',[82] and links this exclusivism with religious and political authoritarianism. Muslim thinkers, he asserts, must 'prod believers to go beyond the normative community, to foster a cross-cultural discourse in which the Islamic tradition, along with Christianity and Judaism, provides a credible voice of guidance, not governance.' This 'going beyond' the normative community seems to imply the necessity of attacking not just religious fundamentalism but also religious 'conservatism'—Sunni and Shiʿi alike.[83]

---

[82] A. Sachedina, *Islamic Roots*, p. 40.

[83] *Ibid.*, p. 45. As Muhammad Legenhausen notes in his review of the book, 'Democratic Pluralism in Islam? A Critique', in *Transcendent Philosophy* (vol. 3, no. 4, 2002), 'I do not want to suggest that the views of traditional clerical authorities must be accepted without question as definitive of Islam, but a rejection of their views should not be made a precondition for friendly relations.' (p. 401) Most of Sachedina's aims are, needless to say, laudable, and one cannot but sympathise deeply with him over the *fatwa* issued against him

From our point of view, it is of the utmost importance to distinguish clearly between conservative Islam and extremist or fanatical Islam; to blur this distinction, and treat the former automatically as if it were the latter is to run the risk of making a self-fulfilling prophecy: that is, of driving more and more conservatives into the arms of the extremists—of proving true, that is, the accusation that 'the West', and its corrupt lackeys in the Muslim world, is indeed opposed to 'Islam'. It thus reinforces the stereotypes on both sides, and feeds directly into assumptions underlying the Huntington scenario of the 'Clash of Civilizations'. The most effective way of dealing with the fanaticism and ideologization of Islam is to strengthen, not weaken, the forces of traditional, moderate, conservative Islam.[84]

---

in 1998; despite this edict, his efforts in the cause of 'better inter-communal relationships through mutual tolerance, respect and acceptance of the religious value on all world religions' (p. xi) must surely be supported wholeheartedly.

[84] Insufficient attention has been given to the almost unanimous condemnation of terrorism by Islamic scholars in the Muslim world and the West. As regards the West, one should refer readers again to the rapidly growing influence of the dynamic group of Islamic scholars associated with Imam Hamza Yusuf and the Zaytuna Institute in California. Mostly converts, these scholars—Imam Zaid Shakir, Shaykh Abdal Hakim Murad, Imam Siraj Wahhaj, Shaykh Nuh Keller etc.—are both steeped in the traditional sources of Islam and also fully conversant with contemporary western norms of discourse. It is precisely their faithful adherence to the tradition that elevates their credibility as spokespersons and leaders of Muslims in the West, and which makes their arguments more salient in the minds of Muslim youth; those, in particular, who are committed deeply to Islam, traumatized by the on-going injustices against Muslims worldwide, and thus susceptible to the propaganda of the Jihadists. It is such religious leaders as Hamza Yusuf that successfully 'deconstruct' the false premises of fanatical 'Jihadism', doing so from within the tradition. Such principled Muslim arguments are far more effective in the 'war against terror' than bombs and missiles. See, for examples of this kind of argument, the following articles: 'Jihad is not Perpetual Warfare', by Zaid Shakir, in *Seasons—Semiannual Journal of Zaytuna Institute*, vol. 1, no. 2, pp.53-64; 'Generous Tolerance in Islam and its effects on the Life of a Muslim', by Hamza Yusuf, in *Seasons—Semiannual Journal of Zaytuna Institute*, vol. 2, no. 2, 2005, pp.26-42; 'The Poverty of Fanaticism' by Timothy

In the context of this discussion, the task for the Muslim universalist who sees the need to include the particularist even while *spiritually* 'going beyond' particularism, is to affirm conservatism at the same time as opening it up, both inwardly and outwardly, to the other. This is best done by compromise and not confrontation; that is, by reinforcing and building upon the strong tradition of tolerance in Islam, encouraging an openness to dialogue, while helping to cultivate an appreciation of the deeper aspects of the religion of the other—that is, giving evidence of the devotion, virtue, piety, beauty and sanctity residing in other religions. All of this, we believe, is far more likely to cultivate those resources within conservative Islam which constitute such a crucial bulwark against fanatical, extremist interpretations of Islam. If, instead, the guardians of religious orthodoxy are opposed and their authority undermined by perceived 'outsiders' acting in the name of such ideological shibboleths of our times as 'progress', 'liberalism', and 'freedom', then the resulting insecurity and defensive reflexes on the part of orthodox conservatives can only harden existing rigidities rather than attenuate them, thus inadvertently helping to transform religious exclusivism into various forms of political extremism.

In this connection it is useful to take note of the following point made by a western scholar, Leonard Swidler, editor of *Muslims in Dialogue: The Evolution of a Dialogue*, cited earlier. In his introduction he states the purpose behind the book: to trace the entrance of Muslims into dialogue, doing so by reference principally to articles written by Muslims in the *Journal*

Winter, in Joseph Lumbard, *Islam, Fundamentalism and the Betrayal of Tradition*, pp. 283-295; Abdal Hakim Murad, 'Recapturing Islam from the Terrorists' on the website 'Islam for Today' (www.islamfortoday.com/murad01). See also the excellent work by Vincente Olivetti, *Terror's Source* (Birmingham: Amadeus Books, 2002). Finally, the works of Khaled Abou El-Fadl must be mentioned, particularly his cogent arguments against terrorism in *Conference of the Books—The Search for Beauty in Islam* (Lanham/New York/Oxford: University Press of America, 2001), chapters 4, 16, 29; and his *The Place of Tolerance in Islam* (Boston: Beacon Press, 2002).

of Ecumenical Studies from the 1960s through to the 1990s. He refers to the appointment of Professor Ismail Raji al-Faruqi as Associate Editor of the journal in 1969 as a significant event, referring to him as 'a traditionally orthodox Muslim... a highly knowledgeable Islamicist who did an immense amount to break open Islam to dialogue.' He then adds this important observation: 'It was Ismail's very traditional orthodoxy that allowed him to accomplish this so effectively. His often highly skeptical religious confreres trusted him implicitly not to "give away" anything Islamic, and hence were open to being coaxed into joining the dialogue, although most often rather defensively.'[85]

Adherence to formal orthodoxy, then, far from impeding dialogue, facilitates it by encouraging those who might otherwise be averse to dialogue for fear of 'giving something away' or compromising one's faith. It would be appropriate to add here that, in the framework of the Islamic faith, the notion of 'orthodoxy' does not have the same centrality or set of connotations as it does within the Christian faith, heavily defined as Christianity has traditionally been by a single magisterium responsible for defining 'official' dogma as the basis of orthodoxy, 'right opinion'. In Muslim contexts, *orthopraxy*, the correct formal practice of the faith, has always been more important than the holding of right opinions, and indeed, has traditionally been deemed to constitute, in and of itself, a compelling existential argument in favour of the 'orthodoxy' of the individual, whatever his or her 'opinions' may be. For in Islam it is not theology but the Law that dominates the exoteric framework, and thus correct formal observance of the Law that, in practice, defined one's place within the Muslim community.

As mentioned already, it was precisely their strict adherence to the Law that ensured that the mystical ideas of the Sufis studied here were not totally dismissed by the exoteric authorities; for the bedrock of these authorities, the Law, was not being directly

[85] Leonard Swidler, 'The Evolution of a Dialogue', Introduction to *Muslims in Dialogue*, p. v.

challenged by the ideas in question. In today's context such Muslim universalists as Nasr stand a greater chance of being taken seriously by conservative authorities within the faith, both in intra- and inter-faith dialogues, precisely on account of the rigour with which he upholds the essential elements of the Law, and, more importantly, the stress he places on the faithful practice of the rites: as Nasr never tires of repeating in his writings and discourses, one cannot follow the 'path', *al-ṭarīqa*, leading to spiritual reality, *al-ḥaqīqa*, outside of the framework of the revealed law, *al-sharīʿa*: 'Man cannot aspire to the spiritual life, to walking upon the path to God (*Ṭarīqah*), without participating in the *Sharīʿah*.'[86] This is one of the most essential differences between Nasr's traditional form of universalism and the modern liberal type of pluralism: the practice of the form, for Nasr, is a *sine qua non* of any degree of realization of the Truth which transcends all forms, whereas for most liberal pluralists, if they are not embarrassed by the formal *praxis* of the faithful, evince very little solidarity with it.

One is not pretending that the official representatives of Muslim 'orthodoxy' will enthusiastically embrace universalist principles simply because they are accompanied by a stress on observance of the Law. Nonetheless, it is realistic to hope that respect for lawful *praxis* will make less unpalatable some of the spiritual implications of the clear verses of the Qur'ān upon which the universalist conception of Islam is based. Also, it is worth making the effort to present this perspective, which might help to open up points of view within a discourse that, in the absence of such efforts, risks being closed in on itself. Moreover, there is clear evidence that many formal scholars of Islam are by no means closed to the principle of universality. One may cite in this regard the high regard in which the late and much revered Shaykh of Al-Azhar, ʿAbd al-Ḥalīm Maḥmūd, held the person and the writings of René Guénon, one of the founders of the

[86] *Ideals and Realities of Islam* (Cambridge: Islamic Texts Society, 2001), p. 112.

school of *sophia perennis*, to which Nasr belongs.[87] This paragon of Muslim 'orthodoxy' went so far as to say that Guénon was one of those personalities who have rightfully taken up their place in history, and that 'Muslims place him close to Ghazālī and his like (*yaḍaʿuhu al-muslimūn bi-jiwār al-imām al-Ghazālī wa-amthālihi*)'.[88] It is interesting to note also that Frithjof Schuon is mentioned by Shaykh ʿAbd al-Ḥalīm as a 'formidable scholar (*ʿālim ḍalīʿ*)';[89] and he refers also to Schuon's important exposition of the *sophia perennis* entitled *L'Œil du Coeur.*[90]

Whatever be the result on this level of intra-faith dialogue, however, the point of principle remains irrefutable: it is becoming increasingly urgent for this universalist, tolerant side of Islam, clearly rooted in the Qur'ānic discourse, to be brought to the fore, lest it be eclipsed altogether by those groups for whom this aspect of Islamic thought is an inconvenience—the Islamophobes from without, and the fanatics from within the tradition. The words of the great Emir, ʿAbd al-Qādir al-Jazā'irī, uttered over a century ago, have never been more true than they are today:

> 'When we think how few men of real religion there are, how small the number of defenders and champions of the truth—when one sees ignorant persons imagining that the principle of Islam is hardness, severity, extravagance

[87] See ʿAbd al-Ḥalīm Maḥmūd, *Qaḍiyyat al-Taṣawwuf—al-Madrasat al-Shādhiliyya* (Cairo: Dār al-Maʿārif, 1999), where an entire chapter—one of only four—is devoted to Guénon (pp. 281-362) in this book on the Shādhilī order. One should also note that many exoteric authorities in al-Azhar today remain deeply committed to Sufism, and that the school of Ibn ʿArabī has a significant following among these scholars of the Law.

[88] *Ibid.*, p. 301.

[89] *Ibid.*, p. 297.

[90] This was first published in Paris by Gallimard in 1950; see the most recent edition of the English translation, *The Eye of the Heart* (Bloomington: World Wisdom Books, 1997).

and barbarity—it is time to repeat these words: *Patience is beautiful, and God is the source of all succour.*' (XII: 18)[91]

Beautiful Discourse

The Prophet is instructed in the Qur'ān as follows: *Call unto the way of thy Lord with wisdom and fair exhortation, and debate*[92] *with them in the finest manner...* (XVI: 125). It is beauty that is stressed in these words: on the one hand, the kind of 'exhortation' or 'preaching' is *al-mawʿiẓa al-ḥasana*, that is 'beautiful', 'fair', or 'fine' exhortation, and it is the quality indicated by the superlative of the same word, *aḥsan*, 'most beautiful', that must characterise the mode of discourse or argumentation of the Muslim who wishes to follow in the footsteps of the Prophet. Applied to the

---

[91] This statement was made in a letter written by the Emir in 1860, and is quoted in Charles Henry Churchill, *The Life of Abdel Kader* (London: Chapman & Hall, 1867), p. 323. The true character of Jihad was revealed by this remarkable figure in whom one finds combined the qualities of the saint and the warrior. To quote Churchill on the Emir's heroic defence of the Christians living in Damascus during the civil war of 1868: 'All the representatives of the Christian powers then residing in Damascus, without one single exception, had owed their lives to him. Strange and unparalleled destiny! An Arab had thrown his guardian aegis over the outraged majesty of Europe. A descendant of the Prophet had sheltered and protected the Spouse of Christ.' (p. 318)

[92] The Arabic *jādilhum* has been translated in a variety of ways: 'reason with them' (Pickthall); 'argue with them' (Yusuf Ali); 'dispute with them' (Arberry). One prefers the term 'debate' in this context, given that it is to be carried out in 'the finest', 'most excellent', or 'most beautiful' (*aḥsan*) manner; it is difficult to combine the notions of 'disputation' and 'beauty'. Zamakhsharī comments on this manner of discourse as follows: '... [do this] in the best way among the ways of discourse/argument/debate (*mujādila*), with kindness and gentleness, avoiding harshness (*faẓāẓa*) and vehement censure (*taʿnīf*).' *Tafsīr al-kashshāf* (Beirut: Dār al-Kutub al-ʿIlmiyya, 1995), vol. II, p. 619. Also relevant here is the following verse addressed to the Prophet: *It was by the mercy of God that thou wast gentle with them. For if thou hadst been stern and hard of heart they would have dispersed from round about thee* (III: 159).

contemporary situation, we are urged to use our judgement, our *wisdom*, to debate with the other in the most appropriate manner, taking into account both the particular conditions in which the dialogue is being conducted, and the principial priority that must be accorded to universal realities—so clearly affirmed in the Qur'ān—over historical, communal and even theological contingencies. In other words, insofar as one's orientation to the religious other is determined by spiritual, rather than exclusively theological or legal considerations, one should give priority to those verses which are of a clearly principial or universal scope, as opposed to those which are clearly contextual in nature.

By 'contextual' is meant those verses which relate to the plane of theological exclusivism or inter-communal conflict—the very plane that is transcended by the vision that unfolds from the verses stressed and commented upon in the previous two chapters.[93] The first thing to say, then, to the exclusivist, is that there is no warrant in the Qur'ān, even with an exclusivist reading, for any brand of religious intolerance, and still less, persecution of non-Muslims. Not only are these phenomena intrinsically ugly and lacking any 'fairness'—in the sense of beauty as well as equity; they directly contravene clear verses

[93] It should be noted that this stress on certain verses—those which are universal in content, and which promote peace and harmony between the different faith communities, as opposed to those which are more aggressive in tone, and which reflect particular historical situations or specific theological controversies—is not unrelated to Ghazālī's principle of the 'variance in the excellence of the Qur'ānic verses.' See his *The Jewels of the Quran—Al-Ghazali's Theory* (A translation, with an introduction and annotation, of al-Ghazali's *Kitāb Jawāhir al-Qur'ān*) (tr. M. Abul Quasem) (Kuala Lumpur: National University of Malaysia, 1977), pp. 64–5. Needless to say, for Ghazālī, the Qur'ān in its entirety is of a revealed substance, so each verse is equal to all others in respect of revelation; but some verses are of more profound import and of greater theurgic value than others, as attested by the Prophet in many sayings. Ghazālī refers to the 'light of insight' that helps us to see 'the difference between the Verse of the Throne (II: 255) and a verse concerning giving and receiving loans, and between the Sūra of Sincerity (CXII) and the Sūra of Destruction (CXI)...' p. 64.

in the Qur'ān itself. For Muslims are enjoined to defend not just the 'People of the Book' but also, as seen above, *cloisters and churches and oratories*—all such places of worship being described by the Qur'ān as places *wherein the name of God is oft invoked* (XXII: 40). The Prophet stressed the need to really 'protect' those given the status of 'protected minority' (*ahl al-dhimma*): 'On the Day of Judgement I myself will act as the accuser of any person who oppresses a person under the protection (*dhimma*) of Islam, and lays excessive burdens on him.'[94] One should also cite in this connection the historically recorded acts of tolerance manifested by the Prophet himself—for example, in the treaty of Medina, in which the Jews were given equal rights with the Muslims; in the treaty signed with the monks of St. Catherine's monastery in Sinai;[95] and, especially, in the highly symbolic fact that, when the Christian delegation arrived from Najrān (an important centre of Christianity in the Yemen), to engage the Prophet in theological debate—principally, over the issue of the nature of Christ—they were permitted by him to perform their liturgical worship in his own mosque.[96] One observes here a perfect example of how disagreement on the plane of dogma can

[94] Quoted in Balādhurī, *Futūḥ al-buldān*, p. 162 (Hitti, *Origins of the Islamic State*, vol. 1, p. 162); cited in Sachedina, *Islamic Roots*, p. 66.

[95] A copy of the document is displayed to this day in the monastery itself, which is the oldest continually inhabited monastic establishment in Christendom, and which—it is of considerable interest to note—includes within its precincts a mosque, constructed by the monks for the local Bedouins. See J. Bentley, *Secrets of Mount Sinai* (London: Orbis Books, 1985), pp. 18-19. One should note that in this document the Prophet makes it incumbent upon every Muslim to accept the Christians, to help them accomplish their rituals at Church, and not to come between the Christians and their faith (*ʿalayhi bi-tamkīnihā fī al-ṣalāt fī biyaʿihā wa-lā yaḥūla baynahā wa-bayna dīnahā*). Copied by this writer from the document kept in the monastery museum.

[96] See A. Guillaume (tr.) *The Life of Muhammad—A Translation of Ibn Isḥāq's Sīrat Rasūl Allāh* (Oxford: Oxford University Press, 1968), pp. 270-277. It is of interest to note that in the village of Ḥawrān, Syria, a church named after the Christians of Najrān remained a site of pilgrimage for both Christans and Muslims throughout the Middle Ages: 'Who will make a votive offering to

co-exist with a deep respect on the superior plane of religious devotion.

The incident is all the more remarkable in that the dispute between the Prophet and the Christians over the nature of Christ was not resolved by any compromise formula containing elements of the Muslim and the Christian conception of Christ. Each party continued to adhere to its own position, even when the Christian Bishop advised against accepting the revealed challenge (*mubāhala*) to invoke God's curse upon the liars: *Truly for God the likeness of Jesus is as the likeness of Adam: He created him of dust, then He said to him, Be, and he was.* [This is] *the truth from thy Lord, so be not of those who waver. And whoever disputeth with thee concerning him, after the knowledge which hath come to thee, say: Come, let us summon our sons and your sons, and our women and your women, and ourselves and yourselves, then let us humbly pray, and lay the curse of God upon the liars* (III: 59-61). The mutual curse did not take place, the Bishop cautioning against it; instead a practical agreement was arrived at, in terms of which full religious rights together with political protection was granted to the Christians in return for the payment of a tribute.

This example of the prophetic *sunna*, or conduct, is a good background against which one can evaluate the following important passage from the *Discourses* of Rūmī. As mentioned earlier, he clearly takes a Christian to task for continuing to believe in the idea that Jesus is God, but this disagreement on the plane of dogma does not blind Rūmī from his majestic vision of the spirit above all religious forms—a theme that recurs so often in his poetry—nor does it preclude discourse with Christians;

Blessed Najrān?' was the cry of a group of travellers throughout the region collecting votive offerings. See Josef W. Meri, *The Cult of Saints Among Muslims and Jews in Medieval Syria* (Oxford: Oxford University Press, 2002), p. 212. This work is a mine of information detailing the remarkable mutual tolerance that characterized Muslim-Jewish relations on the plane of practical piety, and demonstrating a spiritual culture in which the manifestations of the sacred—whatever be its religious source—provided a focus for devotion which often took precedence over the divergence of formal beliefs.

on the contrary, mutual inspiration between believers is an ever-present possibility. As discussed earlier, a certain particularism on the plane of theology can go hand in hand with a universalism on the plane of spirituality. Here, we should note that Rūmī's 'theological' attitude towards Christianity does not prevent him from asserting, in his poetry and elsewhere, the limitations of the plane on which such an attitude has any meaning; and such an assertion presupposes a perspective that transcends that plane of theological alternativism. In Rūmī's words:

> 'I was speaking one day amongst a group of people, and a party of non-Muslims was present. In the middle of my address they began to weep and to register emotion and ecstasy. Someone asked: What do they understand and what do they know? Only one Muslim in a thousand understands this kind of talk. What did they understand, that they should weep? The Master [i.e. Rūmī himself] answered: It is not necessary that they should understand the form of the discourse; that which constitutes the root and principle of the discourse, that they understand.[97] After all, every one acknowledges the Oneness of God, that He is the Creator and Provider, that He controls everything, that to Him all things shall return, and that it is He who punishes and forgives. When anyone hears these words, which are a description and commemoration (*dhikr*) of God, a universal commotion and ecstatic passion supervenes, since out of these words come the scent of their Beloved and their Quest.'[98]

[97] We have taken the liberty of substantially altering Arberry's translation in this sentence. He translates the Persian, *nafs-i īn sukhan* as 'the inner spirit of these words'; whereas Rūmī's contrast between the *nafs* of the 'words' and the *aṣl* of the 'words' makes it clear that the latter is in fact the 'inner spirit' and the former is something relatively superficial; here, the *nafs* is the formal correlate of the *aṣl*, the supra-formal principle, or the 'inner spirit'.

[98] *Discourses*, p. 108.

In this passage the notion of creative, spiritual dialogue is given clear definition. Receptivity to innate spirituality, such as is rooted in the *fiṭra*, constitutes the inalienable substance of the human soul; and this innate spirituality recognises no confessional boundaries. Rūmī is not so much denying the fact that Muslims and non-Muslims disagree over particular dogmas, as affirming the ever-present validity of spiritual dialogue, a mode of dialogue which bears fruit despite theological disagreement, and which serves to limit the negativity arising out of that disagreement, while turning to spiritual account the common, underlying devotional orientation to the transcendent that articulates the deepest aspirations of all believers.

This mode of dialogue is possible because the receptivity embedded within spiritual aspiration is of infinitely greater import than the limitations that circumscribe all mental conceptions. This is how one can understand the following statement, in which both faith and infidelity are transcended by something more fundamental than the plane on which this formal dichotomy exists: '. . . all men in their inmost hearts love God and seek Him, pray to Him and in all things put their hope in Him, recognizing none but Him as omnipotent and ordering their affairs. Such an apperception is neither infidelity nor faith. Inwardly it has no name.'[99]

In other words, both belief and unbelief, by the very fact of their opposition as mental constructs, are far from the existential quality of spiritual perception, a perception of the reality of God that is one with the very being of the believer, rather than being restricted to the form taken by this perception on the mental plane. This perception 'has no name', because it is essentially of the same substance as that reality which it perceives and thus knows with unshakable certainty: one has absolute certainty of the Absolute because, in the final analysis, it is the Absolute itself which bears witness to itself through the heart of the believer:

[99] *Ibid.*, p. 109.

God beareth witness that there is no god but Him (III: 18).[100] That kind of belief which can be expressed by thought, alone, is wholly relative, as is the faculty with which it is expressed; as such, it is susceptible to being opposed, on the same plane of thought, by its opposite, unbelief. Heartfelt certitude, by contrast, cannot be shaken by any thought from without. The orientation towards God generated by this degree of certitude is one with the very being of the believer, and cannot therefore be negated—except by non-being, which is, precisely, nothing.

This perspective on the essential, unifying dimension of inward orientation towards God is reinforced by the following statements from the same work. Prayer, Rūmī says, changes from religion to religion, but 'faith does not change in any religion; its states, its point of orientation and the rest are invariable.'[101] Similarly, as regards love of God: '. . . love for the Creator is latent in all the world and in all men, be they Magians, Jews or Christians. . . '[102]

In other words, disagreement on the plane of theology and law has no place when it comes to spiritual realities. Even if one regards the religion of the other lacking in some respects—and even if one invites the other to embrace Islam—one can never prejudge the individual believer, of whatever faith. This takes us back to the discussion about the *fiṭra*: it remains intact whatever be the formal religious affiliation of the individual. This being the case, the degree to which this primordial nature—this love of the Creator that is 'latent in all the world and in all men'—is brought to fruition cannot be determined in advance by any

[100] The verse continues: *as do the angels and those of knowledge, upright in justice* . . . From the esoteric point of view the attestation of the angels and of mankind is but the attestation of the one and only reality by the one and only reality, through these different grades of being, and not *by* them. This relates to the mystery of God's knowing His 'hidden treasure' through an apparent 'other'.

[101] *Ibid.*, p. 43. Arberry translates the word *qibla* as locus; but it is preferable to translate this word as 'point of orientation' in the above sentence.

[102] *Ibid.*, p. 214.

formula—dogmatic, juridical or speculative. Thus we arrive at a position which upholds an initial unconditional spiritual equality as between souls of different religions, a position that can be held even by those who are compelled by personal conviction to grant privileged and normative status to their own religion. It is important to add that, even if this position does not preclude belief in the *inequality* between the different faiths, it should ensure that this belief does not translate into fanaticism or chauvinism, pride or arrogance: for, in the very measure that one acknowledges the primordial and innately holy predisposition of each human soul, on the one hand, and believes in the imprescriptible rhythms and modalities of divine grace, on the other hand, no Muslim can presume to prejudge the spirituality, the intrinsic morality, or the posthumous status of the non-Muslim other.

Such a position emerges naturally from reflection on the aspect of the Qur'ānic discourse that has been highlighted in this book. In addition to the verses cited earlier, the following ones should be carefully noted. In indicating the common spiritual ground which unites all believers—that of sincerity, depth, devotion, piety—one is led, by spiritual logic, or an 'aesthetic' sense of proportions, to attribute more significance to this common ground than to the formal differences of dogma, or to the perceived errors on the plane of dogma. The Qur'ānic order to engage in constructive dialogue, and to avoid harsh disputation, is given added depth by these affirmations of the presence of piety and sincere faith in other religious traditions. For example:

> *And do not debate with the People of the Book except in that which is most excellent, save with those who do wrong. And say: We believe in that which hath been revealed to us and revealed to you. Our God and your God is one, and unto Him we surrender* (XXIX: 46)
>
> *They are not all alike. Of the People of the Book there is a staunch community who recite the revelations of God in the watches of the night, falling prostrate. They believe in God and*

> *the Last Day, and enjoin right conduct and forbid indecency, and vie with one another in good works. These are of the righteous. And whatever good they do, they will not be denied it; and God knows the pious* (III: 113–114)
> *Thou wilt find the nearest of them* [the People of the Book] *in affection to those who believe to be those who say: Verily, we are Christians. That is because there are among them priests and monks, and they are not proud* (V: 82)
> *I believe in whatever scripture God hath revealed, and I am commanded to be just among you. God is our Lord and your Lord. Unto us our works and unto you your works; no argument between us and you. God will bring us together and unto Him is the journeying* (XLII: 15).

And finally, it is worth repeating the following verse, which can justifiably be put forward as altogether definitive in respect of dialogue: *Call unto the way of thy Lord with wisdom and fair exhortation, and debate with them in the finest manner* (XVI: 125).

For those wishing to engage in dialogue with other faiths and their representatives, the key question devolves upon the way in which one understands that which is 'finest', 'most excellent' or 'most beautiful'. One is urged to use one's own intelligence, in an aesthetic as well as analytical way, to arrive at what accords most logically and harmoniously with the conditions of one's own 'dialogical' situation. The verse also links the 'call' to the way of God with holding discourse with adherents of other belief-systems. Thus dialogue can itself be seen not as contrary to the Muslim duty of bearing witness to his or her faith, but, as argued above, it can be regarded as an *aspect* of that duty, and also possibly the wisest way of performing that duty in today's world. In an age when, in the words of Frithjof Schuon, 'the outward and readily exaggerated incompatibility of the different religions greatly discredits, in the minds of most of our contemporaries, all religion',[103] a 'call to God' which is based

[103] F. Schuon, *The Transcendent Unity of Religions*, p. 14. Schuon does not pretend that the incompatibility between the different religions can be

on universal inclusivity rather than dogmatic exclusivity is much more likely to be heeded.

This universality springs directly from 'that which is finest' for, in one of the two verses in which this phrase occurs in connection with discourse, the Muslim is instructed to commence the 'finest' discourse with the following words: *We believe in that which hath been revealed to us and revealed to you. Our God and your God is one, and unto Him we surrender.* (XXIX: 46)

The universality of the phenomenon of revelation, together with the unique Absolute in which it is rooted, are given here as the twin principles upon which to build a dialogue or discourse characterised by 'that which is finest'. It is the Absolute that must be accorded absolute significance, and it is this common adherence to the Absolute—whatever be the name given to it—that binds together the different faith-communities; whereas a dialogue that proceeds exclusively from the differences between the communities can only lead to relativities, at best, and conflict at worst. The Absolute must be treated as absolute; then, relativities assume their proper proportions, and are treated as such. The fact of having received revelation, likewise, is of more significance in this perspective, than the different rulings contained within the revelations.

Let us recall the comment on verse V: 48 by Ibn ʿArabī: 'All religion comes from God, even if some of the rulings are diverse. Everyone is commanded to perform the religion and to come together in it... As for the rulings which are diverse, that is because of the Law which God assigned to each one of the messengers.' But this formal, outward diversity does not preclude inner unity, for the different rulings 'are not diverse in the

---

ignored, for the differences and mutual exclusions are real on their own level. What matters for him, though, is the fact that 'each religion is inherently a totality', and that its 'most profound content' is not diminished on account of what it excludes. *Form and Substance in the Religions* (Bloomington: World Wisdom Books, 2002), p. 213.

fact that you have been commanded to come together and to perform them.'[104]

That which unites the believers—belief in an Absolute, and an orientation to the Absolute determined by a revelation proceeding therefrom—is of infinitely greater value than that which differentiates them. This principle will be accepted by all those for whom the Absolute truly takes precedence over the relative—all those for whom the Absolute is alone absolute, and everything else is relative. Those, by contrast, who are inclined to give absolute importance to relative things—and who cannot fail, by consequence, to relativise the Absolute—will stress differentiation over unity. The unity in question here, however, must not in any way be confused with uniformity: the unity is that of the transcendent Absolute, while diversity is the characteristic of the formal revelations, each of which recapitulates within itself something of the inimitable uniqueness of its source—whence the absoluteness of the claims made by each revelation; whence also the exclusivism that accompanies every religion, like a shadow that follows an illuminated object. The light illuminating the objects is one, the objects illuminated are many; the shadows are thus differentiated and 'exclusive', but this mutual exclusion still demonstrates, in its own way, the oneness of the light upon which they all depend for their very existence: *And in the earth are neighbouring tracts, and gardens of vines, and fields sown, and palms in pairs, and palms single, watered with one water. And We have made some of them to excel others in fruit. Surely herein are signs for a people who understand* (XIII: 4).

The rich diversity of 'fruit' bears witness to but one water: differences of form, to the oneness of vivifying essence. Thus, there is no question here of a bland levelling out of formal differences in the name of a putative essence residing at the level of forms. As was seen in Chapter III, the Qur'ānic discourse explicitly refers to the incoherence and illogicality of confessional or denominational pride, and affirms truths of a universal nature,

[104] Quoted in Chittick, *Sufi Path of Knowledge*, p. 303.

doing so, moreover, with an insistence and in a manner that is unparalleled among world scriptures. It is therefore uniquely situated, in intellectual terms, to assist in the resolution of the contemporary problems of inter-faith dialogue, which are to such a high degree generated by mutually exclusive religious claims.

Wisdom is explicitly called for in the verse cited above; and wisdom is not something that can be defined or promulgated in advance of all the concrete and unique situations in which wisdom needs to be applied, as if it were a formal rule or a blueprint. In Qur'ānic terms: on the one hand wisdom is described as a gift from God: *He giveth wisdom to whom He will; and he to whom wisdom is given hath been granted great good* (II: 269). And on the other, it is a quality that can be cultivated, acquired or learnt; this is implied in the following verse, where the Prophet is described as one who teaches and imparts not just the formal message, but the wisdom required to understand and creatively apply that message: *He it is Who hath sent among the unlettered ones a Messenger of their own, to recite unto them His revelations and to make them grow in purity, and to teach them the Scripture and wisdom...* (LXII: 2). Dialogue is closely connected with wisdom for, in the words of the *ḥadīth*: wisdom is the stray camel of the believer. He has a right to it wherever he may find it.[105]

One of the most important aspects of wisdom taught by the scripture of the Qur'ān and the conduct of the Prophet is tolerance of those with belief-systems different from one's own; a tolerance grounded in a consciousness of the reality which transcends all systems of belief, one's own included, and yet is also present, not only within all such systems, but also,

[105] Kāshānī refers to this saying in his comment on II: 25: *And give good tidings to those who believe and perform virtuous acts, that theirs are Gardens underneath which rivers flow; whenever they are provided with food of the fruit thereof they say: This is what was given us before, and it is given to them in resemblance.* The sustenance 'given us before' is wisdom and spiritual sciences that were firmly rooted in the heart, but forgotten, thus 'lost', through preoccupation with worldly affairs. (vol. I, p. 23)

mysteriously, in the depths of each human soul. It is this innate respect for the individual soul as such, based upon the inalienable substance of the *fiṭra* that constitutes the spiritual foundation of each soul, that can lead to authentic dialogue between individuals who represent different religions and civilisations. Spiritually transforming dialogue—as opposed to merely expedient or pragmatic discussion—emerges more naturally if this presence of God in all human beings is respected. And there is no contradiction, it must be stressed, between the two types of dialogue. For the practical aspects of dialogue cannot but be enhanced and rendered more efficacious when the basis of the dialogue is deepened by the spiritual vision of the divine *Face* within the other.

For Muslims living at a time when the alternative to dialogue is not just diatribe but violent clash, the imperative of highlighting that which unites the different religions, of upholding and promoting the common spiritual patrimony of mankind, is of the utmost urgency. There is ample evidence in the Qur'ānic text itself, and compelling commentaries on these verses by those most steeped in the spiritual tradition of Islam, to demonstrate that the Qur'ān not only provides us with a universal vision of religion, and thus with the means to contemplate all revealed religions as 'signs' (*āyāt*) of God; it also opens up paths of creative, constructive dialogue between the faithful of all the different religious communities, despite their divergent belief-systems. It provides us with the basis for dialogue and mutual enrichment on aspects of religious life and thought that go beyond the outward forms of belief, yielding fruit not only in the practical domain of peaceful coexistence, but also and above all, in the fertile fields of metaphysical insight, immutable values, contemplative inspiration and spiritual realization.

Epilogue

It seems fitting for us to conclude this book by citing a passage from the pen of Professor Rusmir Mahmutćehajić, former vice-President of Bosnia & Herzegovina, who resigned from his post out of a refusal to condone the partition of the country along religious lines, manifesting thereby his fidelity to the principle of 'unity of diversity' which has characterized the past six hundred years of Bosnian history.[1] If, historically, Bosnian culture bears witness to this ideal, the continuing adherence to it by Bosnians today—after the most horrific crimes perpetrated against them in the name of its very opposite: virulent ethnic-religious exclusivism—is powerful testimony to the compassion and wisdom that flow forth as the expression of this Qur'ānically-based universalism, and reveal the extraordinary force of that 'transcendently ordained tolerance' called for by T. J. Winter.[2]

---

[1] 'Bosnian history in all its manifestations can be understood as a belief that the three main religious routes can and should be seen in relation to Unity, to their common origin... This belief has never achieved full expression in explicit policy terms, but it is deeply rooted in people's perception of the world. The interweaving of different holy forms is a local fact of life...' *The Denial of Bosnia* (trs. Francis R. Jones & Marina Bowder), (University Park, PA: The Pennsylvania State University Press, 2000), p. 17.

[2] See the introduction of this book. One should also refer here to other Bosnian scholars noted for their Sufi-inspired ethics. See in particular the works of Enes Karić, Rasid Hafizović and Nevad Kahteran. The following remarkable statement also testifies to the power of this 'transcendently

Mahmutćehajić's perspective is deeply rooted in the most universal and esoteric teachings of Sufism, as a glance at any of his books would reveal. Therefore, to the question of how practical this kind of Sufi universalism is in the 'real' world, the following remarkable passage is sufficient answer.

> 'More than a thousand of their *masdjids*[3] [sic] have been destroyed, over a hundred and fifty thousand people killed, over fifty thousand women and girls raped, and more than a million people expelled from their homes. The dark forces of human evil have touched every aspect of their existence—hence the danger of their becoming so radicalised by suffering that they take on the nature of the perpetrators. The other choice is to realise the true meaning of the first image, the *masdjid*, and to hold by it, while facing the immediate need to confront, analyse and identify this evil. The image of the *masdjid*, and the fact of the killings, offer a spectrum of possibilities, ranging from the highest—the Vertical Path—to the lowest—descent into rage. The slaughter must be understood for the ascent to be achieved. Only then can this command be followed with confidence: "Not equal are the good deed and the

ordained tolerance'; it is the simple answer given by Mustafa Cerić, Mufti of Bosnia—following his 'Message to the Muslims of Britain' delivered at the Muslim Parliament, London, May 1994—to the question of whether the Bosnians could bear to live with the Serbs after the atrocities they inflicted upon the Muslims. 'We have to live with them, even if we do not want to, because of what the Qur'ān teaches us.' Cited in *Bosnia: Destruction of a Nation, Inversion of a Principle* (London: Islamic World Report, 1996) ed. R. Shah-Kazemi, p. ix.

[3] The mosque is presented by Mahmutćehajić as the paradigm of universal worship, in accordance with its etymology, *masjid* meaning literally, 'place of prostration'. His use of this word in this paradigmatic sense is based, on the one hand, on the verses which tell us that everything in creation *prostrates to God* (see for example, XIII: 15; XVI: 49; XXII: 18); and on the other, the *ḥadīth* which says that God had made the whole of the earth a *masjid*.

evil deed. Repel evil with that which is fairer[4] and behold, he between whom and thee there is enmity shall be as if he were a loyal friend: Yet none shall receive it, except the steadfast; none shall receive it, except a man of mighty fortune." In contrast, rendering evil for evil means to become agents in the spread of corruption.

The conspiracy among Bosnia's enemies to build a totalitarian uniformity through destruction is a denial of Unity, for Unity can only be confirmed by the pluriformity which they are striving to destroy. "Had God not driven back the people, some by means of others, there had been destroyed cloisters and churches, synagogues and mosques, wherein God's name is much mentioned."[5] This plurality of ways is a confirmation of the unity of the truth, thus denial of any one of them is at the same time denial of the truth. All people have the right to resist any kind of effort to exclude or deny this diversity: "To those against whom war is made, permission is given to fight, because they have been wronged. . . They are those who have been expelled from their homes in defiance of right, for no cause except that they say: Our Lord is God."[6] This is the most important reason to take up arms, for without defence of that freedom, "the earth had surely become corrupted." [7]

The fact that Bosnia has survived intact down the ages shows the will to preserve the monasteries, churches, synagogues and mosques. This has only been possible through the consensus that the elements of her diversity and constant dialogue about their nature lead to one and the same goal. This awareness is sown in every human self and is reflected in the creed, "We believe in what has

---

[4] The Arabic is, again, *aḥsan*; the verses being cited are XLI: 34–35.

[5] Q. XXII: 40.

[6] Q. XXII: 39–40.

[7] Q. II: 251.

been sent down to us, and what has been sent down to you; our God and your God is One, and to Him we have surrendered."[8]

Unity is confirmed by the multitude of paths that lead towards it, just as peace is confirmed by a multitude of voices. The monasteries, churches, synagogues and mosques give outer form to this multitude of paths and voices and show their underlying Unity. "Checking one set of people by means of another" points to the constant flow of dialogue between faiths and peoples which prevents anything, even a path towards Unity, from being commandeered as a means of reaching their goal. To those who see only their own goal, their own and any other path is irrelevant. Only through relinquishing their goal would they come closer to God; but instead, by deifying their goal, they refuse to see the truth that "no associate has He".[9] This is an unforgivable attitude, the source of all corruption. When narrow-mindedness becomes a god, the resulting arrogance displays itself as ignorance, which passes itself off as knowledge, and weakness, which comes in the guise of violence.

It is only possible to break this cycle if one accepts the overriding fact of humanity's quest for Perfection. Learning a sacred language means acknowledging the fact that there are other languages. Every person follows his or her own path: the messenger reveals the message, but humans have freedom in how they read it. Individuals, therefore, are subject to two conditionalities, one greater and one lesser—in the words of the Torah, the Gospels, and the Kur'an [sic], believing in God and doing good. The ascending motion brings them closer to Completeness; but this motion is shown by the goodness of their acts, for God is always infinitely close to

[8] Q. XXIX: 46.

[9] Q. VI: 163.

humankind, but humankind is always infinitely far from God. A person's position is shown by the relationship of dialogue with those who are close to that person. And this relationship rests on trust, for submission to God binds the individual to the goodness of man, in accordance with the command: "Thou shalt love thy neighbour as thyself: I am the Lord".'[10]

[10] Leviticus: 19: 18. Rusmir Mahmutćehajić, *Bosnia the Good—Tolerance and Tradition* (tr. Marina Bowder), (Budapest & New York: Central European University Press, 2000), pp. 144-145.

Bibliography

Abu Rabi', Ibrahim M., *Intellectual Origins of Islamic Resurgence in the Modern Arab World*, Albany, State University of New York Press, 1996.

Adang, Camilla, *Muslim Writers on Judaism and the Hebrew Bible from Ibn Rabban to Ibn Hazm*, Leiden, E. J. Brill, 1996.

Addas, Claude, *Quest for the Red Sulphur—The Life of Ibn ʿArabī* (tr. P. Kingsley), Cambridge, Islamic Texts Society, 1993.

Ajmal, Mohammad, 'Sufi Science of the Soul', in S. H. Nasr (ed.), *Islamic Spirituality*, vol. 1 Foundations, London, Routledge & Kegan Paul, 1987.

ʿAlī b. Abī Ṭālib, *Nahj al-balāgha* (compiled by al-Sharīf al-Raḍī, ed. Shaykh ʿAzīzullāh al-ʿUtārdī), Tehran, Nahj al-Balāgha Foundation, 1993.
———*Peak of Eloquence* (translation of *Nahj al-balāgha* by Sayed Ali Reza), New York, Tahrike Tarsile Qur'an, 1996.

Allen, Douglas, 'Phenomenology of Religion' in the *Encyclopedia of Religion*, New York, Macmillan, 1987.
———*Structure and Creativity in Religion*, The Hague, Mouton, 1978.

Almond, Ian, 'The Honesty of the Perplexed: Derrida and Ibn ʿArabi on "Bewilderment"', *Journal of the American Academy of Religion*, vol. 70, no. 3, 2002.

Āmulī, Sayyid Ḥaydar, *Kitāb jāmiʿ al-asrār wa-manbaʿ al-anwār* (*La philosophie Shi'ite*), ed. H. Corbin and O. Yahia, Tehran & Paris, Bibliothèque Iranienne, 1969.
———*Al-Muḥīṭ al-aʿẓam wa'l-baḥr al-khiḍamm fī ta'wīl kitāb Allāh al-ʿazīz al-muḥkam*, 4 vols., Qom, al-Maʿhad al-Thaqāfī Nūr ʿAlā Nūr, 1380 Sh./2001.

Arkoun, Mohammed, *The Concept of Revelation: From the People of the Book to the Societies of the Book*, Claremont, Cal., Claremont Graduate School, 1987.
———*The Unthought in Islamic Thought*, London, Saqi Books, 2002.

Arnold, Thomas, *The Preaching of Islam*, London, Luzac, 1935.

Asad, Muhammad, *The Message of the Qur'ān*, Bristol, The Book Foundation, 2003.

Askari, Hasan, 'Within and Beyond the Experience of Religious Diversity', in J. Hick and H. Askari (eds.), *The Experience of Religious Diversity*, Aldershot, Gower Press, 1985.

Aslan, Adnan, *Religious Pluralism in Christian and Islamic Philosophy—The Thought of John Hick and Seyyed Hossein Nasr*, Richmond, Curzon Press, 1998.

Ayoub, Mahmoud, 'Jesus the Son of God: A Study of the Terms *Ibn* and *Walad* in the Qur'ān and *Tafsīr* Tradition' in Yvonne Y. Haddad and Wadi Z. Haddad (eds.), *Christian-Muslim Encounters*, Gainesville, University Press of Florida, 1995.

———*The Qur'ān and Its Interpreters*, Albany, State University of New York Press, 1984.

al-Baḥrānī, Kamāl al-Dīn b. Maytham, *Sharḥ Nahj al-balāgha*, 5 vols., Beirut, Dār al-Thaqalayn, 1999.

Baker, Robert, and Henry, Gray (eds.), *Merton and Sufism—The Untold Story*, Louisville, Fons Vitae, 1999.

Basinger, David, *Religious Diversity—A Philosophical Assessment*, Aldershot, Ashgate, 2002.

Bauman, Lynn C., 'Mystery and Scriptural Text in the Post-Modern Age', *Sacred Web*, no. 3, June 1999.

Bernstein, Richard, 'Metaphysics, Critique and Utopia', *The Review of Metaphysics*, no. 42, 1988.

Boullata, Issa, '*Fa-stabiqū 'l-khayrāt*: A Qur'anic Principle of Interfaith Relations', in Yvonne Y. Haddad and Wadi Z. Haddad (eds.), *Christian-Muslim Encounters*, Gainesville, University Press of Florida, 1995.

Böwering, Gerhard, *The Mystical Vision of Existence in Classical Islam: The Qur'ānic Hermeneutics of the Ṣūfī Sahl al-Tustarī*, Berlin & New York, Walter de Gruyter, 1980.

———*Sufi Hermeneutics in Medieval Islam*, Tokyo, Sophia University, 1987.

Braybrooke, Marcus, 'Inter-faith Work Needs Its Mystics', in *World Faiths Encounter*, no. 16, 1997.

al-Bukharī, Muḥammad b. Ismāʿīl, *Ṣaḥīḥ al-Bukhārī*, (tr. M. M. Khan), 9 vols., Chicago, Kazi Publications, 1976–1979.

Burckhardt, Titus, *Introduction to Sufi Doctrine* (tr. D. M. Matheson), Wellingborough, Thorsons, 1976.
———*Mirror of the Intellect* (tr. & ed. William Stoddart), Cambridge, Quinta Essentia, 1987.
———*Sacred Art in East and West*, Louisville, Fons Vitae, 2002.
———*The Art of Islam, Language and Meaning* (tr. Peter Hobson), London, World of Islam Festival Trust, 1976.

Burton, John, 'Abrogation', in *Encyclopedia of the Qur'ān* (ed. Jane D. McAuliffe), Leiden, E. J. Brill, 2001.

Chittick, William C., 'Divine Names and Theophanies' in M. Chodkiewicz (ed.), *Les Illuminations de La Mecque/The Meccan Illuminations*, Paris, Sindbad, 1988.
———*Imaginal Worlds: Ibn al-ʿArabī and the Problem of Religious Diversity*, Albany, State University of New York Press, 1994.
———*The Self-Disclosure of God*, Albany, State University of New York Press, 1998.
———*The Sufi Path of Knowledge*, Albany, State University of New York Press, 1989.

Chodkiewicz, Michel, *An Ocean Without Shore—Ibn Arabi, the Book and the Law* (tr. David Streight), Albany, State University of New York Press, 1993.
———*Seal of the Saints: Prophethood and Sainthood in the Doctrine of Ibn 'Arabī* (tr. Liadain Sherrard), Cambridge, Islamic Texts Society, 1993.

Churchill, Charles Henry, *The Life of Abdel Kader*, London, Chapman & Hall, 1867.

Clarke, Kelly James, 'Perils of Pluralists', in *Faith and Philosophy*, vol. 14, no. 3, 1997.

Coomaraswamy, Ananda K., *Coomaraswamy 2: Selected Papers: Metaphysics* (ed. Roger Lipsey), Princeton, Princeton University Press, 1977.

Corbin, Henri, *Creative Imagination in the Sufism of Ibn ʿArabī* (tr. R. Mannheim), Princeton, Princeton University Press, 1969.
———*En Islam iranien*, 4 vols., Paris, Gallimard, 1971–2.

Cutsinger, James S., '*Hesychia*: An Orthodox Opening to Esoteric Ecumenism' in James S. Cutsinger (ed.), *Paths to the Heart*, Bloomington, World Wisdom, 2002.
———'The Mystery of the Two Natures' in *Sophia: The Journal of Traditional Studies*, vol. 4, no. 2, 1998.

Dahlen, Ashk, 'Transcendent Hermeneutics of Supreme Love: Rumi's Concept of Mystical Appropriation' in *Orientalia Suecana* , vol. 52, 2003.

Dakake, David, 'The Myth of a Militant Islam', in J. Lumbard (ed.), *Islam, Fundamentalism and the Betrayal of Tradition*, Bloomington, World Wisdom Books, 2004.

Danner, Victor, *The Islamic Tradition*, New York, Amity House, 1988.

D'Costa, Gavin, 'The Impossibility of a Pluralist View of Religions', in *Religious Studies*, no. 32, 1996.
———*The Meeting of Religions and the Trinity*, Edinburgh, T & T Clark, 2000.
———*Theology and Religious Pluralism*, Oxford, Blackwell, 1986.

Detmer, David, 'Ricoeur on Atheism: A Critique' in *The Philosophy of Paul Ricoeur*, The Library of Living Philosophers, ed. Lewis E. Hahn, Chicago, Open Court, 1995.

al-Dhahabī, Muḥammad Ḥusayn, *al-Tafsīr wa'l-mufassirūn*, 2 vols., Cairo, Dār al-Kutub al-Ḥāditha, 1961.

Dionysius the Areopagite, *Mystical Theology and the Celestial Hierarchies*, Fintry, The Shrine of Wisdom Press, 1965.

Donovan, Peter, 'The Intolerance of Religious Pluralism', *Religious Studies*, vol. 29, 1993.

Eaton, Gai, *Remembering God: Reflections on Islam*, Cambridge, Islamic Texts Society, 2000.

Eck, Diana L., *Encountering God: A Spiritual Journey from Bozeman to Banares*, Boston, Beacon Press, 1993.

Eckhart, Meister, *Meister Eckhart: Sermons & Treatises* (tr. Maurice O'Connell Walshe), 3 vols., Dorset, Element Books, 1979.

El-Fadl, Khaled Abou, *Conference of the Books: The Search for Beauty in Islam*, Lanham/New York/Oxford, University Press of America, 2001.
———*Speaking in God's Name: Islamic Law, Authority and Women*, Oxford, Oneworld, 2001.
———*The Place of Tolerance in Islam*, Boston, Beacon Press, 2002.

Eliade, Mircea, *The Sacred and the Profane*, Harcourt, Brace & Co., 1959.

Ernst, Carl W., *Words of Ecstasy in Sufism*, Albany, State University of New York Press, 1984.

Esack, Farid, *Qur'an, Liberation and Pluralism*, Oxford, Oneworld, 1997.

Esmail, Aziz, *The Poetics of Religious Experience*, London, Institute of Ismaili Studies—Occasional Papers 1, 1998.

Fastiggi, Robert L., 'The Incarnation: Muslim Objections and the Christian Response', *The Thomist*, vol. 57, no. 3, July 1993.

Gardet, Louis, '*Dhikr*', in *Encyclopedia of Islam* (2nd Edition), Leiden, E. J. Brill, 1960-2002.

Gellner, Ernest, *Reason and Culture*, Oxford, Blackwell, 1992.

al-Ghazālī, Abū Ḥāmid, *Iḥyā' ʿulūm al-dīn*, 6 vols., Beirut, Dār al-Jīl, 1992.
———*The Book of Knowledge* (Book I of *The Revival of the Religious Sciences*, translated by N. A. Faris), Lahore, Sh. Muhammad Ashraf, 1966.
———*The Recitation and Interpretation of the Qur'ān* (Book VIII of *The Revival of the Religious Sciences*, translated by M. Abul Quasem), London & Boston, Routledge & Kegan Paul, 1984.
———*Al-Ghazālī Invocations and Supplications* (Book IX of *The Revival of the Religious Sciences*, translated by K. Nakamura), Cambridge, Islamic Texts Society, 1990.
———*The Faith and Practice of al-Ghazālī* (translation of *Al-Munqidh min al-ḍalāl* by W. Montgomery Watt), London, George Allen & Unwin, 1953.
———*Al-Ghazālī: The Niche of Lights* (translation of *Mishkāt al-anwār* by D. Buchman), Provo, Utah, Brigham Young University Press, 1998.
———*The Jewels of the Quran* (translation of *Kitāb Jawāhir al-Qur'ān* by M. Abul Quasem), Kuala Lumpur, National University of Malaysia, 1977.

Giulio Basetti-Sani, *The Koran in the Light of Christ*, Chicago, Franciscan Herald Press, 1977.

Gril, Denis, 'Le terme du voyage', in M. Chodkiewicz (ed.), *Les Illuminations de La Mecque/The Meccan Illuminations*, Paris, Sindbad, 1988.

Grondin, Jean, *Introduction to Philosophical Hermeneutics*, New Haven & London, Yale University Press, 1994.

Guénon, René, *The Multiple States of Being* (tr. J. Godwin), New York, Larson Publications, 1984.
———*The Reign of Quantity and the Signs of the Times*, New York, Sophia Perennis, 2004.

Habil, Abdurrahman, 'Traditional Esoteric Commentaries on the Qur'ān', in S. H. Nasr (ed.), *Islamic Spirituality*, vol. 1 Foundations, London, Routledge & Kegan Paul, 1987.

Heidegger, Martin, *Being and Time* (trs. J. Macquarrie & E. Robinson), Oxford, Blackwell, 2000.

Henzell-Thomas, Jeremy, *The Challenge of Pluralism and the Middle Way of Islam*, Occasional Papers, no. 1, Richmond, The Association of Muslim Social Scientists (UK), 2002.

Hick, John, *The Metaphor of God Incarnate—Christology in a Pluralistic World*, London, SCM Press, 1993.
———'The Possibility of Religious Pluralism: A Reply to Gavin D'Costa', in *Religious Studies*, no. 33, 1997.

Hodgson, Marshall G. H., *The Venture of Islam: Conscience and History in a World Civilization*, Chicago & London, University of Chicago Press, 1977.

Homerin, Th. Emeril, 'Ibn ʿArabī in the People's Assembly' in *Middle East Journal*, vol. 40, no. 3.

al-Hujwīrī, ʿAlī, *The Kashf al-Maḥjūb: The Oldest Persian Treatise on Sufiism* (tr. R. A. Nicholson), Lahore, Islamic Book Service, 1992.

Huntington, Samuel, 'The Clash of Civilizations' in *Foreign Affairs*, vol. 72, no. 3, 1993.

Ibn ʿArabī, Muḥyī al-Dīn, *Fuṣūs al-ḥikam*, Cairo, Maṭbaʿat al-Maymaniyya, 1321/1903.
———*Bezels of Wisdom* (translation of *Fuṣūs al-ḥikam* by Ralph Austin), New York, Paulist Press, 1980.
———*The Ringstones of Wisdom* (translation of *Fuṣūs al-ḥikam* by Caner Dagli), Chicago, Kazi Publications, 2004.
———*Al-Futūḥāt al-makkiyya*, 4 vols., Cairo, Dār al-Kutub al-ʿArabiyya al-Kubrā, 1911.
———*Journey to the Lord of Power: A Sufi Manual on Retreat* (translation of

Risālat al-anwār fī mā yumnaḥ ṣāḥib al-khalwa min al-asrār by Rabia T. Harris), New York, Inner Traditions International, 1981.
———*Le Livre de l'extinction dans la contemplation* (translation of *Kitab al-fanā' fi'l-mushāhada* by Michel Valsan), Paris, Les Editions de l'Œuvre, 1984.
———*The Tarjumān al-Ashwāq: A Collection of Mystical Odes* (tr. R. A. Nicholson), London, Theosophical Publishing House, 1978.

Ibn ʿAṭā'illāh al-Iskandarī, *Ibn ʿAṭā'illāh's Sufi Aphorisms* (translation of *Kitāb al-ḥikam* by Victor Danner), Leiden, E. J. Brill, 1973.
———*The Key to Salvation: A Sufi Manual of Invocation* (translation of *Miftāḥ al-falāḥ wa miṣbāḥ al-arwāḥ* by Mary A. K. Danner), Cambridge, Islamic Texts Society, 1996.

Ibn Isḥāq, *The Life of Muhammad—A Translation of Ibn Isḥāq's Sīrat Rasūl Allāh*, tr. A. Guillaume, Oxford, Oxford University Press, 1968.

al-Iṣfahānī, al-Rāghib, *Muʿjam mufradāt alfāẓ al-Qur'ān*, Beirut, Dār al-Fikr, n.d.

Izutsu, Toshihiko, *Sufism and Taoism—A Comparative Study of Key Philosophical Concepts*, Berkeley, Los Angeles, University of California Press, 1983.

Jabre, Farid, *La notion de la maʿrifa chez Ghazali*, Beirut, Librarie Orientale, 1958.

al-Kalābādhī, Abū Bakr, *The Doctrine of the Ṣūfīs* (translation of *Kitāb al-taʿarruf li-madhhab ahl al-taṣawwuf* by A. J. Arberry), Cambridge, Cambridge University Press, 1935.

Kamali, M. Hashim, *Freedom of Expression in Islam*, Cambridge, Islamic Texts Society, 1997.
———*Principles of Islamic Jurisprudence*, Cambridge, Islamic Texts Society, 1991.

al-Kāshānī, ʿAbd al-Razzāq, *Tafsīr al-Qur'ān al-Karīm*, Beirut Dār al-Yaqaẓa, 1968.
———*Tafsīr al-Shaykh al-Akbar*, Cairo, al-Maktaba al-Tawfīqiyya, n.d. (reprint of the Cairo 1283/1866 edition).

al-Kharrāz, Abū Saʿīd, *The Book of Truthfulness* (edition and translation of *Kitāb al-ṣidq* by A. J. Arberry), London & New York, Oxford University Press, 1937.

Küng, Hans, *Projekt Weltethos* (tr. J. Bowden, *Global Responsibility: In Search of a New World Ethic*), New York, Crossroad, 1991.

Lāhījī, Shams al-Dīn Muḥammad, *Mafātīḥ al-iʿjāz fī sharḥ-i gulshan-i rāz*, Tehran, Intishārāt-i Zuwwār, 2000.

Landolt, Hermann, 'Ghazali and "*Religionswissenschaft*"—Some Notes on the *Mishkāt al-Anwār* for Professor Charles J. Adams', *Etudes Asiatiques*, XLV, no. 1, 1991.

Lane, Edward W., *Arabic-English Lexicon*, Cambridge, Islamic Texts Society, 1984.

Lazarus-Yafeh, H., *Studies in Ghazālī*, Jerusalem, Magnes Press, 1975.

Legenhausen, Muhammad, 'Democratic Pluralism in Islam? A Critique', in *Transcendent Philosophy*, vol. 3 no. 4, 2002.
———*Islam and Religious Pluralism*, London, Al-Hoda, 1999.

Lewis, Bernard, *The Jews of Islam*, New Jersey, Princeton University Press, 1984.

Lewisohn, Leonard, *Beyond Faith and Infidelity: The Sufi Poetry and Teachings of Maḥmūd Shabistarī*, London, Curzon Press, 1995.
———(ed.), *The Heritage of Sufism*, 3 vols., Oxford, Oneworld, 1999.

Lings, Martin, *A Sufi Saint of the Twentieth Century: Shaikh Aḥmad al-ʿAlawī, His Spiritual Heritage and Legacy*, Cambridge, Islamic Texts Society, 1993.
———*Sufi Poems—A Mediaeval Anthology*, Cambridge, Islamic Texts Society, 2004.
———*What is Sufism?*, London, George Allen & Unwin, 1975.
———*Ancient Beliefs and Modern Superstitions* London, Archetype, 2001.

Lory, Pierre, *Les Commentaires ésotériques du Coran d'après 'Abd ar-Razzāq al-Qāshānī*, Paris, Les Deux Océans, 1980.

Lumbard, Joseph (ed.), *Islam, Fundamentalism and the Betrayal of Tradition*, Bloomington, World Wisdom Books, 2004.

MacIntyre, Alasdair, *After Virtue*, London, Duckworth, 1981.
———*Three Rival Versions of Moral Enquiry*, London, Duckworth, 1990.
———*Whose Justice? Which Rationality?*, London, Duckworth, 1988.

Madelung, Wilferd, *Religious Schools and Sects in Medieval Islam*, London, Variorum Reprints, 1985.

Maḥmūd, ʿAbd al-Ḥalīm, *Qaḍiyyat al-Taṣawwuf—al-Madrasat al-Shādhiliyya*, Cairo, Dār al-Maʿārif, 1999.

Maʿrifat, Muḥammad Hādī, *Tafsīr wa-mufassirān*, 2 vols., Qom, Mu'assisa Farhangī al-Tamhīd, 1379–1380/2000–2001.

Maritain, Jacques, *The Degrees of Knowledge*, New York, Charles Scribner's Sons, 1959.

Massignon, Louis, *Essay on the Origins of the Technical Language of Islamic Mysticism* (tr. B. Clark), Indiana, University of Notre Dame, 1997.
———*The Passion of al-Ḥallāj* (tr. H. Mason), 4 vols., Princeton, Princeton University Press, 1982.

Mayer, Toby, 'Review Article: *The Qur'ān and its Interpretive Tradition*, by A. Rippin', in *Journal of Qur'ānic Studies*, vol. IV, no. 2, 2002.

McAuliffe, Jane D., 'Exegetical Identification of the Ṣābi'ūn', *The Muslim World*, vol. 72, 1983.
———*Qur'ānic Christians: An Analysis of Classical and Modern Exegesis*, Cambridge, Cambridge University Press, 1991.

Michon, Jean-Louis, 'Titus Burckhardt and the Sense of Beauty', in *Sophia: The Journal of Traditional Studies*, vol. 5, no. 2, 1999.
———'The Spiritual Practices of Sufism', in S. H. Nasr (ed.), *Islamic Spirituality*, vol. 1 Foundations, London, Routledge & Kegan Paul, 1987.

Morris, James Winston, 'Ibn ʿArabi's "Esotericism": The Problem of Spiritual Authority', in *Studia Islamica*, LXXI (1990).
———'Ibn ʿArabi's Spiritual Ascension', in M. Chodkiewicz (ed.), *Les Illuminations de La Mecque/The Meccan Illuminations*, Paris, Sindbad, 1988.

Murad, Abdal Hakim, 'Recapturing Islam from the Terrorists' on the website 'Islam for Today' (www.islamfortoday.com/murad01).

Murata, S., *The Tao of Islam: A Sourcebook on Gender Relationships in Islamic Thought*, Albany, State University of New York Press, 1992.
———Murata, Sachiko and Chittick, William, *The Vision of Islam*, New York, Paragon House, 1994.

Muṭahharī, ʿAllāma, 'ʿIrfān: Islamic Mysticism', in his *Understanding Islamic Sciences*, London, Islamic College for Advanced Studies, 2002.

Nasr, Seyyed Hossein, *The Heart of Islam: Enduring Values for Humanity*, New York, HarperCollins, 2002.
———*Ideals and Realities of Islam*, Cambridge, Islamic Texts Society, 2001.
———*Introduction to Islamic Cosmological Doctrines*, London, Thames & Hudson, 1978.

———*Islamic Art and Spirituality*, Ipswich, Golgonooza Press, 1987.
———*Knowledge and the Sacred*, Albany, State University of New York Press, 1989.
———*Science and Civilization in Islam*, Cambridge, Islamic Texts Society, 1987.
———*Sufi Essays*, London, George Allen & Unwin, 1972.
———*Three Muslim Sages: Avicenna, Suhrawardī, Ibn ʿArabī*, Delmar, Caravan Books, 1976.
———*Traditional Islam in the Modern World*, London & New York, Kegan Paul, 1987.
———'Intellect and Intuition: Their Relationship from the Islamic Perspective', in *Studies in Comparative Religion*, vol. 13, nos. 1, 2, Winter-Spring, 1979.
———'The Heart of the Faithful is the Throne of the All-Merciful', in James S. Cutsinger (ed.), *Paths to the Heart: Sufism and the Christian East*, Bloomington, World Wisdom, 2002.
———'The Qur'ān as the Foundation of Islamic Spirituality', in *Islamic Spirituality*, vol. 1 Foundations, London, Routledge & Kegan Paul, 1987.
———'Reply to Hossein Ziai', in *The Philosophy of Seyyed Hossein Nasr*, The Library of Living Philosophers, vol. XXVIII, (eds. Lewis Edwin Hahn, Randall E. Auxier, Lucian W. Stone Jr.) Chicago & La Salle, Ill., Open Court, 2001.
———'Reply to Sallie B. King', in *Ibid.*

al-Nawawī, Yaḥyā b. Sharaf al-Dīn, *An-Nawawī's Forty Hadith* (trs. E. Ibrahim & D. Johnson-Davies), Cambridge, Islamic Texts Society, 1997.

Nettler, Ronald, *Sufi Metaphysics and Qur'ānic Prophets: Ibn ʿArabī's Thought and Method in the* Fuṣūṣ al-ḥikam, Cambridge, Islamic Texts Society, 2003.

Netton, Ian R., *Allah Transcendent—Studies in the Structure and Semiotics of Islamic Philosophy, Theology and Cosmology*, London, Routledge/Curzon, 1994.

Neuhas, Richard, 'Review of Bat Ye'or, *The Decline of Eastern Christianity Under Islam: From Jihad to Dhimmitude*', in *First Things*, no. 76, October 1997.

Nwyia, Paul, *Exégèse coranique et langage mystique*, Beirut, Dār al-Mashreq, 1970.

Oldmeadow, Kenneth, 'Metaphysics, Theology and Philosophy', in *Sacred Web*, no. 1, July 1998.

Olivetti, Vincente, *Terror's Source*, Birmingham, Amadeus Books, 2002.

Pallis, Marco, *The Way and the Mountain*, London, Peter Owen, 1991.

Parrinder, Geoffrey, *Jesus in the Qur'an*, Oxford, Oneworld, 1996.

Perry, Whitall, *Treasury of Traditional Wisdom*, London, George Allen & Unwin, 1971.

al-Qushayrī, Abu'l-Qāsim, *Principles of Sufism* (partial translation of *al-Risāla al-Qushayriyya* by B. R. von Schlegell), Berkeley, Mizan Press, 1990.

Race, Alan, *Christians and Religious Pluralism*, London, SCM, 1983.

Radtke, Bernard and John O'Kane, *The Concept of Sainthood in Early Islamic Mysticism: Two works by al-Ḥakīm al-Tirmidhī*, Richmond, Curzon Press, 1996.

Rayshahrī, Muḥammad (ed.), *Mīzān al-ḥikma*, Tehran/Qom, Maktab al-Iʿlām al-Islāmī, 1362SH/1983.

al-Rāzī, Fakhr al-Dīn, *Tafsīr al-kabīr*, 11 vols., Beirut, Dār Iḥyā' al-Turāth al-ʿArabī, 2001.

Richie, J. M., 'Christianity in the Qur'ān', in *Encounter: Documents for Muslim-Christian Understanding*, no. 81, 1982.

Ricoeur, Paul, *Figuring the Sacred* (tr. Mark Wallace), Minneapolis, Fortress Books, 1995.
———*Freud and Philosophy* (tr. D. Savage), New Haven & London, Yale University Press, 1970.
———*Hermeneutics and the Human Sciences* (ed. & tr. J. B. Thompson), Cambridge, Cambridge University Press, 1981.

Rifkin, Jeremy, 'Dialogue is a Necessity', *The Guardian*, November 13, 2001.

Rosenthal, Franz, *Knowledge Triumphant: The Concept of Knowledge in Medieval Islam*, Leiden, E. J. Brill, 1970.

Rūmī, Jalāl al-Dīn, *The Discourses of Rūmī* (*Fīhi mā fīhi*) (tr. A. J. Arberry), London, John Murray, 1961.
———*Mathnawī-i maʿnawī* (ed. ʿAbd al-Ḥamīd Mashāyikh Ṭabāṭabā'ī), Tehran, Nashr-i Ṭulūʿ, n.d.
———*The Mathnawī of Jalāl ud-Dīn Rūmī* (tr. R. A. Nicholson), 3 vols., London, Luzac, 1926, 1930, 1934.

Rūzbihān Baqlī Shīrāzī, *Kitāb ʿabhar al-ʿāshiqīn*, (eds. H. Corbin & M. Mo'in), Tehran, Intishārāt-i Manuchihrī, 1987.

Sachedina, Abdulaziz, *The Islamic Roots of Democratic Pluralism*, Oxford, Oxford University Press, 2001.
———'Is Islam an Abrogation of Judeo-Christian Revelation?' in *Concilium: International Review of Theology*, no. 3, 1994.

Sacks, Jonathan, *The Dignity of Difference—How to Avoid the Clash of Civilizations*, London & New York, Continuum, 2002.

al-Sadiq, Sayyid Rida, 'At War with the Spirit of Islam', in *Dialogue*, December 2002.

Safi, Omid (ed.), *Progressive Muslims: On Justice, Gender and Pluralism*, Oxford, Oneworld, 2003.

Samsel, Peter, 'A Unity With Distinctions: Parallels in the Thought of St Gregory Palamas and Ibn al-ʿArabī', in James S. Cutsinger (ed.), *Paths to the Heart: Sufism and the Christian East*, Bloomington, World Wisdom, 2002.

al-Sarrāj, Abū Naṣr, *Kitāb al-lumaʿ* (ed. R. A. Nicholson), E. J. Gibb Memorial Series XXII, London, Luzac, 1963.

Schimmel, Annemarie, *Deciphering the Signs of God: A Phenomenological Approach to Islam*, Albany, State University of New York Press, 1994.
———*Mystical Dimensions of Islam*, Chapel Hill, University of North Carolina Press, 1975.

Schleifer, S. A., 'Jihād and Traditional Islamic Consciousness' in *Islamic Quarterly*, vol. XXVII, no. 4, 1983.

Schuon, Frithjof, *Christianity/Islam: Essays on Esoteric Ecumenism*, Bloomington, World Wisdom Books, 1985.
———*The Eye of the Heart*, Bloomington, World Wisdom Books, 1997.
———*Form and Substance in the Religions*, Bloomington, World Wisdom, 2002.
———*Light on the Ancient Worlds*, Bloomington, World Wisdom, 1984.
———*Logic and Transcendence*, London, Perennial Books, 1984.
———*Spiritual Perspectives and Human Facts*, London, Perennial Books, 1987.
———*The Transcendent Unity of Religions*, Wheaton, Illinois, Theosophical Publishing House, 1993.
———*Understanding Islam*, Bloomington, World Wisdom, 1994.

Sells, Michael, *Mystical Languages of Unsaying*, Chicago and London, Chicago University Press, 1994.

Shah-Kazemi, Reza, (ed.), *Bosnia: Destruction of a Nation, Inversion of a Principle*, London, Islamic World Report, 1996.

———'From the Spirituality of Jihad to the Ideology of Jihadism', in *Seasons: Semiannual Journal of Zaytuna Institute*, vol. 2, no. 2, 2005

———'Review of *The Philosophy of Seyyed Hossein Nasr*' in *Sophia: The Journal of Traditional Studies*, vol. 8, no. 2, Winter, 2002.

———'The Metaphysics of Interfaith Dialogue: Sufi Perspectives on the Universality of the Quranic Message', in James S. Cutsinger (ed.), *Paths to the Heart: Sufism and the Christian East*, Bloomington, World Wisdom, 2002.

———'The Notion and Significance of *Maʿrifa* in Sufism', in *Journal of Islamic Studies*, vol. 13, no. 2, 2002.

———'The Spiritual Function of Tradition: A Perennialist Perspective', in *Sacred Web: A Journal of Tradition and Modernity*, no. 7, 2001.

al-Shaibi, Kamil Mustafa, *Sufism and Shi'ism*, Surbiton, LAAM, 1991.

Shakir, Zaid, 'Jihad is not Perpetual Warfare', in *Seasons: Semiannual Journal of Zaytuna Institute*, vol. 1, no. 2.

Shankaracharya, *Samkara on the Absolute* (tr. A. J. Alston), London, Shanti Sadan, 1987.

———*The Mandukyopanisȧd with Gaudapada's Karika and Sankara's Commentary* (tr. S. Nikhilananda), Mysore, Sri Ramakrishna Ashrama, 1974.

Siddiqui, Ataullah, *Christian-Muslim Dialogue in the Twentieth Century*, London, Palgrave MacMillan, 1997.

Sirāj ad-Dīn, Abū Bakr, *The Book of Certainty*, Cambridge, Islamic Texts Society, 1992.

Smith, Huston, *Beyond the Postmodern Mind*, Wheaton, Il, Quest Books, 1989.

Smith, James, 'Determined Violence: Derrida's Structural Religion', in *The Journal of Religion*, vol. 78, no. 2, 1998.

———'Re-Kanting Postmodernism? Derrida's Religion Within the Limits of Reason Alone', in *Faith and Philosophy*, vol. 17, no. 4, 2000.

Spencer Trimingham, J., *The Sufi Orders in Islam*, Oxford, Oxford University Press, 1998.

Stiver, Dan, *The Philosophy of Religious Language*, Oxford, Blackwell, 1996.

Studstill, Randall, 'Eliade, Phenomenology and the Sacred', in *Religious Studies*, vol. 36, 2000.

al-Sulamī, ʿAbd al-Raḥmān, *Tafsīr al-Sulamī*, 2 vols., Beirut, Dār al-Kutub al-ʿIlmiyya, 2001.

Suzuki, D. T., *Studies in Zen*, London, Rider, 1986.

Swidler, Leonard, ed., *Muslims in Dialogue: The Evolution of a Dialogue*, Lewiston/Queenston/Lampeter, The Edwin Mellen Press, 1992.

al-Ṭabarī, Abū Jaʿfar Muḥammad b. Jarīr, *Jāmiʿ al-bayān ʿan ta'wīl ay al-Qur'ān*, 16 vols., Beirut, Dār Iḥyā' al-Turāth al-ʿArabī, 2001.

Talbi, Mohamed, 'Possibilities and Conditions For a Better Understanding Between Islam and the West', in Leonard Swidler (ed.), *Muslims in Dialogue: The Evolution of a Dialogue*, Lewiston/Queenston/Lampeter, The Edwin Mellen Press, 1992.

Tarnas, Richard, *The Passion of the Western Mind*, London, Pimlico Press, 1991.

Taylor, John, 'Jaʿfar al-Ṣādiq: Forebear of the Sufis', in *Islamic Culture*, vol. XL, no. 2, 1966.

Uždavinys, Algis, 'Through the Idols of Twilight: Postmodernism and Tradition', *Sophia—A Journal of Traditional Studies*, vol. 5, no. 1, Summer 1999.

Vahiduddin, Syed, 'Islam and Diversity of Religions' in *Islam and Christian-Muslim Relations*, vol. 1, no. 1, 1990.

Versteegh, C. H. M., *Arabic Grammar and Qur'ānic Exegesis in Early Islam*, Leiden, E. J. Brill, 1993.

Voll, John O., 'Sufi Orders' in *The Oxford Encyclopedia of the Modern Islamic World*, vol. 4, Oxford, Oxford University Press, 1994.

Waley, Muhammad-Isa, 'Contemplative Disciplines in Early Persian Sufism' in Leonard Lewisohn (ed.), *The Heritage of Sufism*, vol. 1, Oxford, Oneworld, 1999.

Ware, Bishop Kallistos, 'How Do We Enter the Heart?', in James S. Cutsinger (ed.), *Paths to the Heart*, Bloomington, World Wisdom, 2002.

Watt, W. Montgomery, *Early Islam: Collected Articles*, Edinburgh, Edinburgh University Press, 1990.

Wensinck, A. J., 'Al-Khaḍir (al-Khiḍr)', in *Encyclopedia of Islam*, 2nd edition, Leiden, E. J. Brill, 1960-2002.

Winter, T. J., 'Islam and the Threat of Europe' in *World Faiths Encounter*, no. 29, 2001.
———'The Poverty of Fanaticism' in Joseph Lumbard (ed.), *Islam, Fundamentalism and the Betrayal of Tradition*, Bloomington, World Wisdom Books, 2004.

Yahia, Osman, *Histoire et classification de l'œuvre d'Ibn 'Arabī*, Damascus, Institut Français de Damas, 1964.

Yazdi, Mehdi Ha'iri, *The Principles of Epistemology in Islamic Philosophy: Knowledge by Presence*, Albany, State University of New York Press, 1992.

Yusuf, Hamza, 'Generous Tolerance in Islam and its effects on the Life of a Muslim', in *Seasons—Semiannual Journal of Zaytuna Institute*, vol. 2, no. 2, 2005.

al-Zamakhsharī, *Tafsīr al-kashshāf*, 4 vols., Beirut, Dār al-Kutub al-ʿIlmiyya, 1995.

Index to Qur'ānic Quotations

Index